SOURCES OF COHERENCE IN READING

Edited by

ROBERT F. LORCH, JR.
University of Kentucky

EDWARD J. O'BRIEN
University of New Hampshire

 LAWRENCE ERLBAUM ASSOCIATES, PUBLISHERS

1995   Hillsdale, New Jersey   Hove, UK

Lawrence Erlbaum Associates, Inc., Publishers
365 Broadway
Hillsdale, New Jersey 07642

Library of Congress Cataloging-in-Publication Data
Sources of coherence in reading / edited by Robert F. Lorch, Jr. and
   Edward J. O'Brien
        p.   cm.
      Includes bibliographical references and index.
      ISBN 0-8058-1339-X (cloth)/ISBN 0-8058-1637-2 (pbk.) (acid-free paper)
      1. Reading, Psychology of.   2. Reading comprehension.   3. Cohesion
(Linguistics)   I. Lorch, Robert Frederick, 1952–   .   II. O'Brien,
Edward J.
      BF456.R2S68 1994
      418'.4—dc20   94-6857
                                                                CIP

Books published by Lawrence Erlbaum Associates are printed on acid-free paper,
and their bindings are chosen for strength and durability.

Printed in the United States of America
10   9   8   7   6   5   4   3   2   1

Contents

Contributors

Jason E. Albrecht
Department of Psychology
University of Massachusetts
Amherst, MA 01003

Paul A. Baligian
Department of Psychology
Amherst College
Amherst, MA 01002

Eugenie L. Bertus
Department of Psychology
Memphis State University
Memphis, TN 38152

Charles P. Bloom
U.S. West Advanced Technologies
4001 Discovery Drive
Boulder, CO 80303

Susan T. Chrysler
Traffic Control Materials Division
Building 582-1-15
3M Center
St. Paul, MN 55144-1000

Cynthia Connine
Department of Psychology
SUNY-Binghamton
Binghamton, NY 13901-6000

Jennifer A. Deaton
Department of Psychology
1202 West Johnson Street
University of Wisconsin
Madison, WI 53706-1696

Stephen Dopkins
Department of Psychology
George Washington University
2125 G Street NW
Washington, D.C. 20052

Susan A. Duffy
Department of Psychology
Amherst College
Amherst, MA 01002

William K. Estes
Department of Psychology
Harvard University
33 Kirkland St.
Cambridge, MA 02138

Charles R. Fletcher
Department of Psychology
University of Minnesota
75 E. River Road
Minneapolis, MN 55455

Marita Franzke
Department of Psychology
University of Colorado
Boulder, CO 90309-0345

Jonathan M. Golding
Department of Psychology
University of Kentucky
Lexington, KY 40506-0044

Arthur C. Graesser
Department of Psychology
Memphis State University
Memphis, TN 38152

Jerry Hauselt
Department of Psychology
Southern Connecticut State University
501 Cresent Street
New Haven, CT 06515

Andrew F. Hundley
Department of Psychology
Amherst College
Amherst, MA 01002

Elizabeth Husebye-Hartmann
Minnesota Center for Health Statistics
Minnesota Department of Health
717 Delaware Street SE
Minneapolis, MN 55440

Albrecht Werner Inhoff
Department of Psychology
SUNY-Binghamton
Binghamton, NY 13901-6000

Rachna Jain
Department of Psychology
The University of Chicago
5848 S. University Avenue
Chicago, IL 60637

Tracy M. Jennings
IBM Santa Teresa Lab
555 Bailey Ave. D89/F145
San Jose, CA 95141

Caren Jones
Department of Psychology
University of Massachusetts
Amherst, MA 01003

Eleen N. Kamas
Department of Psychology
Carnegie-Mellon University
Pittsburgh, PA 15213

Janice M. Keenan
Department of Psychology
University of Denver
Denver, CO 80208

Walter Kintsch
Department of Psychology
University of Colorado
Boulder, CO 90309-0345

Madeline A. Klusewitz
Department of Psychology
University of Kentucky
Lexington, KY 40506-0044

Elizabeth Pugzles Lorch
Department of Psychology
University of Kentucky
Lexington, KY 40506-0044

Robert F. Lorch, Jr.
Department of Psychology
University of Kentucky
Lexington, KY 40506-0044

Joseph P. Magliano
Department of Psychology
The University of Chicago
5848 S. University Avenue
Chicago, IL 60637

Keith M. Millis
Department of Psychology
Northern Illinois State University
Dekalb, IL 60115-2864

John D. Murray
Department of Psychology
Landrum Box 8041
Georgia Southern University
Statesboro, GA 30460-8041

Johanna Nordlie
Psychology Department
Barnard College
3009 Broadway
New York, NY 10027-6598

Edward J. O'Brien
Department of Psychology
University of New Hampshire
Durham, NH 03824

Paula Payton
Department of Psychology
The University of Chicago
5848 S. University Avenue
Chicago, IL 60637

Alexander Pollatsek
Department of Psychology
University of Massachusetts
Amherst, MA 01003

Gary E. Raney
Department of Psychology
1007 W. Harrison St.
University of Illinois at Chicago
Chicago, IL 60607-7137

Keith Rayner
Department of Psychology
University of Massachusetts
Amherst, MA 01003

Lynne M. Reder
Department of Psychology
Carnegie-Mellon University
Pittsburgh, PA 15213

Kirsten Risden
Center for Research in Learning,
    Perception & Cognition
205 Elliott Hall
75 East River Road
University of Minnesota
Minneapolis, MN 55455

Sandra A. Sego
Department of Psychology
University of Kentucky
Lexington, KY 40506-0044

Murray Singer
Department of Psychology
University of Manitoba
Winnipeg, MB R3T 2N2
Canada

Soyoung Suh
Department of Psychology
The University of Chicago
5848 S. University Avenue
Chicago, IL 60637

Tom Trabasso
Department of Psychology
The University of Chicago
5848 S. University Avenue
Chicago, IL 60637

Paul van den Broek
Department of Educational Psychology
University of Minnesota
Burton Hall
178 Pillsbury Drive, SE
Minneapolis, MN 55455

Preface

In the last 20 years, interest in the study of processes underlying discourse comprehension has increased dramatically. In that time, there have been several shifts in theoretical perspective, as well as increasingly sophisticated techniques for the study of on-line processes in reading. Each new shift has resulted in a deeper understanding of those processes and greater respect for their complexity. The last few years have produced many new and exciting discoveries. The purpose of this book is to present the current state of cognitive theory and research on discourse comprehension process.

Although the scholarly purposes for assembling this text justify the effort, we were motivated to take on the task by the occasion of the retirement of our mentor, Jerome L. Myers. This volume is dedicated to him. Therefore, we would like to attempt to convey some sense of Jerry to those readers who have not had the privilege of knowing him personally.

Jerry did his graduate work at the University of Wisconsin between 1953 and 1957. The methodological rigor that characterized graduate training in "the dust bowl of empiricism," as Wisconsin was known at the time, has always been a hallmark of Jerry's empirical research. During his graduate training, David Grant was a major influence on Jerry's professional development. Grant's encouragement of intellectual curiosity led Jerry to topics he might otherwise not have explored, and the example Grant provided is one Jerry has emulated in his own teaching career. It was Grant's seminar covering Bush and Mosteller's (1955) text that initiated Jerry's love affair with math modeling. In 1962–1963, Jerry spent a year at Stanford as a United States Public Health Service Special Fellow at the Institute of Mathematical Studies in the Social Sciences with colleagues such as Dick Atkinson, Gordon Bower, Bill Estes, and Pat Suppes. That experience permanently established his commitment to math modeling.

A major early research interest for Jerry was probability learning. The subject matter was a natural choice for someone with his methodological skills and quantitative interests. As the fledgling discipline of cognitive psychology began to emerge in the late 1960s, Jerry's research attention shifted to basic questions concerning memory retrieval. Using network representations as a general framework, his research examined memory search processes, semantic and episodic priming mechanisms, and the role of integration of information on subsequent retrieval of the information. In the 1980s, Jerry's research shifted to some degree to the more complex representations and processing required for text comprehension. Although much current research in discourse processing focuses on representational issues, Jerry has remained concerned with the basic processing assumptions and search mechanisms that must be a part of any representational system. Jerry's current work has been instrumental in developing and constraining models of discourse comprehension.

Along with his substantive program of research, Jerry has also maintained active research interests in experimental design and statistical analysis. He has published numerous papers testing and expanding on basic statistical assumptions. He has also maintained one of the premier graduate-level books in research design and statistics. He wrote three editions of *Fundamentals of Experimental Design* (1979) and coauthored a book with Arnie Well titled *Experimental Design and Statistical Analysis* (1991). In addition, he has served as editor of the quantitative section of the *Psychological Bulletin*. Finally, he has taught statistics to several generations of University of Massachusetts graduate students, many of whom have gone on to teach graduate-level statistics.

Jerry was a driving influence in the development of the program in cognitive psychology at the University of Massachusetts. When Jerry came to the university, he joined a program that was developing strengths in human factors approaches to psychology. He shaped it more to his own interests, first recruiting Jim Chumbley, whose interests in math modeling fit Jerry's own. Next, he recruited Chuck Clifton, whose specialty of psycholinguistics was one that Jerry thought would become respectable some day. At this time in the late 1960s, the University of Massachusetts psychology department was growing rapidly, but its primary areas of growth were in biopsychology and clinical psychology. Jerry convinced the department that it needed more statistics instructors, and promptly recruited two more young cognitive psychologists—Sandy Pollatsek and Arnie Well. Jerry thus built around himself an active group of cognitive psychologists with interests and approaches that were very congenial to his own. This group has had the good fortune to be augmented by other very fine researchers, including Keith Rayner, David Rosenbaum, Caren Jones, and Scott Johnson. Jerry has always been the heart and the conscience of the cognitive group.

Jerry's contributions to the department at the University of Massachusetts extend beyond his influence on the development of the cognitive program. In the mid 1970s, the university was going through the first of the budget crises that have beset state universities ever since that time. Jerry's colleagues recognized that he was the only member of the faculty tough enough and respected enough to force it to make the choices it had to make. He agreed to serve as acting chair of the department and, in the course of his 18-month tenure, succeeded in reshaping it into a leaner, stronger department.

Nancy Myers has played a special role in Jerry's career and life. Jerry and Nancy have been together since their meeting in graduate school. With their mutual support, each has earned an international reputation in their respective areas. Early on, when their scholarly interests overlapped, they collaborated on grants and publications. Together, they were instrumental in the growth and development of the University of Massachusetts psychology program into one of the elite departments in the country. And even when their research programs have diverged, they have supported each other through the trials that academic life can bring and they have shared its joys, too.

Although this book was assembled to honor Jerry Myers, it is not a festschrift in the conventional sense. This book is not a compilation of research by Jerry's students; rather, it focuses on a single area of research in which Jerry is very active and the contributors have a variety of professional relationships and personal ties to Jerry. Bill Estes' pioneering use of math models to formalize theory and direct empirical research had a seminal influence on Jerry's research philosophy. Walter Kintsch and Jerry have shared research interests and a personal acquaintance for many years. Keith Rayner and Sandy Pollatsek are friends and colleagues of Jerry's at the University of Massachusetts. Jason Albrecht, Steve Dopkins, Susan Duffy, and John Murray did postdoctoral work with Jerry. Albrecht Inhoff, Cindy Connine, and Betty Lorch did their graduate work at the university. Several contributors have become acquainted with Jerry through their common research interests, including Randy Fletcher, Art Graesser, Jonathan Golding, Jan Keenan, Lynne Reder, Murray Singer, Tom Trabasso, and Paul van den Broek. The editors of this book are privileged to have had Jerry as a mentor. This text is a sincere "thank you" to Jerome L. Myers from his students, colleagues, and friends for his contributions to the field and to each of us personally.

Finally, we will indulge our prerogative as editors to acknowledge Jerry's influence on us. If you ask Jerry why he chose an academic career, he has a stock reply: "I wasn't big enough to play for the Knicks, so I chose the best alternative." We have never heard Jerry admit to any of his other weaknesses on the court (i.e., poor inside game, no outside shot, and an unwillingness to give up the ball), but his answer accurately communicates the love he exhibits for research and teaching. Any colleague or student who has discussed research with Jerry knows the overwhelming enthusiasm he has for his subject. Whenever either of us has tried to acknowledge our debt to him, he has always deflected our attempts with: "Good students are worth it; they make it fun." Perhaps our real motivation for editing this book was to acknowledge Jerry in a way he cannot deflect: If good students are worth it, a good teacher is invaluable. Thanks for making it fun, Jerry.

ACKNOWLEDGMENTS

We wish to thank Nancy A. Myers and Charles E. Clifton, Jr. for their contributions to the preface of this book. Chuck wrote the paragraphs concerning Jerry's contributions to the Department of Psychology at the University of Massachusetts. Nancy pointed out factual errors in earlier drafts of the manuscript and made innumerable suggestions for the improvement of the preface.

REFERENCES

Bush, R. R., & Mosteller, F. (1955). *Stochastic models for learning*. New York: Wiley.
Myers, J. L. (1979). *Fundamentals of experimental design, 3rd ed*. Boston: Allyn and Bacon.
Myers, J. L., & Well, A. D. (1991). *Research design and statistical analysis*. New York: Harper Collns.

Introduction: Sources of Coherence in Reading

Robert F. Lorch, Jr.
University of Kentucky

Edward J. O'Brien
University of New Hampshire

What does it mean to comprehend a story, or a book, or a set of instructions? We generally credit a reader with understanding a text if the reader constructs a connected mental representation of the text that is consistent with the representation intended by the author. This definition of comprehension establishes as central to the study of reading those processes by which connections are made among related representational elements. Thus, a great deal of cognitive research on reading can be viewed as an attempt both to identify the types of information readers use to link related text elements, and to characterize the processes by which those links are represented in memory. This book presents the current state of our knowledge concerning such sources of coherence in reading. The purposes of this introduction are to provide a historical context for the work presented in the subsequent chapters, and to give an overview of the chapters.

A BRIEF HISTORICAL CONTEXT

Kintsch and van Dijk's (1978) theory of text comprehension was one of the earliest cognitive theories of reading; several key components of the theory continue to influence research on reading. Central to the theory is the assumption that a reader can maintain only a limited amount of information in active memory. Connections among text propositions are hypothesized to be constructed within working memory, but only a few propositions can be actively maintained in working memory at any point in time. Thus, working memory limitations require: (a) that readers have effective strategies for maintaining text propositions as a potential context for integrating new information; and (b) that readers have efficient strategies for identifying appropriate antecedents in long-term memory, or making appropriate bridging inferences when the contextual information available in working memory does not provide an adequate context for integrating new information.

Kintsch and van Dijk emphasized one particular source of coherence in reading: Readers are hypothesized to construct a propositional network representation of a text using *coreference* as the basis for identifying related propositions. The emphasis on coreference as a source of coherence was motivated by two considerations. First, coreference is a simple, explicit way of indicating a relation between two propositions, thus it is likely to be an important cue employed by readers to identify such relations. Second, coreference is likely to covary with other sources of coherence; for example, causally related events are likely to have common referents (Fletcher, Chrysler, van den Broek, Deaton, & Bloom, this volume; Trabasso & van den Broek, 1985). Thus, Kintsch and van Dijk relied on coreference as an indicator of interconnections among propositions to keep tractable the problem of analyzing text structure. This allowed them to focus on the processes by which readers construct a representation of that structure.

Kintsch and van Dijk's theory was concerned with how readers construct a representation of a text. As such, their theory naturally emphasized what we call *text-based* sources of coherence (cf. Kintsch & Franzke, this volume). We use the term text-based to refer to devices and conventions employed by writers to communicate relations among text elements. These include coreference, the use of connectives (e.g., and, because), signals (e.g., headings), and other devices. By referring to some sources of coherence as text-based, we do not intend to remove from readers the responsibility for constructing a text representation. After all, if readers do not respond appropriately to these indicators of relations among propositions, their text representations will not be coherent. However, we do wish to emphasize that some sources of coherence in reading are direct attempts by the writer to facilitate the comprehension attempts of the reader. Several of the chapters in this book address such text-based sources of coherence and their effects on reading and memory (see the chapters by: Dopkins & Nordlie; Fletcher et al.; Golding, Millis, Hauselt, & Sego; Murray; and O'Brien).

Kintsch and van Dijk intentionally limited the scope of their theory to questions concerning how readers process the content of a text. They implicitly assumed that the reader's goal is to construct a representation that is faithful to the text. They purposely minimized the role of the reader's prior knowledge in the comprehension process at this level of representation. Although readers were hypothesized to use background knowledge to make bridging inferences, such inferences were considered a last resort for maintaining coherence.

Since the 1980s, there has been a clear shift of theoretical perspective from viewing reading comprehension as a process of representing the text (as in Kintsch and van Dijk's, 1978, textbase model) to viewing comprehension as a process of representing what the text is about (as in a situation model; cf. Kintsch & Franzke, this volume). Recent theories generally retain the processing assumptions of the Kintsch and van Dijk model, but they have increasingly emphasized the role of the reader's prior knowledge in the process of understanding discourse. The greater emphasis on the interaction between the reader and the text has led to a better understanding of the complexity of the reader's task.

With the shift in focus from the role of textbase models to the role of situation models in reading comprehension, there has been increasing emphasis on *reader-based* sources of coherence in reading. By "reader-based sources of coherence," we refer to the knowledge and strategies readers bring to the task of constructing a coherent text representation. For example: Readers identify causal relations among events to construct coherent representations of narratives; the perspective a reader adopts in reading a story influences how the reader integrates events during reading; and readers draw on their background knowledge to integrate text statements with each other and with their prior knowledge. Several of the chapters in this book are concerned with such reader-based sources of coherence in reading comprehension (see the chapters by: Albrecht & O'Brien; Graesser, Bertus, & Magliano; Jones; Kintsch & Franzke; Lorch; Lorch, Klusewitz, & Lorch; Singer; Trabasso, Suh, Payton, & Jain; and van den Broek, Risden, & Husebye-Hartmann).

AN OVERVIEW OF THE CHAPTERS

The chapters of the book are organized roughly by the distinction between text-based versus reader-based sources of coherence. Most of the chapters in the first half of the book address text-based sources of coherence and the chapters in the second half address reader-based sources of coherence. However, not all of the chapters fit into this categorization scheme and, within subsets of the chapters, several other themes are developed.

Chapters 1 and 2 are concerned with methodological issues in the study of comprehension processes. In chapter 1, Rayner, Raney, & Pollatsek present a strong case for the potential of eye movement methodologies in the study of discourse processing. Eye movement procedures have been used with great success to examine basic visual processing and the control of eye movements during reading (see Inhoff & Connine, this volume). However, relatively few researchers have exploited the potential of the paradigm for studying discourse processes. Rayner et al. cite several examples from their lab illustrating the power of the paradigm for resolving difficult issues concerning topics such as parsing of syntax, the selection of the appropriate sense of a lexically ambiguous word, inference processes, and other discourse processes.

Priming procedures have been widely used to study inference processes during reading. In chapter 2, Keenan and Jennings carefully consider appropriate control conditions for priming experiments. A typical application of the paradigm involves having subjects read a sentence or short text, then presenting them with a target word that denotes a key concept in the inference that is being tested. The dependent measure is latency to respond to the target word in some manner (e.g., lexical decision, naming, or recognize whether the word occurred in the preceding text). For example, after reading a text ending with the sentence "Bobby pounded the boards together with nails," subjects might have to verify whether the word *hammer* occurred in the text. If latency to respond is speeded relative to an appropriate control condition, the conclusion is that subjects must have made the inference that a hammer was the instrument used to do the pounding. A threat to the validity of the procedure is that the baseline condition used to evaluate inferencing may not adequately rule out the possibility of differences between the experimental and control conditions in the amount of word-based priming they produce. Keenan and Jennings report two experiments that demonstrate the importance of controlling for word-based priming effects. Their experiments also indicate that some of the available evidence suggesting that instrumental inferences are made during reading in fact reflects word-based priming effects rather than inference processes.

In chapter 3, Estes presents a detailed analysis of how subjects make choice responses in categorization tasks. The general issue at hand is the relation between mental representations and responses based on those representations. Estes observes that cognitive science lacks a general model of how individuals generate responses. This theoretical gap is apparent in research on reading. As one example, there has been considerable debate concerning appropriate methods for detecting whether inferences are made on-line (cf. Keenan & Jennings, this volume). The use of probe procedures based on binary-choice tasks (e.g., lexical decision, word recognition) has been criticized as being too vulnerable to context-checking strategies to allow a reliable assessment of the state of a reader's representation of a text. At another level of analysis, theoretical models of how readers integrate new information into their text representations generally focus on memory search processes (e.g., Albrecht & O'Brien, this volume). The emphasis of these models is on factors influencing the relative accessibility of information in memory that is relevant to the comprehension of new text information. However, the available models have paid far less attention to the question of how a single context is selected from the many potential contexts onto which a new statement might be mapped. That is, how does the reader chose one representational "response" from several alternative options?

In chapter 4, Inhoff and Connine examine the nature of bottom-up processing of visual information during reading. They argue that information concerning the spatial layout of print (e.g., word length, spacing) dominates attention and oculomotor control during reading. In the subsequent chapter, Duffy, Hundley, and Baligian look at top-down influences on encoding processes. They demonstrate that reading a sentence presented in inverted type is greatly facilitated if the preceding sentence has a strong causal relation to the target sentence. This result is consistent with the hypothesis that readers can compensate for disruptions of visual information by relying on other sources of information (i.e., context) to encode a sentence.

Chapters 6 and 7 are both concerned with one particular type of text-based source of coherence. The chapters by Murray and by Golding, Millis, Hauselt, and Sego examine effects of logical connectives on reading and memory for causally related sentence pairs. The findings of the two studies are remarkably consistent. Relative to a control condition of no explicit connective, adversative connectives (e.g., but) facilitate reading of the second sentence of a pair, but do not affect integration of the two sentences as assessed by a cued recall test. Both investigators found no evidence that causal connectives (e.g., therefore) influence reading or memory, and Murray also found no evidence that additive connectives (e.g., and) influence reading or memory.

The chapters by Dopkins and Nordlie, O'Brien, and Kamas and Reder address a variety of issues, but present similar hypotheses concerning mechanisms underlying the identification of related concepts in a text. Dopkins and Nordlie consider the question of how noun anaphors are resolved during reading. They propose a distinction between bottom-up and top-down processes operating to identify the antecedent of a noun anaphor. Bottom-up processes focus on information in the anaphoric expression (e.g., gender and phonological information) as the basis for identifying its referent; top-down processes focus on information in the discourse prior to the anaphor, including information about syntactic constraints, discourse focus, and various heuristics that may be used to identify referents of anaphors.

Dopkins and Nordlie argue that general memory search processes are responsible for the identification of referents of anaphors. The nature of such search processes is the focus of O'Brien's chapter 9. He proposes that a resonance mechanism can account for many of the findings concerning how anaphors are resolved during reading. A resonance process is also hypothesized to drive the detection of connections and inconsistencies among statements in a text that do not co-occur in active memory. It is used to explain much of the evidence for on-line inferencing, both necessary and elaborative.

Kamas and Reder also emphasize the centrality of automatic memory search processes to reading. According to their featural familiarity hypothesis, the retrieval process generates information from the prior text and from background knowledge that is related to the current contents of attention. They propose that readers often use familiarity information resulting from this process as a heuristic to monitor their comprehension and guide their responses in a variety of circumstances.

In chapter 11, Fletcher and his colleagues separate the effects of co-occurrence, coreference, and causal relatedness as contributors to the coherence of sentence pairs. They demonstrate that coreference contributes to coherence above and beyond any effects of simple co-occurrence of two statements in working memory. However, causal relatedness has little effect on coherence beyond that of coreference except when the causal relation between the two related statements is explicitly encoded.

Trabasso, Suh, Payton, and Jain argue persuasively for a role for verbal protocol methods in the study of inferencing and other on-line processes. They present findings from studies of adults and third graders who produced talk-aloud protocols and free recalls for narratives. The talk-aloud responses were categorized in four ways: Subjects either (a) explained an event, often by retrieving an earlier event in the story; or (b) they maintained an event in short-term memory; or (c) they associated an event with background knowledge; or (d) they predicted an upcoming event from the current event in the narrative. The operations of maintaining, explaining, and retrieving an event were highly intercorrelated and were predictive of text recall. Trabasso and his colleagues suggest that readers use operations of maintenance, explanation, and retrieval to integrate information in working memory, with the result of a coherent representation and good subsequent recall.

In chapter 13, Singer reviews his program of research concerning how readers use their background knowledge to validate their inferences during reading. It is well-documented that readers routinely make bridging inferences, especially causal inferences, to connect events in their mental representations of text. It is assumed that bridging inferences are based on the reader's general knowledge. Singer presents his model of how general knowledge is used to make bridging inferences and reviews evidence relevant to the evaluation of the model.

In chapter 14, Albrecht and O'Brien extend the resonance mechanism described in O'Brien's chapter to include the processing of goal-based information. They suggest that readers maintain elements in explicit focus representing actions or events relevant to unsatisfied goals. These elements serve as discourse pointers, pointing to goal-relevant information in implicit focus. Incoming information relevant to an unsatisfied goal is mapped onto all relevant goal information in both explicit and implicit focus. Albrecht and O'Brien caution that goals should not be defined by the goals of the protagonist; it is often the case that the goals of the reader and the goals of a protagonist are not the same. In those cases, the goals of the reader will govern what is maintained in explicit and implicit focus.

Just as Albrecht and O'Brien argue that processing of goal information in narratives is central to constructing a globally coherent text representation, Lorch argues that readers of expository text must identify and interrelate superordinate topics as they read. He demonstrates that when readers are interrupted just before encountering a new discourse topic, they resume reading more easily if they are reminded of the last-encountered topic than if they are given no reminder or are reminded only of the most superordinate topic that is relevant. He interprets his findings as demonstrating that readers relate new text topics to related text topics in the process of constructing a globally coherent text representation.

In chapter 16, Graesser, Bertus, and Magliano review the literature and theories on knowledge-based inferencing during comprehension of narrative. They review six models that make different predictions concerning the types of inferences that are made on-line. They summarize the literature as showing that inferences about causal antecedents, superordinate goals, and character emotions are made on-line, whereas inferences about causal consequences, subordinate goals, states, and instruments of actions are not routinely made during reading. These results are consistent with a constructionist theory of knowledge-based inferencing.

Like several other authors in this book, Kintsch and Franzke are interested in the role of background knowledge on reading and memory for text. They examine the influence of prior knowledge about a specific domain on recall of information from a domain-relevant news story. They report that subjects' recalls were good if general background knowledge was adequate to support comprehension. However, when understanding of text content required specialized domain knowledge, recall was directly related to the amount of domain-relevant information subjects were presented before reading and recalling the target story. Kintsch and Franzke interpret their results as consistent with the hypothesis that readers construct two representations based on their reading of a text: a textbase representation whose construction depends only on general background knowledge, and a situation model whose construction relies more heavily on domain-specific background knowledge.

In chapter 18, Jones argues that the shift in research focus to the mental model (or situation model) level of representation raises some serious questions about the nature of that representation. She argues that it is not enough to simply provide evidence that such a level of representation exists; we need to begin to specify both the nature of that representation and the processes necessary to construct such a representation. Without a better understanding of exactly what a mental model is and how it is constructed, the usefulness of the mental model construct is called into question.

The final two chapters emphasize the reader's role in determining what constitutes adequate comprehension of a text. Van den Broek, Risden, and Husebye-Hartmann propose that readers have multiple, flexible "standards of coherence" that directly influence the connectedness of the representation they construct as they read. Depending on factors such as motivation, relevant background knowledge, and purposes for reading, the standards that readers adopt as their criteria for comprehension may vary in strictness. Standards for coherence may be expected to vary for the same reader across different reading situations and across different individuals in the same reading situation.

In the final chapter, Lorch, Klusewitz, and Lorch use clustering analyses to organize readers' perceptions of the cognitive requirements of a wide variety of reading situations. They distinguish 14 types of reading situations, with most of the distinctions being based on systematic differences in readers' goals across the types. Systematic differences in readers' standards for coherence (van den Broek, Risden, & Husebye-Hartmann, this volume) may explain some of the distinctions among types found in Lorch et al.'s study. The authors suggest that their typology of reading situations may provide a useful framework for organizing theory and research on reading strategies.

REFERENCES

Kintsch, W., & van Dijk, T. A. (1978). Toward a model of text comprehension and production. *Psychological Review, 85*, 363–394.

Trabasso, T., & van den Broek, P. (1985). Causal thinking and the representation of narrative events. *Journal of Memory and Language, 24*, 612–630.

1 Eye Movements and Discourse Processing

Keith Rayner
Gary E. Raney
Alexander Pollatsek
University of Massachusetts

Understanding the processes whereby readers comprehend text has been extremely important to cognitive psychologists over the past 20 years. Theoretical and methodological advances have been made and there continues to be considerable interest in the topic. In this chapter, we argue that examinations of eye movements as people read text have been underutilized as sources of data to investigate discourse processing. For example, in their excellent analysis of tasks used to detect whether or not inferences are made during reading, Keenan, Potts, Golding, and Jennings (1990) did not list eye movement measures as one of the major techniques; they do mention the use of eye movement data, but only in passing.

Our goal is to review some basic facts about eye movements during reading, particularly as they relate to discourse processing. For much of this chapter, we use the term *discourse processing* in its broadest sense (i.e., all processes that go into comprehending discourse). Thus, we begin by discussing comprehension broadly, briefly reviewing effects such as text difficulty and then examining in some more detail (a) how reading is facilitated when people reread a passage of text and (b) how processing of earlier parts of the text facilitates reading later parts of the text. The last part of the chapter examines how eye movements have been used to investigate discourse processing in its narrower sense (i.e., the processes beyond lexical access that go into comprehending discourse). Although eye movements have been important in the investigation of several areas, our focus is primarily on anaphora and elaborative inference.

BASIC CHARACTERISTICS OF EYE MOVEMENTS
DURING READING

During reading, we make a series of *fixations* and *saccades* as our eyes move from one location in the text to another. Eye movements are necessary because of acuity limitations in the visual system. In order to process a new part of the text, we move our eyes so as to place the fovea (or central region of vision) over that part of the text we wish to process next. Fixations, which average around 250 ms, are the periods of time when we acquire new information from the text. Separating the fixations are rapid movements of the eyes (called saccades) from one place to another in the text; on average, the eyes move about 8–9 character spaces with each saccade. The actual saccades are very rapid, ballistic movements that typically take on the order of 20–50 ms during reading. During saccades, no useful information is acquired from the text because the eyes are moving so rapidly. Although the majority of eye movements during reading are in the forward direction (or from left-to-right for readers of English), about 10% to 15% of the time we move our eyes back to look at text that our eyes have already passed over; these movements back in the text are referred to as *regressions*.

Perhaps the most important characteristic of eye movements during reading is that there is considerable variability—both within and between readers—in the duration of fixations, length of saccades, and frequency of regressions. That is, individual fixation durations for a given reader range from under 100 ms to over 500 ms and saccade lengths range from 1 character space to about 15–20 character spaces (although saccade lengths greater than 12 characters typically follow a regression). Similarly, there is also considerable between–reader variability in basic eye movement characteristics.

There is now a great deal of evidence to suggest that the variability in fixation duration within readers is due to cognitive processes associated with comprehending text (Rayner & Pollatsek, 1989); likewise, short saccades and frequent regressions are typically indicative of some type of processing difficulty. In general, text difficulty exerts a powerful influence on eye movement behavior: As text difficulty increases, readers make more and longer fixations, saccade length decreases, and regression frequency increases. Figure 1.1 shows frequency distributions for fixation durations for easy and difficult text: the average fixation duration is 252 ms for the easy text and 288 ms for the difficult text. As is obvious in Fig. 1.1, the distribution of fixations shifts as a function of text difficulty.

Eye movements during reading are also very much influenced by characteristics of the orthography. All of the values that we have described are for readers of English. However, when eye movements are examined across languages, some striking differences emerge (see Rayner & Pollatsek, 1989, for further discussion). In particular, saccade length for ideographic languages, such as Chinese

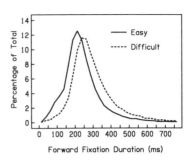

FIG. 1.1. Average forward fixation duration when readers read easy and difficult text. Text difficulty for these data was manipulated by using different video displays that varied in the extent to which the letters were clearly defined. Similar distributions have been obtained in our lab using text rated as "easy" or "difficult" according to readability formulas.

and Japanese, tend to be shorter and fixation durations tend to be longer than is the case for readers of English. Readers of Hebrew, which is a more densely packed orthography than English, tend to fall between Japanese and English on both measures: fixation durations are longer and saccade lengths shorter than for English.

As we read, our eyes move left-to-right across each line of text. At the end of the line, we make a return sweep to the beginning of the next line. The last fixation on a line is typically about five to six characters from the end of the line, and the first fixation on the next line is typically five to six characters from the first letter in the line; thus, about 80% of the line generally falls within the extreme fixations. The first fixation on a line is usually a bit longer than other fixations, presumably because the reader has not had any preview of the word prior to fixating on it. On the other hand, the last fixation on the line is generally a bit shorter, presumably because the reader does not have to compute where to fixate next on the line nor engage in extensive parafoveal processing.

Research on the perceptual span—the area of effective vision during each fixation—has documented that the region from which readers obtain useful information is quite restricted (see Rayner & Pollatsek, 1989, for a review). Experiments using eye contingent display-change techniques, in which the experimenter controls how much information the reader sees on each fixation, have shown that the span of effective vision extends from the beginning of the currently fixated word, but no more than three to four character spaces to the left of fixation, to about 14 to 15 character spaces to the right of fixation for readers of English. The perceptual span is asymmetric in the opposite direction for readers of Hebrew because it is read from right-to-left (Pollatsek, Bolozky, Well, & Rayner, 1981). Finally, readers obtain information from the currently fixated line and do not obtain useful information below the line they are reading (Inhoff & Briihl, 1991; Inhoff & Topolski, 1992; Pollatsek, Raney, LaGasse, & Rayner, 1993). More fine-grained analyses of the perceptual span have revealed that, on most fixations, readers identify the word they are currently fixating and extract information from the word to the right as well. On some fixations, the word to the right is fully processed and skipped, but the more usual case appears to be that readers partially process the word to the right of the fixated word and this "preview" shortens fixation time on the word when they later fixate it (Blanchard, Pollatsek, & Rayner, 1989; Inhoff & Rayner, 1986; Rayner, Well, Pollatsek, & Bertera, 1982).

We think the data just mentioned and the data discussed later, indicating that fixation times are sensitive to word frequency, are most naturally explained by assuming that lexical access of the fixated word usually initiates both an eye movement program and a shift of covert attention to the word to the right of fixation. Thus, because there is an appreciable latency between the decision to move the eye and the actual execution of the saccadic eye movement, attention moves to the word to the right of fixation prior to the actual eye movement. A model based on these assumptions explains much of the data on eye movements (Morrison, 1984, adapted by Rayner & Pollatsek, 1989). An additional assumption—that a later eye movement program can "cancel" an earlier one if it follows it closely in time—can account for both the phenomenon that short, easily processed words are commonly skipped and that the fixation time before the skip is lengthened (Hogaboam, 1983; Pollatsek, Rayner, & Balota, 1986). Recent research, however, suggests that when processing of the foveal word is difficult, readers extract little useful information from the parafoveal word (Henderson & Ferreira, 1990; Inhoff, Pollatsek, Posner & Rayner, 1989; Rayner, 1986).

Research on eye movement control in reading also suggests that fixation duration and saccade length are computed somewhat independently from each other. Fixation duration appears to be influenced primarily by the ease or difficulty associated with processing the fixated word (or words), whereas the location where the eyes move to appears to be computed based on word length information acquired parafoveally (Morris, Rayner, & Pollatsek, 1990; Pollatsek & Rayner, 1982; Rayner & Morris, 1992).

FIXATION MEASURES OF COGNITIVE PROCESSES

The fixation time on a word seems to reflect at least some cognitive processes associated with understanding that word. For example, fixation times on high frequency words are shorter than those on low frequency words even when word length is controlled (Inhoff & Rayner, 1986; Rayner & Duffy, 1986). This type of result demonstrates that the *eye–mind span* during reading must be relatively short (Just & Carpenter, 1980): If there were a large gap between the completion of a cognitive process such as lexical access and when an eye movement could be executed contingent on that process, then the effect of a variable such as word frequency would not be seen when the word was fixated, but on some later fixation (if at all). Because the eye–mind span appears to be short, we assume that the eye movement record is a fairly direct indicator of the cognitive processes in reading. Hence, if the effect of some discourse processing variable is delayed beyond when it could first logically appear, we assume that the underlying cognitive processing is also delayed.

The computation of the processing time associated with each word in a text would be straightforward if readers fixated once and only once on each word. But, as noted earlier, some words are frequently skipped and some words receive more than one fixation before the reader moves on to the next word. We think the best solution (see Rayner, Sereno, Morris, Schmauder, & Clifton, 1989) is to compute three different fixation time measures: first-fixation duration, gaze duration, and total time. Certainly, the average fixation duration on an individual word makes little sense as a measure of processing time for that word.

First-fixation duration represents the duration of the initial fixation on a word. If a reader makes two or more fixations on the word before moving on to the next word, only the first fixation would be used in computing the mean time on target words. When the reader makes only a single fixation on the target word, that value is used in computing the mean. Gaze duration represents the sum of all fixations on a word prior to moving the point of fixation to another word. This measure does not include the duration of any regressions made to the target word. On the other hand, the total time measure is the sum of all fixations made on a target word, including the duration of any regressions to the word. All of these measures are contingent on the word being fixated (i.e., when the word is skipped, the trial is removed from the analysis rather than a duration of zero being counted on that trial). This implies that one needs to also report the probability that a word is fixated (in addition to the previously mentioned three duration measures) to adequately reflect processing of the target word. Sometimes the probability of regressing back to the target word is a useful measure as well.

In many studies dealing with discourse processes, however, the unit of analysis is larger than a single word and can encompass a clause or an entire sentence. In such cases, it has often proved useful to distinguish between first-pass and total reading times. First-pass reading time on a region is analogous to gaze duration on a word: it is the sum of all forward fixations in a region prior to an eye movement out of that region. The total reading time (as with individual words) includes the first-pass time plus any rereading time that occurs as a result of regressing back to a region. To equate for differences in region size, a milliseconds-per-character measure is often used in which the total time is divided by the number of letter spaces in the region. The millisecond-per-character measure tacitly assumes that processing letters is the rate-determining step in reading, whereas total time on the region tacitly assumes that processing words (or "idea units") is the rate-determining step. Because neither assumption is likely to be true, it is usually prudent to report more than one measure (see Rayner et al., 1989).

To summarize, when global effects are examined, factors such as words per minute, average fixation duration, average saccade length, and probability of regressions are reasonable measures to examine. However, when more local effects are being examined, then factors such as first-fixation duration, gaze duration, total fixation time, probability of fixation, and probability of a regression are the most reasonable measures to examine.

DISCOURSE EFFECTS OF EYE MOVEMENTS

We have already noted that eye movement characteristics are dramatically influenced by global text difficulty. Table 1.1 shows how the topic of a passage influences eye movements; reading a passage from a physics or biology text is considerably more difficult for college students than reading light fiction. Such a comparison confounds several variables, however. In general, the less technical material will deal with concepts that the reader is more familiar with and topics that he or she has more real-world knowledge about. However, there may also be some sense in which the more technical passages are intrinsically harder (e.g., the syntax may be more complex, the ideas conveyed may be intrinsically harder, there may be a greater density of idea units).

The points just made suggest that familiarity with the material allows people to read text faster (i.e., speeds their discourse processing). This facilitation, of course, could occur at several levels (e.g., faster identification of individual words, greater familiarity with certain syntactic constructions, better underlying pragmatic knowledge to understand the discourse as a whole). However, more local or short-term familiarity appears to have effects as well. We discuss two examples.

First, there are data that indicate that when people reread a passage of text, they read it faster during the second reading. Second, there are data indicating

TABLE 1.1
Mean Fixation Duration (in ms), Mean Saccade Length (in Character Spaces), Percentage of Fixations That Were Regressions, and Reading Rate (in Words per Minute) for 10 College-Age Readers Reading Different Types of Text

Topic	DUR	SL	% REG	WPM
Light fiction	202	9	3	365
History	222	8	4	321
Psychology	216	8	11	308
Economics	233	7	11	268
Physics	261	7	17	238
Biology	264	7	18	233
Mean	233	7.6	11	289

Note. DUR = fixation duration, SL = saccade length, REG = regressions, WPM = words per minute.

that people's reading tends to speed up as they get further into a passage. In both cases, it appears that the act of reading creates a context that facilitates later reading.

REREADING A PASSAGE OF TEXT

One simple way to manipulate the difficulty associated with discourse processing is to ask readers to reread the same passage of text. We (Raney & Rayner, in press) conducted a study in which readers were asked to read a passage and then immediately read it over again. Some of the results reported in this chapter are reported in Raney and Rayner (in press), whereas other results are presented here for the first time.

We first examine the overall difference between the first and second reading to give a feeling for the size and nature of the speed-up when a text is read more than once. Table 1.2 shows various measures of reading performance for the first and second reading of the passages. (We discuss the line-by-line data later.) In this study, the average reading rates were 225 and 257 words per minute (wpm) for the first and second reading, respectively, representing a 14% speedup on the second reading. (These rates are somewhat below average for college-age readers, probably because the passages were fairly detailed.) As can be seen, the increase in reading rate was due to multiple changes in reading performance. During the second reading, the average duration of forward fixations decreased by 2% (or 4 ms), the number of fixations decreased by 9%, and forward saccade length increased by 7%. Although small, each of these changes was statistically significant, and thus consistent across readers.

Benefits from rereading have also been shown using texts written in other languages. For example, Hyona and Niemi (1990) examined rereading using Finnish subjects. When their data are averaged across passages (collapsing across their two experiments), average reading rates for the first and second readings were 194 wpm and 211 wpm, respectively, which represents a 9% increase in speed. The relatively slow reading rate might reflect language differences between Finnish and English: Finnish words tend to be longer, Finnish has no articles, and compound words are common (Hyona, Niemi, & Underwood, 1989). Increased reading speed was again reflected by several eye movement parameters. Across passages, the average fixation duration decreased by 3% (8 ms), the average number of fixations decreased by 5%, and forward saccade length increased by 6.5% (saccade length was reported only for their Experiment 2). Given that their texts were in a language quite different from English, these values are remarkably similar to those of Raney and Rayner (in press). This demonstrates that overall rereading benefits may not be large, but the benefits consistently occur.

TABLE 1.2
Mean Reading Rate (in WPM), Fixation Duration (in ms), Number of Fixations, and Saccade
Length (in Characters) for Forward and Regressive Fixations During the First and Second
Reading of Short Passages. Data are Presented for Each Line of the Texts

		Forward Fixation			Regressive Fixation		
Line	WPM	DUR	N	SL	DUR	N	SL
First Reading							
1	207	246	8.0	8.0	240	1.7	7.0
2	236	250	7.3	8.8	240	1.4	5.9
3	242	254	7.3	8.7	234	1.4	6.2
4	248	248	7.0	8.9	236	1.3	6.6
5	241	254	7.3	8.9	237	1.5	6.3
6	243	253	7.2	8.8	234	1.5	6.3
7	240	250	7.3	8.8	231	1.3	6.2
8	244	251	7.3	8.8	229	1.4	6.2
9	239	252	7.4	8.9	236	1.4	6.1
10	236	252	7.2	8.7	238	1.5	6.0
11	258	249	7.3	9.1	228	1.4	6.2
12	254	249	7.0	9.0	234	1.3	5.9
13	235	256	7.1	9.1	243	1.4	6.5
14	252	248	7.0	9.1	225	1.1	6.3
15	203	276	6.1	9.4	249	1.3	6.4
Mean	225	252	7.2	8.8	237	1.4	6.3
Second Reading							
1	251	237	7.0	8.6	220	1.0	6.6
2	260	245	6.8	9.3	243	1.2	6.7
3	269	251	6.7	9.1	226	1.1	6.2
4	275	247	6.5	9.4	237	.9	6.3
5	270	251	6.6	9.3	231	1.1	6.1
6	269	252	6.7	9.2	238	1.1	5.7
7	269	246	6.7	9.4	242	1.1	6.2
8	279	249	6.5	9.5	226	1.1	6.7
9	266	252	6.6	9.7	241	1.2	6.8
10	269	247	6.6	9.1	223	1.1	6.0
11	296	243	6.6	9.6	227	1.1	6.0
12	289	250	6.4	9.8	235	1.2	6.0
13	288	247	6.3	9.8	222	.8	6.5
14	298	246	6.1	10.0	234	.9	6.2
15	251	260	5.5	10.0	223	.9	6.5
Mean	257	248	6.5	9.4	234	1.1	6.3

Note. WPM = words per minute, DUR = fixation duration, N = number, SL = saccade length

READING SPEED CHANGES WITHIN A PASSAGE

As we mentioned earlier, readers typically speed up the further they get into a
passage. We examined the data from the previous passages to see whether such a
speedup occurred in our data. For this analysis, we examined reading time on

each of the 15 lines of text. Table 1.2 shows how reading rate changes across successive lines of the passage in the first and second reading. It is interesting that even on the second reading, readers were slower on the first few lines of the passage, then were fairly constant in rate for a number of lines, and then finally increased their rate toward the end of the passage (although they slowed down for the last line).

When average fixation duration on each line was examined, it did not differ much across lines; on each line, the average fixation duration was about 250 ms. The exception was the last line, which had significantly longer average fixation durations, even on the second reading. Thus, except for the last line, the change in reading rate was a result of readers making fewer fixations and regressions per line as they progressed through the passage (see Table 1.2).

Both the slower reading rate and the longer fixations on the last line suggest that there is something special about it. Part of the effect may be an artifact because the last fixation was terminated by a key press instead of an eye movement: Because the latency for manual movements is longer than for eye movements, this would artificially increase the reading time per line. However, there appears to be a real effect, generally described as a *wrap-up* effect. That is, it appears that the slowdown is largely a result of subjects attempting to "rehearse" and consolidate their knowledge of the passage, probably because they knew that they would receive comprehension questions after the passage was removed. There are several pieces of data that support this hypothesis. First, readers made a number of fixations, separated by short saccades, at the end of the passage, as though they were making sure that they had comprehended the passage. Furthermore, some subjects made regressions back to earlier segments of the passage, apparently to verify that they had comprehended the material. (We discuss wrap-up effects more fully in the next section.)

From these findings, one might conclude that fixation time is a relatively insensitive measure of processing time. We should caution the reader, however, that this measure is the average duration of all fixations on a line rather than one of the measures we discussed previously that reflects fixation time on a single word. The average fixation duration measure may be relatively insensitive to changes in text difficulty for the following reason. When text is easier, readers tend to refixate words less often and skip words more often. However, refixations on words tend to be short and fixations before skips tend to be long. Hence, as the text gets easier, "normal" fixations (i.e., those other than refixations and before skips) may get shorter, but this speedup could be masked by decreasing numbers of (short) refixations and increasing numbers of (long) fixations before skips. In fact, as we see later, the other measures of fixation time that we discussed before indicate that, when analyzed properly, fixation time does decrease during rereading.

WHAT IS BEING SPED UP?

We have documented that, in the normal course of reading a passage, the process is sped up either by having read the whole passage previously or by having read the first part of the passage. We have also indicated that there are many possible reasons for these speedup effects. This section examines to what extent these effects can be accounted for by repetition of words or concepts either within a passage or from one reading to the next. First, let us consider the case of rereading.

Within each passage of text, Raney and Rayner (in press) included a target word, which was either a high or low frequency word. On the second reading of the passage, the target word either remained the same or was replaced by a synonym, which in turn was either a high or low frequency word. Thus, for example, the target word *archaic* (a low frequency word) could either remain the same during the second reading of the passage or be replaced by the word *ancient* (a high frequency word) and the target word *light* (a high frequency word) could either remain the same or be replaced by the word *scant* (a low frequency word) on the second reading of the passage. Word length was closely matched for the high and low frequency words, with low frequency words having a frequency of 15 or less (mean = 7.3) and high frequency words having a frequency greater than 60 (mean = 135) according to the Francis and Kucera (1982) norms.

Table 1.3 shows the gaze duration data for each of the conditions. Two findings are apparent. First, there is a large frequency effect: Readers looked at the low frequency words 48 ms longer than the high frequency words during the first reading and 49 ms longer during the second reading. Second, there was a repetition effect: On average, fixations were 16 ms shorter on the second reading for low frequency words and 17 ms shorter on the second reading for high frequency words. Importantly, the size of the repetition effects for identical words and synonyms were roughly equivalent. (The pattern for first fixation duration data was the same.) These data indicate that one cause for the speedup

TABLE 1.3
Gaze Duration (in ms) on Target Words as a Function of Condition and First Versus
Second Reading of the Passage

	Frequency of Target Word	
Condition	Low	High
First reading	323	275
Second reading (average)	307	258
Second reading (identical)	310	255
Second reading (synonym)	304	261

during rereading is repetition of individual items. However, what seems to be most important is the repetition of the basic concept rather than the orthographic form, as the same speedup occurs for synonym repetition as for identical repetition.

We also examined repetition effects by seeing how the fixation time on a word changes as a function of the number of times a word is repeated within a passage. Specifically, we examined fixation times on 14 high frequency words and 14 low frequency words, which were five to six letters long and repeated throughout our passages (see Table 1.4). We limit ourselves here to repetitions during the initial reading of the passages. As is clear in Table 1.4, there is a repetition effect as fixation time on the target words gets shorter from the first to the third occurrence. There is also a word frequency effect: On the initial encounter with a high or low frequency word, readers' gaze durations were about 40 ms longer on the low frequency words than on high frequency words (there was about a 20 ms difference for first fixation duration). On the second encounter, however, the frequency effect was reduced to about 20 ms for gaze duration and to zero for first fixation duration; thus, word frequency effects on the second encounter are completely explained by more refixations on the low frequency words. By the time the word is seen for the third time in the passage, the frequency effect completely disappears; apparently a floor effect emerges, such that there is no improvement for high frequency words beyond the second encounter and no improvement for low frequency words beyond the third encounter.

The repetition effects just mentioned could be due either to repetition of the orthographic form or to repetition of the concept (or both). One way to separate these effects is to compare fixation times on a word when its second occurrence in a passage is consistent with its first mention versus when the second occurrence is not consistent with its first mention. For example, suppose you read a passage where the concept *wine bottle* is mentioned early in the passage and then later in the passage *beer bottle* is mentioned. Obviously, the word *bottle* is not referring to the same object in the two cases. We had subjects read a set of

TABLE 1.4
Gaze Duration (in ms) on Target Words as a Function of Frequency and Number of Occurrences
of the Word During the First Reading of a Passage

	Number of Occurrences			
	1	*2*	*3*	*4+*
Low	325 (274)	291 (250)	271 (241)	273 (250)
High	284 (252)	271 (251)	267 (243)	270 (248)

First fixation duration (in ms) is shown in parentheses.

passages of this format and measured fixation times on the target concepts.[1] The basic findings were straightforward. When *wine bottle* was repeated, gaze durations on both the adjective (*wine*) and the noun (*bottle*) were reduced (by 12–20 ms). When the second occurrence of the word *bottle* referred to a beer bottle, there was no facilitation on either the adjective or noun.

Two points are worth discussing. First, facilitation either occurred for both the adjective and the noun or for neither word. If repetition effects applied to individual words, without regard to how words are related, then when *beer bottle* is mentioned (after first encountering *wine bottle*) there should have been facilitation for *bottle* but not for *beer*. The lack of facilitation for *beer bottle* supports the importance of conceptual repetition for producing word repetition effects. Even though the word *bottle* is repeated when *beer bottle* is mentioned, the concept *beer bottle* is not the same as *wine bottle*.

A second interesting point is the role distance played in the repetition effect. When the interval between the two repetitions of *wine bottle* was roughly two sentences or less, the majority of the repetition effect occurred on the adjective. When the interval between repetitions was increased to roughly four or more sentences, the repetition effect was equal for the adjective and noun. What does this mean? At short intervals, subjects appeared to recognize the repeated phrase as soon as the adjective was read, and consequently, repetition benefits were largest on the adjective (and fixation time was longer on the adjective than on the noun). When the interval was long, subjects might not have recognized the repetition as soon as the adjective was fixated, therefore repetition benefits were spread across the adjective and noun. This result illustrates the ability of eye fixation data to localize discourse level effects during reading.

A second way of examining repetition effects involves repeating lexically ambiguous words and comparing cases in which the meaning remains consistent from one encounter to the next with cases in which the intended meaning changes. Binder and Morris (1993) asked subjects to read passages of text in which an ambiguous word such as *club* was used. Consider the following example: "There was a lot of excitement at the bars downtown. Crowds of people were gathered outside the **club** on the street. An hour earlier, a man was struck on the head with a **club** and robbed. The police had been called." The first occurrence of the word *club* refers to a meeting place, whereas the second occurrence refers to a weapon. Binder and Morris compared fixation times on the second occurrence of the target word when it was consistent with the earlier mention (so that in both cases the reference would be to a place for social gatherings) to when the second occurrence was inconsistent with the first (as in the example). When the two meanings were consistent, the gaze duration was 258 ms, whereas when they were inconsistent, it was 297 ms.

---

[1]The study described here was carried out in a collaboration consisting of Ed O'Brien, Jason Albrecht, and the first two authors of this chapter.

Binder and Morris performed a follow-up experiment that attempted to diagnose whether the difference just observed was best explained by facilitation due to the repetition of the word's meaning (independent of orthographic repetition) or to inhibition when the word's meaning is changed. This experiment included passages where a control word replaced the first mention of the ambiguous word (*home*, in the example passage replaced the first mention of *club*). In these passages, the gaze duration on *club* at the end of the passage—this was now the first mention of club—was 291 ms for the "weapon" meaning of *club*. As there was little difference between the 291 ms gaze duration on *club* (when it meant "weapon") between the control passage and the gaze duration of 297 ms when its meaning was inconsistent with its previous meaning in the passage, there is little evidence for inhibition due to the change in meaning from first to second mention. Thus, the most parsimonious explanation of the 40 ms difference between the two conditions in the original experiment is a facilitation effect due to concept repetition.

Summary of Repetition Effects

So far, we have examined discourse effects in terms of increased familiarity (due to prior exposure) of whole passages and individual words in the passage. Although it is hard to make a definitive statement about which linguistic processes are being facilitated, we think some plausible inferences can be drawn.

In the case of rereading, we showed that there was only about a 16 ms speedup on the gaze duration of key target words, which is only about a 5% reduction in fixation time. If this reduction (a) can be ascribed to lexical access and (b) is typical for all words in the passage, then it seems that at least some of the 15% decrease in overall reading time from the first to the second reading of the passage is due to discourse processes beyond lexical access. Furthermore, there appears to be no additional benefit in rereading for a repetition of the orthographic form above the benefit for re-encountering the same meaning. These relatively small effects also suggest that many repetition-priming effects with isolated words (using similarly long delays) may be operating largely on postlexical processes.

Also note that although frequency effects were not reduced on a second reading of the passage, they were smaller than those found for words presented in the context of a single sentence. For example, Rayner and Duffy (1986) reported an 87 ms word frequency effect for gaze duration for words embedded in single sentences (in contrast to the 48 ms effect discussed in the Raney and Rayner study). Perhaps the additional context provided by passages reduced differences in integration difficulty between low and high frequency words. This conclusion is speculative because the same target words were not used in each study. But if true, it suggests that part of the word frequency effect observed in reading individual sentences may not only be tapping lexical access, but discourse level processes as well.

Another point worth noting is that Raney and Rayner (1993) found no overall difference between synonym repetition and identical repetition, suggesting that only repetition of the concept is important in rereading. In this study, subjects appeared to be unaware of the wording changes (as evidenced by self-report after the experiment). In contrast, Levy, DiPersio, and Hollingshead (1992) showed that if subjects notice word substitutions, even for synonyms, reading time slows during rereading. Thus, it appears that when subjects notice a surface change, the benefit attained from conceptual repetition is outweighed by the cost of the "double take." Clearly, more work is needed to determine the conditions under which wording changes are noticed and the way in which this noticing process interacts with conceptual repetition.

There appears to be a real effect of speedup as readers get into a paragraph-length passage. At least some of this speedup appears to be due to repetitions in the paragraph. The data indicate that the crucial aspect (as in rereading) is repetition of the meaning rather than of the orthographic form of the word. These repetition effects appear to be about 20–50 ms and thus substantially bigger than the repetition effects in rereading. This is not surprising, because the lag between two instances is much less than in rereading a whole passage. Moreover, the repetition of concepts is an important ingredient in forming a discourse structure (e.g., Kintsch & van Dijk, 1978). Thus, the repetition effects we observed on gaze duration may not only be operating at the lexical level; when a concept is repeated for the second time (over relatively short lags), there may be less time needed to tie it into the discourse structure than when it is mentioned for the first time.

Let us close this section with a final comment about rereading. Looking at savings in reading a passage a second time has been viewed as an implicit memory test of reading comprehension (Kolers, 1975; Levy et al., 1992). That is, one can make various changes in the text (as with the synonym change manipulation) to see what aspects of the text are "remembered." Examining the differences between reading and rereading promises to be a more sensitive test of memory for detail of passages than the usual explicit memory tests now commonly used. Moreover, the use of eye movements in examining how rereading differs from original reading should dramatically enhance the power of this paradigm.

SENTENCE AND CLAUSE WRAP-UP

Just and Carpenter (1980) reported that fixation times on words occurring at the end of a sentence were unusually long. However, their study did not provide a direct comparison of fixation time on the same word when it ended a sentence and when it did not. A study reported by Rayner et al. (1989) specifically examined gaze duration on a target word when it ended a sentence or did not end a sentence. Consider the following two examples:

> The chairman told Hoffman to take his time in deciding. Hoffman made his decision about the new offer later, after he had returned to **Boston**. He explained the possibilities to his wife. She agreed that it was probably for the best.

> The chairman told Hoffman to take his time in deciding. Hoffman made his decision about the new offer later. After he had returned to **Boston**, he explained the possibilities to his wife. She agreed it was probably for the best.

The target word *Boston* occurs at the end of a sentence in the first passage, but not in the second passage. Gaze durations were 53 ms longer on the target word when it ended a sentence than when it did not.

In a second study reported by Rayner et al. (1989), subjects read sentences where a target word either ended a clause or did not end it. For example, consider the following two sentences:

> Before the large and impressive dinosaurs which we see preserved in museums ruled the **planet**, tiny primative mammals called therapsids had already been present for a long time.

> Before the large and impressive dinosaurs which we see preserved in museums ruled the **planet** billions of years ago, tiny primative mammals called therapsids had already been present for a long time.

Here, the target word *planet* ends a clause in the first sentence, whereas in the second sentence it does not. Readers fixated 31 ms longer on the target word when it ended a clause than when it did not.

These studies basically replicate results reported by Just and Carpenter (1980). Although the magnitude of the effect was not nearly as large as they reported, the results provide clear evidence that there is often additional processing associated with reaching the end of a clause or sentence, as the reader apparently engages in tying together or integrating information with the clause or sentence. More recently, Magliano, Graesser, Eymard, Haberlandt, and Gholson (1993) reported a decrease in gaze duration for end-of-clause words. In their experiment, the texts (easy narratives) were much more predictable than the texts used by Just and Carpenter (1980) and by Rayner et al. (1989). They argued that the end-of-clause effect obtained in the prior studies was a result of the unpredictable passages that were used that provoked considerable higher level processing at the end of clauses. It will be interesting in future research to see how these "local" discourse processing phenomena are affected by the characteristics of the text.

ANTECEDENT SEARCH

A fundamental assumption of most models of discourse structure is that the reader is building a discourse structure online by hooking up content words to the structure that has already been built up. An important part of this process is antecedent search, in which the reader searches his or her mental representation of the prior text to determine whether the current word is an anaphor (i.e., has an antecedent in the text already read). This section discusses the two simplest forms of that search: (a) when a pronoun is encountered that refers to a prior noun phrase and (b) when a noun refers directly to a prior noun phrase (either as a repetition or synonym). The next section discusses a somewhat more complex process, where an "elaborative inference" is needed to establish that the current noun has an antecedent in the text.

Pronominal reference and noun-to-noun reference involve the simplest kind of connection, in which a word refers back to a single word that was mentioned earlier in the text. For example, when a reader encounters the pronoun *she* in the course of reading a passage, a search of the mental discourse representation for some mention of the specific female that *she* is referring to may be initiated. Similarly, some nouns require an antecedent. For example, if a reader encounters *the bird*, a search for a previous mention of a particular bird may be initiated. However, the process of establishing an antecedent may also entail drawing an inference about some earlier information. That is, the reader may have to "fill in" information that is not explicitly stated in the text in order to successfully make a connection. A number of reading-time experiments have shown that those processes necessary to establish an antecedent can be time consuming (see Sanford & Garrod, 1981). Eye movement data can address the question of where this extra time is being spent in reading.

Ehrlich and Rayner (1983) found evidence to suggest that antecedent search processes can be initiated immediately upon encountering a pronoun; the fixation on which the pronoun was encoded was significantly longer (about 20 ms) than the previous fixation. However, they also found that such processing was not always completed before the reader moved on to another word. In particular, when there was some distance between the pronoun and anaphor, there was evidence of spillover effects; the next couple of fixations following the pronoun were increased. Ehrlich and Rayner concluded that antecedent search may be initiated while the reader is fixating the pronoun, but might not be completed until one or two fixations following the pronoun.[2]

Is there a similar pattern for nouns requiring antecedents? It may be that pronouns are special lexical items that elicit a strategy of delaying antecedent

---

[2]Blanchard (1987) and Clifton and Ferreira (1987) subsequently demonstrated that the "distance effect" in the Ehrlich and Rayner (1983) study was due to a topic change. However, for our present purposes the precise locus of the effect is not an issue.

search until more information is available. In contrast, nouns typically have more semantic content, presumably making the immediate search for an antecedent much easier. Duffy and Rayner (1990) recently examined this issue. Consider the following two paragraphs:

> Fred stepped carefully onto his front porch. An unexpected snowstorm had hit the night before. Drifts covered the yard. The snow had drifted onto the porch. In fact Fred had worried that it might pile up against the front door. Fred found a *robin (goose)* huddled under a porch chair. The *bird* was in a protected spot. Fred could tell that it was cold, but still alive.

> Fred stepped carefully onto his front porch. An unexpected snowstorm had hit the night before. Drifts covered the yard. Fred found a *robin (goose)* huddled under a porch chair. The snow had drifted onto the porch. In fact Fred had worried that it might pile up again the front door. The *bird* was in a protected spot. Fred could tell that it was cold but still alive.

The target noun was always a category name (such as *bird*). Preceding the target noun was an antecedent that was always an exemplar of the category. The exemplar was either high (such as *robin*) or low (such as *goose*) in typicality with respect to the category. In addition, the distance between the antecedent and target noun was varied as in the two example passages just given (the first and second passages are examples of a close and distant condition, respectively). Table 1.5 shows the gaze durations on the target noun as well as the time spent on the post-target region. Turning first to the time spent on the post-target region, readers were reliably slower when the exemplar was low in typicality. More importantly, the experimental factors clearly affected the gaze duration on the target noun itself. Gaze durations on the close–high typical target were shorter than those on the target words in the other three conditions. This pattern differs from that of Ehrlich and Rayner (1983), who found no effect of distance of antecedent on the fixation directly on the target pronoun.

One possible explanation for the results is that gaze durations in this situation reflect a priming effect that results from the proximity of a highly related lexical item. In the close–high typical condition, a lexical item that was highly related to the target word was in close proximity to the target word and this was not true for the other three conditions. As a result, processing for the target word would be facilitated in the close–high condition. This priming could be having its effect either on lexical access for the target word or on an early stage of anaphor resolution in which relatedness can be taken as an indicator of possible core-ference. Another possibility is that gaze durations reflect a more controlled process of anaphor resolution (in which a search process is automatically triggered) that is initiated when the reader encounters a definite noun phrase regardless of whether a related word has recently been read.

In a subsequent study reported by Duffy and Rayner (1990), an attempt was

TABLE 1.5
Gaze Durations (in ms) on the Target Word and the Posttarget Region (ms per Character) as a
Function of Typicality and distance of Antecedent in the Duffy and Raymer (1990) Experiments

	Experiment 1	
Target Nouns	Close	Distant
High typical	269	294
Low typical	306	294
Posttarget region		
High typical	25	26
Low typical	28	28
	Experiment 2	
Target Nouns	Close	Distant
Category	249	270
Empty noun	275	270
Posttarget region		
Category	24	25
Empty	25	25

made to differentiate between the possibilities outlined in the preceding paragraph. In Experiment 2, distance and target anaphor were manipulated as in the prior study. The target manipulation was changed, however. The target was either a category name (as in Experiment 1) or a more semantically empty noun that could replace the category name in a sentence. In the example that follows, the target was either *weapon* or *object* and the antecedent was *sword*. Empty noun anaphors were included because they could be clearly signalled as anaphors using the determiner *the*, but they were not strongly semantically related to their antecedents. The following is an example passage from the study with the distant condition:

> Bill was ushered by the butler across the marble hall and into the millionaire's lavish living room. Above the fireplace he noticed a gleaming *sword* hanging from red velvet ropes. He took a deep breath and nervously rubbed his hands as he paced. The *weapon* (*object*) drew his attention as he stood waiting for the millionaire to interview him.

As seen in Table 1.5, readers spent less time fixating category names when their antecedents were close than when they were distant in the text. This replicates the gaze duration pattern for the high typicality condition in the first experiment. In contrast, there was no effect of distance of antecedent on gaze duration for the empty nouns. This pattern is consistent with the hypothesis that the distance effect is a priming effect reflecting the recent encounter of a semantically related noun.

The data presented in this section are consistent with the following overall picture of the anaphor resolution process for category nouns. Although still fixated on the anaphoric noun, readers complete lexical access and go on to complete an initial process in anaphor resolution that identifies one or more candidate antecedents for the anaphor. This process is facilitated if a word that is semantically related to the target word has recently been encountered. The eyes then move on to fixate the next words in the sentence. It is during these later fixations that a candidate is actually verified as the intended antecedent of the anaphor.

ELABORATIVE INFERENCES

In this section, we describe two sets of studies that examine elaborative inferences during reading. Many of the current models of discourse comprehension assume that readers activate relevant world knowledge in order to comprehend text, and that this results in a text representation that incorporates what the reader infers or "fills in" as well as the information that is explicitly stated. The critical difference between the elaborative inference process and antecedent search processes described in the prior section is that an elaborative inference involves generating information online that has not been explicitly stated in the text up to that point. Antecedent search, on the other hand, involves building a connection between two explicitly stated concepts. For example, in one version of the passage that follows, the word *weapon* is encountered prior to any explicit mention of what the weapon is. Later, the word *knife* appears and the meaning of the passage can be comprehended only if the reader understands that the weapon referred to earlier was the knife. The reader is said to draw an elaborative inference if he or she made the inference that the weapon was a knife before such an inference was necessary (i.e., when encountering the word *knife* later in the passage). This process is considered different than noun anaphor, because one does not infer in the same sense that a goose is a bird or a weapon is an object. Those "inferences" are logical entailments of the meanings of *goose* and *weapon*. In contrast, a weapon (even in conjunction with stabbing) is not necessarily a knife: it could be a sword, icepick, or some other sharp object.

Although readers clearly need to make inferences to fully understand the meaning intended by the author, there are currently claims (McKoon & Ratcliff, 1992) that very few inferences are necessarily made when reading. Indeed, much of the literature on inferences suggests that readers usually make inferences only when they are forced to by the text (Rayner & Pollatsek, 1989, chapter 8). In the case of elaborative inferences, the evidence for online inference is weak because

TABLE 1.6
Gaze Duration (in ms) on Target Words in the Different Experimental Conditions of the
O'Brien et al. (1988) Study

	Experiment 1	Experiment 2	Experiment 3
High context-explicit	207	217	201
High context-implicit	212	214	227
Low context-explicit	211	210	214
Low context-implicit	234	242	244

Note. The first fixation duration data were very similar to the gaze duration data.

the data used to demonstrate it are typically obtained from an end-of-sentence task or a probe task, and therefore open to the alternative explanation that the inference was made only when it was probed for.

O'Brien, Shank, Myers, and Rayner (1988) reported some experiments that used eye movement data to investigate elaborative inference processes. In their studies, subjects read passages of text such as: "All the mugger wanted was to steal the woman's money. But when she screamed, he *stabbed (assaulted)* her with his *knife (weapon)* in an attempt to quiet her. He looked to see if anyone had seen him. He threw the knife into the bushes and ran away." When subjects read this passage, either *stabbed* or *assaulted* was present and either *knife* or *weapon* was present. Thus, there were four conditions: high-context explicit (*stabbed–knife*), high-context implicit (*stabbed–weapon*), low-context explicit (*assaulted–knife*), and low-context implicit (*assaulted–weapon*). Table 1.6 shows the results across three different experiments. As indicated earlier, the implicit conditions are the ones in which the reader is given an opportunity to draw an elaborative inference.

The central question in the research was whether or not readers' fixation time on *knife* in the final sentence of the passage was the same in the implicit condition and in the explicit condition. If the fixation time were the same in the two conditions, then one could infer that the elaborative inference (that *the weapon* was a knife) had been drawn before *knife* was encountered in the last sentence. If the fixation times were longer in the implicit conditions, then it would be likely that the reader was waiting at least some of the time to make the inference until he or she encountered *knife*.

As seen in Table 1.6, the finding in two of the three experiments[3] reported by O'Brien et al. (1988) was that the critical high- context implicit condition did not differ from the explicit condition. In all three experiments, the low-context explicit condition yielded fixation times like the high-context explicit condition; apparently, the explicit mention of the target word earlier in the passage facili-

---

[3]In Experiment 1 of the O'Brien et al. (1988) paper, there was a distance manipulation. However, because this manipulation had little effect, the data are collapsed across that variable in Table 1.8.

tated processing of the word when it was repeated (in other words, we have further evidence of a repetition effect). Across all of the experiments, the low-context implicit condition yielded the longest fixation times.

We turn now to the difference between Experiment 2 and Experiment 3. In Experiment 2, the passages contained what O'Brien et al. (1988) referred to as a "demand sentence" that may have required the readers to think about the possible inference in the passage. Consider the following passage:

> Joan was delighted when Jim gave her a ring with a diamond (large stone) in it. (1. He had asked her to marry him, and now they were officially engaged.) (2. He often bought her expensive and unusual gifts, and this was no exception.) She went to show her father. [He asked what kind of gem it was]. She excitedly told him that it was a diamond from her boyfriend.

The context early in the passage was manipulated the same way in Experiments 2 and 3. In the high-context condition, subjects would see Sentence 1, whereas in the low-context condition they would see Sentence 2 instead. Sentence 1 is highly related to the topic of diamond rings, whereas Sentence 2 fits with the overall passage but it does not invite the inference of a diamond ring. The sentence in square brackets was the demand sentence; it was included in Experiment 2, but not in Experiment 3.

The results of Experiment 3 clearly indicate that readers were no longer completing the elaborative inference in the implicit condition when the demand sentence was removed. Thus, even the strong cue of *engaged* was not enough in itself to cause the readers to infer *diamond*. As noted earlier, the demand sentence was included to encourage the reader to infer the target (by requiring them to reinstate the target concept). However, the necessity of reinstating the concept *large stone* does not require the inference of *diamond*. Hence, although the demand sentence strongly prompts the reader to infer *diamond* (which requires use of material from the *engaged* sentence as well as the *diamond* sentence), it is not really an inference necessary to maintain coherence in the passage.

In a follow-up study, Garrod, O'Brien, Morris, and Rayner (1990) noted that some of O'Brien et al.'s (1988) passages contained an anaphoric relation between a target word and its prior mention and others did not. Garrod et al. therefore varied (a) whether or not there was an anaphoric relation between a target word and its prior mention and (b) the explicitness of the prior mention. This was done by varying whether or not a definite or indefinite article was used. The following is an example paragraph from their study:

> When Julie saw the crocuses and budding bushes, she thought that spring couldn't be far off. She was convinced when she saw a cute red-breasted *bird* (*robin*) in her back yard. There were also several other signs that winter was ending. She hoped *the robin* (*a robin*) would build a nest in her yard.

TABLE 1.7
Gaze Duration (in ms) on Target Words in the Different Experimental Conditions of the
Garrod et al. ((1990) Study

	Explicit Antecedent	Implicit Antecedent
Anaphoric	234	237
Nonanaphoric	236	269

When the definite article was used, *the robin* is anaphoric on *bird*, whereas when the indefinite article is used there is not a clear anaphoric relationship. Table 1.7 shows the mean gaze duration on the target word (*robin*) in the last sentence. The results indicate that readers use either definite reference or repetition of the noun to equate two concepts, but they do not equate them when both definite reference and repetition are missing.

Garrod et al. (1990) argued that elaborative inferences only occur when there is a clear anaphoric relationship in the text and that the two text characteristics that O'Brien et al. manipulated (a strong biasing context or a demand sentence) may have produced different types of elaborative inferencing. Garrod et al. further suggested that a biasing context results in a passive form of elaborative inference, involving setting up a context of interpretation, whereas the presence of a demand sentence invites the reader to actively predict a subsequent expression.

Given that either a demand sentence or a strong anaphoric relationship seems to be needed to obtain evidence of anaphoric inferencing in these studies, the results of the O'Brien et al. (1988) and Garrod et al. (1990) studies are consistent with the idea that readers are not constantly generating elaborative inferences, or that elaborative inferences are only minimally encoded (McKoon & Ratcliff, 1986, 1992). The studies also clearly demonstrate the utility of using eye movement data to study higher order discourse processes (see also Rayner & Morris, 1990).

ON THE USE OF EYE MOVEMENTS TO STUDY DISCOURSE PROCESSES

In this chapter, we have reviewed some basic facts about eye movements during discourse processing. We have also presented some examples of how eye movements can be used to examine interesting questions about online processes during reading. Our hope and expectation is that more and more studies utilizing eye movements to study discourse processes will start to appear.

In our laboratory, in addition to the studies that have been reviewed in this chapter, we have also used eye movement data to examine topics such as:

1. The resolution of lexical ambiguity (Dopkins, Morris, & Rayner, 1992; Duffy, Morris, & Rayner, 1988; Pacht & Rayner, 1993; Rayner & Duffy, 1986; Rayner & Frazier, 1989; Sereno, Pacht, & Rayner, 1992).
2. The influence of contextual constraint on word processing (Balota, Pollatsek, & Rayner, 1985; Ehrlich & Rayner, 1981; Schustack, Ehrlich, & Rayner, 1987).
3. The processing of syntactically ambiguous sentences (Ferreira & Clifton, 1986; Frazier & Rayner, 1982; Rayner, Carlson, & Frazier, 1983; Rayner & Frazier, 1987).

In all of these areas, it is our sense that eye movement data have become particularly important in adjudicating between different theoretical positions. Let us be a bit more specific with respect to this last point.

There is now a major theoretical controversy concerning the extent to which contextual and discourse variables can influence the initial parsing decisions that readers make when faced with strings of words that are syntactically ambiguous. Although all current models of sentence parsing accept that discourse variables play an important role in sentence processing, they differ markedly in the way they construe the scheduling of these effects. Some accounts maintain that discourse factors guide initial parsing decisions and that they exert their influence before any other factors come into play. Other accounts claim that discourse information is brought to bear after an initial analysis has taken place based on principles related to the rules of grammar and limitations of short-term memory.

With respect to these issues, some evidence (Ferreira & Clifton, 1986; Ferreira & Henderson, 1990; Rayner et al., 1983; Rayner, Garrod, & Perfetti, 1992) favors the view that discourse influences are delayed so that the reader makes an initial parse independent of discourse factors, with such factors influencing reanalysis procedures. Other evidence (Altmann, Garnham, & Dennis, 1992; Altmann, Garnham, & Henstra, 1994; Trueswell, Tanenhaus, & Kello, 1993) favors the view that contextual information is used immediately in parsing. Still other evidence (Britt, Perfetti, Garrod, & Rayner, 1992; Rayner & Sereno, 1994) suggests that under some situations discourse factors influence initial parsing decisions, whereas under other situations they do not. Although there are currently some apparently conflicting findings, it has also become evident that a clearer picture of how parsing strategies operate has emerged from the research and some resolution of the issues is now beginning to appear likely.

The point of the present discussion is that all of the experiments cited in the preceding paragraph utilized eye movement data to establish the conclusions that were made. Whereas all of the original studies dealing with sentence parsing were initially conducted in our lab, more recently many other studies have been conducted in other laboratories because it has become apparent that the best way to obtain data concerning online processes is to use eye movement data. We would be pleased if, in the realm of discourse processing in general, more research from laboratories other than our own were undertaken using eye movements to study the moment-to-moment processes that occur as readers comprehend text. Perhaps there is a trend developing in this direction (see Garrod, Freudenthal, & Boyle, 1994). We certainly hope so and believe that eye movement data can serve a valuable function in further enlightening us concerning discourse processing.

ACKNOWLEDGMENTS

Preparation of this chapter was supported by Grant DBS-9121375 from the National Science Foundation and Grant HD26765 from the National Institute of Health. The second author was supported on an NIMH Training Grant awarded to the University of Massachusetts.

REFERENCES

Altmann, G. T. M., Garnham, A., & Dennis, Y. (1992). Avoiding the garden path: Eye movements in context. *Journal of Memory and Language, 31*, 685–712.

Altmann, G. T. M., Garnham, A., & Henstra, J. A. (1994). Effects of syntax in human sentence parsing: Evidence against a structure-based proposal mechanism. *Journal of Experimental Psychology: Learning, Memory, and Cognition, 20*, 209–216.

Balota, D. A., Pollatsek, A., & Rayner, K. (1985). The interaction of contextual constraints and parafoveal visual information in reading. *Cognitive Psychology, 17*, 364–390.

Binder, K. S., & Morris, R. K. (1993). *Lexical ambiguity: An investigation of access, integration, and inhibition.* Manuscript submitted for publication.

Blanchard, H. E. (1987). Pronoun processing during fixations: Effects on the time course of information utilization. *Bulletin of the Psychonomic Society, 25*, 171–174.

Blanchard, H. E., Pollatsek, A., & Rayner, K. (1989). The acquisition of parafoveal word information in reading. *Perception & Psychophysics, 46*, 85–94.

Britt, M. A., Perfetti, C. A., Garrod, S., & Rayner, K. (1992). Parsing and discourse: Context effects and their limits. *Journal of Memory and Language, 31*, 293–314.

Clifton, C., & Ferreira, F. (1987). Discourse structure and anaphora: Some experimental results. In M. Coltheart (Ed.), *Attention and Performance* (Vol. 12, pp. 635–654). London: Lawrence Erlbaum Associates.

Dopkins, S., Morris, R. K., & Rayner, K. (1992). Lexical ambiguity and eye fixations in reading: A test of competing models of lexical ambiguity resolution. *Journal of Memory and Language, 31*, 461–477.

Duffy, S. A., Morris, R. K., & Rayner, K. (1988). Lexical ambiguity and fixation times in reading. *Journal of Memory and Language, 27*, 429–446.

Duffy, S. A., & Rayner, K. (1990). Eye movements and anaphor resolution: Effects of antecedent typicality and distance. *Language and Speech, 33*, 103–119.

Ehrlich, K., & Rayner, K. (1983). Pronoun assignment and semantic integration during reading: Eye movements and immediacy of processing. *Journal of Verbal Learning and Verbal Behavior, 22*, 75–87.

Ehrlich, S. F., & Rayner, K. (1981). Contextual effects on word perception and eye movements during reading. *Journal of Verbal Learning and Verbal Behavior, 20*, 641–655

Ferreira, F., & Clifton, C. (1986). The independence of syntactic processing. *Journal of Memory and Language, 25*, 75–87.

Ferreira, F., & Henderson, J.M. (1990). The use of verb information in syntactic processing: A comparison of evidence from eye movements and word-by-word reading. *Journal of Experimental Psychology: Learning, Memory, and Cognition, 16*, 555–568.

Francis, W. N., & Kucera, H. (1982). *Frequency analysis of English usage: Lexicon and grammar.* Boston: Houghton Mifflin.

Frazier, L., & Rayner, K. (1982). Making and correcting errors during sentence comprehension: Eye movements in the analysis of structurally ambiguous sentences. *Cognitive Psychology, 14*, 178–210.

Garrod, S., Freudenthal, D., & Boyle, E. (1994). The role of different types of anaphor in the on-line resolution of sentences in a discourse. *Journal of Memory and Language, 33*, 39–68.

Garrod, S., O'Brien, E. J., Morris, R. K., & Rayner, K. (1990). Elaborative inferencing as an active or passive process. *Journal of Experimental Psychology: Learning, Memory, and Cognition, 16*, 250–257.

Henderson, J. M., & Ferreira, F. (1990). Effects of foveal processing difficulty on the perceptual span in reading: Implications for attention and eye movement control. *Journal of Experimental Psychology: Learning, Memory, and Cognition, 16*, 417–429.

Hogaboam, T. W. (1983). Reading patterns in eye movement data. In K. Rayner (Ed.), *Eye movements in reading: Perceptual and language processes* (pp. 309–332). New York: Academic Press.

Hyona, J., & Niemi, P. (1990). Eye movements during repeated reading of a text. *Acta Psychologica, 73*, 259–280.

Hyona, J., Niemi, P., & Underwood, G. (1989). Reading long words embedded in sentences: Informativeness of word halves affects eye movements. *Journal of Experimental Psychology: Human Perception and Performance, 15*, 142–152.

Inhoff, A. W., & Briihl, D. (1991). Semantic processing of unattended text during selective reading: How the eyes see it. *Perception & Psychophysics, 49*, 289–294.

Inhoff, A. W., Pollatsek, A., Posner, M. I., & Rayner, K. (1989). Covert attention and eye movements during reading. *Quarterly Journal of Experimental Psychology, 41A*, 63–89.

Inhoff, A. W., & Rayner, K. (1986). Parafoveal word processing during eye fixations in reading: Effects of word frequency. *Perception & Psychophysics, 40*, 431–439.

Inhoff, A. W., & Topolski, R. (1992). Lack of semantic activation from unattended text during passage reading. *Bulletin of the Psychonomic Society, 30*, 365–366.

Just, M. A., & Carpenter, P. A. (1980). A theory of reading: From eye fixations to comprehension. *Psychological Review, 87*, 329–354.

Keenan, J. M., Potts, G. R., Golding, J. M., & Jennings, T. M. (1990). Which elaborative inferences are drawn during reading? A question of methodologies. In D.A. Balota, G.B. Flores d'Arcais, & K. Rayner (Eds.), *Comprehension processes in reading* (pp. 377–402). Hillsdale, NJ: Lawrence Erlbaum Associates.

Kintsch, W., & van Dijk, T. A. (1978). Toward a model of text comprehension and production. *Psychological Review, 85*, 363–394.

Kolers, P. A. (1975). Specificity of operations in sentence recognition. *Cognitive Psychology, 7*, 289–306.

Levy, B. A., DiPersio, R., & Hollingshead, A. (1992). Fluent rereading: Repetition, automaticity, and discrepancy. *Journal of Experimental Psychology: Learning, Memory, and Cognition, 18*, 957–971.

Magliano, J. P., Graesser, A. C., Eymard, L. A., Haberlandt, K., & Gholson, B. (1993). Locus of interpretive and inference processes during text comprehension: A comparison of gaze durations and word reading times. *Journal of Experimental Psychology: Learning, Memory, and Cognition, 19*, 704–709.

McKoon, G., & Ratcliff, R. (1986). Inferences about predictable events. *Journal of Experimental Psychology: Learning, Memory, and Cognition, 12,* 82–91.

McKoon, G., & Ratcliff, R. (1992). Inference during reading. *Psychological Review, 99,* 440–466.

Morris, R. K., Rayner, K., & Pollatsek, A. (1990). Eye movement guidance in reading: The role of parafoveal letter and space information. *Journal of Experimental Psychology: Human Perception and Performance, 16,* 268–281.

Morrison, R. E. (1984). Manipulation of stimulus onset delay in reading: Evidence for parallel programming of saccades. *Journal of Experimental Psychology: Human Perception and Performance, 10,* 667–682.

O'Brien, E. J., Shank, D. M., Myers, J. L., & Rayner, K. (1988). Elaborative inferences during reading: Do they occur on-line? *Journal of Experimental Psychology: Learning, Memory, and Cognition, 14,* 410–420.

Pacht, J. M., & Rayner, K. (1993). The processing of homophonic homographs during reading: Evidence from eye movement studies. *Journal of Psycholinguistic Research, 22,* 251–271.

Pollatsek, A., Bolozky, S., Well, A. D., & Rayner, K. (1981). Asymmetries in the perceptual span for Israeli readers. *Brain and Language, 14,* 174–180.

Pollatsek, A., Raney, G. E., LaGasse, L., & Rayner, K. (1993). The use of information below fixation in reading and in visual search. *Canadian Journal of Experimental Psychology, 47,* 179–200.

Pollatsek, A., & Rayner, K. (1982). Eye movement control in reading: The role of word boundaries. *Journal of Experimental Psychology: Human Perception and Performance, 8,* 817–833.

Pollatsek, A., Rayner, K., & Balota, D.A. (1986). Inferences about eye movement control from the perceptual span in reading. *Perception & Psychophysics, 40,* 123–130.

Raney, G. E., & Rayner, K. (in press). Word frequency effects and eye movements during two readings of a text. *Canadian Journal of Experimental Psychology.*

Rayner, K. (1986). Eye movements and the perceptual span in beginning and skilled readers. *Journal of Experimental Child Psychology, 41,* 211–236.

Rayner, K., Carlson, M., & Frazier, L. (1983). The interaction of syntax and semantics during sentence processing: Eye movements in the analysis of semantically biased sentences. *Journal of Verbal Learning and Verbal Behavior, 22,* 358–374.

Rayner, K., & Duffy, S. A. (1986). Lexical complexity and fixation times in reading: Effects of word frequency, verb complexity, and lexical ambiguity. *Memory & Cognition, 14,* 191–201.

Rayner, K., & Frazier, L. (1987). Parsing temporarily ambiguous complements. *Quarterly Journal of Experimental Psychology, 39A,* 657–673.

Rayner, K., & Frazier, L. (1989). Selection mechanisms in reading lexically ambiguous words. *Journal of Experimental Psychology: Learning, Memory, and Cognition, 15,* 779–790.

Rayner, K., Garrod, S., & Perfetti, C. A. (1992). Discourse influences during parsing are delayed. *Cognition, 45,* 109–139.

Rayner, K., & Morris, R. K. (1990). Do eye movements reflect higher order processes in reading? In R. Groner, G. d'Ydewalle, and R. Parham (Eds.), *From eye to mind: Information acquisition in perception, search, and reading.* Amsterdam: North Holland Press.

Rayner, K., & Morris, R. K. (1992). Eye movement control in reading: Evidence against semantic preprocessing. *Journal of Experimental Psychology: Human Perception and Performance, 18,* 163–172.

Rayner, K., & Pollatsek, A. (1989). *The psychology of reading.* Englewood Cliffs, NJ: Prentice Hall.

Rayner, K., & Sereno, S. C. (1994). Regressive eye movements and sentence parsing: On the use of regression contingent analyses. *Memory & Cognition, 22,* 281–285.

Rayner, K., Sereno, S. C., Morris, R. K., Schmauder, A.R., & Clifton, C. (1989). Eye movements and on-line language comprehension processes [Special issue]. *Language and Cognitive Processes, 4,* 21–50.

Rayner, K., Well, A. D., Pollatsek, A., & Bertera, J.H. (1982). The availability of useful information to the right of fixation in reading. *Perception and Psychophysics*, *31*, 537–550.

Sanford, A. J., & Garrod, S. C. (1981). *Understanding written langauge: Explorations in comprehension beyond the sentence*. New York: Wiley.

Schustack, M. W., Ehrlich, S. F., & Rayner, K. (1987). The complexity of contextual facilitation in reading: Local and global influences. *Journal of Memory and Language*, *26*, 322–340.

Sereno, S. C., Pacht, J. M., & Rayner, K. (1992). The effect of meaning frequency on processing lexically ambiguous words: Evidence from eye fixations. *Psychological Science*, *3*, 296–300.

Trueswell, J. C., Tanenhaus, M. K., & Kello, C. (1993). Verb-specific constraints in sentence processing: Separating effects of lexical preference from garden-paths. *Journal of Experimental Psychology: Learning, Memory, and Cognition*, *19*, 528–553.

2 The Role of Word-Based Priming in Inference Research

Janice M. Keenan
University of Denver

Tracy M. Jennings
IBM, Santa Teresa Lab

A popular method for determining whether a subject has made an inference is to test the activation level of the inference concept. For example, to see if a subject inferred the instrument of the action in "Bobby pounded the boards together with nails," the activation level of *hammer* is assessed after reading this sentence versus after reading a sentence in which *hammer* would not be a possible inference (e.g., "Bobby stuck the boards together with glue").

In an earlier article (Keenan, Golding, Potts, Jennings, & Aman, 1990), we noted that there is a major problem with this method of assessing the occurrence of inferences. The problem is that inferencing is not the only way in which the inference concept can be activated. It may also be activated by virtue of reading words that are semantically related to it—in this case, *pounded*, *boards*, and *nails*. When a concept is activated by related words in the text, we refer to it as *word-based priming*. When the activation derives from units of text or knowledge structures larger than the word, such as the knowledge that a hammer is typically used to pound nails into a board, we refer to it as *text-based priming*.

Sharkey and Sharkey (1992) further characterized the distinction between word-based and text-based priming. They said that word-based priming has a rapid onset, whereas text-based priming has a relatively slower onset. This claim derives from homophone studies showing that both meanings of a homophone, like *bug*, are activated immediately; but after 250 ms, only the meaning of the homophone that fits the meaning of the text is still activated (Swinney, 1979). The fact that the inappropriate meaning is initially activated suggests that it takes some time for the text to exert its influence.

Sharkey and Sharkey (1992) also claimed that there is a difference between word-based and text-based priming in how long the effects are sustained or how easily they are disrupted. Word-based priming is said to be easily disrupted because, in studies of priming using word lists, one intervening item is sufficient to eliminate any priming effects. Text-based priming, on the other hand, is said to be sustained over several unrelated words, dissipating only when there is a change in topic.

In recent years, researchers have recognized that word-based priming might be a problem in assessing the occurrence of inferences, leading to conclusions that inferences are drawn when in fact the inference concept may have only been activated through word-based priming. As a result, studies using activation measures of inferencing now often try to control for word-based priming (e.g., McKoon & Ratcliff, 1986; Potts, Keenan, & Golding, 1988). This is done by constructing a control version for each text that contains all of the words that the inference version contains that are related to the inference concept, but arranged in such a way so as not to induce the inference. Constructing these controls is difficult, as the following well-known example from McKoon and Ratcliff (1986) illustrates.

McKoon and Ratcliff (1986) used the inference text, "The director and cameraman were ready to shoot close-ups when suddenly the actress fell from the 14th story." They tested for the occurrence of the inference with the target word *dead*. The control version of this text was constructed so that it contained many of the same words but did not imply anything about death: "Suddenly the director fell upon the cameraman, demanding that he get a close-up of the actress on the 14th story." Notice the unusual use of the term *fell* in the control version. This stems from the difficulty of having to construct a passage with the word *fall* but without implying that anything bad happened. Notice another problem: the word *shoot*, perhaps the most highly associated word of all to the target *dead*, was omitted from the control version. This shows that not only are these control versions difficult to construct, but also they are not always successful.

The question we address in this chapter is whether or not it is really necessary to go through the considerable trouble of constructing these word-based priming controls when doing inference research with activation measures. This question arises for two reasons. One is a recent finding by Sharkey and Sharkey (1992) suggesting that word-based priming does not always occur in text. The other is data suggesting that even when word-based priming occurs, it may be too short-lived to be much of a problem for inference researchers (e.g., Carrol & Slowiaczek, 1986).

Sharkey and Sharkey (1992) had subjects read sentences that were interrupted at specific points by the presentation of lexical decision targets. For example, the sentence, *"The boy is sometimes unkind and thoughtless,"* would be interrupted by the target *girl*. They found no priming between highly related concepts like *boy–girl*, even when *girl* immediately followed *boy*. However, when they did another experiment in which they scrambled the words so that they no longer made a sentence but rather a word list, then they obtained priming effects.

Should we conclude from these findings that word-based priming does not occur in texts? No, as Sharkey and Sharkey pointed out, that would be too strong a conclusion, because studies showing that both meanings of homophones are initially activated provide clear evidence that word-based priming does occur in texts. Should we conclude from these results that whatever word-based priming does occur in texts is not enough of a problem to contaminate inference studies? We caution against such a conclusion, as well, because of some methodological problems with Sharkey and Sharkey's study. One is that their experiment showing no word-based priming also had no other significant effects, suggesting a possible problem of statistical power. Another problem is that the critical comparison between intact sentences and scrambled versions was between experiments; perhaps other differences between the experiments, besides the scrambled versus intact sentences, could account for the different results.

Studies of the duration of word-based priming in word-list contexts present a consistent picture of short-lived effects that are disrupted by one intervening unrelated word (Foss, 1982; Gough, Alford, & Holley-Wilcox, 1981; Meyer, Schvaneveldt, & Ruddy, 1972). Studies of word-based priming in discourse contexts, however, present a confusing picture regarding its duration. Foss (1982) compared the duration of word-based priming in lists and discourse. He found that priming effects were quite short lived in a list context, but rather long lived in a discourse context. Specifically, he found as much priming after 12 intervening words in a discourse context as after only 1.5 intervening words in a list context. If word-based priming is this long lived in a discourse context, then it could be a serious contaminant of activation measures of inferencing.

In contrast to Foss (1982), Carrol and Slowiaczek (1986) concluded that effects of word-based priming are short lived, dissipating by the end of a clause. They used a gaze duration methodology with sentences that contained related words like *king* and *queen*. They manipulated whether the two words occurred in the same clause or a different clause of the same sentence, while maintaining the same number of intervening words. They found that *king* primed *queen* only when they occurred in the same clause. These results suggest that any effect of word-based priming should dissipate at the end of a sentence and thus not influence test words presented after the sentence.

It is hard to know how to reconcile the discrepancies between Foss' (1982) and Carrol and Slowiaczek's (1986) conclusions. One possibility is that the effects Foss observed were due not to word-based priming, but rather to the knowledge structures activated by the words when they formed a sentence (i.e., text-based priming). Another possibility is the difference in methodologies. Foss used the lexical decision task to assess priming, whereas Carrol and Slowiaczek used gaze duration. Results from the lexical decision task are subject to the criticism that they may reflect backward context checking, which is brought on by the need to make a dichotomous decision and occurs at the time of test (cf. Keenan, Potts, Golding, & Jennings, 1990). It may be the backward context checking that makes it appear as if the word-based priming effect is so long lived in Foss' study. Yet another possible way to reconcile their results is considered in the "Final Discussion" section.

At this point it is unclear whether there can be word-based priming effects in discourse that are of sufficient potency and duration to contaminate activation measures of inferencing. The purpose of the research reported in this chapter is to help clarify this situation.

Previous studies of inferences have used either one or the other, but not both, of the following types of controls. They either used *no inference control* versions that were not controlled for word-based priming (e.g., McKoon & Ratcliff, 1981) or they used No Inference Control versions that were controlled for word-based priming (e.g., McKoon & Ratcliff, 1986; Potts et al., 1988). For simplicity, we refer to these as the Control version and the Word-Based Priming (WBP) control version. Table 2.1 gives examples of each.

In the present studies, we use both types of controls in the same experiment. This allows us to compare performance across the controls and thereby answer two questions. The first question is whether there is any word-based priming occurring. If there is word-based priming, then latencies to the inference concept should be faster after having read a WBP Control version than after having read the Control version. If there is no word-based priming, then there should be no difference between the two controls. The second question is whether there is any inference or text-based priming occurring. If there is activation of the inference concept from inferencing in addition to that provided by word-based priming, then latencies to the inference target should be faster following the Inference version than the WBP Control. On the other hand, if there is no inferencing and only word-based priming, then performance following Inference versions should be no different than that following WBP Controls.

TABLE 2.1
Sample Paragraph

Initial text:	Bobby got a saw, hammer, screwdriver, and square from his toolbox. He had already selected an oak tree as the site for the birdhouse. He had drawn a detailed blueprint and measured carefully. He marked the boards and cut them out.

Final Sentence Version

Inference:	Then Bobby pounded the boards together with nails.
Control:	Then Bobby stuck the boards together with glue.
Word-Based Priming Control:	He pounded his fist on the boards when he saw that he had no nails.

Note. The inference and control versions are from McKoon and Ratcliff (1981). The WBP control was designed for the current experiments.

The example paragraph in Table 2.1 is taken from McKoon and Ratcliff's (1981) study of instrument inferences. All of the paragraphs used in our studies were adapted from McKoon and Ratcliff's materials. Basically, we just constructed WBP Controls for each of their paragraphs. The reason we chose McKoon and Ratcliff's study as a domain in which to examine the question of word-based priming is that the literature on instrument inferences is so divided on whether or not these inferences are drawn during reading. McKoon and Ratcliff's study is one of the few studies using activation measures that found evidence for subjects making instrument inferences. We wondered, however, to what extent their evidence was really evidence for inferences as opposed to evidence for word-based priming. As Table 2.1 shows, there is a large difference in the potential for word-based priming between their Inference and Control versions. The Inference version contains words highly related to the target word, *hammer*—namely, *pound* and *nails*—whereas the Control version does not. So, a secondary goal of this research was to provide further evidence on the question of the occurrence of instrument inferences.

McKoon and Ratcliff (1981) used a recognition task to assess activation of the instrument inferences. Elsewhere we have argued that recognition measures do not allow one to determine whether the inference was drawn during reading or at the time of test, and consequently, are not the measure of choice in inference research (Keenan et al., 1990). Despite our earlier admonitions, we used recognition in the present experiments. We did this because we wanted to replicate McKoon and Ratcliff's procedure as closely as possible so that we could assess the degree to which word-based priming was affecting their results. Keep in mind, however, that because we are using recognition, any evidence we obtain for inferences above and beyond word-based priming cannot be attributed to inferences occurring during reading; they could also have occurred at the time of the recognition test.

EXPERIMENT 1

This experiment replicates McKoon and Ratcliff's (1981) Experiment 1 on instrument inferences while adding WBP Controls. The goal is to determine whether the activation of instrument inference concepts observed by McKoon and Ratcliff is due to inferencing, word-based priming, or both.

Method

Materials. The materials consisted of 39 of McKoon and Ratcliff's (1981) original 40 paragraphs. As illustrated by the example in Table 2.1, each paragraph consisted of five sentences. The first sentence always mentioned the target instrument. The middle three sentences elaborated the topic, but did not mention the instrument. The final sentence had three possible versions: the Inference version, the WBP Control, and the Control. The Inference version was designed to suggest the target as an instrument of the action. The WBP Control was designed to include all the words contained in the Inference version that were related to the target instrument but not imply the target. For example, for the Inference version, "The teenager was hurriedly digging a grave," which was tested with the target *shovel*, the WBP Control was "The teenager saw a dog digging near the grave." The Control version neither suggested the target instrument nor contained any words related to it.

An attempt was made to make WBP Controls similar in length to Inference and Control versions. However, the difficulty in constructing these sentences and making them fit with the preceding text made it impossible to meet this goal for many of the paragraphs. Consequently, although the Control and Inference version sentences averaged 7 words, the WBP Controls averaged 11 words. For this reason, we do not discuss reading times on the final sentences, even though they were collected, because they were affected by these differences in length.

In order to discourage subjects from anticipating when the target would be tested, filler paragraphs were included that were both shorter and longer than the experimental texts. The fillers were also designed to keep subjects from detecting the fact that the targets for the experimental paragraphs were always instruments. Finally, the fillers provided the targets to which the correct response on the recognition test was "No." There were 63 filler paragraphs.

Design and Subjects.   Final sentence version was a within-subjects factor with three levels: Inference, WBP Control, and Control. The 39 paragraphs were divided into three lists of 13 each. Assignment of materials to list was done using a Latin square with three groups of subjects and 16 subjects per group. The 48 subjects were all University of Denver undergraduates participating for extra credit.

Procedure.   The experiment was run on Kaypro 80286 PCs. It began with a practice session of 90 trials on a lexical decision task. This task was used to get subjects accustomed to responding quickly and accurately to stimuli on the screen. Subjects then read the 102 paragraphs, presented in groups of 6. The paragraphs were presented one sentence at a time. After reading the final sentence of a paragraph, there was a 250 msec delay. Then a line of asterisks appeared on the screen directly above a test word. Subjects decided whether the target word had appeared in the previous paragraph and indicated their response by pressing either the "Yes" or "No" key. Instructions emphasized careful reading so that the subject would be able to understand the meaning of the paragraph and perform well on a comprehension test. A comprehension test occurred after every six paragraphs. It consisted of a test sentence from each of the preceding six paragraphs to which the subject had to respond "True" or "False."

Results

The critical alpha level was set to .05 for all statistical tests. Mean recognition times were computed for correct responses only. Outliers were removed and replaced by the grand mean; this involved less than 2% of the data. No subjects were eliminated from the study because of their performance on the comprehension test. The average performance on the comprehension test was 89% correct.

Recognition Latencies.   Recognition latencies for the target instrument are presented in Table 2.2 as a function of version of the final sentence. Recognition was fastest following the Inference versions, next fastest for the WBP Controls, and slowest for the Controls, $F(2,90) = 8.02$, $MSe = 23,344$ by subjects and $F(2,72) = 7.47$, $MSe = 19,761$ by items.

We replicated McKoon and Ratcliff's (1981) finding that the time to recognize the target instrument was significantly faster following the Inference version than the Control version, $F(1,90) = 15.86$, $MSe = 46,169$ by subjects and $F(1,72) = 14.94$, $MSe = 39,523$ by items. However, it seems that much of the advantage of the Inference version is due to word-based priming. That is because the latencies to the target following WBP Controls were also significantly faster than those following the Controls, $F(1,90) = 5.57$, $MSe = 16,199$ by subjects and $F(1,72) = 3.97$, $MSe = 10,396$ by items. Furthermore, the difference between the Inference and WBP Controls was only marginally significant by items, $F(1,72) = 3.51$, $MSe = 9,284$, $p < .065$, and not significant by subjects, $F(1,90) = 2.64$, $MSe = 7,673$.

In sum, the latency data suggest that there is a significant word-based priming effect. Whether there is also an effect of inferencing on the activation level of inference concepts above and beyond that due to word-based priming is not that clear because the difference was only marginally significant in only the item analysis.

Errors.   The error data are also presented in Table 2.2. They follow the same pattern as the latency data, with Inference versions showing the fewest errors, followed by the WBP Controls, and then the Controls; $F(2,90) = 3.38$, $MSe = 3.26$ by subjects, and $F(2,72) = 2.58$, $MSe = 4.01$ by items. Planned comparisons showed the only significant difference was between the Inference and Con-

TABLE 2.2
Mean Recognition Latencies (ms) and Error Percentages for Experiment 1

Version	Recognition Latency	Errors
Inference	905	9
WBP control	923	12
Control	949	13

trol versions, $F(1,90) = 5.15$, $MSe = 7.99$ by subjects and $F(1,72) = 6.75$, $MSe = 6.49$ by items.

Note that subjects in our study made far fewer errors than in McKoon and Ratcliff's (1981) study. Error rates in McKoon and Ratcliff's study were 30% for Inference versions and 24% for Controls, compared to 9% and 13% in our study. This suggests that subjects in our study responded to our instructions to read carefully. It also suggests that the marginal effect of inferencing observed here cannot be due to subjects not reading as carefully as in McKoon and Ratcliff's study.

Discussion

The goal of this study was to determine whether the activation of instrument inference concepts observed by McKoon and Ratcliff (1981) was due to inferencing, word-based priming, or both. We replicated their finding that instrument inference concepts are recognized faster following Inference versions than following Control versions. However, we also found that these concepts could be recognized almost as fast following a WBP Control that uses the same words as the Inference version but does not imply the use of the instrument. This suggests that much of the activation of inference concepts in these experiments is due to word-based priming.

Our results leave open the question of whether there is also an effect of inferencing. Recognition latencies following Inference versions were faster than those following WBP Controls, but the difference was only marginally significant in the item analysis. If there was no effect of inferencing, that would make these results consistent with other studies showing that instrument inferences are not drawn (e.g., Dosher & Corbett, 1982). McKoon and Ratcliff might counter that their immediate recognition latencies were not their only evidence for the occurrence of instrument inferences; they also had evidence from their delayed priming in item recognition tests (Experiments 3 and 4). However, our attempts to replicate these experiments resulted in no evidence for inferences (Jennings, 1993). So, whether or not instrument inferences occur while reading these paragraphs is still an open question.

Based on Carrol and Slowiaczek's (1986) study, we had thought it possible that word-based priming would dissipate by the end of the final sentence, resulting in no difference in recognition latencies between our Controls and WBP Controls. The fact that our WBP Controls were significantly faster suggests that there is a word-based priming effect that persists beyond the boundaries of the sentence. Furthermore, because we used a 250 ms delay between the subjects' finishing the final sentence and the presentation of the test word, it cannot be said that word-based priming dissipates after 250 ms (Sharkey & Sharkey, 1992). What this means is that researchers wishing to test the effects of inferencing apart from the effects of word-based priming need to incorporate WBP Controls in their studies. The purpose of the next experiment is to provide further evidence on this question.

EXPERIMENT 2

McKoon and Ratcliff (1981) hypothesized that if the instrument in the first sentence was described in such a way that it could not possibly be used as the instrument of the action in the final sentence, then the instrument concept would not be inferred when reading the final sentence. So for the example in Table 2.1, if the hammer was described as broken in the first sentence, then in reading the final sentence that "Bobby pounded the boards together with nails," subjects should not infer that Bobby used a hammer because the hammer is broken. They further hypothesized that if *hammer* is not inferred, then recognition times for *hammer* should be the same after the Inference version as after the Control version. In fact, that is exactly what McKoon and Ratcliff found in their Experiment 5.

At first glance, McKoon and Ratcliff's finding of no difference between inference and Control versions may seem to challenge the conclusions of our Experiment 1 regarding the role of word-based priming. After all, if word-based priming is operating, then latencies to recognize *hammer* should be faster following the Inference version than following the Control version, regardless of whether an inference is drawn, because the Inference version has more words that are related to *hammer* that can activate it. However, McKoon and Ratcliff used a delayed recognition test requiring subjects to read two unrelated paragraphs before taking the recognition test; so the inference concept would not be expected to still be activated, either by word-based or text-based priming, when a paragraph intervenes like this.

The question we asked in Experiment 2 is what will happen with an immediate test involving these materials. As in Experiment 1, we included the Controls originally used by McKoon and Ratcliff and the WBP Controls that we constructed. Assuming that the word-based priming effects observed in Experiment 1 will obtain again in this experiment, we expect recognition latencies to be faster following WBP Controls than following Controls. Because the Inference versions in this experiment differ from Experiment 1 in that the first sentence precludes the target concept from being the instrument of the action in the final sentence, we do not expect the marginal effect of inferencing observed in Experiment 1. If McKoon and Ratcliff (1981) are correct that the first sentence prevents inferring the instrument when reading the final sentence, then latencies following Inference versions should be no different than those following the WBP Controls.

Method

The design, procedure, and number of subjects was exactly as in Experiment 1. The only difference in method was in the materials.

We used McKoon and Ratcliff's (1981) materials from their Experiment 5. These were very similar to the paragraphs we used in Experiment 1. The main difference was that the first sentences were rewritten so as to preclude the target from being the instrument of the action in the final sentence. In rewriting the first sentences, McKoon and Ratcliff also added another sentence following the first sentence. The revised beginning of the example in Table 2.1 was, "Bobby opened his toolbox and pulled out a mallet, a hammer which had been broken earlier that week, and a screwdriver. He also collected the lumber and paint he had bought." Note these versions always included an alternative instrument, in this case the mallet.

Results

Recognition Latencies.   Recognition latencies for the target (e.g., *hammer*) as a function of final sentence version are presented in Table 2.3. The latencies show a difference between the Inference and Control versions, which appears to be due to word-based priming, not inferencing. Support for word-based priming stems from the fact that targets are recognized faster following WBP Controls than Controls. Support for the view that inferencing is not occurring stems from the fact that we found virtually no difference in recognition times between the Inference and WBP Controls. Although this pattern corresponds to our predictions, the differences were not significant. The overall effect of sentence version was $F(2,90) = 1.35$, $MS_e = 2,808$ by subjects, and $F(2,72) < 1$ by items; and the planned comparison of WBP Controls versus Controls was $F(1,90) = 1.61$, $MS_e = 3,370$ by subjects, and $F(1,72) < 1$ by items.

Errors.   The error data are also presented in Table 2.3. Subjects made the fewest errors for the WBP Controls and the most for the controls. The overall difference in error rates was marginally significant by subjects, $F(2,90) = 3.05$, $MS_e = 2.77$ and significant by items $F(2,72) = 3.53$, $MS_e = 3.41$. Planned comparisons of the difference between the WBP Controls and the Controls

TABLE 2.3
Mean Recognition Latencies (ms) and Error Percentages for Experiment 2

Version	Recognition Latency	Errors
Inference	831	10
WBP control	833	7
Control	845	11

showed that difference to be significant both by subjects and items, $F(1,90) = 6.33$, $MS_e = 5.76$ and $F(1,72) = 7.24$, $MS_e = 7.02$. This difference in errors provides further evidence for the facilitating effects of word-based priming.

Discussion

The results of this experiment support McKoon and Ratcliff's (1981) conclusion that a first sentence that precludes the most probable instrument from being the instrument of the action in the final sentence will indeed prevent the inference from occurring. We found no difference in recognition latencies between the Inference versions and the WBP Controls. It should be recognized, however, that having the inferencing effect go away in this experiment may not be all that impressive, because the results of Experiment 1 show that the effect of inferencing was not that much beyond the activation provided by word-based priming alone.

Most important for our purposes is that the results of this experiment support the conclusions of Experiment 1 regarding the role of word-based priming. Again, we found that simply reading a sentence with words related to the instrument target is sufficient to facilitate recognition of the target. Accuracy was significantly better for WBP Controls than for Controls, and the latencies showed a trend in the same direction.

FINAL DISCUSSION

The main question addressed by these experiments is whether word-based priming can affect activation measures of inference. Recent investigations of inferencing have assumed that it can, and consequently, have gone to considerable trouble constructing control versions of texts that control for word-based priming. But recent evidence by Sharkey and Sharkey (1992) suggests that such controls might not be necessary. Given the difficulties in constructing WBP Controls, especially for texts longer than a single sentence, we set out to determine if such controls are necessary. The results of our experiments suggest they are. In both experiments we found clear evidence for word-based priming: Inference concepts were responded to faster following word-based priming controls than following normal controls. If we had not included the WBP Controls, it would have been easy to misattribute the difference in latencies between Inference and Control versions as due to inferencing. With both controls included in this study, it is clear that much of the effect that gets interpreted as inferencing is merely due to word-based priming.

In contrast to Carrol and Slowiaczek (1986), who found that word-based priming did not persist across clause boundaries, we found it persisting beyond sentence boundaries, even after a 250 ms delay. Our findings are thus more compatible with those of Foss (1982), who also found priming across sentence boundaries.

It is difficult to know exactly how to reconcile the various findings regarding the duration of word-based priming in text. We do not think that Carrol and Slowiaczek's (1986) finding is a fluke, because it is rather similar to Dosher and Corbett's (1982) finding no facilitation of semantically related instruments like *broom* following the sentence, "The man swept the floor." Dosher and Corbett interpreted their result as showing that subjects do not infer *broom* while reading the sentence. However, their results also show no word-based priming from *swept* to *broom*.

One possible way to reconcile the results is to examine the number of words in the text that are related to the target. From the materials described in both Carrol and Slowiaczek's (1986) study and Dosher and Corbett's (1982) study, there appears to have been only one word related to the target. In Foss' (1982) examples and in our study, there were two or more related words. For the example in Table 2.1, there are three words related to *hammer*: *pounded*, *nails*, and *boards*. We assume that the more related words there are, the more word-based priming there is. If there needs to be a certain amount of word-based priming before it can be detected, then that could explain the discrepancy in results.

The number of related concepts may be important not only for creating an amount of activation that is sufficient to detect, but also for controlling the duration of word-based priming. If one thinks in terms of a network of concepts with excitatory links, it would make sense that the more concepts feeding activation to the target, the longer the activation could be sustained.

The notion that the number of related concepts controls the detectability and duration of word-based priming can be used to provide a word-based priming account of recent claims for instrument inferences occurring when there is a two-sentence context but not a single-sentence context. For example, Lucas, Tanenhaus, and Carlson (1990) found no evidence that *broom* was activated any more than *closet* when subjects read the single sentence, "John swept the floor every week on Saturday." However, if subjects read that same sentence preceded by the sentence, "There was a broom in the closet," then *broom* was more activated than *closet*. Perhaps what is controlling the effect here is not the presence of a context sentence that induces one to draw the inference, but rather the cumulative activation that *broom* receives from four related concepts (broom, swept, closet, floor) as opposed to only 2 for *closet* (closet, broom).

Similarly, Swinney and Osterhout (1990) found evidence for instrument inferences only with two-sentence texts where the first sentence was what they called script suggestive rather than neutral. For example, for the target sentence, "He cut the juicy meat . . . ," the first sentence was either "John sat down to eat his meal that evening," or "John sat down in his normal chair that evening." They tested for activation of *knife* immediately following the word *meat* in the target sentence. They found that *knife* was inferred only when the target sentence was preceded by the script-suggestive first sentence. Although it may be the case that the difference in activation of *knife* is due to the script knowledge activated by the first sentence, there is an equally plausible word-based priming account of the result. The script version uses more words related to *knife* than the neutral version. Therefore, although the word-based priming coming from *cut* by itself is not sufficient to activate *knife*, when that activation is combined with the activation stemming from the additional related words in the script-suggestive version, then the activation is sufficient to be detected.

It may also be the case that activations are not only cumulative, but they may cause some higher-order concept other than the inference to become activated. This higher-order concept could further help sustain activation. For the example in Table 2.1, for instance, the category concept, *tools*, could get activated and in turn feed activation to *hammer*. In this case, word-based priming induces text-based priming, but the text-based priming is not coming from inferring that *hammer* was the instrument of the action.

In sum, the present experiments show that word-based priming plays a significant role in the activation of instrument inference concepts. We have also shown that it is possible to explain the differences in evidence for the occurrence of instrument inferences by examining the amount of word-based priming. Further research is needed to determine the parameters that control the duration of word-based priming.

REFERENCES

Carrol, P., & Slowiaczek, M. L. (1986). Constraints on semantic priming in reading: A fixation time analysis. *Memory & Cognition, 14*, 509–522.

Dosher, B. A. & Corbett, A. T. (1982). Instrument inferences and verbs schemata. *Memory & Cognition, 10*, 531–539.

Foss, D. J. (1982). A discourse on semantic priming. *Cognitive Psychology, 14*, 590–607.

Gough, P. B., Alford, J. A., & Holley-Wilcox, P. (1981). Words and contexts. In O. Tzeng & H. Singer (Eds.), *Perception of print: Reading research in experimental psychology.* Hillsdale, NJ: Lawrence Erlbaum Associates.

Jennings, T. M. (1993). *The role of word-based priming in instrument inference research.* Unpublished doctoral dissertation, University of Denver.

Keenan, J. M., Golding, J. M., Potts, G. R., Jennings, T. M., & Aman, C. J. (1990). Methodological issues in evaluating the occurrence of inferences. In A. Graesser & G. Bower (Eds.), *Inferences and text comprehension* (pp. 295–312). New York: Academic Press.

Keenan, J. M., Potts, G. R., Golding, J. M., & Jennings, T. M. (1990). Which elaborative inferences are drawn during reading? A question of methodologies. In D. Balota, G. Flores d'Arcais, & K. Rayner (Eds.), *Comprehension processes in reading* (pp. 377–402). Hillsdale, NJ: Lawrence Erlbaum Associates.

Lucas, M. M., Tanenhaus, M. K., & Carlson, G. N. (1990). Levels of representation in the interpretation of anaphoric reference and instrument inference. *Memory & Cognition, 18*, 611–631.

McKoon, G., & Ratcliff, R. (1981). The comprehension processes and memory structures involved in instrumental inference. *Journal of Verbal Learning and Verbal Behavior, 20*, 671–682.

McKoon, G., & Ratcliff, R. (1986). Inferences about predictable events. *Journal of Experimental Psychology: Learning, Memory, and Cognition, 12*, 82–91.

Meyer, D.,Schvaneveldt, R., & Ruddy, M. (1972). *Activation of lexical memory.* Paper presented at the meeting of the Psychonomic Society, St. Louis, MO.

Potts, G. R., Keenan, J. M., & Golding, J. M. (1988). Assessing the occurrence of elaborative inferences: Lexical decision versus naming. *Journal of Memory and Language, 27*, 399–415.

Sharkey, A. J., & Sharkey, N. E. (1992). Weak contextual constraints in text and word priming. *Journal of Memory and Language, 31*, 543–572.

Swinney, D. A. (1979). Lexical access during sentence comprehension: (Re)consideration of context effects. *Journal of Verbal Learning and Verbal Behavior, 18*, 645–659.

Swinney, D. A., & Osterhout, L. (1990). Inference generation during auditory language comprehension. In A. Graesser & G. Bower (Eds.), *Inferences and text comprehension* (pp. 17–33). New York: Academic Press.

3 Response Processes in Cognitive Models

William K. Estes
Harvard University

In an often cited passage, the behaviorally oriented learning theorist E. R. Guthrie (1952) chided the somewhat more cognitively oriented learning theorist E. C. Tolman for leaving his animal subjects buried in thought. In Tolman's theory (1932,1933), the result of an animal's experience in a maze was the formation of "expectations" about what led to what, an idea that seemed intuitively compelling to many psychologists of the period. But Guthrie's point was that the theory included no explicit connection between expectation and behavior and thus was not rigorously testable. In present-day cognitive theory, the term *expectation* has given way to a more formal concept of subjective probability, perhaps better termed *mental representation of probability*. An individual's experience with some collection of objects or events is assumed to lead to the acquisition of knowledge about event probabilities, and this knowledge serves as a determiner of decisions and responses. The theoretical linkage between knowledge and response is critical because it is only by observing responses that we can assess the state of knowledge. How we accomplish this assessment and justify confidence in the results will be the main topic of this chapter.

BACKGROUND

Probability Learning and Probability Matching

A great deal of research and theory development intervened between Tolman's popularization of a rather informal notion of expectancy, or "sign-expectation" (Tolman, 1932, 1933) and the flourishing of well formalized cognitive models in

51

the 1980s and 1990s. The experimental study of learning relative to event probabilities originated in studies intended only to show that principles of simple
learning or conditioning could be extended to situations in which reinforcement
(i. e., the occurrence of rewards or unconditioned stimuli) was uncertain. Dem-
onstrations of the feasibility of such extension were reported almost simultaneously by Brunswik (1939) for the learning of simple mazes by rats and by
Humphreys (1939) for learning by human beings in a situation contrived to be
analogous to conditioning. In Humphreys' situation, which proved to be a proto-
type for much later research on "probability learning," the task for a learner was
to predict on each trial of a series which of two events would occur. The events,
appearance (E1) or nonappearance (E2) of a signal light in Humphreys' study,
occurred with fixed probabilities independently of the subject's behavior. Because the only event probabilities used were 0, .5, and 1, the experiment was
incapable of yielding much insight into the learning of probabilities. However,
the potentialities of Humphreys' paradigm were quickly recognized by other
investigators, and studies by Grant, Hake, and Hornseth (1951) and Estes and
Straughan (1954) yielded evidence that the learning curve, plotted in terms of
proportion of predictions of event E1 per trial block, approached a final level in
which the proportion of E1 predictions by a group of subjects approximated the
probability of E1 occurrence—the phenomenon of "probability matching." This
result aroused much interest because it was predicted by a model for elementary
associative learning (Estes, 1950; Estes & Straughan, 1954) and thus raised a
question that stimulated a substantial volume of research but was still not definitively answered two decades later:

> is there a fundamental probability learning process that develops with practice,
> asymptotes at p [probability of the predicted event], and is directly manifested in
> prediction behavior on early trials, given proper instructions and no tangible pay-
> offs? (Myers, 1976, p. 179)

Myers concluded that there was evidence for such a process but that its operation
is easily obscured by the propensity of subjects to interpret the experimental task
as one of sequence learning rather than one of predicting independent events.

Following a burst of studies in the 1950s that were mainly concerned with
delineating the conditions of probability matching and departures from matching,
research diverged on two paths, one focussing on the learning of temporal
patterns and sequences of events (Gambino & Myers, 1967; Myers, 1970; Restle
& Brown, 1970), the other on the acquisition of knowledge about probabilities
(Estes, 1976). On both paths, research and theory have been concerned primarily
with the what and how of learning. But progress on both paths depends also on
developing a deepened understanding of the connections between behaviors and
states of knowledge. In the following sections, I examine this problem from
several standpoints. I do not limit consideration to research directed specifically

at the learning of probabilities, but, rather, approach the problem in the broader context of research on categorization and classification where probability learning is only one component of a more complex process.

Three Model Frameworks

As a preparatory step, I review very briefly the essentials of three types of models for classification and classification learning, broadly defined—stimulus sampling models, instance-based classification models, and connectionist network models. To apply and test models of these kinds, it is necessary to deal with knowledge-behavior linkage at a quantitative level. I limit this sketch to the simplest model in each family that serves our purposes:

1. the stimulus sampling model for simple probability learning as presented by Estes and Straughan (1954);
2. a simplified version of the exemplar model for category learning originated by Medin and Schaffer (1978) that I have used in other treatments of model-related issues (Estes, 1986, 1994);
3. the adaptive network for categorization formulated by Gluck and Bower (1988).

Readers familiar with these types of models can conveniently skip this review.

1. The Stimulus Sampling Model.   It is convenient to express the learning assumptions of the model in terms of a standard binary prediction experiment with alternative outcome events E1 and E2. On any trial n, the learner's probability, P_1, of predicting E1 changes in accord with the following functions:

$$\text{If E1 occurs, } P_{1,n+1} = P_{1,n} + \theta(1 - P_{1,n}),$$

$$\text{and if E2 occurs, } P_{1,n+1} = P_{1,n} - \theta P_{1,n},$$

where θ represents the fraction of cues (elements or aspects of the stimulating situation) sampled (attended to) by the learner on trial n. It is easy to show that, if E1 and E2 occur with probabilities π and $1 - \pi$ over a series, the expected change in P_1 on any trial n is given by

$$P_{1,n+1} = P_{1,n} + \theta(\pi - P_{1,n}). \tag{1}$$

A well known implication of this recursion is that the learning curve plotted in terms of $P_{1,n}$ is described by an exponential function,

$$P_{1,n} = \pi - (\pi - P_{1,0})(1 - \theta)^n, \tag{2}$$

running from the initial value, $P_{1,0}$, to an asymptote at $P_1 = \pi$. Hence, the model is said to predict probability matching. For our present purposes, it is important to note that on the basis of the learning axioms of the model, the quantity P_1 should be characterized, not as a response probability, but as the proportion of cues in the set being sampled that are associated with the response of predicting E1. The equating of P_1, so defined, with probability of the response of predicting E1 is a convention that has no formal justification in terms of more primitive assumptions.

2. The Exemplar Model for Category Learning. It is assumed that, at the end of each learning trial, a representation of the perceived exemplar in terms of its attributes is stored in the memory array, together with the correct category label. At the beginning of each trial after the first, the subject computes the similarity of the exemplar presented to each member of the current memory array, sums its similarity to all of the members associated with each category, computes the probability of each category, and generates a response based on these probabilities.

The form of the memory array and the computation of probabilities are illustrated in terms of a minimal categorization task in Table 3.1. For concreteness, the category exemplars can be assumed to be light and dark triangles and squares, the entries 1 and 2 under Training Pattern denoting dark and light and entries 1 and 2 in the second column denoting triangle and square. The task has a simple, deterministic structure in which dark stimuli belong to Category A and light stimuli to Category B. The columns of Table 3.1 headed Training Pattern and Category can be taken to represent the memory array we would expect to have been formed after a subject has seen each of the four exemplar patterns once. Entries 1 and 0 under Category indicate that patterns 11 and 12 have been stored in the A column and patterns 21 and 22 in the B column. The tabular

TABLE 3.1
Feature Coding and Category Similarities (Product Rule) for Exemplar Model Applied to Minimal Categorization Problem

Training Patterns	Category		Similarity	
	A	B	to Catagory A	to Catagory B
11	1	0	$1 + s$	$s + s^2$
12	1	0	$1 + s$	$s + s^2$
21	0	1	$s + s^2$	$1 + s$
22	0	1	$s + s^2$	$1 + s$

on test of 11:

$$\text{Probability correct} = \frac{(1 + s)}{(1 + s) + (s + s^2)}$$

$$= 1/(1 + s)$$

arrangement with columns corresponding to categories is just an expository convenience, of course; we assume only that the memory record of the sequence of learning trials includes a feature pattern together with a category tag for each trial.

As the basis for predicting categorization probabilities on tests given at this point in learning, I start by computing the similarity of the first pattern, Pattern 11, to both of the items stored in Category A. The algorithm for computing similarity between two patterns, termed the *product rule*, is to compare them feature by feature, entering a 1 into a product when there is a match and a quantity s (a "similarity parameter," having a value in the range 0 to 1) when there is a mismatch. When we compare Pattern 11 to itself, we obtain $1*1 = 1$, and when we compare it to 12, we obtain $1*s = s$. Thus the summed similarity of test pattern 11 to the current memory array for Category A is $1 + s$. Comparing the same test pattern to the representations stored for Category B yields $s*1 = s$ and $s*s = s^2$ for the comparisons to 21 and 22 and a summed similarity of $s + s^2$. Our prediction of the probability of a correct response (i.e., a Category A response) to pattern 11 is given by the similarity of pattern 11 to Category A divided by the sum of its similarities to Categories A and B , that is,

$$P_{11}(A) = (1 + s)/(1 + 2s + s^2) = 1/(1 + s),$$

which can easily be shown also to be the probability of a correct response to each of the other patterns in this simple case. Thus, our prediction is that, unless s is equal to unity, the probability of a correct response will be greater than 1/2, and if s is equal to zero the probability correct will be unity.

More generally, for any stimulus pattern Π in a binary categorization, the probability of a Category A response in the presence of Π is given by

$$P_{\Pi}(A) = \text{Sim}(\Pi,A)/[\text{Sim}(\Pi,A) + \text{Sim}(\Pi,B)] \tag{3}$$

where $\text{Sim}(\Pi,A)$ and $\text{Sim}(\Pi,B)$ are the total similarities of pattern Π to the patterns stored in Categories A and B in the memory array.

3. The Adaptive Network Model.   In the simple version of this model for categorization introduced by Gluck and Bower (1988), one assumes the same featural representation of stimulus patterns as in the exemplar model, so we can use Table 3.1 again for illustrative purposes. It is convenient to number the features, denoting dark and light by f_1 and f_2 and triangle and square by f_3 and f_4, and to rename Categories A and B as Categories 1 and 2. For a network representation of the task, we define a memory node, n_i, corresponding to each feature, f_i, and a category node, C_i, corresponding to each category. The network includes a path from each memory node to each category node, and a weight, w_{ij}, is associated with the path from n_i to C_j. Presence of f_i in the stimulus pattern of a trial activates n_i, and n_i sends activation to each category node, the strength of activation of C_j being proportional to w_{ij}. The weights are all important, for it is in them that memory resides, and it is by them that responses are determined.

At the outset of the task, all of the weights are equal to 0, but on each learning trial, the values of the weights are adjusted by a competitive learning algorithm known as the delta rule. On a trial when, for example, n_1 and n_3 are active, the weight on the path from n_1 to C_j increases according to

$$w'_{1j} = w_{1j} + \beta(1 - w_{1j} - w_{3j}) \tag{4}$$

if Category C_j is correct and decreases according to

$$w'_{1j} = w_{1j} - \beta(w_{1j} + w_{3j}) \tag{5}$$

if Category C_j is not correct. The terms w_{ij} on the right sides of these equations are the values at the beginning of the given trial and the w'_{ij} on the left are the new values at the end of the trial; β is a learning parameter with a value in the range 0 to 1.

The outputs of the network to C_1 and C_2 at the start of the trial are

$$o_1 = w_{11} + w_{31}$$

$$\text{and } o_2 = w_{12} + w_{32},$$

respectively. These outputs (each transformed by the exponential function $o'_j = e^{co_j}$ to avoid negative quantities) determine the probability, $P(1)$, of a Category C_1 response by the formula

$$P(1) = o'_1/(o'_1 + o'_2). \tag{6}$$

Because this formula has the same form as that given in Equation 3 for the exemplar model, it can be assumed that all conclusions drawn about connections between memory states and responses in the next section will apply similarly to the exemplar and network models.

THE MICROSTRUCTURE OF RESPONSE PROCESSES

In the vast majority of studies of classification learning, the learner's task on each trial is to make a choice from a set of alternatives, most often two in number, to indicate his or her expectation about the outcome of the trial. The outcome may be a to-be-predicted event or a label for the category to which a stimulus presented on the trial should be assigned. Although more complex cases have been studied, I limit attention here to the standard paradigm in which the probabilities of the outcomes are constant over trials and independent of the learner's behavior, and in which the learner's sole source of information about the outcome probabilities is trial-by-trial observation of outcome occurrences. The question at issue is whether an estimate of the learner's choice probabilities derived from his or her observed sequence of choices constitutes a valid measure of the learner's knowledge concerning the probabilities of the alternative outcomes. Consider, for example, the classic two-choice prediction experiment, with outcomes E1 and E2 having probabilities .75 and .25, respectively. If a learner predicts outcome E1 on 75% of trials late in a learning series, do we have evidence that he or she has in some sense acquired knowledge of the true probability of E1? Or, consider the currently more popular binary categorization experiment in which category exemplars are probabilistically related to categories.[1] The learner views on each trial one member of a set of stimulus patterns, indicates which of two categories, A or B, the pattern belongs to, and then is shown the correct category label. In a variant that is especially relevant here, the design includes some patterns that occur equally often in both categories; however, the category base rates (probabilities with which the categories are sampled over the series) differ from .5, so a learner can improve his or her categorization performance by taking account of the base rate. In a study reported by Gluck and Bower (1988), for example, an equal-frequency pattern was included and Categories A and B were sampled in the ratio .75:.25. Over the learning series, their subjects' probability of assigning this pattern to Category A approached .75 quite closely. Again, we wish to know whether the observed probability matching justifies a conclusion that the subjects had formed a veridical mental representation of the category probability. Lacking a window that would allow direct observation of the learner's state of knowledge, we can attack the question only by examining it from different standpoints and seeking converging lines of relevant evidence.

A Canonical Format for Choice Probability

We can sharpen the problem at issue and broaden our approach by taking advantage of the fact that, in a wide variety of cognitive models, the theoretical connection between cognition and action takes a common form. Regardless of the characteristics of a particular task, an individual confronted by a choice among a set of K alternatives is assumed to have some strength of preference for each alternative. The strength for alternative i has some value that may be denoted v_i, and the individual's probability of choosing alternative i is assumed to be given by the expression

$$p_i = v_i/(v_1 + v_2 + \ldots + v_K). \tag{7}$$

With differing definitions for the v_i, this formula has been the standard expression for choice probability in behavioral and cognitive models since the early 1950s. In stimulus sampling theory, v_i is the number of elements or aspects of a stimulating situation that are associated with response i (Estes, 1950). In the

---

[1]A set of stimulus patterns, for e., g., symptom combinations, is sampled on each trial of a series, the patterns having one set of probabilities on trials when Category A is correct and a different set of probabilities on trials when Category B is correct.

choice model of Luce (1959, 1963), v_i is defined simply as strength of preference for alternative i, and the axioms of the model guarantee that the expression will have the formal properties of a probability measure. In current models of categorization deriving from Medin and Schaffer (1978), v_i is the global similarity of a stimulus pattern to all pattern representations stored in memory as members of Category i. In the network model for categorization (Gluck & Bower, 1988), v_i is the sum of weights on paths from active input nodes to the output node corresponding to Category i. In each case, the assumptions of the model, together with estimates of its parameters, enable one to compute a value for p_i on any trial of an experiment. Most commonly the model is tested by comparing these predicted values with choice proportions computed from experimental data.

A question of central interest here, although rarely raised in the literature, is whether response proportions are valid estimators of p_i. How could the assumption be wrong? The first possibility to be examined is that the response process might actually be deterministic, in which case the observed proportion of choices of alternative i could not be expected to provide a measure of p_i. For any group of subjects observed on some trial n of an experiment, each subject might have some criterion value of p_i above which probability of response i would equal 1 and below which probability of response i would equal 0. If the criterion or the value of p_i, or both, vary over subjects, then the observed proportion is a montage that does not provide a measure of any of the p_i or even of their average. Clearly, we need to seek sources of evidence about the relation between p_i and response probability.

The Issue of Probabilistic Versus Deterministic Responding

Taking this route, I begin by considering the nature of the choice response and, in particular, asking whether it is generated by a deterministic or a probabilistic decision mechanism. By *deterministic*, we mean that, knowing the learner's current state of knowledge, we can predict his or her response with certainty. By *probabilistic*, we mean that, knowing the learner's current state of knowledge, we can only assign probabilities to hisor her alternative responses.

In research in psychophysics, there are many well-studied experimental situations for which one can reasonably assume that a subject's response probability depends solely on conditions, such as stimulus parameters, that can be held constant over a series of trials, so that the data take the form of binomial distributions from which response probabilities can be estimated. But in experiments on category or probability learning, matters are more complex, because a subject's response probabilities must be expected to vary over trials. The data obtained from a prediction experiment, for example, could arise from either type of mechanism. It might be that a subject's probability $P(i)$ of predicting event Ei is a graded quantity, corresponding directly to P_i in equation 1, that increases or decreases from trial to trial as a function of trial outcomes. Then, if informative feedback were discontinued at some point, the current value of $P(i)$ would predict the proportion of occurrences of response i over a subsequent block of trials. We would characterize the decision process as probabilistic and could reasonably conclude that the learner had formed a mental representation of the outcome probabilities.

In contrast, it might be that the learner's probability of predicting Ei is either 1 or 0 on any trial and switches back and forth between these values as a function of trial-to-trial feedback.[2] If, then, feedback were discontinued at some point, the ensuing sequence of responses would be either all predictions of E1 or all predictions of E2, and we would characterize the decision process as deterministic. In this case, we could not meaningfully speak of the learner's having formed a mental representation of the event probabilities. A parallel argument can obviously be given for the category learning paradigm.

An experiment conducted in my laboratory (described in the Appendix) was designed to provide an empirical test of the deterministic versus probabilistic assumptions. The task was presented as a simulation of medical diagnosis in order to encourage the subjects to attend closely to the trial outcomes. On each trial of a learning series, the subject saw a stimulus pattern in the form of a chart representing the symptoms of a hypothetical patient and responded by predicting whether the patient would prove to have Disease A or Disease B; following the response, the correct disease label was displayed. A number of different symptom patterns appeared in a random sequence during the learning series, and for each pattern there was some fixed probability, 0, .25, .50. .75, or 1.00, that Disease A would be correct. At the end of the learning series, a series of test trials was given, with each pattern appearing five times on randomly selected trials. The test trials differed from learning trials only in that the correct disease labels were not displayed following subjects' responses.

Results obtained with all of the pattern types led to the same conclusions, so I present data only for the two .50 patterns, which yielded the most divergent predictions from the probabilistic and deterministic hypotheses. With data pooled over the .50 patterns for all subjects, the percentages of cases in which a Category A response occurred 0, 1, 2, 3, 4, or 5 times on the five tests of a pattern are as shown by the white bars in both panels of Figure 3.1. Using the observed overall proportion of A responses as an estimate of the theoretical probability of response A in either a probabilistic or a deterministic decision model, computer simulations of the data to be expected from a probabilistic model yielded the dark bars shown in the upper panel of Figure 3.1 and simulations for a deterministic model yielded those shown in the lower panel. Clearly

---

[2]In fact, a study by Yellott (1969) produced compelling evidence that under some conditions a model assuming such a process closely describes the fine structure of human probability learning data.

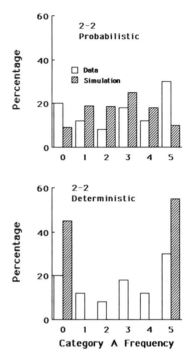

FIG. 3.1. Frequency distributions of Category A responses over five test trials on tests of .50 (2-2) items and predictions from simulations based on probabilistic or deterministic response modes.

the data are much better approximated by a probabilistic than by a deterministic process, although neither could be said to yield a close fit.

How should this result be interpreted? It does not make sense to think of a process intermediate between probabilistic and deterministic, but it is a reasonable hypothesis that the data represent a mixture in which, for some patterns tested on some subjects, responses are generated by a probabilistic process and for the remainder by a deterministic process. To evaluate this idea, we defined a "mixture coefficient" α representing the proportion of subject-item combinations that conformed to a probabilistic process and used a computer routine to ascertain what mixture would best approximate the data. The estimate of a obtained was .61, signifying a mixture of 61% probabilistic and 39% deterministic responding. Weighting the theoretical values in the upper and lower panels of Figure 3.1 by .61 and .39, respectively, we obtain the fit to the observed distribution of Category A response frequencies shown in Figure 3.2. Similar analyses of the data for the other patterns yielded a very similar estimate of α, .70, for the combined .75 and .25 cases and a somewhat smaller estimate, .55 for the combined 1.00 and 0 cases. Thus, we have no support for the idea that either the probabilistic or the deterministic hypothesis holds in general, and we have a rather strong suggestion that data pooled over subjects and stimuli commonly represent a mixture of probabilistic and deterministic responding.

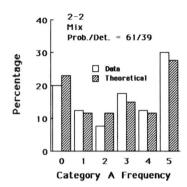

FIG. 3.2. Frequency distribution of Category A responses over five test trials on tests of .50 (2-2) items and predictions from a mixture of probabilistic and deterministic response modes.

A question that immediately arises is whether this result reflects a mixture of two types of individuals in our subject population,—some who respond probabilistically and some who respond deterministically. To obtain some relevant evidence, I set 0 or 5 Category A responses on the five test trials on a pattern as the criterion for deterministic responding and classified the performance of each subject as deterministic (D) or probabilistic (P) for each of the two .50 patterns separately.

Considering the data for individual subjects over both test blocks for both patterns, only 1 of the 20 subjects was consistently deterministic (i.e., produced either five Category A or five Category B responses in every test block), 4 were consistently probabilistic, and the full frequency distribution was very close to the binomial distribution expected on the hypothesis of independence.[3]

The picture emerging from this analysis seems reasonably clear, but one may still ask whether the predominantly probabilistic responding might be limited to the special condition in which responses are not followed by informative feedback. We cannot hope to obtain similarly direct evidence from the data of an ordinary learning series, but there might be possibilities in a model-based approach. Given a model that provides a good description of learning data, we can formulate two alternative versions of the model that differ only in the response process assumed. The exemplar model is suitable for this purpose, and it is straightforward to program two forms of the model that are identical up to the representation of response probability on any trial but differ in the route from this representation to response production. It will suffice for our present purposes to consider only a binary categorization. For any sequence of learning trials up to a trial n, on which exemplar i occurs, both versions will compute the same value of the quantity

$$p_{iA,n} = \text{Sim}_{i,A}/(\text{Sim}_{i,A} + \text{Sim}_{i,B}), \tag{8}$$

[3]Observed frequencies of 0, 1, 2, 3, or 4 probabilistic blocks were 1, 4, 5, 6, and 4, respectively, and the expected frequencies 0.5, 3.1, 6.9, 6.9, and 2.6.

where $Sim_{i,j}$ denotes total similarity of exemplar i to all exemplar representations stored in Category j in the memory array. In the probabilistic form of the model (the one generally assumed in published applications of the model), the probability that exemplar i will be assigned to Category A by the learner on trial n is equal to $p_{iA,n}$. In the deterministic form this probability is equal to unity if $p_{iA,n}$ is greater than $p_{iB,n}$ and otherwise equal to zero.

For the desired analysis, we define a "mixture parameter," ρ, and assume that for any learning series, responding is probabilistic on a proportion ρ of trials and deterministic on the remaining proportion $1 - \rho$. The assumption is vacuous, of course, until a value is specified for ρ, but in the contemplated analysis of a set of learning data, we will use an analysis program that computes the optimal value of r for the given data (i.e., the value that yields the best fit of the model to the data by a least-squares criterion). Applied to the learning data of the experiment just described, this procedure yields an estimate of 1.0 for ρ in the first series and .93 in the replication.

A possible reservation about this last result is that the analysis was based on average response percentages for a group of subjects so we cannot draw direct inferences about response modes of individual subjects. An obvious tactic to meet this reservation is to apply the same analysis to protocols of individual subjects. The data from this experiment are not suitable for the purpose because the learning series included too few trials on each stimulus pattern to allow reliable parameter estimates. However, another experiment conducted in my laboratory will serve. A full description of the study is given in Estes (1994, Chap. 4). The task was simulated medical diagnosis. On each of 60 learning trials, a subject saw a symptom pattern, responded by designating one of two disease categories, then was shown the label of the correct category. For the desired analysis, I applied the exemplar model with the mixture parameter, first to the group data, then to the data for each of the 24 subjects singly. For two replications of the experiment, the analysis of the group data yielded estimates of .95 and .94 for the mixture parameter, ρ. Measures of goodness of fit of the model in terms of root-mean-square deviations between observed and predicted response percentages were 10.91 and 11.33 for the standard exemplar model (equivalent to the mixture model with $\rho = 1$) and 10.88 and 11.27 for the mixture model.

Turning to the analyses for individual subjects, the mean estimates of ρ for the two replications were .74 and .77,—somewhat smaller than the estimates from the group data but still signifying preponderantly probabilistic responding. Six subjects In the first replication and eleven in the second yielded ρ estimates of 1.0, indicating uniform probabilistic responding, and none in either replication yielded an estimate of 0, which would have signified uniform deterministic responding. In the total 48 individual analyses, 38 yielded ρ estimates signifying probabilistic responding on a majority of trials. Thus, both the model-free analysis of the test data and the model-based analyses of the learning data yield the same picture of predominantly probabilistic responding.

The conclusions reached here may have a fair degree of generality. The stimuli and category structures used in my experiments are typical of a great part of current research on categorization and category learning,[4] and it seems likely that we can expect the probabilistic response mode to be predominant in most studies using meaningful stimuli defined on multiple attributes. Analyses of individual subject data in simple probability learning experiments (Estes, 1964; Friedman et al., 1964) suggest that the same characterization holds there also, although there may be a shift toward deterministic responding when learning series are very long or when rewards are given for correct responding (Myers, 1970, 1976). The one important exception to our conclusions is associated with studies of categorization of very simple stimuli (e.g., line segments or angles), defined on continuous sensory dimensions. For that type of study, Ashby and his associates have produced clear evidence of deterministic responding (Ashby, 1992; Ashby & Lee, 1991). A critical difference between the two types of studies may be that, when stimuli are defined on only one or two sensory dimensions, subjects can discover a criterion that defines category membership (e.g., all angles greater than 45° belong to Category A) and recode stimuli in terms of their relation to the criterion, whereas with complex, multiattribute stimuli such recoding may be difficult or impossible.

The Problem of Inference From Response to Cognition

In many of the models that use Equation 1 as the basis for prediction of choices, it is assumed that the observed proportion of occurrences of response i in a subject's data should directly estimate p_i, and that, if the response process is probabilistic, the probability of response i should be given by p_i. A critical question concerns the justification for assuming that p_i, computed from Equation 7, rather than some transformation of it, should represent response probability. This question was considered by Estes, Campbell, Hatsopoulis, and Hurwitz (1989) in the course of applying the exemplar model to a set of category learning data. They first fit their data with p_i, computed from the right-hand side of Equation 8, interpreted as response probability. Then they compared the result with a fit of the model changed only by defining the v_i in Equation 7 as

$$v_i = e^{c \text{Sim}(i)}, \tag{9}$$

where c is a scaling parameter, and basing predictions on the modified form of Equation 8

$$p_{iA,n} = e^{c \text{Sim}_i,A}/(e^{c \text{Sim}_i,A} + e^{c \text{Sim}_i,B}). \tag{10}$$

---

[4]For reviews, see Estes (1994); Medin and Florian (1992); Nosofsky (1992); Nosofsky, Kruschke, and McKinley, 1992; Smith and Medin (1981).

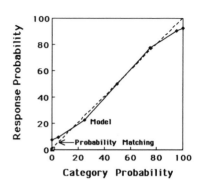

FIG. 3.3. Theoretical Category A probabilities, on a percentage scale, computed from the exemplar model with the standard expression for response probability (dashed line) or with a modified expression in which similarities are subjected to an exponential transformation (solid curve).

The fit of this modified version of the model proved to be actually slightly better than that of the standard version.

The way in which this modification of the choice function alters predictions is illustrated in Figure 3.3. The straight dashed line in the figure represents asymptotic probability of choosing Category A computed from Equation 8 for various true probabilities of Category A. The solid curve represents the same theoretical probability computed from Equation 10[5]. An alternative modification that might deserve consideration is to alter Equation 7 by subjecting p_i, rather than v_i, to an exponential transformation. That is, with p_i defined by

$$p_{i,A} = \text{Sim}_{i,A}/(\text{Sim}_{i,A} + \text{Sim}_{i,B}),$$

probability of response A to stimulus i would be given by the expression $e^{cp_{i,A}}/(e^{cp_{i,A}} + e^{cp_{i,B}})$. This function is plotted in Figure 3.4 for two values of the parameter c and will be seen to deviate from the dashed diagonal line in much the same way as the function shown in Figure 3.3.

It is not easy to determine whether either of these transformations would improve our predictions of probability learning data, for there are almost no reported studies that have employed enough trials to yield measures of asymptotic response probability together with enough different event probabilities to yield meaningful functions for comparison with those in Figures 3.3 and 3.4. The one relevant study I have found was reported by Voss, Thompson, and Keegan (1959, Experiment 3). Subjects learned a list of nine paired-associate items with the unusual feature that for each stimulus there were two response alternatives, one of which was correct with probability π and the other with probability $1 - \pi$, with π varying from .1 to .9. A plot of asymptotic response proportions versus π values exhibited a sigmoid form very similar to the function for $c = 4$ in Figure 4.

A number of categorization experiments yield suitable data, because the category structures typically include sets of exemplar patterns for which the validity

---

[5]For this computation, $\text{Sim}_{i,A} + \text{Sim}_{i,B}$ was set equal to 10 and c was set equal to 4.

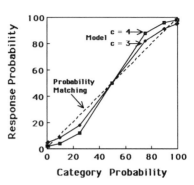

FIG. 3.4. Theoretical Category A probabilities, on a percentage scale, computed from the exemplar model with the standard expression for response probability (dashed line) or with a modified expression in which the standard exemplar model expression for response probability is transformed as described in the text.

(e.g., probability of a category in the presence of the pattern) varies over a wide range. One such case was reported by Gluck and Bower (1988, Experiment 1). Estimates of asymptotic categorization response probabilities for that experiment are plotted against true category probabilities in Figure 3.5, and a similar plot for a semi replication of Gluck and Bower's study reported by Estes et al. (1989, Experiment 1) is given in Figure 3.6. Data from another study of generally similar design done in my laboratory (Estes, 1994, Chap. 5, Experiment 5.2) yield the function shown in Figure 3.7. In all three cases, a very large percentage of the variance in the data values can be accounted for by a linear "probability matching" function (the dashed diagonal line in each figure).[6] However, all of the functions deviate somewhat from linearity in the direction of the theoretical functions of Figures 3.3 and 3.4, suggesting that there may be some error in using observed response proportions to estimate values of the theoretical quantity p_i, which is assumed in both stimulus sampling and exemplar models to represent response probability.

Subject Estimation of Event Probabilities

Although theoretical response probabilities have been estimated from observed response frequencies in nearly all research on probability learning and category learning, a few studies have used the presumably more direct procedure of having experimental subjects generate estimates of event probabilities. In two relevant studies of probability learning, subjects were run in binary prediction experiments with standard procedures (as those of Edwards, 1961; Estes & Straughan, 1954; Friedman et al., 1964; Grant et al., 1951) except that, on each trial, the subject gave a numerical estimate of the probabilities of the outcome events (Bauer, 1972; Neimark & Shuford, 1959). Both studies included groups that made prediction responses in the standard fashion and groups that both

---

[6]In these and other figures that include data, both theoretical probabilities and response measures are expressed on a percentage scale.

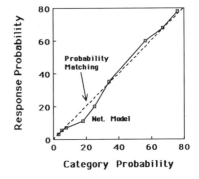

FIG. 3.5. Predictions from the Gluck and Bower (1988) model for Category A percentages at the asymptote of learning (solid curve) compared with exemplar model prediction of probability matching (dashed line).

predicted the trial outcome and estimated its probability; Bauer's study also included a group that only gave estimates. In both studies, all of the learning curves for probability estimates resembled those obtained for response proportions in groups that only made predictive responses. Over a 400-trial learning series in Bauer's study and over a 300-trial series in Neimark and Shuford's, these curves approximated probability matching closely over the later trial blocks, event probability being .70–.30 and .67–.33 in the two studies, respectively. In contrast, in both studies, learning curves for prediction responses for the groups that both predicted events and estimated probabilities rose more steeply and reached levels in the range .80–.85, considerably above probability matching. It would have been easy for subjects who both predicted and estimated to adopt a deterministic response mode, predicting E1 whenever its estimated probability was appreciably higher than .50 and predicting E2 whenever the estimated E1 probability was appreciably lower than .50.

Neither of the probability learning studies used enough different event probabilities to allow a comparison of asymptotic response proportions and probability estimates over a significant range of values. However, relevant data are obtainable from a few category learning studies. One is the Estes et al. (1989, Experi-

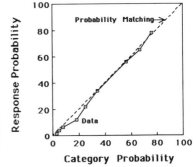

FIG. 3.6. Asymptotic Category A percentages from the study of Estes et al. (1989) compared to predictions computed on the hypothesis of probability matching (dashed line).

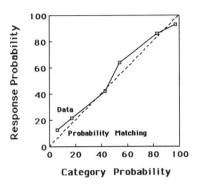

FIG. 3.7.   Asymptotic Category A percentages from a category learning study cited in the text compared to predictions computed on the hypothesis of probability matching (dashed line).

ment 1) study. On learning trials, their subjects made binary choices, assigning exemplars (symptom patterns) to categories. On blocks of interspersed test trials (on which the stimuli were single symptoms), only half of the subjects made binary choices, whereas the other half gave numerical estimates of category probabilities. Test results for both groups are shown in Figure 3.8, with response proportions for one group and mean probability estimates for the other plotted as a function of true category probability. The function for categorizing deviates from linearity in the same way seen previously for the learning data (see Fig. 3.6), and looks much like the theoretical function for $c = 4$ in Figure 3.4. In contrast, the function for estimating probability parallels the probability-matching diagonal, but runs somewhat above it, indicating some overall bias toward Category A.[7] Clearly, categorization response proportions and category probability estimates cannot both correspond directly to theoretical responses computed from a model (although it has been tacitly assumed that they do in applications of models to categization data).

Given that the response proportions and probability estimates are not even linearly related, which should be the preferred empirical dependent variable in tests of models? In discussions of this question with other investigators, I have found that many use response proportions without much concern about their validity as measures of theoretical quantities, partly because research on category learning has traditionally been focused on the prediction of categorization performance, and partly because of the lack of any satisfactory theoretical account of how individuals generate numerical estimates of probabilities. The first reason does not impress me as a good one, for progress toward the goal of adequate prediction of categorization performance must depend on having sound proce-

---

[7]Biases of this kind appear to occur only when subjects are asked to estimate probabilities in the absence of suitable preparation for the task. When subjects have experience in making estimates in a situation where they receive trial-by-trial informative feedback, as in the study of Neimark and Shuford (1959), such biases characteristically disappear.

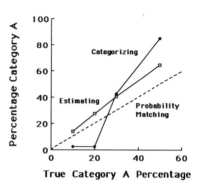

FIG. 3.8. Comparison of data from categorization test trials on which subjects in one condition made categorization responses in the usual manner and those in the other condition gave numerical estimates of category probabilities. From Estes et al. (1989).

dures for estimating theoretical variables of models from data. The second reason points to a problem that deserves attention, but not only in connection with probability estimation, for we do not yet have a theoretical account of how individuals generate responses. In modern cognitive psychology, notable progress toward characterizing properties of mental representations has been accompanied by some neglect of their linkage to the behavior that is not only what we wish to predict and explain but also the principal source of information about cognitive structures and processes.

SUMMARY

To summarize the implications of the various attempts to clarify the connections between theoretical variables and behavioral measures that have been discussed in this chapter, we can first offer some comfort for the many investigators who assume direct relations between theoretical and observed probabilities without worrying much about the basis for the assumption. It appears that, in many commonly studied experimental paradigms, the assumption of probabilistic responding is satisfied to a fairly good approximation, and there has been progress toward delineating some of the conditions under which deterministic responding predominates. Less comforting are the indications that estimates of the theoretical probabilities defined in models derived from subjects' response proportions or from their estimates of event probabilties apparently are neither identical nor even linearly related. It seems that either response measure can be expected to be serviceable when one's predictions from models concern qualitative or semiquantitative aspects of data, but that some uncertainty should be attached to conclusions derived from quantitative fits of models to data until we have a better grasp of the connections between theoretical variables and behavior.

APPENDIX

Experiment on Probabilistic Versus Deterministic Responding

The purpose of the experiment was to determine whether a learner who has probabilities p and $1 - p$ of assigning a stimulus pattern x to Categories A and B, respectively, at a given stage of learning will, if the pattern is repeated on n trials, generate a binomial distribution of responses with mean pn or will make the same response (the one with higher probability) on every trial. These alternative results would be taken to signify probabilistic or deterministic responding, respectively.

Method. The task was simulated medical diagnosis. The stimuli were bar charts, representing symptom patterns, that were to be assigned to disease Categories A or B. The subjects were 20 Harvard undergraduates, assigned to two groups of 10 that differed only with respect to the set of specific symptom patterns and the order of presentation. The heights of bars, two values in each of six chart positions, signified high or low degrees of various symptoms, and the patterns used for each subgroup were a random subset of 12 of the 64 possible patterns. The charts were shown on a microcomputer screen and responses were typed on the keyboard.

For each subject, the experiment constituted a series of 200 trials, two blocks of 50 learning trials each followed by a block of 50 test trials. Frequencies of presentation of symptom patterns in categories were as follows within each block of learning trials. (Two additional patterns were included in the learning series, one occurring once in Category A and one occurring once in Category B. These patterns were not tested, so they will be ignored in the remainder of this exposition.)

Number of Patterns	Category A	B
1	4	0
1	0	4
2	3	1
2	1	3
1	6	2
1	2	6
2	2	2

Thus it was expected that the learner's probabilities of assigning different patterns to Category A would approach different levels, ranging from 0 to 1, by the end of the learning series. Each of these 10 patterns was presented five times in each test block, with the presentations of different patterns intermixed in a quasi-random sequence.

On each learning trial, a pattern was displayed and the subject entered a categorization response on the keyboard, following which the correct category label for the trial appeared on the display screen. Test trials were exactly the same except that the correct category label was not shown.

ACKNOWLEDGMENTS

The research reported and preparation of this article were supported by Grant BNS 90–09001 from the National Science Foundation. I am indebted to Nicholas Hatsopoulis, Joshua B. Hurwitz, and W. Todd Maddox for assistance with the research.

REFERENCES

Ashby, F. G. (1992). Multidimensional models of categorization. In F. G. Ashby (Ed.), *Multidimensional Models of Perception and Cognition* (pp. 449–483). Hillsdale, N J : Lawrence Erlbaum Associates.

Ashby, F. G., & Lee, W. W. (1991). Predicting similarity and categorization from identification. *Journal of Experimental Psychology:General*, *120*, 150–172.

Bauer, M. (1972). Relations between prediction- and estimation- responses in cue-probability learning and transfer. *Scandinavian Journal of Psychology*, *13*, 198–207.

Brunswik, E. (1939). Probability as a determiner of rat behavior. *Journal of Experimental Psychology*, *25*, 175–197.

Edwards, W. (1961). Probability learning in 1000 trials. *Journal of Experimental Psychology*, *62*, 385–394.

Estes, W. K. (1950). Toward a statistical theory of learning. *Psychological Review*, *57*, 94–107.

Estes, W. K. (1964). Probability learning. In A. W. Melton (Ed.), *Categories of Human Learning* (pp. 89–128). New York: Academic Press.

Estes, W. K. (1976). The cognitive side of probability learning. *Psychological Review*, *83*, 37–64.

Estes, W. K. (1986). Array models for category learning. *Cognitive Psychology*, *18*, 500–549.

Estes, W. K. (1994). *Classification and Cognition*. Oxford: Oxford University Press.

Estes, W. K., Campbell, J. A., Hatsopoulis, N., & Hurwitz, J. B. (1989). Base-rate effects in category learning: A comparison of parallel network and memory storage-retrieval models. *Journal of Experimental Psychology: Learning, Memory, and Cognition*, *15*, 556–571.

Estes, W. K., & Straughan, J. H. (1954). Analysis of a verbal conditioning situation in terms of statistical learning theory. *Journal of Experimental Psychology*, *47*, 225–234.

Friedman, M. P., Burke, C. J., Cole, M., Keller, L., Millward, R. B., & Estes, W. K. (1964). Two-choice behavior under extended training with shifting probabilities of reinforcement. In R. C. Atkinson (Ed.), *Studies in Mathematical Psychology* (pp. 250–315). Stanford, CA: Stanford University Press.

Gambino, B., & Myers, J. L. (1967). Role of event runs in probability learning. *Psychological Review*, *74*, 410–419.

Gluck, M. A., & Bower, G. H. (1988). From conditioning to category learning: An adaptive network model. *Journal of Experimental Psychology: General*, *117*, 225–244.

Grant, D. A., Hake, H. W., & Hornseth, J. P. (1951). Acquisition and extinction of a verbal conditioned response with differing percentages of reinforcement. *Journal of Experimental Psychology*, *42*, 1–5.

Guthrie, E. R. (1952). *The Psychology of Learning*, Revised Edition. New York: Harper and Brothers.

Humphreys, L. G. (1939). Accquisition and extinction of verbal expectations in a situation analogous to conditioning. *Journal of Experimental Psychology*, *25*, 294–301.

Luce, R. D. (1959). *Individual Choice Behavior*. New York: Wiley.

Luce, R. D. (1963). Detection and recognition. In R. D. Luce, R. R. Bush, & E. Galanter (Ed.), *Handbook of Mathematical Psychology*. Vol. 1, pp. 103–189. New York: Wiley.

Medin, D. L., & Florian, J. E. (1992). Abstraction and selective coding in exemplar-based models of categorization. In A. Healy, S. M. Kosslyn, & R. M. Shiffrin (Ed.), *From Learning Processes to Cognitive Processes: Essays in Honor of William K. Estes* (pp. 207–234). Hillsdale, N J : Lawrence Erlbaum Associates.

Medin, D. L., & Schaffer, M. M. (1978). Context theory of classification learning. *Psychological Review*, *85*, 207–238.

Myers, J. L. (1970). Sequential choice behavior. In G. H. Bower (Ed.), *The Psychology of Learning and Motivation: Advances in Research and Theory*. Vol. 4, pp. 109–170. New York: Academic Press.

Myers, J. L. (1976). Probability learning and sequence learning. In W. K. Estes (Ed.), *Handbook of Learning and Cognitive Processes*, Vol. 3 (pp. 171–205). Hillsdale, N J : Lawrence Erlbaum Associates.

Neimark, E. D., & Shuford, E. H. (1959). Comparison of predictions and estimates in a probability learning situation. *Journal of Experimental Psychology*, *57*, 294–298.

Nosofsky, R. M. (1992). Exemplars, prototypes, and similarity rules. In A. Healy, S. M. Kosslyn, & R. M. Shiffrin (Eds.), *From Learning Theory to Connectionist Theory: Essays in Honor of William K. Estes* (pp. 149–167). Hillsdale, N J : Lawrence Erlbaum Associates.

Nosofsky, R. M., Kruschke, J. K., & McKinley, S. (1992). Combining exemplar-based category representations and connectionist learning rules. *Journal of Experimental Psychology: Learning, Memory, and Cognition*, *18*, 211–233.

Restle, F., & Brown, E. R. (1970). Serial pattern learning. *Journal of Experimental Psychology*, *83*, 120–125.

Smith, E. E., & Medin, D. L. (1981). *Categories and Concepts*. Cambridge, MA: Harvard University Press.

Tolman, E. C. (1932). *Purposive Behavior in Animals and Men*. New York: Appleton-Century.

Tolman, E. C. (1933). Sign-gestalt or conditioned reflex? *Psychological Review*, *40*, 246–255.

Voss, J. F., Thompson, C. P., & Keegan, J. H. (1959). Acquisition of probabilistic paired associates as a function of S-R1 S-R2 probability. *Journal of Experimental Psychology*, *58*, 390–399.

Yellott, J. I., Jr. (1969). Probability learning with noncontingent success. *Journal of Mathematical Psychology*, *6*, 541–575.

4
Perceptual Similarity and Salience in the Accessing of Lexical Meaning

Albrecht Werner Inhoff
Cynthia Connine
State University of New York at Binghamton

This chapter primarily focuses on modality-specific sources of information that contribute to the recognition of words during reading, as the retrieval of word meanings must precede more molar language comprehension processes. We will discuss how characteristics unique to visual language are exploited in this process. A brief comparison with one aspect of auditory word recognition is used to argue that similar principles may guide language recognition in the two domains but that different signal characteristics force modality specific implementations of these principles. Finally, we consider the possibility that modality-specific codes are included, or are part of, readers' molar text representations.

SIGNAL VARIABILITY AND THE REPRESENTATION OF MEANING

Derivation of meaning from the acoustic speech signal requires complex attentional, perceptual, and linguistic skills. The acoustic properties of the basic, linguistically defined speech unit, the phoneme, vary across speakers, speaking rates, and phoneme contexts. The speech signal, produced by fluent speakers, is nearly devoid of any segmentation clues and the temporal structuring of speech provides little, if any, information pertaining to word onsets and offsets. Furthermore, listeners must be able to understand spoken language under a wide range of signal presentation rates as the speaker, rather than the listener, controls the rate of signal presentation. Because listeners experience little difficulty in understanding spoken language, research in this domain has to a large degree focused on their apparent success at contacting knowledge representations with noisy acoustic signals.

The signal in visually presented language, in the form of distinct graphemes (letters) and word sequences, appears to be substantially less noisy. In the realm of printed language, a grapheme's spatial layout is generally unaffected by the presence of surrounding graphemes and, across writing systems, graphemic variability is relatively small; the visual signal is stationary and is generally segmented into spatially distinct letter, word, and sentence units. Two other aspects of visually presented language symbols appear to benefit the recognition processes: First, the individual who learns to read is usually quite mature and can draw on well established language encoding and comprehension skills in the auditory domain. Second, the reader (encoder), rather than the writer (signal source), controls the rate of signal presentation. Yet, learning to read progresses at a relatively slow pace and more developmental difficulties are associated with the perception and comprehension of written language than with the perception and comprehension of spoken language.

Closer examination of the visuospatial signal, as available to the reader, reveals several sources of signal variability (noise). The visual signal, in the form of letter and word sequences, is projected onto a retinal structure with vast differences in visual acuity. High-acuity vision is confined to a small concentric area that is projected onto the fovea and adjacent parafovea. At a typical eye text distance of approximately 40 cm and a font size of 10 characters per inch, approximately 3 to 5 horizontal character spaces to the right and left of a fixated character space, and adjacent character spaces on lines above or below the fixated character space, are projected onto the fovea and adjacent parafovea. Within this range, fine grained letter discrimination is possible as needed; for instance, when *house* is to be distinguished from *horse*. However, even within this area, there is a distinct center-to-periphery acuity gradient, with highest acuity for the directly fixated letter. To apply high acuity vision to segments of text beyond the foveal-near parafoveal area, readers must execute eye movements, called saccades. After each saccade, the eyes are relatively stationary (fixated) and useful linguistic information is obtained. Two types of saccades are generally discriminated: frequently occurring regular (forward) saccades that move the eyes to novel text and occasional regressions that move the eyes to previously read text.

Saccade lengths are quite variable and move the focus of vision to various intraword locations. As can be seen for six-letter words in Fig. 4.1, center letters are the most likely recipient of a fixation but other letters are also frequently fixated (Inhoff, 1989a; O'Regan, 1981; Rayner, 1979). Because there are large changes of visual acuity even within the fovea, variability in intraword fixation location will introduce variability in the available visual signal. For instance, the word *mirror* will provide a different retinal signal to the language recognition system when fixated near the second letter than when fixated near the fifth letter.

Six Letter Word Fixation Location

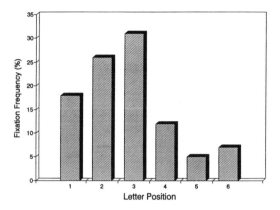

FIG. 4.1.   The frequency with which letters 1–6 of a six-letter word are fixated during sentence reading. The data were obtained by Inhoff (1989a). Adapted by permission of the American Psychological Association.

Fixation location effects are found in word-naming latencies with shorter naming times when optimal intraword locations are fixated, with optimal corresponding to a word center fixation for short words and a fixation slightly left to the center for long words (O'Regan, 1983).

Fixation location effects are also found in word viewing times, with shorter gaze durations for fixations at optimal locations (O'Regan & Levy-Schoen, 1987; O'Regan, Levy-Schoen, Pynte, & Brugaillere, 1984), and in the frequencies with which words are refixated during reading, with fewer refixations following optimal fixations (McConkie, Kerr, Reddix, Zola, & Jacobs, 1989; Vitu, 1991; Vitu, O'Regan, & Mittau, 1990).

Another source of variability in the visual signal is related to readers' acquisition of visual information beyond the boundaries of the directly fixated word. Although the visual acuity of these adjacent words (subsequently called *parafoveal words*) is generally insufficient for fine grained letter discriminations, some useful visual information is obtained. Fig. 4.2 shows the proportion of words skipped during the reading of short 80- to 100-word passages of text that were presented line by line on a computer screen while eye movements were recorded (Vitu, O'Regan, Inhoff, & Topolski, 1994). As can be seen, a substantial proportion of words did not receive a fixation, with skipping rates of approximately 70% for very short words. When word skipping occurs, all perceptual and linguistic analyses pertaining to the skipped word must have been based on a low-acuity, high-noise parafoveal signal.

Visual and auditory sources of information thus provide noisy, yet informative, signals. For each modality, the symbol-representation system must thus

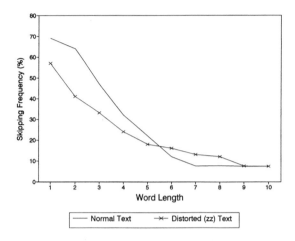

FIG. 4.2.   The skipping rate as a function of letter string length. Two text conditions are shown. One in which normal passages of text were read and one in which text was distorted by replacing all letters of text with the letter z.

discover means of discerning linguistically informative signal components from noise. In this discovery, the usefulness of a signal component for accessing meaning may be a function of its perceptual distinctiveness within a particular modality, with salient signal components being less affected by noise than non-salient components. Identification of perceptually salient features could dominate the recognition process in that their use may precede and constrain the acquisition of perceptually less salient signal components. Because some linguistic features may be perceptually salient when the signal is presented in one modality but not in another, language processing could thus be shaped to a large extent by domain-specific processes.

USE OF SPATIAL LAYOUT DURING SKILLED READING

The visual modality dominates the representation of spatial information. When different modalities are provided with conflicting spatial cues, visual input prevails. Colavita's (1974) work illustrates this phenomenon when inputs from visual and auditory domains are in competition. After matching simple visual and auditory stimuli for intensity, a modality selection task was introduced in which subjects were instructed to press one key when a visual stimulus was presented and another key when an auditory stimulus was presented at the same location. On some trials, the two stimuli were presented concurrently. In these "conflict" situations, subjects almost exclusively signalled the presence of a visual stimulus. However, a reversal of perceptual dominance, with auditory input dominating visual input, is obtained for temporal rate perception (Welch, DuttonHurt, & Warren, 1986), presumably because the auditory domain is more effective at temporal discriminations.

Writing conventions have been adopted in which the visuospatial layout of language symbols provides important information. For European languages, "spatio-linguistic" conventions include the ordering of lines from top to bottom, the ordering of words from left to right, the ordering of letters from left to right, and the use of blank spaces to signal the onset and offset of word units. Blank spaces also define word length, a spatial cue that may provide important linguistic constraints. O'Regan (1979) noted that his examination of the Kucera and Francis (1967) word frequency norms shows that "knowledge of a word's first and last letters, and its length decreases the number of possible choices to less than 19 words 75% of the time" O'Regan continued "if grammatical constraints and crude information about inside letters further diminish the number of choices, then perceptibility may approach 1.0 for many of the letters in the word (p. 502)." Word length is also correlated with several linguistic features (e.g., with word frequency, as short words occur more often in printed language; with syntactic word category, as short words are often function words; with a word's syllable and morpheme structure, as short words generally contain fewer syllables and morphemes, and with neighborhood density, as short words occur in larger lexical neighborhoods).

Word length has a profound effect on readers' oculomotor activity. Interword saccade size decreases when information specifying parafoveal word length is denied (McConkie & Rayner 1975; Morris, Rayner, & Pollatsek, 1990; Rayner & Bertera, 1979; Rayner, Inhoff, Morrison, Slowiaczek, & Bertera, 1981; Rayner, Well, Pollatsek, & Bertera, 1982). When length is specified, interword saccades are larger when a long word is to be fixated than when a short word is to be fixated (Inhoff, 1989a; O'Regan, 1980; Rayner, 1979; see also Fig. 4.3 below).

Profound effects of length on oculomotor activity are also evident in a more systematic investigation in which we (Vitu et al., 1994) measured skilled readers' eye movements while they read short passages that were either shown unaltered or distorted. Distortion was accomplished by replacing all letters of text with the letter z. For instance, the normal phrase "the acquisition of drugs is too . . . " corresponded to the distorted phrase "zzz zzzzzzzzzzz zz zzzzz zzz . . . ". Each subject read half of the passages in normal display mode, with each passage reading followed by a comprehension-related question. The remaining passages were read in distorted mode and were not followed by questions. Subjects were asked to "read" distorted text as if it were normal. Passages that were shown as normal text for one subject were shown as distorted text for the following subject, and vice versa. Normal and distorted passages were thus identical in their spatial layout with identical line orderings, word lengths, and

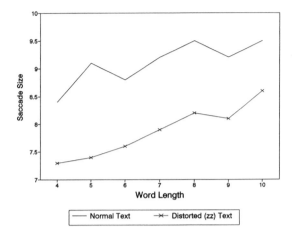

FIG. 4.3.   Saccade size as a function of the length of the subsequently
fixated letter string. Two text conditions are shown. One in which
normal passages of text were read and one in which text was distorted
by replacing all letters of text with the letter *z*.

word length orderings, but differed radically in the availability of other linguistic
information, including lexical, linguistic, and structural information.

Skipping rates for distorted text are shown in Fig. 4.2. A comparison with
skipping rates for normal text, also shown in Fig. 4.2, reveals remarkably similar
rates for the two text presentation conditions. Hence, the spatial layout of text
appears to the major determiner of oculomotor activity. There were, though,
significant differences for short words, with higher skipping rates in the normal
text condition. Presumably, this occurred because the skipping of short words is
related to the high probability with which they can be identified when parafoveally available.

The similarity of oculomotor activity during the reading of normal and distorted text is also evident in Fig. 4.3 which shows the size of saccades to
parafoveal stimuli of four or more characters in the normal and distorted text
conditions, given that these stimuli received at least one fixation. Consistent with
earlier findings, saccade size increased with the length of the parafoveal stimulus
in the normal text condition. Notably, the same tendency was evident when
distorted text was read. Again, however, effects of text type emerged for short
stimuli, presumably because parafoveally available short words provided useful
linguistic information that contributed to saccade specification.

These findings show that the spatial layout of text is a major source of
oculomotor control during reading. The spatial layout of text is also exploited by
selective attentional processes that determine the level of representation of encoded signals.

SPATIAL SHIFTS OF VISUOSPATIAL ATTENTION

Given the concentric shape of the fovea and of the adjacent parafoveal area, visual information can be obtained from more than one horizontal line of text during each fixation. For instance, when a fixated word is sandwiched between two distractor words, and the display is shown for a short duration to prevent eye movements, the semantic processing of the fixated word is affected by its vertical neighbors (Kahneman & Chajczyk, 1983). In contrast to this, several recent studies showed that acquisition of semantic information is more selective during reading and that useful information is obtained only from words located at the fixated line of text (Inhoff & Briihl, 1991; Inhoff & Topolski, 1992; Pollatsek, Raney, LaGasse, & Rayner, 1993)

We (Inhoff & Briihl, 1991) asked subjects to read short interleaved passages of text for comprehension. Two passages were presented concurrently via successive two-line displays with one line pertaining to one story and the second line pertaining to another story. Subjects were requested to read the top line and to disregard the bottom line. The results of a subsequent recognition test, which was administered after each attended/unattended passage reading, showed that readers obtained semantic information from both the attended and unattended passages. This global result replicates an earlier study (Willows & MacKinnon, 1973) and suggests that useful visual information was obtained from more than one line of text. However, more fine grained fixation location analyses revealed that readers sometimes inadvertently moved their eyes to the to-be-disregarded lines. Furthermore, correct recognition of unattended text elements was generally related to an eye movement to the corresponding "unattended" text segment. When these confounding instances were removed, the recognition data showed that useful semantic information was obtained only from fixated (attended) lines of text.

Results of two subsequent studies, which measured fixation durations on one line of text as a function of linguistic materials shown on the line (or lines) below (Inhoff & Topolski, 1992; Pollatsek et al. 1993), also failed to show semantic cross talk between lines. These results converge in showing that spatial cues, in the form of vertical line structure, guide spatially selective processes to confine the acquisition of useful visual information during reading.

In contrast to vertically available linguistic information, which is inhibited by selective attention, lateral shifts of spatial attention to new text appear to facilitate the acquisition of useful information. This facilitative effect is expressed in two major findings. As noted previously, a larger proportion of very short words is skipped when normal text is read than when distorted text is read, presumably because highly familiar, short words can be identified via low-acuity (noisy) parafoveal vision. Furthermore, when the next word in the text is not skipped but fixated, its viewing time is a function of its prior parafoveal availability, as word viewing times increase when parafoveal previews are denied prior to fixation (e.g, Blanchard, Pollatsek, & Rayner, 1989), presumably because lateral shifts of attention faciliated the acquisition of parafoveal word information prior to the previewed word's subsequent fixation (Pollatsek, Bolozky, Well, & Rayner, 1981; Inhoff, Pollatsek, Posner, & Rayner, 1989).

Spatial cues thus appear to support two distinct attentional functions: One that inhibits the acquisition of clearly visible, but potentially disruptive, visual information from spatially adjacent lines of text, and one that facilitates the acquisition of low-acuity and noisy, yet useful, linguistic information from the next word in the text.

SPATIAL LANDMARKS AND THE STORAGE OF LINGUISTIC INFORMATION

Parafoveal preview benefits, which are expressed in shorter word-viewing times when the word was parafoveally available prior to fixation, imply intersaccadic storage of useful information. This storage must be of relatively short duration, as most fixations last between 200 ms and 400 ms and as saccades themselves are of extremely short duration, lasting between 10 ms and 30 ms.

To specify the format of this short-duration storage, Rayner (1975) manipulated the relationship between parafoveally available target previews and the identity of the subsequently fixated target. Target viewing times revealed relatively large benefits when a parafoveal preview was visually similar to the subsequently fixated target (e.g., a preview of *traitor*, or of *tcaober* followed by the fixation of *teacher*), irrespective of whether previews were similar words or nonwords. Visually dissimilar previews, in contrast, yielded no benefit. Two other studies (Balota, Pollatsek, & Rayner, 1985; Rayner, Pollatsek, & Balota, 1986) confirm that visual similarity of previewed and subsequently fixated stimuli determined the magnitude of preview benefits. Both studies reveal that a parafoveally available nonword (e.g., *scmg*) that was visually similar to the target (e.g., *song*) was almost as effective as preview of the target word itself. Again, preview of a visually dissimilar word (e.g., *tune*) yielded virtually no benefit, even when it was semantically related to the target.

Rayner (1975) accounted for similarity effects by assuming that parafoveally obtained information was stored in a low-level, pre-linguistic visual buffer. Buffered information reinforced, or complemented, visual information obtained during the following fixation. The hypothesis was, however, abandoned because word identification and sentence reading were relatively unimpaired when case changes (e.g., from *HoUsE* to *hOuSe*) occurred during successive fixations (McConkie & Zola, 1979; Rayner, McConkie, & Zola 1980). Furthermore, the visual buffer hypothesis could not accommodate findings that show that some linguistic properties of parafoveal previews affected the magnitude of preview benefits. Specifically, parafoveal previews of high frequency words are more effective than previews of low frequency words (Inhoff & Rayner, 1986) and previews are more effective when prior contextual constraints are high than when they are low (Balota et al., 1985). Recent revisions of the buffer model emphasize the abstract, lexical nature of intersaccadic storage (Inhoff, Bohemier, & Briihl, 1993; Pollatsek & Rayner, 1993).

Our current view of intersaccadic storage falls in between the original visual buffer hypothesis (Rayner, 1975) and recent revisions that stress the abstract format of intersaccadic storage. In contrast to the "abstract storage" hypothesis, we propose that the initial representation of a to-be-recognized word is dominated by visuospatially salient word properties (landmarks), which are least subject to noise in the low-acuity parafoveal signal. Encoding of perceptually salient landmarks will precede and constrain the acquisition of less salient sources of parafoveal information. When salient parafoveal word-form properties are sufficiently familiar and constraining, parafoveal word identification and subsequent word skipping can occur. When parafoveally encoded visual information does not yield successful word identification, the acquired word-form information is stored across the saccade and used during the following fixation. We further propose that retention of visuospatially salient form properties across saccades is accomplished via the activation of a set of lexical units that share these features. In the following discussion, we refer to this view as the landmark storage hypothesis of intersaccadic memory. According to the hypothesis, preview benefits accrue when parafoveally activated lexical form representations and representations activated during the following fixation converge upon the same lexical unit.

Similar to the original visual buffer hypothesis, our view of intersaccadic storage thus emphasizes visuospatial form properties of intersaccadic storage; hence, it can account for effects of visual similarity. Like the abstract, lexical storage hypothesis, we propose that intersaccadic storage consists of the activation of lexical representations. Furthermore, we assume that lexical activation is dominated, first, by visuospatial landmarks and second, by the linguistic properties of these landmarks; hence, it can account for some effects of the parafoveal signal's linguistic status. For instance, perceptually salient features may be more useful when high frequency words are parafoveally available; similarly, effects of contextual constraints could indicate that use of landmarks is more effective when contextual constraints are high.

Small or negligible effects of case changes on reading rate and parafoveal preview benefits (McConkie & Zola, 1979; Rayner, McConkie, & Zola, 1980) that were damaging to the visual buffer hypothesis also seem to pose difficulties for the landmark hypothesis of intersaccadic memory. However, in defense of effects of visual similarity (or lack thereof), it should be pointed out, first, that upper- and lower-case letter features are generally correlated and, second, that some studies obtained detrimental effects of letter case changes on word recognition (Marchetti & Mewhort, 1986). Furthermore, case changes do not affect the usefulness of important visuospatial landmarks as they neither affect word length, nor the identity of beginning and/or ending letters, nor the identity of position specific letter clusters. Hence, small or negligible effects of case changes on fixation durations cannot be used to reject the landmark model.

However, the landmark model has difficulty accounting for one recently reported finding that showed that homophonic previews are more effective than visually matched nonhomophonic previews. For instance, parafoveal preview of *reins* followed by a fixation of *rains* (*reins/rains*) was more effective than preview of *ruins* followed by the fixation of *rains* (*ruins/rains*) when the duration of the first fixation on the target word (*rains*) was measured (Pollatsek, Lesch, Morris, & Rayner, 1992; Experiment 2). Visuospatial characteristics of non-homophonic and of homophonic parafoveal previews were thus closely matched, yet reliable preview differences emerged.

Closer examination of the results reveals, however, some peculiarities. First, subanalyses of the items revealed an anomalous reversal of similarity effects. Specifically, when a "similar" preview and the subsequently fixated target shared the first letter (*bean/bare*), first fixations on the target were 19 ms LONGER than when parafoveal preview and the subsequently fixated target were visually dissimilar (*town/bare*). This is in direct opposition to previously reported similarity effects from the same laboratory. In Balota et al.'s (1985) first fixation data, targets with visually similar previews (*cahc/cake*) were 18 ms SHORTER than first fixations preceded by dissimilar previews (*picz/cake*). Rayner, Balota, and Pollatsek (1986) did not report first fixations, but their gaze data reveal nearly identical viewing times when preview and fixated words were visually similar (*sorp/song*) and identical (*song/song*). Dissimilar previews (*door/song*), in contrast, yielded substantially longer viewing times (a 44 ms increase over the identical condition). As indicated earlier, these similarity effects were not related to the lexical status of parafoveal previews.

Another subresult of the Pollatsek et al. (1992) study violates the claim of homophonic preview superiority. Specifically, visually similar nonhomophonic previews were MORE effective than visually similar homophonic previews when preview and target shared the first two letters in the corresponding conditions. Specifically, preview of a nonhomophonic word (e.g., *mall*) resulted in 13 ms shorter first fixation durations on the subsequently fixated target (e.g., *mail*) than preview of a visually matched homophonic word (e.g., *male*). Abnormalities in Pollatsek et al.'s (1992) results could have contributed to an underestimation of nonhomophonic similarity effects and, by comparison, to an overestimation of homophonic preview benefits. Consequently, these data may not warrant rejection of the landmark hypothesis.

SPATIOLINGUISTIC LANDMARKS: PARAFOVEAL
WORD LENGTH AND LETTER POSITION

Parafoveally available word length is perceptually salient and, as shown before, determines skipping rates and saccade size. Pollatsek and Rayner (1982) also showed that the length of a foveal word is encoded relatively early during a fixation. We (Inhoff, Topolski, Bohemier & Wang, 1994) extended this finding and examined effects of parafoveally available word length. In the study, subjects read sentences containing high and low frequency target words.

Parafoveal preview of these targets either provided nearly accurate word length information (e.g., when the parafoveal preview of *movement* consisted of *movment*) or inaccurate length information (e.g., when the corresponding preview consisted of *mov ment*). Irrespective of preview accuracy the "missing" letter (*e* in the example just given), was inserted at the proper intraword location while the eyes were moved onto the target, and the intact target word was visible during the following target fixation. The results show that target-viewing times were substantially increased when the previously available spatial pattern had been incorrectly specified. This disruption was equally detrimental to the recognition of high and low frequency target words. Parafoveally available linguistic information thus appears to be used within the context of visuospatial specifications.

Interword spaces also reduce detrimental effects of lateral masking in the parafovea (Bouma, 1973). Consequently, beginning and ending (exterior) letters of parafoveally available words that are adjacent to blank spaces are perceptually salient and should serve as landmarks in the use of parafoveally available linguistic information. Results of two recent experiments are consistent with this view (Briihl & Inhoff, in press). In the study, parafoveal previews revealed either the beginning, ending, exterior, or center letters of subsequently fixated target words (e.g., preview of *thunder* consisted of *xxxnder*, *thxxxxr*, and *xxundxx*, respectively, followed by the fixation of *thunder*). Preview of the complete parafoveal word, *thunder*, was used as a full preview control condition and preview of a length matched string of xs, *xxxxxxx*, was used as a no preview baseline. Analyses of the viewing time on the subsequently fixated (intact) target revealed preview benefits when perceptually salient exterior and beginning letters were visible prior to fixation but not when nonsalient center letters had been visible. Moreover, the largest preview benefits were obtained when center letters were viewed in the context of exterior letters, as occurred in the full preview condition. This suggests a spatio-temporal gradient in the acquisition of parafoveal information, with the acquisition of salient exterior letters preceding and constraining the encoding of nonsalient center letters.

THE CONTRIBUTION OF SUBWORD STRUCTURE TO WORD RECOGNITION IN READING

Word length and exterior letters are perceptually salient and may serve as landmarks. Subword structure, such as a word's morphemic or syllabic composition, in contrast, is not salient. Consistent with the landmark hypothesis, a review of the literature indicates that nonsalient linguistic sources of information do not contribute to the recognition process when these sources are parafoveally available.

The first study to examine effects of the morphemic composition on parafoveally available words (Inhoff, 1987) appears to show somewhat larger preview benefits when the parafoveally available letter sequence formed a morpheme (*cow* of *cowboy*) than when it formed a pseudomorpheme (*car* of *carpet*). However, two subsequent studies with more controlled stimulus materials (Inhoff, 1989b; Lima, 1987) failed to obtain morpheme-related preview effects. Subanalyses of Inhoff's (1989b) follow-up study also failed to show any syllable-based preview effects. In Lima's (1987) study, parafoveally available words were either prefixed (e.g., *resist*) or pseudoprefixed (e.g., *relish*); parafoveal previews of prefixes were as effective as preview of pseudoprefixes. However, during the following target fixation, more time was spent viewing pseudoprefixed words. Finally, Lima and Inhoff (1985) examined whether word-initial letter constraints affected the usefulness of parafoveal previews. Their results reveal nearly identical parafoveal preview benefits from parafoveally available familiar word-initial trigrams that were compatible with a large number of words (e.g., *roo*) and from less familiar trigrams that were compatible with few words (e.g., *dwa*). During the following target fixation, however, more time was spent on words with less familiar beginning letter sequences.

In contrast to large effects of spatial landmarks on the usefulness of parafoveal previews, a word's internal structure thus appears to have no effect when parafoveally available, presumably because word structure is not perceptually salient. Different types of processes could give rise to effects of subword structure during a word's subsequent fixation. For instance, subword structure could be used during a verification process that preliminarily identified words are subjected to (e.g., Becker, 1979; Paap, Newsome, McDonald, & Schvaneveldt, 1982), and/or it could consist of post-recognition processes in which a word's meaning is tuned to a particular sentence and passage context.

SPOKEN WORD RECOGNITION: PERCEPTUAL SALIENCE AND SIMILARITY

As indicated previously, the acoustic signal in spoken word recognition has different signal characteristics than the visual signal in the recognition of printed language. Yet, a series of recent findings suggest that similar processing principles may govern the acquisition of lexical information in the two domains.

Auditory language is ordered in the temporal domain in a way that is similar to the spatial ordering of visually coded language. The beginnings of sentences are uttered prior to the ends of sentences and initial phoneme sequences in words are uttered prior to the ends of words; hence, beginnings of words reach the perceiver prior to the ends of words. As a result of the temporal ordering of spoken language, initial information can constrain the number of possible lexical completions. Specifically, the beginnings of words can be used to entertain a set of lexical hypotheses; as more of the input is heard, the set of lexical hypotheses can be narrowed based on mismatches with the incoming speech. For some (long) words, this sequential constraint can effectively reduce the number of lexical hypotheses to one possibility before the complete word has been heard. This observation concerning the temporal nature of speech has guided theoretical conceptions of spoken word recognition in that word beginnings are presumed to play a privileged role in recognition (Marslen-Wilson & Welsh, 1978).

Although this assumption is intuitively appealing in that it respects the serial nature of speech, there are a number of indications that suggest it is incorrect in its strongest form. In general, word beginnings are not unambiguously available from the physical signal. They are not marked by distinct onsets and offsets of the acoustic signal and co-articulatory forces from prior segments often obscure the segmental identity of word-initial phonemes. Furthermore, the speech signal can be masked or distorted by environmental noise and the disruption of the speech signal may occur in any sequential position.

Because word beginnings are not perceptually salient in spoken word recognition, lexical activation may occur even when an accurate acoustic-phonetic description of the word initial segment is not available. To test this hypothesis, we (Connine, Blasko, & Titone, 1993) used a cross modal priming paradigm in order to investigate whether the acoustic-phonetic similarity of a nonword relative to a word modulates activation of that word. Subjects performed a lexical decision on a semantically related or unrelated visually presented target word following an auditory stimulus. Auditory stimuli consisted of one set of base words and two sets of derived nonwords. One set of derived nonwords, minimal nonwords, consisted of stimuli where the initial phoneme was altered by one or two linguistic features (e.g. *SEVEN-ZEVEN*). A second set of derived nonwords, maximal nonwords, consisted of stimuli where the initial phoneme was altered by five or more linguistic features (e.g. *SEVEN-SHEVEN*). A major finding was that the similarity relationship between the acoustic input and a lexical representation determined the robustness of the obtained priming effect. The base words showed the largest priming effect whereas minimal nonwords showed an intermediate but significant priming effect and maximal nonwords showed no significant priming effect (see also Marslen-Wilson & Zwiterslood, 1988, for a similar demonstration for maximal nonwords). These results are inconsistent with the hypothesis that lexical activation hinges on the successful use of the word-initial stimulus segment.

A weaker version concerning the importance of nonsalient word onsets incorporates the temporal characteristics of speech via an advantage in activation of a word whose initial sounds match the input. That is, a lexical representation that matches the input at word onset will have a consistent activation advantage throughout processing compared to a word whose initial sounds do not match precisely. The weaker version of the 'onsets are special' hypothesis is compatible with the class of connectionist word-recognition models such as the TRACE model (McClelland & Elman, 1986). The TRACE model assumes interconnections within and between phoneme and lexical levels in a fashion such that initial information tends to dominate activation levels. However, additional experiments we have conducted using the cross modal priming paradigm disconfirm the weak version of the importance of word onsets We found comparable priming effects for minimal nonwords where the altered phoneme was in initial or in medial positions (Connine et al., 1993). These results suggest that intact information in medial nonwords does not serve to reinforce consistent lexical hypotheses (those words beginning with the same initial phonemes) at the expense of other lexical hypotheses. In general, the operative metric for lexical activation appears to the goodness of fit (similarity) between the acoustic-phonetic signal and the corresponding word-form representation.

CONCLUSION

Our studies on visual and auditory word recognition thus indicate that, irrespective of modality, sensory input is mapped onto form-based representations with representational activation being determined by the degree of overlap, or goodness of fit, between input features and a short duration, modality specific representation of lexical forms. Our results also suggest that the perceptual distinctiveness of input features is exploited during this phase of the language recognition process, with perceptually salient features dominating lexical activation. Word beginnings and endings are salient in the visual domain and appear to play a privileged role during intersaccadic storage and the initial phase of the word recognition process in reading. Medial word segments, in contrast, are not perceptually salient and play a less prominent role. In the auditory domain, word beginnings are not distinct and acoustic-phonetic information specifying word initial and medial segments contribute equally to the word recognition process. Though similar principles (i.e., perceptual salience and goodness of fit) may determine the success of the recognition process in the visual and auditory domains, application of these principles will result in modality specific recognition processes.

REFERENCES

Balota, D., Pollatsek, A., & Rayner, K. (1985). Prafoveal visual information and semantic contextual constraints. *Cognitive Psychology, 17,* 364–390.

Becker, C. (1979). Semantic context effects and word frequency effects in visual word recognition. *Journal of Experimental Psychology: Human Perception and Performance, 5,* 252–259.

Blanchard, H., Pollatsek, A., & Rayner, K. (1989). The acquisition of parafoveal word information in reading. *Perception & Psychophysics, 46,* 85–94.

Bouma, H. (1973). Visual interference in the parafoveal recognition of initial and final letters of words. *Vision Research, 13,* 767–782.

Briihl, D. & Inhoff, A. W. (in press). Integrating information across fixations during reading: The use of orthographic bodies and of exterior letters. *Journal of Experimental Psychology: Learning, Memory, and Cognition.*

Colavita, F. (1974). Human sensory dominance. *Perception & Psychophysics, 16,* 409–412.

Connine, C., Blasko, D., & & Titone, D. (1993). Do the beginnings of spoken words have a special status in auditory recognition? *Journal of Memory and Language, 32,* 193–210.

Inhoff, A. W. (1987). Parafoveal word perception during eye fixations in reading: Effects of visual salience and word structure. In M. Coltheart (Ed.), *Attention and Performance, Vol. 12.* (pp 403–420). Hillsdale, NJ: Lawrence Erlbaum Associates.

Inhoff, A. W. (1989a). Parafoveal processing of words and saccade computation during eye fixations in reading. *Journal of Experimental Psychology: Human Perception and Performance, 15,* 544–555.

Inhoff, A. (1989b). Lexical access during eye fixations in reading: Are word access codes used to integrate lexical information across interword fixations? *Journal of Memory and Language, 28,* 444–461.

Inhoff, A. W., Bohemier, G., & Briihl, D. (1993). Integrating text across fixations in reading and copytyping. In K. Rayner (Ed.), *Eye movements and visual cognition: Scene Perception and Reading.* (pp. 355–369). New York: Springer Verlag.

Inhoff, A. W., Topolski, R. Bohemier, G. & Wang, J. (1994). Integrating word length information across fixations: The function of interword spaces during reading. Manuscript submitted for publication.

Inhoff, A., & Briihl, D. (1991). Semantic processing of unattended text during selective reading: How the eyes see it. *Perception & Psychophysics, 49,* 289–294.

Inhoff, A. W., Pollatsek, A., Posner, M., & Rayner, K. (1989). Covert attention and eye movements in reading. *Quarterly Journal of Experimental Psychology, 41A,* 63–89.

Inhoff, A. W., & Rayner, K. (1986). Parafoveal word processing during eye fixations in reading: Effects of word frequency. *Perception & Psychophysics, 40,* 431–439.

Inhoff, A., & Topolski, R. (1992). Lack of semantic activation from unattended text during passage reading. *Bulletin of the Psychonomic Society, 30,* 365–366.

Kahneman, D., & Chajczyk, D. (1983). Tests of automaticity of reading: Dilution of Stroop effects by color irrelevant stimuli. *Journal of Experimental Psychology: Human Perception and Performance, 9,* 497–509.

Kucera, H., & Francis, W. N. (1967). *Computational analysis of present-day American English.* Providence, RI: Brown University Press.

Lima, S. (1987). Morphological analysis in sentence reading. *Journal of Memory and Language, 26,* 84–99.

Lima, S., & Inhoff, A. W. (1985). Lexical access during eye fixations in reading: Effects of word-initial letter sequence. *Journal of Experimental Psychology: Human Perception and Performance, 11,* 272–285.

Marchetti, F., & Mewhort, D. (1986). On the word superiority effect. *Psychological Research*, *48*, 23–35.

Marslen-Wilson, W., & Welch, A. (1978). Processing interactions and lexical access during word recognition in continuous speech. *Cognition*, *8*, 1–71.

Marslen-Wilson, W., & Zwitserlood, P. (1988). Accessing spoken words: On the importance of word onsets. *Journal of Experimental Psychology: Human Perception and Performance*, *15*, 576–585.

McClelland, J., & Elman, J. (1986). The TRACE model of speech perception. *Cognitive Psychology*, *18*, 1–86.

McConkie, G., Kerr, P., Reddix, M., Zola, D., & Jacobs, A. (1989). Eye movement control during reading. II: Frequency of refixating a word. *Perception & Psychophysics*, *46*, 245–253.

McConkie, G. &. Rayner, K. (1975). The span of the effective stimulus during a fixation in reading. *Perception & Psychophysics*, *17*, 578–586.

McConkie, G., & Zola, D. (1979). Is visual information integrated across successive fixations in reading? *Perception & Psychophysics*, *25*, 221–224.

Morris, R., Rayner, K., & Pollatsek, A. (1990). Eye movement guidance in reading: The role of parafoveal letter and space information. *Journal of Experimental Psychology: Human Perception and Performance*, *16*, 268–281.

O'Regan, J. (1979). Eye guidance in reading: Evidence for the linguistic control hypothesis. *Perception & Psychophysics*, *25*, 501–509.

O'Regan, J. (1980). The control of saccade size and fixation duration in reading: The limits of linguistic control. *Perception & Psychophysics*, *28*, 112–117.

O'Regan, J. (1981). The convenient viewing position hypothesis. In D. Fischer, R. Monty & J. Senders (Eds.), *Eye movements: Cognition and visual perception* (pp. 289–298). Hillsdale, NJ: Lawrence Erlbaum Associates.

O'Regan, J. (1983). Elementary perception and eye movement control processes in reading. In K. Rayner (Ed.), *Eye movements in reading: Perceptual and language processes* (pp. 121–138). New York: Academic Press.

O'Regan, J., & Levy-Schoen, A. (1987). Eye movement strategy and tactics in word recognition and reading. In M. Coltheart (Ed.), *Attention and Performance, Vol. 12: The psychology of reading* (pp. 363–383). Hillsdale, NJ: Erlbaum Associates.

O'Regan, J., Levy-Schoen, A., Pynte, J., & Brugaillere, J. (1984). Convenient fixation location within isolated words of different length and structure. *Journal of Experimental Psychology: Human Perception and Performance*, *10*, 250–257.

Paap, K., Newsome, S., McDonald, J., & Schvaneveldt, R. (1982). An activation verification model for letter and word recognition: The word superiority effect. *Psychological Review*, *89*, 573–594.

Pollatsek, A., Bolozky, S., Well, A., & Rayner, K. (1981). Asummetries in the perceptual span for Israeli readers. *Brain and Language*, *14*, 174–180.

Pollatsek, A., Lesch, M., Morris, R., & Rayner, K. (1992). Phonological codes are used in integrating information across saccades in word indentification and reading. *Journal of Experimental Psychology: Human Perception and Performance*, *18*, 148–162.

Pollatsek, A., Raney, G., LaGasse, L., & Rayner, K. (1993). The use of information below fixation in reading and visual search. *Canadian Journal of Psychology*, *47*, 179–200.

Pollatsek, A., & Rayner, K. (1982). Eye movement control in reading: The role of word boundaries. *Journal of Experimental Psychology: Human Perception and Performance*, *8*, 817–833.

Pollatsek, A., & Rayner, K. (1993). What is integrated across fixations? In K. Rayner (Ed.), *Eye movements and visual cognition: Scene perception and reading* (pp. 166–191). New York: Springer Verlag.

Rayner, K. (1975). The perceptual span and peripheral cues in reading. *Cognitive Psychology*, *7*, 65–81.

Rayner, K. (1979). Eye guidance in reading: Fixation locations within words. *Perception, 8,* 21–30.

Rayner, K., Balota, D., & Pollatsek, A. (1986). Against parafoveal semantic processing during eye fixations in reading. *Canadian Journal of Psychology, 40,* 473–483.

Rayner, K., & Bertera, J. (1979). Reading without a fovea. *Science, 206,* 468–469.

Rayner, K., Inhoff, A., Morrison, R., Slowiaczek, M., & Bertera, J. (1981). Masking of foveal and parafoveal vision during eye fixations in reading. *Journal of Experimental Psychology: Human Perception and Performance, 7,* 167–179.

Rayner, K., McConkie, G., & Zola, D. (1980). Integrating information across eye movements. *Cognitive Psychology, 12,* 206–226.

Rayner, K. &. Pollatsek., A. (1987). Eye movements in reading: A tutorial review. In M. Coltheart (Ed.), *Attention & Performance: Vol. 12. The psychology of reading* (pp. 327–362). Hillsdale, NJ.: Lawrence Erlbaum Associates.

Rayner, K., & Pollatsek, A. (1989). *The Psychology of Reading.* Englewood Cliffs, NJ: Prentice Hall.

Rayner, K., Well, A., Pollatsek, A., & Bertera, J. (1982). The availability of useful information to the right of fixation in reading. *Perception & Psychophysics, 31,* 537–550.

Vitu, F. (1991). The influence of parafoveal preprocessing and linguistic context on the optimal landing position effect. *Perception & Psychophysics, 50,* 58–75.

Vitu, F., O'Regan, K., Inhoff, A.W., & Topolski, R. (1994). *Mindless reading: Eye movements are similar in scanning strings and reading texts.* Manuscript submitted for publication.

Vitu, F., O'Regan, J., & Mittau, M. (1990). Optimal landing position in reading isolated words and continuous text. *Perception & Psychophysics, 47,* 583–600.

Welch, R., DuttonHurt, L., & Warren, D. (1986). Contributions of audition and vision to temporal rate perception. *Perception & Psychophysics, 39,* 294–300.

Willows, D., & MacKinnon, G. (1973). Selective reading: Attention to the "unattended" lines. *Canadian Journal of Psychology, 27,* 292–304.

5 Inferencing Upside Down

Susan A. Duffy
Andrew F. Hundley
Paul A. Baligian
Amherst College

It should surprise no one to be told that reading comprehension is a complex process in which many events (from eye movements to access of the mental dictionary to the generation of inferences) must be appropriately scheduled. Some processes are likely to depend on the completion of others: A particular word cannot be integrated into a sentence as a whole until it is identified; a particular bridging inference cannot be drawn until the relevant sentence information has been analyzed. In the skilled reader, this scheduling is carried out quite efficiently under normal circumstances. But what happens when one process, on which other processes are dependent, is temporally disrupted? For example, what happens when the process of analyzing the perceptual information for word recognition is delayed? Such a delay presumably occurs when the reader is a beginning reader who is as yet unskilled at decoding words based on their perceptual information. For skilled readers, a similar delay might occur when the letters of each word are perceptually degraded or transformed so that the normal perceptual processes are disrupted.

Current models of reading emerging from the literature on good versus poor readers have two complementary predictions about what happens to the system when the critical process of perceptual analysis of words is delayed. The first prediction is that other kinds of information are used to compensate for the delay in availability of perceptual information. In particular, there is much evidence to

This research was supported in part by NIMH Grant 5 R03 MH46855 and a grant from Amherst College to the first author, by NIMH Grant 1 R01 MH40029 to Jerome Myers, and by a Ford Foundation Honors Grant for honors thesis research to the second author. Experiment 1 was presented at the 31st Annual Meeting of the Psychonomic Society, New Orleans, November 1990.

suggest that semantic context is used by poor readers to help identify words when perceptual processes fail (Stanovich, 1980). As a result, such models are labelled *interactive compensatory* models because the claim is made that the system has the capacity to use both semantic and perceptual information in the word-recognition process, and that the former can compensate for the lack of the latter (Perfetti, 1988; Stanovich, 1980).

The second prediction of interactive-compensatory models is that a delay in pulling out the perceptual information needed for word recognition has consequences for higher level comprehension processes. Stanovich (1980) suggested that when there is difficulty analyzing the perceptual information, limited resources that would usually be used for higher level inferencing processes must be diverted to word recognition, and thus higher level processing suffers. For example, Lesgold and Perfetti (1978) suggested that beginning readers have to rehearse the phonemes of the current word in working memory in order to put the word together for recognition. As a result, the preceding words in the sentence are lost from working memory.

THE INVERSION OF TEXT

There is in the literature, of course, a great deal of work focusing on differences in good and poor readers and the extent to which such an interactive compensatory model drawing on limited resources sheds light on these differences. But there is also a great deal of work on another circumstance in which perceptual processing of words is delayed for skilled readers; this is the work on the perceptual transformation of text. This work begins with Kolers' (1975) study on the comprehension of inverted text. Two findings have been replicated in later studies: Readers spend longer reading inverted text than normal text (not surprisingly), and readers remember more of the inverted text than the normal, uninverted text.

More recent work in the inverted-text paradigm provides evidence that this better memory is the result of an increased conceptual processing of the text, as opposed to increased perceptual processing. For example, Masson and Sala (1978) found that subjects were faster to reread in inverted form sentences that they had earlier read in inverted form. This rereading effect did not differ whether the reread sentences were verbatim or paraphrased versions of the earlier sentences. Graf and Levy (1984) found a similar effect for paragraphs. Graf (1981) found that the memory advantage for rotated sentences disappeared when the sentences were anomalous. Thus, the claim is that a more elaborated conceptual memory representation is stored for the inverted text because conceptual processing has compensated for the lack of useful perceptual information.

The finding that text inversion leads to more conceptual processing is congruent with one assumption of the interactive-compensatory models of reading. Under these models, one would expect that the processing difficulty that results from reading inverted text would lead the reading system to compensate with an increased use of semantic context to help in decoding. Thus, the inversion literature converges nicely with the literature on these models if the additional conceptual processing consists of the use of semantic context to aid in word recognition.

This additional conceptual processing at the word level, however, should not necessarily lead to better memory for the text. An additional assumption of interactive-compensatory models is that when difficulty is encountered at the word recognition level, resources normally used for integrating propositions into coherent memory representations are diverted to the word recognition process. Thus, a finding that memory for inverted text is worse than memory for text in normal typography would be more congruent with these models. Yet the memory advantage for inverted text has been replicated in many studies.

In the current experiments we set out to address this apparent contradiction. We reasoned that the higher level processes most likely to suffer when resources are diverted to word recognition would be those involved in integrating information across sentences. Such processes would seem to require resources for a number of reasons. For example, resources are needed to maintain in working memory selected information from earlier sentences while the current sentence is being read (Kintsch & van Dijk, 1978), to find antecedents for anaphors encountered in the current sentence (Garrod & Sanford, 1977), and to draw causal inferences about why a particular event has occurred (Myers, Shinjo, & Duffy, 1987). Much of the prior research on inverted typography focused on recognition memory for individual sentences read in normal or inverted type. The few studies in which longer texts were used (e.g., Graf & Levy, 1984) tested memory through general comprehension questions and rereading. In none of these studies was memory for particular inferences targeted. As a result, it seemed possible that this earlier research had missed the effect of inversion on the reader's ability to carry out integrative processes across sentences.

CAUSAL INFERENCE

We chose to focus on one particular integrative process—the discovery of a causal relationship between one sentence and its immediate predecessor. Consider, for example, the process of comprehending the following pair of sentences as a coherent pair:

1a. Joey got angry at his brother in a game.
2. The next day his body was covered with bruises.

The reader must draw a bridging inference (Clark, 1977) to fully comprehend the connection between the messages in the two sentences. Presumably, the inference is a causal one, that Joey and his brother had a physical fight that was caused by the anger and had as its consequence the bruises. Consider some alternative first sentences for the pair:

1b.   Joey's brother punched him again and again.

1c.   Joey went to play baseball with his brother.

With Sentence 1b as the first sentence, the reader needs no bridging inference because the event in the first sentence directly causes the bruises in Sentence 2. With Sentence 1c as the first sentence, the reader is unlikely to draw any bridging inference because the event in the first sentence does not provide enough constraints for determining what happened to cause the bruises in Sentence 2.

In a series of studies, Myers, Shinjo and Duffy explored the time course of reading pairs of sentences like those just mentioned and the resulting memory representations for these sentences (Myers et al., 1987). They found that readers spent more time on the second sentence as the first sentence became less related to it. For moderately related pairs like 1a-2, they argued that this additional time reflected time to form a bridging inference. For low-related pairs like 1c-2, they argued that this additional time reflected time spent failing to find an obvious inference. This claim was supported by the recall results. When readers were given the first sentence and asked to recall the second (and vice versa), memory was best for the moderately related sentences—those that were most likely to elicit bridging inferences (replicating results of Keenan, Baillet, and Brown, 1984). Myers et al. argued that the memory representation for the moderately related sentences contained more propositions (because of the inference) and more interconnections among propositions. Thus it was easier for readers to find a path from the first sentence of the pair to the second.

Further evidence was provided in a second set of studies (Duffy, Shinjo, & Myers, 1990). Subjects were asked to write an elaboration sentence that could reasonably come between the two sentences of each pair in a story. This ensured that an elaborative inference was generated for every sentence pair at every level of relatedness. Subjects spent the least amount of time generating an elaboration for the moderately related sentences, as expected, because these are the sentences that invite a bridging inference. Furthermore, the recall advantage for the moderately related sentences disappeared. This again is predicted under the assumption that the generation of any relevant inference will result in a more elaborated memory trace that facilitates cued recall. Because subjects generated these inferences for all pairs, recall did not differ systematically across the pairs.

In all of these studies, one striking finding is the lack of a positive relationship between reading time and recall. Simply spending more time does not always enhance recall. When subjects were instructed to read the sentence pairs (Myers et al., 1987), the pairs that produced the longest reading times (the low-related) had the lowest recall. When subjects were instructed to elaborate, the pairs that produced the longest times (the high- and low-related) had no better recall than those with the shortest times (the moderately related). It is clear, then, that many different kinds of processes contribute to the reading-time measure and not all of these make comparable contributions to recall. Specifically, it is the generation of an elaborated memory trace that enhances recall, not merely the allocation of more time to reading.

THE CURRENT STUDIES

We have continued to use these sentence pairs to explore the relationship between the processes that take place during the initial reading of a text and later memory for what was read. In particular, we have asked subjects to read the Myers et al. (1987) sentence pairs in inverted type (displayed upside down on a computer screen). Examples of the sentence pairs in inverted typography are presented following this paragraph. As can be seen, each individual letter has been inverted and, as a result, subjects always read from left to right. It is fairly difficult to read sentences transformed in this way (more difficult, for example, than reading texts in which every line as a whole has been rotated in the plane of the paper so that subjects read from right to left).

Ɑɥɐɹou qɐɔʞǝp ɥɔ ɔɐɹ ouʇ oɟ ʇɥǝ pɹıʌǝɯɐʎ˙
Ɑɥǝ ʍǝuʇ ʇo ǝu!pıuƃ ʞuɐɥ ɥɔoɖıuƃ ʇo ƃǝʇ ɐ ɟoɐu˙

Ɑ sɥɹouƃ uıƃɥʇ ʍıup ɔɐɯǝ ıu ʇɥǝ ƃuoɹɥs˙
Ɑɥǝ ɖǝɖǝɹs ou ʇɥǝ ɖǝsʞ qɹǝʍ oɟɟ ouʇo ʇɥǝ ɟɟool˙

Drawing on the logic of the limited capacity interactive-compensatory models, we reasoned that it would be difficult for subjects to make any use of the relationship between the two sentences when viewing them in inverted form for two reasons. First, if scarce resources are drawn to word-recognition processes, then insufficient resources would be available for drawing the linking inferences. Second, as the subject begins struggling through the second sentence, the first sentence will be lost from working memory because insufficient resources are available for holding it there (Daneman & Carpenter, 1980). The result should be that the first sentence of the pair will be less available than usual at the point in the second sentence when readers normally notice that a relationship between the two sentences exists. Given this logic, we predicted that the effect of relatedness on reading time and cued recall would be reduced for inverted sentence pairs when compared to their normal-typography counterparts.

EXPERIMENT 1

Methods

Subjects.   Thirty-six students from Amherst College were paid to participate in this experiment.

TABLE 5.1
Examples of Sentence Pairs at Each Level of Relatedness

Level 1 (Low-related)
Sharon backed her car out of the driveway.
She went to the bank hoping to get a loan.

Level 2
Cleo arranged flowers on the table for dinner.
The water spilled on the expensive carpet.

Level 3
Tony had a fight with his friend near a pond.
He walked home soaking wet to change his clothes.

Level 4
Joey began fighting with his older brother.
The next day his body was covered with bruises.

Level 5 (High related)
A strong night wind came in the open window.
The papers on the desk blew off onto the floor.

Materials. Thirty sentence pairs originally created by Myers et al. (1987) were used in this experiment. All pairs were associated with relatedness ratings established in a norming study. The 30 pairs were those selected by Duffy et al. (1990, Experiments 2 and 3) to fall into five levels of relatedness with no overlap in ratings across levels. Examples are given in Table 5.1.

Filler sentences consisted of 20 two-clause sentences (included as part of a different study). An additional four practice items appeared at the beginning of each block of the experiment.

Each subject saw stimuli presented in both normal and inverted typography. Stimuli were blocked by typography. Half of the subjects saw the inverted texts first; half saw the normal texts first. Across the set of subjects, all stimuli appeared equally often in the first and second block of the experiment and in normal and inverted form. Thus, there were four different stimulus lists with each subject assigned to one of the four lists. For each list, the inverted sentences were typed into the stimulus file backwards (e.g., .doirep eht htiw gninnigeb).

Procedure. Subjects sat in front of the computer screen with a keyboard in front of them. Each sentence pair was preceded by a display of two lines that indicated where each sentence would appear. Subjects pressed the space bar to display each sentence. Stimuli were presented one sentence at a time. Subjects were instructed to read each sentence aloud and to press the space bar immediately after completing each sentence. Reading time for each sentence was recorded. For the inverted typography block of the experiment, the computer monitor was physically turned upside down (after assurances from our computing center personnel that inversion would not harm the electronics!). The monitor was returned to its normal upright position for the normal typography block.

An experimenter remained in the room with the subject to monitor the subject's performance. If the subject misread a word, the experimenter indicated this by simply saying "No." The subject then corrected the error and reread the entire sentence correctly.

When subjects completed the reading part of the experiment, they were given a cued recall booklet. This booklet contained the first sentence of every sentence pair they had seen. Subjects were instructed to write down whatever they could remember of the second sentence of each pair. All first sentences were presented in normal typography for the recall test.

Results

Both reading time and cued recall data were analyzed. Results of analyses of variance based on subject variability (F_1) and on item variability (F_2) are reported.

Reading-Time Data.   The mean reading times for the second sentence of each pair are presented in Fig. 5.1. Subjects spent on average about 3 seconds reading the normal sentences and 14 seconds reading the inverted sentences, an 11 second difference that was significant [$F_1(1,34)$ = 158.8, MS_e = 372,573,000, $p < .001$; $F_2(1,25)$ = 128.1, MS_e = 61,979,200, $p < .001$]. There was also an effect of relatedness within the subjects analysis [$F_1(4,136)$ = 12.33, MS_e = 14,357,500, $p < .001$; $F_2(4,25)$ = 1.80; MS_e = 32,572,600, $p > .15$]. This effect interacted with typography within the subjects analysis

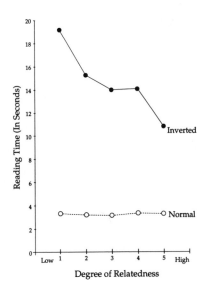

FIG. 5.1. Mean reading times for the second sentence of each pair in Experiment 1 as a function of relatedness and typography.

$[F_1(4,136) = 11.83; MS_e = 14,621,000, p < .001; F_2(4,25) = 1.84; MS_e = 61,979,200, p > .10]$. As a result, we analyzed relatedness separately for the normal and inverted conditions.

Within the normal condition, the effect of relatedness did reach significance in the subjects analysis $[F_1(4,136) = 2.98, MS_e = 52,694, p < .03; F_2 < 1]$, reflecting the slight dip in reading times at Level 3. The striking effect of relatedness, however, appears in the subjects analysis of the inverted condition $[F_1(4,136) = 12.1, MS_e = 28,925,800, p < .001; F_2(4,25) = 1.83; MS_e = 63,477,100, p > .15]$. Here, the second sentences for Level 1 pairs took on average 19 seconds to read aloud; for Level 5 pairs this time was reduced to 11 seconds.

Recall Data.   Mean percentage recall for Sentence 2 of each pair is presented in Fig. 5.2. Overall, subjects recalled on average 27% of the normal sentences and 47% of the inverted sentences. This 20% difference was significant $[F_1(1,34) = 29.42, MS_e = 6,134, p < .001; F_2(1,25) = 56.2, MS_e = 436, p < .001]$. Again, there was a significant effect of relatedness $[F_1(4,136) = 15.99, MS_e = 431, p < .001; F_2(4,25) = 2.55, MS_e = 844, p < .07]$ that also interacted with typography within the subjects analysis $[F_1(4,136) = 3.16, MS_e = 517, p < .02]$. When we analyzed the normal and inverted conditions separately, the relatedness effect was marginal at best within the normal condition $[F_1(4,136) = 2.17, MS_e = 491, p < .08, F_2 < 1]$ and significant within the inverted condition $[F_1(4,136) = 16.35, MS_e = 456, p < .001, F_2(4,25) = 3.60, MS_e = 650, p < .02]$.

Given the pattern of data, in a post hoc analysis we separated off the Level 1 data from the rest. Within just the Level 1 data, inverted sentences did not have a recall advantage over the normal typography sentences (both $Fs < 1$); the advantage did exist within Levels 2–5 $[F_1(1,34) = 38.86, MS_e = 4,344, p < .001, F_2(1,20) = 65.1, MS_e = 443, p < .001]$. Within the Level 2–5 data, there was no significant overall relatedness effect (both $Fs < 1$). Furthermore there was no interaction of relatedness with typography within Levels 2–5.

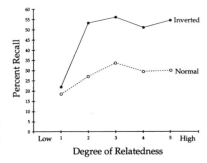

FIG. 5.2.   Mean percent recall for the second sentence of each pair in Experiment 1 as a function of relatedness and typography.

Discussion

Readers spent more time reading inverted text than normal text. Overall, they recalled more of the inverted text. This pattern replicates the results from the transformed text literature. More importantly, however, within the inverted stimuli, there was a clear effect of relatedness on both reading time and recall. Reading time for the inverted pairs decreased with increasing relatedness. Recall was lowest for the low-related inverted sentence pairs.

In the recall data, the interaction between relatedness and typography indicated that the effect of inversion is not constant across all stimuli; low-related pairs did not benefit from inversion. This result is similar to the finding of Graf (1981) that the inversion advantage disappeared for sentences that were anomalous. In addition, the interaction indicated that the effect of relatedness was larger for the inverted than for the normal stimuli. That is, the recall advantage for Levels 2 through 5 compared to Level 1 is much larger for the inverted texts than for the normal texts.

The relationship between reading time and recall is not a simple one. Although subjects did spend longer reading the inverted sentences and had better memory for these pairs, other aspects of the data argue against a claim that memory is simply a function of time. In particular, the sentence pairs that elicited by far the longest reading times (the Level 1 pairs in the inverted condition), were also among the worst recalled. This pattern mirrors that of Myers et al. (1987).

How does the limited-capacity interactive-compensatory model fare? A highly related first sentence (Level 5) reduced the reading time for the second sentence by 8 seconds and increased recall by about 35% (compared with a Level 1, low-related first sentence). The fact that relatedness had such a strong effect on the inverted stimuli (both reading times and recall) suggests that subjects were able to maintain information from inverted Sentence 1 while reading inverted Sentence 2. Furthermore, they were able to make use of Sentence 1 in the reading of Sentence 2. Although the use of semantic context is predicted by the limited-capacity interactive-compensatory models, the limited-capacity assumption is brought into question here with the evidence that processing an inverted Sentence 2 does not interfere with drawing inferences related to Sentence 1.

How is sentence 1 being used to reduce the reading time for inverted Sentence 2 by 8 seconds (comparing the Level 1 and the Level 5 times)? In the Myers et al. (1987) and Duffy et al. (1990) studies using the same texts, the assumption was made that the inferences drawn to link the two sentences were drawn not as a part of the word-recognition process but after such processes had completed. This assumption seems unlikely here. The 8-second difference in reading time for inverted high versus low-related Sentence 2s is obviously much larger than the difference found by Myers et al. (1987). Furthermore, this difference is not reflecting an 8-second pause at the end of the Level 1 sentences while the reader does some inferencing. Readers pressed the space bar immediately after saying the last word of the sentence. Rather, it is more likely in the case of reading inverted text that the elaborating inferences are drawn as part of the word-recognition process. This has two observable results. First, word-recognition time (reflected in reading time) is reduced when some relation can be found between the first sentence and the current words to be recognized in the second sentence. Second, multiple links between sentences are stored in memory during this word-recognition process, and these provide useful retrieval routes when retrieving Sentence 2 at recall.

Finally, we should consider the rather marginal effects of relatedness within the reading time and recall data for the normal typography sentences. Myers et al. (1987) found a striking decrease in reading time with increasing relatedness for sentence pairs presented in normal typography. This effect is not replicated here. Furthermore, Myers et al. found a significant peak in recall for the moderately related pairs that is only marginal here, although the peak for the moderately related pairs is present in the recall means. A major difference in procedure may account for the differing patterns of results. In the Myers et al. study, subjects read the sentences silently. In the current experiment, subjects read each sentence aloud to the experimenter. Thus, the current reading times may primarily reflect articulation rate, which would not be expected to vary across levels of relatedness for normal typography sentences. Furthermore, when the goal is to read sentences aloud, readers may be less focused on creating coherence between sentences. Consistent with this claim is the fact that the overall level of recall for the normal sentences in the current study (27%) is much lower than that in the Myers et al. (1987) study (about 50%).

EXPERIMENT 2

It is clear from the results of Experiment 1 that the memory representation of Sentence 1 is playing a critical role in the processing of inverted Sentence 2 when the two sentences are related. In a follow-up experiment, we explored the nature of that memory representation by asking whether it mattered that Sentence 1 had also been processed in inverted form. That is, suppose Sentence 1 had been presented in normal typography. Would it be as useful a source of context? In this experiment, we used the same sentence pairs and subjects always read Sentence 2 in inverted form. Half the time Sentence 1 was inverted and half the time it was in normal typography.

Three straightforward possibilities occurred to us initially. First, there might be no difference in the semantic representation that results from reading Sentence 1 in inverted or normal typography. In this case, there would be no reason to expect any difference in reading time or memory for Sentence 2 depending on first sentence typography. Second, the representation of inverted Sentence 1 might itself be more elaborated and thus more available for use compared with normal-typography Sentence 1. In this case, there should be a reading-time and memory advantage for the inverted Sentence 1 condition. Third, the representation of inverted Sentence 1 might be somewhat fragmented because of the processing difficulties associated with inverted text (reviving a form of the limited-capacity hypothesis). In this case, there should be a reading-time and memory advantage for the normal Sentence 1 condition.

Method

Subjects.   Thirty-six Amherst College students were paid for their participation in this experiment.

Materials.   Stimuli and design were the same as in Experiment 1 except that the second sentence of each pair was always presented in inverted typography. Only the typography of the first sentence varied.

Procedure.   In order to vary typography within a sentence pair, two cathode-ray tube (CRT) screens were used. The screens were mounted side by side at a comfortable viewing height. The right-hand CRT remained inverted throughout the experiment. The left-hand CRT was upright for the normal condition and turned upside down for the inverted condition. At the beginning of each trial, a line appeared on the left-hand screen indicating the position of the upcoming sentence. A left-pointing arrow appeared on the right-hand screen to remind the subject to begin with the left-hand screen. A press of the space bar caused a display of Sentence 1 on the left-hand screen and a single line on the right-hand screen (which marked the future location of Sentence 2). After reading the first sentence aloud, the subject pressed the space bar, which caused the second sentence to appear on the right-hand screen. Subjects completed the trial by reading this sentence aloud and again pressing the space bar when done. When subjects had completed the reading part of the experiment, they were given the cued recall booklet, as in Experiment 1.

Results

Reading-Time Data.   Reading times for Sentence 2 of each pair (which was always inverted) are displayed in Fig. 5.3. Subjects spent more time on Sentence 2 when it was preceded by an inverted Sentence 1 than when it was preceded by a normal Sentence 1 [$F_1(1,34) = 40.15$, $MS_e = 120,262,000$, $p < .001$; $F_2(1,25) = 28.34$, $MS_e = 21,994,900$, $p < .001$]. As in Experiment 1, reading times increased with decreasing relatedness [$F_1(4,136) = 23.45$, $MS_e = 25,524,300$, $p < .001$; $F_2(4,25) = 2.53$, $MS_e = 76,735,900$, $p < .07$].

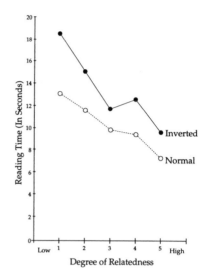

FIG. 5.3. Mean reading times for the second sentence of each pair in Experiment 2 as a function of relatedness and typography of first sentence.

Recall Data. Cued recall means for Sentence 2 of each pair (the sentence that was always inverted) are presented in Fig. 5.4. Subjects displayed better recall for sentences that followed an inverted Sentence 1 than for those that followed a normal-typography Sentence 1 [$F_1(1,34) = 13.8$, $MS_e = 3,099$, $p <$ .003; $F_2(1,25) = 16.5$, $MS_e = 410$, $p < .001$]. Recall also increased as level of relatedness increased [$F_1(4,136) = 20.1$, $MS_e = 395$, $p < .001$; $F_2(4,25) = 3.6$, $MS_e = 754$, $p < .02$].

Discussion

As in Experiment 1, there is an effect of relatedness in both the reading time and the recall data. In the normal and inverted conditions, readers' attempt to read an inverted sentence is facilitated when the preceding sentence is related. Furthermore, memory for that sentence pair is enhanced.

It is also clear that the typography of Sentence 1 has an effect on both the processing and memory of the inverted Sentence 2. The particular pattern of effects, however, is not one that we originally predicted. Subjects spent longer reading inverted Sentence 2 when Sentence 1 was inverted, and recall was better for Sentence 2 in that condition. In our original predictions, we had expected that the reading and recall effects would be inversely related (the condition that produced higher reading times would produce lower cued recall scores).

The finding of better recall for the inverted condition is actually consistent with the inversion literature. Although it was not directly tested, memory for Sentence 1 presented in inverted form should be better than memory for Sentence 1 presented in normal typography. Given that inverted Sentence 1 is easier to locate in memory at recall, Sentence 2 should also be more easily located because of its links to Sentence 1. This could account for better recall for the inverted condition in this experiment.

The puzzle, however, is to explain why our results show longer reading times as well as better memory in the inverted condition. Again, note that this is not a simple pattern in which more reading time leads to better recall. This pattern holds when one considers just the effect of inversion: Reading times are longer and recall is better in the inverted condition. The pattern does not hold when one considers the effect of relatedness: Reading times are longer and recall is worse in the low related conditions.

We have considered two possible accounts of the effect of inversion of Sentence 1 on the reading time for inverted Sentence 2. The first is one of our original hypotheses: The memory representation that results immediately from reading a normal typography sentence is more coherent and more useful in reading inverted Sentence 2. Thus reading time for Sentence 2 is reduced in that condition. This hypothesis, however, would predict a larger inversion effect within the reading times for the high-related condition than for the low-related condition. This interaction pattern did not appear in the data.

A second hypothesis is that subjects need a "recovery period" after reading an inverted sentence. They are slow to move their eyes from the first screen to the second and slow to begin reading the second sentence. This allows time for consolidation of the Sentence 1 memory trace before beginning to read Sentence 2. We have no measure of intersentence time, which would have provided information about this hypothesis. A similar phenomenon, however, was observed by Haberlandt and Bingham (1978). They presented subjects with triples of sentences that were either related or unrelated. As expected, they found increased reading time for the third sentence of the unrelated triple. In addition, they found that reading times for the "ready" message displayed after a triple and for the first sentence of the next triple were also longer when the preceding triple was unrelated. This suggests that subjects continued to process the unrelated triples as they moved on to the next one. A similar carry-over effect resulting from reading a sentence in inverted typography could have occurred in the current experiment.

Regardless of the locus of the inversion effects in this experiment, we should

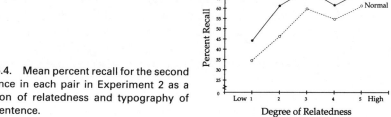

FIG. 5.4. Mean percent recall for the second sentence in each pair in Experiment 2 as a function of relatedness and typography of first sentence.

not lose sight of the replication of the relatedness effect. That is, as in Experiment 1, both reading time and recall performance for inverted second sentences were influenced by the relatedness of the first sentence of the pair. In particular, reading time was reduced and recall was improved as relatedness of the sentences increased.

GENERAL DISCUSSION

In two experiments in which subjects read pairs of sentences that varied in degree of relatedness, we found that both reading time and recall were influenced by relatedness of the pair. This in itself is not a new finding; it replicates results of Keenan et al. (1984), Myers et al. (1987) and Duffy et al. (1990). More importantly, this effect of relatedness was observed when the second sentence was presented in inverted typography. In addition, we found no simple relationship between reading time and recall. Next, we consider the implications of each of these findings.

Effect of Relatedness on the Comprehension of Inverted Text

Focusing on the limited-capacity assumptions of the interactive-compensatory models of reading, we had expected a reduced relatedness effect in the inverted conditions. If the process of decoding words in inverted typography uses up limited resources, then fewer resources would remain for carrying out two resource-demanding operations: drawing elaborative causal inferences to link the two sentences and holding Sentence 1 and the related inferences in working memory while reading Sentence 2. Our results are not consistent with this view.

Our results are consistent, however, with the compensatory assumption of the interactive-compensatory models—the assumption that conceptual processes making use of semantic context compensate for perceptual processing in word recognition. In particular, elaborative inferencing based on the content of Sentence 1 serves the word-recognition process for Sentence 2 when perceptual difficulty prevents the normal operation of this process. This process is facilitated when there is available either a highly related Sentence 1 or a related causal inference that can be drawn. Under this analysis, the effect of relatedness on inverted reading times in the current experiments reflects differences in the availability of semantic context useful for word recognition. In contrast to the moderately and high-related pairs, for the low-related sentence pairs, Sentence 1 provides little information that would be useful in identifying the words in Sentence 2.

This account also calls into question the assumption that subjects reading inverted Sentence 2 would have few resources left over for simultaneously holding Sentence 1 and its related inferences in working memory, where it would be available for use in comprehending Sentence 2. In contrast to this assumption, it is clear that our subjects were making use of their memory for Sentence 1 and/or related inferences in comprehending inverted Sentence 2. Indeed, one by-product of the process of inferencing in the service of lexical access seems to be that the information on which the inferences are based is maintained in an active state. Thus, Sentence 1 and related inferences remain available for use throughout sentence comprehension. Furthermore, these inferences become part of the longer term memory trace for the sentence pair and facilitate later cued recall.

Relationship Between Reading Time and Memory

The results here also contribute to the growing literature on the dissociation between patterns of reading time and patterns of recall. In these experiments in general, increasing the perceptual difficulty of the reading task (by inverting the sentences to be read) resulted in longer reading times and in greater memory. Increasing the conceptual difficulty (by decreasing the relatedness of the sentences) also resulted in longer reading times but in reduced memory. Graf and Levy (1984) observed a similar pattern using longer texts. In their experiments, readers spent more time on the inverted texts than the normal typography texts and on the conceptually difficult texts than the easy texts. But this additional time only enhanced comprehension of the inverted texts; comprehension of the difficult texts was poorer than for the easy texts. Furthermore, on a misspelling-detection task readers were more accurate on the difficult texts than on the easy texts, which was taken to indicate that the increased time was spent in increased perceptual processing. Readers were less accurate detecting misspellings in the inverted text compared with normal text, which Graf and Levy took as evidence that the increased time was spent in increased conceptual processing. Graf and Levy concluded that increased conceptual processing is the key to the enhanced memory for the inverted texts.

We do not have any direct measure here of the extent to which our reading time effects were reflecting differences in conceptual or perceptual processing. The pattern of results, however, is consistent with the claim that subjects compensated with conceptual processing as much as possible when reading inverted text. This produced the memory advantage that Graf and Levy would predict. In the low-related conditions, however, the increased reading time did not produce a memory advantage. Operating with the assumptions of Graf and Levy, this would lead us to conclude that the increased time was reflecting more perceptual processing in the absence of any useful conceptual information. Alternatively, the increased time might also reflect an attempt at conceptual processing that was unsuccessful, a claim made by Myers et al. (1987) to account for the long reading times and low recall for the low-related sentence pairs in their experiments.

Regardless of which explanation is correct, the point is that there are many processes that can produce lengthened reading times. Only some of these processes also produce a memory advantage.

REFERENCES

Clark, H. (1977). Bridging. In P. Johnson-Laird & P. Wason (Eds.), *Thinking: Readings in cognitive science* (pp. 411–420). Cambridge: Cambridge University Press.

Daneman, M., & Carpenter, P. (1980). Individual differences in working memory and reading. *Journal of Verbal Learning and Verbal Behavior, 19*, 450–466.

Duffy, S. A., Shinjo, M., & Myers, J. L. (1990). The effect of encoding task on memory for sentence pairs varying in causal relatedness. *Journal of Memory and Language, 29*, 27–42.

Garrod, S., & Sanford, A. (1977). Interpreting anaphoric relations: The integration of semantic information while reading. *Journal of Verbal Learning and Verbal Behavior, 16*, 77–90.

Graf, P. (1981). Reading and generating normal and transformed text. *Canadian Journal of Psychology, 35*, 293–308.

Graf, P., & Levy, B. A. (1984). Reading and remembering: Conceptual and perceptual processing involved in reading rotated passages. *Journal of Verbal Learning and Verbal Behavior, 23*, 405–424.

Haberlandt, K., & Bingham, G. (1978). Verbs contribute to the coherence of brief narratives: Reading related and unrelated sentence triples. *Journal of Verbal Learning and Verbal Behavior, 17*, 419–425.

Keenan, J. M., Baillet, S. D., & Brown, P. (1984). The effects of causal cohesion on comprehension and memory. *Journal of Verbal Learning and Verbal Behavior, 23*, 115–126.

Kintsch, W., & van Dijk, T. A. (1978). Toward a model of text comprehension and production. *Psychological Review, 85*, 363–394.

Kolers, P. A. (1975). Memorial consequences of automatized encoding. *Journal of Experimental Psychology: Human Learning and Memory, 1*, 689–701.

Lesgold, A. M., & Perfetti, C. A. (1978). Interactive processes in reading comprehension. *Discourse Processes, 1*, 323–336.

Masson, M. E. J., & Sala, L. S. (1978). Interactive processes in sentence comprehension and recognition. *Cognitive Psychology, 10*, 244–270.

Myers, J. L., Shinjo, M., & Duffy, S. A. (1987). Degree of causal relatedness and memory. *Journal of Memory and Language, 26*, 453–465.

Perfetti, C. A. (1988). Verbal efficiency in reading ability. In M. Daneman, G. E. Mackinnon, & T. G. Waller (Eds.), *Reading research: Advances in theory and practice* (Vol. 6, pp. 109–143). San Diego: Academic Press.

Stanovich, K. E. (1980). Towards an interactive-compensatory model of individual differences in the development of reading fluency. *Reading Research Quarterly, 16*, 32–71.

6 Logical Connectives and Local Coherence

John D. Murray
Georgia Southern University

Most researchers in the area of reading agree that a primary activity during reading is connecting the phrase or sentence that is currently being read with the contents of the immediately preceding sentence. If a reader is able to make such a connection, then local coherence is said to have been achieved. Establishing local coherence is a multifaceted process involving many factors, including argument overlap (Kintsch & van Dijk, 1978); causal inferences (Klin & Myers, 1993; Myers, Shinjo & Duffy, 1987; van den Broek, 1990); coreference mechanisms such as anaphora (Carpenter & Just, 1977); and the recognition of local meaning relations among sentences (Black & Bern, 1981; Keenan, Baillet & Brown, 1984).

Other factors that may facilitate local coherence are text devices that explicitly mark how one section of text is related to another. Examples of such devices are numerical or sequence markers such as *first*, *next*, and *finally*; relevance indicators such as *In summary*; or logical connectives such as *and*, *therefore*, and *but*. It seems reasonable to assume that any text device that makes the relation between two sentences explicit would assist a reader in forging a connection between those sentences. In this chapter logical connectives are explored in terms of how these devices may affect local coherence processes during the reading of simple narratives.

WHAT ARE LOGICAL CONNECTIVES?

Logical connectives are a form of text signal commonly found in both narrative and expository text. Often, they are conjunctions such as *and*, *but*, *also*, *as a result*, *in addition*, and *however*. The theoretical importance given them in terms of day to day parlance and in narrative prose varies among researchers. For example, in their classic work on coherence, Halliday and Hasan (1976) placed relatively high importance on connectives stating that their role is to "specify the way in which what is to follow is systematically connected to what has gone before" (p. 227). However, van Dijk (1977) placed less importance on connectives, asserting that their primary function is merely to create composite sentences from simple sentences. Van Dijk maintained that the relation between propositions is determined "by the relatedness of the facts denoted by them" (p. 47)—the implication being that devices such as connectives are relatively unimportant.

Despite differences in opinion among linguists in terms of the precise role of connectives, most writing instructors and researchers of instruction and reading behavior maintain that connectives are critical to communicating how adjacent sentences are related to one another. In fact, the implicit assumption has been that the presence of connectives is essential for adequate text comprehension. Simply, they make the text clearer (Goldman & Murray, 1992). For this reason, writers are encouraged to include them to increase the comprehensibility of their discourse.

LOGICAL CONNECTIVES AND LOCAL COHERENCE

This chapter discusses two ways in which logical connectives may facilitate local coherence. The first way is their role in *signalling* the text that follows them in a narrative. In this context, signalling may be defined as a process whereby a connective like *and*, *thus*, or *but* alerts the reader that the text that follows is related additively (in the case of *and*) causally (*thus*), or adversatively (*but*) to the sentence that was previously read. The second way is their role in facilitating memory *integration* of the sentences surrounding the connective. In integration, the issue is whether the presence of a connective, because it explicitly indicates the nature of the relation between successive sentences, increases the probability that both sentences will be stored together in memory.

Experimental evidence that would support the idea that connectives signal the upcoming text would show that the reading time of text immediately following a connective is faster compared to the reading time of that text when the connective is absent. A reduction in reading time is predicted because the presence of the connective presumably reduces the number of inferences the reader must make in order to comprehend the subsequent text (Britton, Glynn, Meyer, & Penland, 1982). Consistent with this position, Haberlandt (1982) showed that the presence of an adversative or causal connective immediately preceding a target sentence led to faster reading time of that sentence compared to when the connective was absent. In this experiment, the target sentence either confirmed or disconfirmed an expectation created by four preceding sentences. Haberlandt's findings suggest that adversative and causal connectives can act as signals that reduce reading time—at least in a situation where the target line is related to the aggregate content of a group of preceding sentences. It is unclear whether connectives will reduce the reading time of a sentence when it is preceded by a single sentence.

With respect to the integrative benefits of connectives, it seems reasonable to assume that any text device that makes clearer the semantic relation between text units would produce a more accurate and more integrated memory representation of the text material (Loman & Mayer, 1983). This assumption leads to a prediction of better recall of the sentences surrounding the connective compared to a condition where the connective is absent. In fact, evidence in support of integrative benefits is mixed. Although several studies have examined the effects of connectives on recall of text (Britton et al., 1982; Marshall & Glock, 1978; Meyer, Brandt, & Bluth, 1980), precise conclusions regarding their benefits on memory have been difficult to make, in part because of the many text-based and reader-based characteristics that have been manipulated (Lorch, 1989; Saul & Goldman, 1991). Caron, Micko, and Thuring (1988) reported that the presence of the causal connective *because* between two unrelated sentences led to better memory of these sentences than either *and* (an additive connective), *but* (an adversative connective), or no connective, suggesting that *because* fostered greater integration of the sentences surrounding the connective. However, in a recent study using sensible, expository materials, Millis, Graesser, and Haberlandt (1993) reported that the presence of causal connectives actually inhibited memory compared to a no-connective condition.

In sum, conclusions regarding the benefits of logical connectives on local coherence processes are difficult to draw given the current state of research. It appears that connectives may act as signals (i.e., speed up reading) and facilitate intersentential integration, but the extent to which this is true may be limited. To understand these limits, research is needed to examine the effect(s) of different types of connectives on the comprehension of different types of text by different types of readers. The next few sections of this chapter report the findings from research done in my lab that suggest answers to some of these questions. In this research, the benefits of three types of logical connectives were explored in a setting that is common for most readers: simple narratives where successive sentences follow coherently from one another and depict frequently encountered intersentential relations. In this setting the reader is not burdened with making effortful inferences in order to connect adjacent sentences. The passages that were used in the present studies convey common events that are easily understood by most adult readers. Following descriptions of the experiments, a model is described that attempts to account for the results and may serve as a starting point for future research.

INTRODUCTION TO EXPERIMENTS

The experiments to be discussed examine the extent to which three classes of logical connectives affect local coherence through two types of benefits. The first benefit is that of facilitating reading through signalling. The second benefit is that of facilitating recall. As discussed previously, if a connective signals the upcoming text, then that text will be read more quickly when it follows a connective than when it does not. If a connective facilitates in the integration of the text surrounding the connnective, then recall of the sentence pair will be greater when a connective is present versus when a connective is absent.

In three experiments, subjects read simple, two-sentence narratives that were referentially coherent and depicted one of three intersentential relations: additive, causal, and adversative. Table 6.1 displays a sample item. The primary materials were 30 two-sentence passages, and each passage had three versions. As indicated by the sample item, the first sentence differed among the three versions and the second sentence was identical and was designated the "target" sentence. In the "additive" passages, the target sentence elaborated on or extended the content of the first sentence in a noncausal, noncontrastive way. In the "causal" passages, the target sentence stated a result or consequence of an event stated in the first sentence. In the "adversative" passages, the target sentence stated an event that contrasted with the content of the first sentence. The passages were pretested to make sure that they were perceived as sensible.

In addition to the relation between the first and target sentences, another independent variable in these experiments was the presence or absence of a logical connective. Given that the purpose of these experiments was to examine the effects of logical connectives when used appropriately, the connectives used were semantically matched to each sentence pair. In other words, additive connectives were used in the additive passages. Similarly, causal and adversative connectives were used in the causal and adversative passages, respectively.

Four instances from each logical connective category were employed in these

TABLE 6.1
Sample Item

Condition	Item
Additive	Rudy and Tom avoided each other on the bus to the amusement park. Moreover they didn't speak to one another for the rest of the day.
Causal	Rudy and Tom fought with each other on the bus to the amusement park. Therefore They didn't speak to one another for the rest of the day.
Adversative	Rudy and Tom laughted with each other on the bus to the amusement park. Yet they didn't speak to one another for the rest of the day.

TABLE 6.2
Connective Instances Used in Present Experiments and Frequency of Use of
Each Instance (out of 30)

ADDITIVE CONNECTIVES:
moreover (7)
furthermore (8)
also (6)
and (9)

CAUSAL CONNECTIVES:
therefore (7)
so (8)
thus (8)
consequently (7)

ADVERSATIVE CONNECTIVES:
yet (6)
nevertheless (8)
however (8)
but (8)

experiments. Table 6.2 displays the specific connectives that were used along with the number of items in which they were used (out of 30). The connectives were selected so that each category would contain connectives that represent a comparable range of frequency of usage in English (Francis & Kucera, 1982). Within each category, one connective is of relatively low frequency, two are at moderate levels, and one is at a relatively high level.

EXPERIMENT 1

In Experiment 1, 60 participants read 30 experimental sentence pairs one line at a time on a computer in a self-paced task along with 63 "filler" sentence pairs. Of the 30 experimental pairs, 10 were additive, 10 were causal, and 10 were adversative. The filler pairs were sensible and depicted a variety of topics. Approximately one fourth of the filler items contained a verbal connective that preceded the second sentence. In addition, one half of the filler pairs were followed by a yes/no comprehension question, which was based on the content of the filler.

In this experiment, the connective's presence/absence was manipulated between subjects; 30 participants read the experimental items with the connectives intact while the remaining 30 read them with the connectives omitted. The Relation Type factor was manipulated within subjects, and all items were counterbalanced over conditions. The 30 experimental pairs were randomly ordered, and two fillers were interspersed between each experimental passage.

Each participant was run individually and told that his or her main objective while reading the passages was to answer the comprehension questions correctly. Participants were not told which items would be followed by a comprehension question. Passages were read one line at a time and at participants' own pace. Each trial began with a ready signal. When ready to start, a participant pushed the Enter key to clear the screen and bring on the first line of a passage. Participants read each line until it was understood, then pushed a key on the keyboard to replace the current line with the next line of the passage. The lines from each passage were presented in such a way as to appear approximately equal in length. The target sentence appeared in its entirety on one line, however this was not necessarily the case with the first sentence. For the participants who read the experimental passages with the connectives present, the first word of the target sentence (the connective) appeared at the end of the immediately preceding line so that the text contained in the target sentence would be identical across all conditions. The experimental session began with three practice passages followed by 90 passages. The reading session lasted approximately 20 minutes.

Immediately after completing the reading task, participants were presented with an unexpected memory test. In this test, the first sentence of each of the 30 experimental passages was presented in a booklet in random order followed by a blank line. For each item, participants were asked to write down as much as they could remember of the target sentence using the first sentence as a cue. Participants had unlimited time to do the memory task.

Reading Time Results

The mean reading times (RTs) for the target lines from participants in the connectives absent and connectives present groups are displayed in Table 6.3. As can be seen from the row means, the overall mean RT for the connective present group was not faster than the RT for the connective absent group, $F < 1$, suggesting that connectives did not result in a general signalling advantage. (All reported F scores are based on subject variability and, unless otherwise noted, were also significant by items.) However, the group X Relation Type interaction was signif-

TABLE 6.3
Mean Reading Times of Target Line (in msec) for Experiment 1

| | Type of Relation | | | |
	Additive	Causal	Adversative	Mean
Connectives Present	2132	2063	2080	2092
GROUP				
Connectives Absent	1980	1960	2253	2064
Mean	2056	2012	2166	

icant, F (2,116) = 8.36, $p < .001$. The pattern of means suggests that only the adversative connectives led to a decrease in reading time of the target sentence. The presence of additive and causal connectives was associated with a moderate increase in reading time. Because of a lack of statistical power, however, none of these between-subject comparisons were significant (all $ps > .1$).

The reading-time data from this experiment suggest that when connectives are placed between sentences that are relatively easy to integrate, their effects on the processing of subsequent text depends on the nature of the relation between the adjacent sentences. Specifically, among the relations examined in this experiment, connectives only decreased the reading time of the target sentence when that sentence was adversatively related to the first sentence. When sentence relations were additive or causal in nature, the presence of connectives offered no reading-time advantage and perhaps a slight processing liability.

Cued Recall Results

With respect to cued recall, each participant's recall protocol was examined by a judge who was blind to the purposes of the experiment. The judge scored participants' response to each memory test item as 1 if the gist was recalled and 0 if the gist was not recalled. The mean number of recalled items in each condition for each group (maximum = 10) is displayed in Table 6.4. As can be seen by examining the row means, no overall difference between groups was observed in terms of the average number of target sentences recalled, $F < 1$. The lack of a main effect implies that (a) overall integrative benefits from connectives were not observed, and (b) inferential connections between the sentences of all three types of sentence pairs were relatively easy to make and did not depend on the presence of the connective.

The column means indicate that there were differences in recall among the different types of intersentential relations, F (2, 116) = 45.32, $p < .001$. Furthermore, the group X Relation Type interaction was significant, F (2, 116) =

TABLE 6.4
Mean Number of Items Recalled (Out of 10) in Experiment 1

	Type of Relation			
	Additive	Causal	Adversative	Mean
Connectives Present	4.3	6.6	7.3	6.1
GROUP				
Connectives Absent	5.4	6.2	7.3	6.3
Mean	4.85	6.4	7.3	

4.3, $p < .02$. Upon close examination of the means, the interaction was found to be based on a difference in recall between the causal and additive targets for participants in the connective present group. However, because this interaction did not replicate in Experiment 2, it is discussed no further.

The cued recall data offer no direct support for the hypothesis that logical connectives facilitate in the integration of adjacent sentences that are coherent. There is little or no indication that the presence of connectives was associated with improved recall in any of the types of intersentential relations examined. Of course, one limitation with the present experimental design is that any integrative benefits attributable to the connectives may have been masked because the sentence pairs were easy to comprehend. Only by examining the recall data and the reading-time data together does indirect evidence emerge in support of adversative connectives facilitating intersentential integration. Specifically, the same level of recall for the adversative targets was observed for the connectives present and connectives absent groups, but the target reading times for the former group were faster than for the latter group. For additive and causal targets, the relationship between processing effort and recall did not differ for the different participant groups. Specifically, small differences in RT were associated with small differences in recall for both additive and causal targets.

EXPERIMENT 2

The purpose of Experiment 2 was to replicate the reading-time findings of Experiment 1 in a completely within-subjects design, and to examine memory with a free-recall procedure. The same two factors examined in Experiment 1 (presence/absence of connective and relation type [Additive, Causal, Adversative]) were employed in this experiment. With the same pool of 30 items, participants were now exposed to five items per condition. The 42 participants read the 30 experimental items on the computer in a self-paced reading task. No fillers were presented. Consequently, the experimental instructions were slightly changed: Instead of reading each passage in order to answer an immediately following question, participants were told to expect comprehension questions at the end of the session. After reading all of the passages, participants did a short distractor task that was followed by a surprise free-recall test for all 30 passages they had read on the computer.

Reading-Time Results

Table 6.5 displays the mean RTs. A quick glance at these means shows that overall reading times are considerably longer than in Experiment 1. Whereas this was not expected, it seems possible that the slight change in the instructions may have led to this increase.

TABLE 6.5
Mean Reading Times of Target Line (in msec) for Experiment 2

	Type of Relation			
	Additive	Causal	Adversative	Mean
Connectives Present	2708	2697	2780	2728
Connectives Absent	2722	2466	3047	2745
Mean	2715	2582	2914	

Despite the overall increase in RT relative to Experiment 1, the pattern of means remains very much the same. As observed before, the RTs did not differ between connective present and connective absent conditions, $F < 1$. In addition, the interaction was significant, $F (2, 82) = 5.18, p < .01$. The pattern of means is very similar to that in Experiment 1 and nicely replicates those findings. The adversative targets were read significantly faster when preceded by a connective than when not preceded by a connective [$t (41) = 2.17, p < .05$]. No such advantage was found with additive or causal targets. This finding strongly supports the hypothesis that when adjacent sentences are relatively easy to integrate, only an adversative connective acts as a signal for the upcoming text. In addition, the inhibitory effect of the causal connective observed in Experiment 1 was echoed in Experiment 2 [$t (41) = 1.79, p = .08$]. In Experiment 1, a slight (103 ms) increase in processing time on the target line was associated with the presence of a causal connective. In Experiment 2, this pattern emerged again and did so more strongly (231 ms) suggesting that the causal connective may be imposing some sort of processing liability on the subsequent text (see also Millis et al., 1993). With the additive targets, the difference in reading time observed in Experiment 1 failed to replicate in Experiment 2 so it is not discussed further.

Free-Recall Results

The question of whether the presence of a connective facilitates the integration of adjacent sentences was examined by scoring each participant's recall protocol in terms of the number of items where at least one proposition from both the first sentence and the target sentence was recalled (maximum = 5). The means are displayed in Table 6.6.

No overall differences in recall emerged between the connective present and connective absent conditions, $F < 1$. Furthermore, significant differences in recall were found among the different relation type conditions, $F (2, 82) = 7.2, p = .001$. However, in contrast to Experiment 1, no interaction emerged, $F < 1$.

These data corroborate the conclusions from Experiment 1 with respect to the

TABLE 6.6
Mean Number of Items (out of 5) Where at Least One Proposition From Both Sentences Was
Recalled in Experiment 2

	Type of Relation			
	Additive	Causal	Adversative	Mean
Connectives Present	.52	.69	.86	.69
Connectives Absent	.50	.57	.98	.68
Mean	.51	.63	.92	

integrative benefits of connectives: that the presence of additive, causal, or adversative connectives between sentences conveying like relations offers no memory facilitation compared to a condition where the connective is absent. The lack of an interaction in Experiment 2 strengthens this argument. Only when we examine the reading time and recall data together do we have indirect evidence in support of the assumption that adversative connectives facilitate integration. Consistent with the findings from Experiment 1, a similar level of recall in Experiment 2 was observed for adversative targets whether they were preceded by a connective or not. This same level of recall occurred despite the fact that significantly less processing time was devoted to adversative targets preceded by a connective. Interestingly, for causal targets we found a contrasting result: more or less equal recall despite less processing time devoted to targets not preceded by a connective. For additive targets, reading-time and recall appear not to differ as a function of the presence of an additive connective. The role of connectives in integration is discussed more extensively later on.

EXPERIMENT 3

Experiment 3 was conducted in order to elucidate how logical connectives may affect readers' conscious perceptions of local coherence. Two possibilities were explored: The first is that if connectives increase the comprehensibility of text, then readers should judge target sentences preceded by connectives as following more sensibly from the first sentence than sentences not preceded by connectives. The second possibility is that if (as the findings from Experiments 1 and 2 suggest) connectives facilitate (i.e., speed up) reading only when the target sentence is adversatively related to the immediately prior sentence, then readers should judge such a sentence as following less sensibly from the preceding sentence if it does not contain an adversative connective. However, the sensibility of target sentences should not be as strongly affected by the presence of additive or causal connectives.

The possibilities just mentioned were investigated by having a group of 54 participants read the 30 experimental sentence pairs used in Experiments 1 and 2 along with 20 filler sentence pairs. In contrast to the fillers used in Experiment 1, those employed in this experiment were not sensible (together, the two sentences did not make sense). A sample filler might read: "Ralph couldn't understand what the speaker's point had been. Recently, he had been typing on his computer."

The same 2 × 3 within-subjects design employed in Experiment 2 was used in Experiment 3. The 50 sentence pairs were randomly ordered and presented in a booklet. Beside each pair was a blank line for participants to write a number between 1 and 5 reflecting the extent to which the second sentence of the pair "followed sensibly" from the first sentence (1 = does not follow at all; 5 = follows extremely well).

Results

The mean rating for each condition is displayed in Table 6.7. The first prediction was confirmed in that participants rated targets preceded by a connective as following significantly more sensibly from the preceding sentence than those targets not preceded by a connective, $F (1, 53) = 135.8, p < .001$. However, consistent with the second prediction, the greatest difference between the presence and absence of the connective clearly lies in the ratings of the adversative targets, as indicated by a significant interaction, $F (2, 106) = 50.8, p < .001$. In addition, differences in perceived sensibility were found among the different types of target sentences, $F (1, 106) = 164.3, p < .001$. The column means show that the causal targets were perceived as following more sensibly from the preceding sentences than either additive or adversative targets.

TABLE 6.7
Mean Ratings for Target Lines (by Condition)

	Type of Relation			
	Additive	Causal	Adversative	Mean
Connectives Present	3.15	3.81	3.14	3.37
Connectives Absent	2.76	3.60	2.04	2.80
Mean	2.96	3.71	2.59	
	(Filler = 1.35)			

The results from Experiment 3 are consistent with and extend the findings of Experiments 1 and 2. The rating data corroborate the reading-time data from the first two experiments with respect to the assumption that adversative connectives operate as signals of upcoming contrastive text. In addition, the rating data alone suggest that the presence of all three types of connectives is associated with greater perceived sensibility of the sentence pair. This finding is consistent with the well-accepted notion that connectives facilitate comprehension of relations among sentences.

The greater perceived sensibility of the additive and causal targets that were preceded by a connective may seem at odds with the reading-time findings pertaining to these targets. I argue that the rating task is tapping into readers' general syntactic preferences and does not necessarily reflect online processes affecting local coherence. It seems reasonable that readers, because of prior writing instruction and experience, would perceive as more sensible a coherent sentence pair that includes an appropriately placed connective than one that does not contain a connective. However, the reading-time data from Experiments 1 and 2 indicate that the online consequences of additive and causal connectives are short-lived and do not affect the conscious perception of intersentential coherence.

DISCUSSION

What conclusions about the role of logical connectives in local coherence processes can be gathered from these experiments? Before discussing this issue, it is important to re-emphasize that these experiments examine connectives in a setting where their usage was appropriate, and where they were placed between sentences that were coherent and relatively easy to integrate. This setting allows the opportunity to make some important observations about the effects of connectives when they appear in a frequently encountered setting. However, this setting is also limited because additional theoretical questions remain unanswered. These theoretical issues are discussed later. In this section, conclusions about the effects of connectives on signalling and integration of easy-to-integrate text are discussed. This discussion is followed by a description of a model based on the present findings.

Do Logical Connectives Signal the Upcoming Text?

At the beginning of this chapter, a logical connective was defined as a signal if its presence led to a reduction in the reading time of the subsequent text. With respect to this definition, the data reported in this chapter strongly support the notion that adversative connectives do indeed act as signals when the target sentence is adversatively related to the preceding sentence.

However, not all text signals are associated with a reduction in reading time. Text signals can also be what Lorch (1989) referred to as "importance indicators," and as such can lead to an increase in reading time of the text that follows them. Theoretically, this type of signal exists for the purpose of flagging the upcoming text as something to which the reader should devote extra processing. The findings from Experiments 1 and 2 indicate that the presence of a causal connective led to a moderate increase in the reading time of the text that followed the connective. These findings suggest that a causal connective may serve as an importance indicator in narrative texts, signalling the reader to pay greater attention to the target sentence. This interpretation is consistent with the well-established finding that readers grant a special status to causally related text events (Trabasso & Sperry, 1985; Trabasso & van den Broek, 1985).

In contrast to adversative and causal connectives, no evidence was obtained to support the notion that additive connectives act as signals of any sort. Over two experiments, the presence of an additive connective led to no reliable increase or decrease in reading time compared to a condition where the connective was absent. The lack of a reliable reading-time effect in the additive targets is not particularly surprising when one considers the relative uninformativeness of additive connectives in general, and the few semantic constraints they impose on the content of the subsequent text (Goldman & Murray, 1992; Saul & Goldman, 1991; van Dijk, 1977). The additive connectives used in these experiments merely indicate a nonspecific elaboration of the content of the preceding text and little else.

Do Logical Connectives Facilitate Text Integration Processes?

The present experiments indicate that of the three types of connectives examined in this research, only the adversatives facilitate in the integration in memory of the sentences surrounding the connective. This conclusion stems from the finding that the presence of an adversative connective led to faster target reading time but equal target memory compared to the RT and memory associated with adversative targets not preceded by a connective. No similar processing time/recall relationships were observed for additive or causal targets.

Processing Model

The proposed model is based on the assumption that narrative text processing proceeds as a process of seeking and establishing causal connections between adjacent propositions. Many researchers in the area of text processing have obtained evidence in support of the central role that causality plays in the comprehension of narratives (Goldman & Varnhagen, 1986; Myers, 1990; Myers &

Duffy, 1991; Trabasso & Sperry, 1985; Trabasso & van den Broek, 1985; van den Broek, 1990).

Given this assumption, the model first stipulates that different classes of connectives are associated with different knowledge bases. This knowledge consists of (a) constraints pertaining to how the sentence that immediately follows the connective is likely to relate to the immediately prior sentence, and (b) procedural knowledge of how to combine these constraints with the contents of the immediately prior sentence to create an expectancy of the content of the postconnective sentence. The model proposes that this knowledge and expectancy-generation process will influence the reading time of the post-connective sentence. Following is a list of descriptions of the constraints presumed to be associated with the types of connectives used in the present experiments and the nature of the generated expectancy:

1. Adversative connectives are highly constrained. They specify solely that the subsequent text is likely to contrast or limit the scope of the content of the preceding text. The content of the immediately preceding sentence combines with these constraints to create the expectancy that the subsequent sentence is likely to contrast with the preceding sentence.

2. Causal connectives are moderately constrained. The subsequent text may be related in several ways to the preconnective sentence. One type of relation is cause and effect; an expectancy consistent with this relation is that the upcoming text will bear a causal relation to the prior text, either by stating a consequence of an event stated in the preceding sentence or by stating the cause for an event that was stated in the preceding sentence.

A second type of relation indicated by a causal connective is that the upcoming text will elaborate in a nonspecific way on the prior text. Evidence that readers may interpret causal connectives in this manner comes from research by Goldman and Murray (1992), where readers were asked to select which one of four types of connectives best "fit" between adjacent sentences. These adjacent sentences reflected additive, causal, adversative, or sequential (i.e., temporal) relations. It was found that readers heavily "over selected" causal connectives, especially in the context of "actual" additive relationships. This finding suggests that readers do not always associate true "cause and effect" relationships with the presence of causal connectives, and tend also to see merely elaborative relations as possibly causal.

3. Additive connectives are highly unconstrained. As mentioned previously, additive connectives signify that the subsequent text merely elaborates or extends what has been just previously stated. Expectations of the content of the postconnective sentence are highly undefined and/or highly variable, and the relation between the pre- and postconnective text is most likely one of mere elaboration.

Following the activation of the connective-appropriate knowledge and the generation of an expectancy for the postconnective sentence, it is proposed that the reader then attempts to integrate the postconnective text with the immediately preceding sentence. The model stipulates that the probability of the connective facilitating online local coherence processes (i.e., decreasing reading time) is a joint function of (a) the degree to which the postconnective text "matches" the expectancy generated during the constraint-activation phase and (b) the constraint level associated with the previously encoded connective.

The model predicts that connective instances possessing a high constraint level, like adversatives, would most likely lead to a decrease in reading time of the subsequent text when that text is adversatively related to the prior sentence (i.e., a high match). Inhibitory effects would be expected from an adversative connective if the subsequent text were not adversatively related to the prior text (low match). With moderately constrained connectives, like causals, a moderate level of facilitation would be expected if the subsequent text met expectations activated by the connective; and a moderate level of inhibition would result if expectations were not met. And finally, with very unconstrained connectives, like additives, very little facilitation or inhibition would result from their presence primarily because of the low level of semantic constraints associated with additives.

With respect to the joint influence of (a) and (b) on integrative processes (or those local coherence processes to which cued and free recall are sensitive), the model assumes that these factors are less important than the amount of elaboration that results from their confluence in addition to the degree to which a coherent connection can be forged between the adjacent sentences (Duffy, Shinjo, & Myers, 1990; Myers et al., 1987). In other words, the degree to which connectives will positively affect memory is based on the factors previously described only to the extent that their confluence results in a well-elaborated and coherent memory representation of the sentence pair.

Explaining the Data With the Model

With respect to the effects of connectives on reading time, the observed facilitation from adversative connectives and the lack of facilitation from additive connectives is highly consistent with the model's assumptions. The high level of semantic constraint associated with adversative connectives combined with a high match between what a reader expects and what is actually presented after encoding the connective constitutes a situation that would yield high connective facilitation. The low level of semantic constraint associated with an additive connective predicts very low connective facilitation.

The observed inhibitory effects associated with the presence of causal connectives are more difficult for the model to explain. The model predicts that the moderate meaning constraints associated with a causal connective coupled with a reasonable "match" between readers' expectations of the upcoming text and their perception of that text once encoded should lead to moderate connective facilitation; and a lesser match should result in moderate inhibition. It is proposed that the observed inhibition was possibly due to readers' variable expectations of the kind of text that follows a causal connective. Goldman and Murray's (1992) findings suggest that readers frequently perceive as sensible the presence of a causal connective between sentences that convey an additive relationship. Therefore it seems possible that when readers in the present studies encoded the causal connectives, their expectations of the upcoming text may have included something other than what was represented by the target sentence. Such a mismatch between expectations and reality would lead to the somewhat "noisy" effects that were observed. Another possibility that was mentioned previously is that causal connectives may be unique in their tendency to signal importance, thus leading to a slower reading time. Future research is needed that carefully explores the semantic attributes of causal connectives.

With respect to the memory findings, the present studies found evidence for only the adversative connectives facilitating in the integration of the pre- and postconnective text. These findings are consistent with the model in that the online effects of the connective were substantial enough to impact memory processing. The lack of facilitation from additive connectives is not surprising due to their uninformativeness regarding the connection between the pre- and postconnective sentences. However, the lack of integrative facilitation from causal connectives seems at odds with research showing that readers rate causally related statements among the most important in narrative texts (Trabasso & Sperry, 1985; Trabasso & van den Broek, 1985). As alluded to earlier, it may be the case that the online effects of causal connectives may not be as clear cut as with other types of connectives. Because readers' expectations are quite variable regarding the type of text that follows a causal connective (Goldman & Murray, 1992), it is possible that the resulting text representation was relatively incoherent and consequently difficult to retrieve. Another possibility is that readers may simply be finding the causal relationship between the events stated in the pre- and postconnective text difficult to understand. If this is the case, the connective would have no effect. As previously stated, future research focusing on causal connectives is necessary.

Because the present experiments only tested sentence pairs where the target text matched the expectations activated by the connective, additional research is needed to evaluate the model's predictions when the match is poor. This research is currently in progress. Some recent evidence with respect to memory has been reported by Caron et al. (1988) and is consistent with the model. These researchers found that, when placed between sentences that were highly unrelated, the causal connective *because* led to greater recall relative to a no-connective condition. No facilitation was observed when the connective was *but* or *and*. The model accounts for the lack of facilitation from the adversative connective by asserting that adversative connectives are quite poor in facilitating integrative processes when the coherence between adjacent sentences is low. The lack of facilitation from the additive connective is explained by the impoverished meaning constraints associated with *and*. The facilitation observed with *because* is based on the moderate meaning constraints associated with *because* and the fact that readers' threshold for the perception of two events as being causally related is quite low. Hence, a moderate level of constraint coupled with a probable match between the constraints activated by the connective and the text, should yield relative facilitation.

FINAL COMMENTS

The model was proposed for the purpose of providing a reasonable interpretation of the findings reported in the present experiments as well as to provide a theoretical starting point for additional research. As mentioned in the previous section, future research is needed to examine the reading-time consequences associated with a poor match between activated connective constraints and the target text. Another aspect of the model to be validated includes a thorough exploration of connective constraints, especially causal connectives, and their specific impact on processing. Research in this area should attempt to pinpoint the specific constraints associated with specific classes of connectives. A related question is whether connectives within a class (e.g., additives) differ in their constraints.

Finally, an important limitation of the model and the experiments presented in this chapter is their focus on logical connectives and local coherence processes in the context of short narratives. In narratives, the inferential connections that must be forged are often quite easy to make and are based on the activation of generic world knowledge. One area that has been the focus of recent research is how readers utilize connectives in content domains with which they are highly unfamiliar (i.e., expository text). In this setting, one may make the prediction that text devices that make the relation between concepts explicit would be more useful to the reader. On the other hand, it may be the case that when reading in an unfamiliar domain readers choose to devote all available processing resources to understanding the semantic relationships being conveyed by the content words in the text. As a result, function words may be ignored or even a nuisance to the reader (see Millis et al., 1993). Further research is needed in this area in order to gain a more complete understanding of the conditions under which connectives are used in reading.

ACKNOWLEDGMENTS

The initial pilot study for the research reported in this chapter was funded by NIMH grant 1R1MH40029 awarded to Jerome L. Myers, and NIMH Postdoctoral Training Grant 5-T32-MH16745-09 awarded to the University of Massachusetts. Thanks go to Elena Mustakova-Naydenova, Robin Yuronis, and Dahlia Chesnoff for help with data scoring. Also, thanks go to Jerome Myers and Celia Klin for ideas with the research and to Susan Goldman, Elizabeth Saul, and Lisa Farwell for comments on earlier versions of this manuscript.

REFERENCES

Black, J. B., & Bern, H. (1981). Causal inference and memory for events in narratives. *Journal of Verbal Learning and Verbal Behavior*, *20*, 267–275.

Britton, B. K., Glynn, S. M., Meyer, B. J. F., & Penland, M. J. (1982). Effects of text structure on use of cognitive capacity during reading. *Journal of Educational Psychology*, *74*, 51–61.

Caron, J., Micko, H. C., & Thuring, M. (1988). Conjunctions and the recall of composite sentences. *Journal of Memory and Language*, *27*, 309–323.

Carpenter, P. A., & Just, M. A. (1977). Reading comprehension as the eyes see it. In M. A. Just & P. A. Carpenter (Eds.), *Cognitive Processes in Comprehension*. (pp. 109–139) Hillsdale, NJ: Lawrence Erlbaum Associates.

Duffy, S. A., Shinjo, M., & Myers, J. L. (1990). The effect of encoding task on memory for sentence pairs varying in causal relatedness. *Journal of Memory and Language*, *29*, 27–42.

Francis, W. N., & Kucera, H. (1982). *Frequency analysis of English usage*. Boston: Houghton Mifflin.

Goldman, S. R., & Murray, J. D. (1992). Knowledge of connectors as cohesion devices in text: A comparative study of native English and ESL speakers. *Journal of Educational Psychology*, *84*, 504–519.

Goldman, S. R., & Varnhagen, C. K. (1986). Memory for embedded and sequential story structures. *Journal of Memory and Language*, *25*, 401–418.

Haberlandt, K. (1982). Reader expectations in text comprehension. In J. Le Ny & W. Kintsch (Eds.), *Language and Comprehension* (pp.239–249). Amsterdam: North-Holland.

Halliday, M. A. K., & Hasan, R. (1976). *Cohesion in English*. London: Longman.

Keenan, J. M., Baillet, S. D., & Brown, P. (1984). The effects of causal cohesion on comprehension and memory. *Journal of Verbal Learning and Verbal Behavior*, *23*, 115–126.

Kinstch, W., & van Dijk, T.A. (1978). Toward a model of text comprehension and production. *Psychological Review*, *85*, 363–394.

Klin, C. M., & Myers, J. L. (1993). Reinstatement of causal information during reading. *Journal of Experimental Psychology: Learning, Memory, and Cognition*, *19*, 554–560.

Loman, N. L., & Mayer, R. E. (1983). Signaling techniques that increase the understandability of expository prose. *Journal of Educational Psychology*, *75*, 402–412.

Lorch, R. F. (1989). Text signaling devices and their effects on reading and memory processes. *Educational Psychology Review*, (Vol. 1, pp. 209–234). NY: Plenum.

Marshall, N., & Glock, M. D. (1978). Comprehension of connected discourse: A study into the relationships between the structure of text and information recalled. *Reading Research Quarterly*, *14*, 10–56.

Meyer, B. J. F., Brandt, D. M., & Bluth, G. J. (1980). Use of top- level structure in text: Key for reading comprehension of ninth-grade students. *Reading Research Quarterly*, *16*, 72–103.

Millis, K. K., Graesser, A. C. & Haberlandt, K. (1993). The impact of connectives on the memory for expository texts. *Applied Cognitive Psychology*, *7*, 317–339.

Myers, J. L. (1990). Causal relatedness and text comprehension. In D.A. Balota, G. B. Flores d'Arcais, & K. Rayner (Eds.) *Comprehension processes in reading* (pp. 361–375), Hillsdale, NJ: Lawrence Erlbaum Associates.

Myers, J. L., & Duffy, S. A. (1991). Causal inferences and text memory. In A. C. Graesser & G. H.

Bower (Eds.) *The Psychology of Learning and Motivation*, (Vol. 25, pp. 159–173). Orlando, FL: Academic Press.

Myers, J. L., Shinjo, M., & Duffy, S. A. (1987). Degree of causal relatedness and memory. *Journal of Memory and Language*, *26*, 453–465.

Saul, E. U. & Goldman, S. R. (1991). *Representation and use of logical connectors*. Paper presented at the Annual Meeting of the American Psychological Society, Washington, DC.

Trabasso, T., & Sperry, L. L. (1985). Causal relatedness and the importance of story events. *Journal of Memory and Language*, *24*, 595–611.

Trabasso, T., & van den Broek, P. (1985). Causal thinking and the representation of narrative events. *Journal of Memory and Language*, *24*, 612–630.

van den Broek, P. (1990). The causal inference maker: Towards a process model of inference generation in text comprehension. In D. A. Balota, G. B. Flores d'Arcais, & K. Rayner (Eds.) *Comprehension Processes in Reading* (pp. 423–445). Hillsdale, NJ: Lawrence Erlbaum Associates.

van Dijk, T. A. (1977). *Text and context*. New York: Longman.

7 The Effect of Connectives and Causal Relatedness on Text Comprehension

Jonathan M. Golding
University of Kentucky

Keith M. Millis
Northern Illinois University

Jerry Hauselt
Sandra A. Sego
University of Kentucky

CAUSAL RELATEDNESS AND TEXT COMPREHENSION

Several studies have documented the importance of causality on text comprehension. These studies have shown that statements that are causally related or lie on the primary causal chain of a narrative are remembered better than statements that are not causally related or that do not lie on the narrative's causal chain (Black & Bern, 1981; Trabasso & van den Broek, 1985). Keenan, Baillet, and Brown (1984) conducted one of the first studies to demonstrate the role causal relations have on text comprehension. In their study, Keenan et al. (1984) measured the reading time and incidental memory for the second sentence (cued by the first sentence) of sentence pairs that varied across four levels of causal relatedness. Table 7.1 presents an example of sentence pairs that illustrates four levels of causal relatedness. Keenan's experiment resulted in two important findings. First, the reading time for the second sentence increased as the causal relatedness between the sentence pairs decreased. Second, the memory for the second sentence followed a quadratic, U-shaped function; memory was best for moderately related sentence pairs (Levels 2 and 3) and lowest for the lowest level of relatedness (Level 1) and highest level of relatedness (Level 4).

Keenan's findings were interesting to text researchers for several reasons. The reading-time data indicates that readers had more difficulty understanding the

TABLE 7.1
Example of Sentence Pairs Involving Different Levels of Causal Relatedness
(From Myers et al., 1987)

Sentence 1:	
Joey went to play baseball with his brother.	(Level 1)
Joey got angry at his brother in a game.	(Level 2)
Joey began fighting with his older brother.	(Level 3)
Joey's brother punched him again and again.	(Level 4)
Sentence 2:	
The next day his body was covered with bruises.	

Note. Level 4 = highly related.

sentence pairs as intersentence causality decreased. This interpretation was consistent with the memory data that showed lowered recall for the lowest levels of relatedness (barring the decline in recall at the highest level of causal relatedness). This pattern of data alone challenged the predominant assumption at the time that coreference was necessary and sufficient to establish textual coherence (see Kintsch & van Dijk, 1978). Another interesting finding was that the memory for the second sentence followed a quadratic function, specifically an inverted-U function. Not only did recall decrease at the lowest level of causal relatedness compared to the middle levels, but it decreased for the highest level.

Myers and his colleagues have replicated and extended Keenan's findings in several published studies (Duffy, Shinjo, & Myers, 1990; Myers & Duffy, 1990; Myers, Shinjo, & Duffy, 1987). In the first study, Myers et al. (1987) addressed limiting factors (e.g., the small number of texts) that might have confounded or otherwise affected the results obtained by Keenan et al. (1984). Using a set of polynomial regression analyses to predict reading times, Myers et al. found that the reading time of the second sentence of the sentence pairs increased as causal relatedness decreased. These analyses resulted in a highly significant linear component, and also a small, yet highly reliable quadratic component. The cued recall results, for both sentences of the pair, were also analyzed using regression. They produced the same U-shaped function as Keenan et al., resulting in a significant quadratic component across recall of both the first and second sentences. Therefore, this study found additional support for the notion of a continuum of causal relatedness, using different materials and measuring recall of both sentences.

Myers and his colleagues have argued that reader-generated elaborations account for the pattern of data observed in the levels of causal relatedness studies. This hypothesis assumes that elaborations (e.g., bridging inferences) stored in the text representation facilitate retrieval, partly because they provide additional retrieval routes from one sentence of the pair to the other at the time of the cued recall test. To account for the results, it must be assumed that subjects elaborated the moderately related pairs more than either the lowest or highest related pairs. Myers et al. (1987) speculated that subjects would naturally have difficulty elaborating the low-related texts because it is not clear what particular inference the author had in mind. Readers would also have difficulty elaborating the high-related sentence pairs because they would already be causally related; no additional elaboration would be required for coherence. Only the moderately related stories would require elaborations that the subjects could readily generate.

Additional support for the elaboration hypothesis was found in a series of experiments by Duffy et al. (1990). When subjects were required to write down elaborations after each sentence pair, subjects' recall of the text did not show the familiar inverted-U function. Being forced to elaborate the sentence pairs led to a flattening of the inverted-U curve found in earlier studies (see also Myers & Duffy, 1990). Moreover, this flattening pattern was very strong, persisting up to 48 hours after sentence presentation. Apparently, forcing subjects to elaborate raised the recall of the low- and high-related sentence pairs to a level comparable with the moderate-related levels, thereby flattening out the curve.

We extend the research on causal relatedness by investigating whether connectives affect the impact of causal relatedness on reading time and memory. Because authors use connectives, such as *therefore*, to indicate a causal relation among clauses, the effect of a connective on reading time and memory would likely vary with levels of causal relatedness. Before presenting the experiments, however, we discuss prior research on the role of connectives on text comprehension.

CONNECTIVES AND TEXT COMPREHENSION

Connectives are words or short phrases that interrelate two statements or clauses in a text by explicitly specifying a conceptual relationship between the statements (Haliday & Hasan, 1976). The most common categories of connectives are causal (e.g., *therefore*, *because*), adversative (e.g., *but*, *however*), temporal (e.g., *before*, *then*), and additive (e.g., *and*, *or*). Because connectives explicitly specify a particular interstatement relation, readers must interpret the conjoined clauses in a way consistent with the meaning of the connective (see Townsend, 1983; Townsend & Bever, 1978, 1983). For example, if a sentence read "Susan walked to her neighbor's house because she ran out of ice for the party," the reader must interpret the clauses as being causally related as the causal connective *because* linked the two clauses. In the absence of the connective, the reader is not obligated to impose a causal relation among the statements (e.g., "Susan walked to her neighbors house. She ran out of ice for the party.").

What impact do connectives have on comprehension and memory? Some researchers have argued that the presence of connectives should facilitate the comprehension of and memory for text. According to this position, connectives are facilitative because they help make explicit the logical relations between text units (i.e., they signal the content of the subsequent text), and therefore aid in the construction of a coherent text representation (Beck, McKeown, Sinatra, & Loxterman, 1991; Haliday & Hasan, 1976; Hirsch, 1977; Lorch, 1989; Segal, Duchan, & Scott, 1991; Smith & Frawley, 1983). Consequently, connectives lessen the need for a reader to make resource-consuming inferences, such as bridging inferences (e.g., Haviland & Clark, 1974; Keenan & Kintsch, 1974).

Several researchers have found empirical support for the claim that connectives facilitate the comprehension of text. Haberlandt (1982) reported that readers took less time to read a sentence when it began with a causal or adversative connective than if there was no connective. Murray (this volume) has also found that the presence of adversative connectives lead to faster reading time. Britton, Glynn, Meyer, and Penland (1982) showed that subjects who read paragraphs with logical connectives (e.g., *hence*) used less cognitive capacity than subjects who read paragraphs with no connectives. In regard to the strength of the resulting text representation, Caron, Micko, and Thuring (1988) found consistent evidence that two unrelated sentences conjoined by the connective *because* led to better recall than if the sentences were not joined by a connective or were conjoined by the connective *and*. Presumably, the presence of the causal connective had elicited elaborations that later aided in the retrieval of the text (see Murray, this volume).

Despite the theoretical and empirical support for facilitation due to connectives, there is some evidence that connectives do not always facilitate text comprehension and memory. Murray (this volume) has found that, for narratives consisting of two sentences, the presence of a causal connective slows reading time relative to having no connective, and that the presence of a causal or adversative connective does not increase cued and free recall (see also Noordman, Vonk, & Kempff, 1992). Millis, Graesser, and Haberlandt (1993) found that connectives do not improve memory for expository texts describing scientific mechanisms. Instead, texts without connectives resulted in slightly greater recall than texts containing causal or intentional connectives, and significantly greater recall than texts containing temporal connectives. They argued that the semantics of the connectives constrained the amount of elaborative processing normally performed by the reader if the connectives had been absent. For example, because temporal connectives are semantically less complex than causal connectives (see Brent, 1989), temporal connectives may have inhibited the reader from computing more complex elaborations involving causality. Because the texts used by Millis et al. described scientific mechanisms, the causal connectives may not have strongly affected recall because they may have been redundant with elaborations that the readers would have generated when the connectives were absent.

EXPERIMENT 1: THE IMPACT OF CAUSAL CONNECTIVES AND LEVELS OF RELATEDNESS ON TEXT COMPREHENSION

Experiment 1 examined whether the presence of the causal connective *therefore* would alter the effect of levels of relatedness on the comprehension of text. When texts are presented without a connective, as in the texts used previously to study causal relatedness, subjects must rely solely on their world knowledge about the events conveyed in the text to compute the causal relatedness between the statements. However, if the two statements are conjoined by a connective, the reader is explicitly told to interpret the clauses causally, regardless of the meaning of the clauses. Therefore, it is possible that the presence of a connective would alter the normal effect that causal relatedness has on comprehension.

Previously, there has only been one study that has addressed the question of whether connectives and causal relatedness interact during comprehension. In an experiment conducted by Millis and Just (1994, Experiment 3), subjects read moderately related or unrelated statement pairs that were either joined or not joined by the causal connective *because*. They found that the presence of the connective decreased final-word reading times when the statements were related but increased them when the statements were unrelated. Overall, the data suggested that the presence of the connective sped up processing for the related statements because they signalled a relation that was appropriate for the related statements. However, when the statements were unrelated, the presence of the connective led the readers down a garden path, causing the readers to perform an extensive, but unsuccessful, search of long-term memory to construct a coherent representation of the statements.

The primary purpose of the present study was to investigate whether results similar to Millis and Just (1994, Experiment 3) would be found when there was a continuum of causal relatedness (using the Myers et al., 1987 materials), and whether subjects' recall of the statement pairs would follow the quadratic trend reported by Keenan et al. (1984) and Myers and his colleagues. We used the causal connective *therefore* instead of *because* as *therefore* preserves the natural ordering of the statements used in Myers et al. (1987). To use the connective *because*, one would have to reverse the order of statements (i.e., Statement 2 because Statement 1), but this is not true when *therefore* is used (i.e., Statement 1 therefore Statement 2). This was an important consideration because we were interested in comparing the reading times for the second statement when the connective had joined the two statements and when it had not.

How might the presence of the causal connective *therefore* alter the effect of levels of causal relatedness on reading time and recall? Assuming that the connective leads the reader to construct a causal interpretation of the text, we expect that at low levels of relatedness, the presence of the connective would slow down the processing time of the second statement (relative to the no-connective condition) because the subjects would have to take time to search long-term memory for an appropriate causal interpretation of the text. However, the connective may speed up processing time or have no effect when the texts are highly related. This is essentially the result that Millis and Just (1994, Experiment 3) found using two levels of causal relatedness.

In regard to recall, the no-connective versions should result in the quadratic, inverted-U curve reported by Myers et al. (1987). To the extent that the connectives do *not* elicit elaborative processing, the same quadratic curve should occur for the connective conditions as well. If connectives elicit elaborative processing, it is possible that the recall will vary across the levels of relatedness such that the inverted-U function will be eliminated. For example, the high level of relatedness may show an increase in recall compared to other studies (e.g., Myers et al., 1987), because the causal connective forces subjects to elaborate to a greater degree during reading. In addition, the low level of causal relatedness may be recalled better than previous studies because readers may successfully reprocess the text in an attempt to integrate the unexpected consequence with the cause concept of the text (see O'Brien & Myers, 1985). Because prior research has found evidence for (Caron et al., 1988) and against (Millis et al., 1993) the finding that connectives increase memory, we do not have an a priori prediction on the magnitude of the recall scores.

Method

We had 96 subjects read the 40 two-sentence texts from Myers et al. (1987). Of these 40, 32 were "experimental" texts and eight were "filler" texts. For each subject, one half of the experimental texts included the connective *therefore*, which joined the two sentences into a single sentence as follows:

> Joey's brother punched him again and again, therefore the next day his body was covered with bruises.

(The two parts of each single sentence in the connective condition are referred to as Statement 1 and Statement 2.) The other half of the experimental texts were shown without the connective, constituting two separate sentences as they had been displayed in Myers et al. (For the two sentences in the no-connective versions, we refer to the first sentence as Statement 1 and the second sentence as Statement 2.) Each text had four versions, each corresponding to a different level of causal relatedness (see Table 7.1 for an example). Each version of a text was presented to an equal number of subjects with and without the presence of the connective. The subjects read the texts in a random order.

The filler texts were the same used in Myers et al. (1987), except that half of them were modified to include the connective *therefore*. Each of the fillers included a Yes–No comprehension question after Sentence 2. These questions were used to insure that subjects were reading the sentences for comprehension. This was found to be the case, with subjects answering seven of these eight questions correctly, on average.

Subjects read the texts at their own pace, one statement at a time, answering the comprehension questions as they appeared. The computer recorded the time that the subjects took to read Statement 2 of the experimental texts. After reading the texts, the subjects were informed that they would be asked to recall part of what they had just read. The subjects were randomly assigned to one of two recall conditions. Subjects in the "recall Statement 1" condition were presented with the second statement of each experimental text, and were asked to recall the first statement associated with each one. Subjects in the "recall Statement 2" condition were given the first statement of each experimental text, and were asked to recall the second statement. Subjects were asked to write down as much as they could remember and to guess if necessary. The presentation order of the statement cues were randomized for each subject.

The subjects' recall protocols were scored in the following manner. Subjects' recall protocols were first parsed into propositional units. The recalled propositions were then scored as to whether they matched the propositions in the experimental texts. For each subject, a memory score was assigned to each statement that the subject was required to recall. The memory score was simply the percentage of propositions in that statement correctly recalled by the subject. The protocols were scored by a single trained scorer. In order to assess reliability, a second trained individual scored a random 10% of the recall protocols. The reliability between the two scores was 92% for recall of Statement 1, and 95% for recall of Statement 2.

The primary dependent variables of interest were Statement 2 reading times and the recall of the two statements. These variables were analyzed in two ways. First, *t*-tests were computed between the connective and no-connective conditions on the overall means. This analysis allowed us to inspect the overall impact that the presence of the connective had on reading times and recall. Second, regression analyses were performed on each subjects' data to assess the trend that the dependent variables produced across the levels of relatedness (see Myers et al., 1987). In these analyses, the mean relatedness rating obtained by subjects in Myers et al. for each text version served as the predictor variable. Separate analyses were conducted on the texts containing the connective and those that did not. Because regression equations were conducted separately for each subject, the regression equation for each analysis (connective vs. no-connective) was based on 16 experimental texts. The regression analyses obtained the least-squares estimates of linear, quadratic, and cubic trends in that order. The mean of the obtained coefficients associated with each trend were then tested to see if they differed significantly from zero (Lorch & Myers, 1990). Differences between the connective and no-connective condition coefficients for each trend were also tested.

Results

Reading Times. The reading time results for Sentence 2 are presented in Fig. 7.1. To present the data most clearly, the results are presented with respect to eight levels of relatedness, even though relatedness was coded as a continuous variable in the regression analysis. The eight levels are the result of dividing the ratings for all 32 texts into eight equal groups. The results found no difference in reading time between texts that had a connective ($M = 2{,}723$ ms) and those texts that had no connective ($M = 2{,}711$ ms), $t(95) < 1$.

For the regression analyses, the results were collapsed across the recall Statement 1 and 2 conditions, after initial analyses found no differences between recall conditions with respect to the linear, quadratic, and cubic coefficients, all ts $(94) < 1.39$, all ps $> .17$. The reading-time results across the levels of relatedness generally show the predicted pattern of results. The overall pattern of reading times replicated the findings reported by Myers et al. (1987) and Keenan et al. (1984). That is, reading times generally decreased as the causal distance decreased. For the no-connective condition, there was a significant linear component, $t(95) = 3.42$, $p < .01$, and a significant quadratic component, $t(95) = 3.18$, $p < .01$. The cubic component for the no-connective condition was not

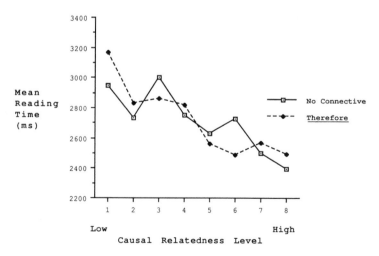

FIG. 7.1.   Mean Statement 2 reading times (ms) as a function of causal relatedness level and connective condition for Experiment 1.

significant, $t(95) < 1$. For the connective condition, the linear component was also significant, $t(95) = 5.19$, $p < .01$, supporting the previous findings of Millis and Just (1994, Experiment 3). Neither the quadratic component, $t(95) = 1.43$, $p = .16$ nor the cubic component, $t(95) < 1$ were significant.

Comparisons of the components between the connective and no-connective conditions indicated that the reading-time functions did not vary for the linear component, $t(95) < 1$, or the cubic component, $t(95) < 1$. However, the quadratic component did vary across these conditions, $t(95) = 2.96$, $p < .01$. It is likely that subjects in the no-connective condition performed a quick assessment of whether elaborations could benefit the coherence of the text. If these elaborations were not fairly accessible to the reader, as in the lowest levels of relatedness, the subjects may not have attempted to elaborate the texts, thus decreasing reading time. Interestingly, the connective condition did not show evidence of this quadratic component. This suggests that the connective made subjects attempt some elaborative processing at all levels of relatedness.

Recall.   Overall, the presence of the connective did not have a strong impact on recall. For the recall of Statement 1, the connective versions resulted in a similar level of recall ($M = 40\%$) as the no-connective versions [($M = 42\%$), $t(47) = 1.44$, $p < .16$]. For the recall of Statement 2, the connective versions led to higher recall ($M = 37\%$) than the no-connective versions [($M = 33\%$), $t(47) = 1.97$, $p < .05$].

Because recall of Statement 1 and Statement 2 led to the same pattern of effects of relatedness [all $ts(94) < 1.51$, $ps > .13$], we collapsed over statements. The resulting recall percentages are presented in Fig. 7.2, again with respect to one of eight levels of relatedness.

The recall percentages in Fig. 7.2 nicely show the quadratic function originally found by Keenan et al. (1984) and replicated by Myers et al. (1987). The regression analyses on the present data resulted in significant linear and quadratic components for both connective and no-connective versions [linear: $t(95) = 6.32$, $p < .01$, and $t(95) = 4.59$, $p < .01$ for the connective and no-connective versions, respectively; quadratic: $t(95) = 3.34$, $p < .01$, and $t(95) = 2.72$, $p < .01$ for the connective and no connective versions, respectively]. The cubic components were not significant for either the connective, $t(95) < 1$, or the no-connective version, $t(95) = 1.92$, $p = .06$. Comparisons of the components between the connective and no-connective conditions indicated that the reading-time functions did not vary for any of the components, $ts(95) < 1$.

The recall scores were virtually identical for both connective and no-connective conditions. On the basis of the reading times, one might have expected an advantage for connective versions at the lower levels of relatedness. Although there is some evidence for this (e.g., a 6% advantage at Level 2), it is not consistent across the other low levels of relatedness. This finding suggests that if subjects were indeed attempting to elaborate the connective versions at the

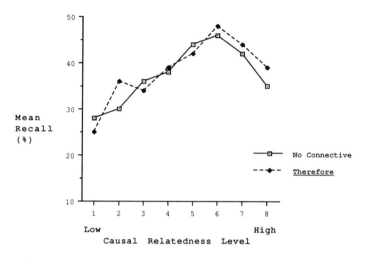

FIG. 7.2.   Mean percentage recall as a function of causal relatedness level and connective condition for Experiment 1.

lower levels of relatedness, they were not successful at establishing effective elaborations.

In summary, the results of Experiment 1 indicate that the presence of the connective *therefore* only had a minor impact on comprehension. The presence of the connective changed the nature of the reading-time function: The quadratic component was significant for the no-connective versions, but it was not significant for the connective versions. The difference appears to be primarily located in the lowest related texts, with the reading times in the connective versions not decreasing as much as in the no-connective versions. This pattern is consistent with the findings reported by Millis and Just (1994, Experiment 3). They reported that the connective *because* increased end-of-sentence reading times when the statements were unrelated, but decreased reading times when the statements were moderately related. With regard to recall, the connective only increased overall recall of Statement 2, but not Statement 1. This implies that Statement 2 was the focus of any elaborative processing engendered by the connective. However, this additional elaboration did not alter the familiar inverted-U function (e.g., Myers et al., 1987).

Of course, there are several potential reasons why we failed to find more differences between the connective and no-connective conditions. One is that readers may naturally attempt to impose a causal interpretation among statements, regardless of the presence or absence of a connective. This would, of course, lead to similar results between the conditions. A second reason is that subjects may not interpret the connective *therefore* as denoting causality, but rather as denoting a logical ordering (e.g., premise → conclusion). The connective *therefore* then would not affect comprehension in the same way as other causal connectives (e.g., *because*). A third reason is that readers may ignore the meaning of the connective during comprehension. Although this is unlikely, the connective may not directly affect the elaborative processing that is assumed to affect recall.

EXPERIMENT 2: THE IMPACT OF ADVERSATIVE CONNECTIVES AND LEVELS OF RELATEDNESS ON COMPREHENSION

In this experiment, we explored the effect of the adversative connective *but* on comprehension. Adversatives generally convey the meaning "contrary to expectation" and "in spite of the fact" (Haliday & Hasan, 1976). Consequently, adversatives place complex semantic relations among the constituents, including temporality, causality, and negation. For example, consider the sentence "Joey's brother hit him again and again, but the next day his body was not covered with bruises." In order to understand this sentence, the reader must determine that (a) Event 1 (conveyed by Statement 1) occurs before Event 2 (conveyed by Statement 2), (b) under normal circumstances Event 1 causes Event 2 to some degree (reflected by the ratings of causal relatedness by Myers et al., 1987), and (c) the consequence did not occur—it was negated (see Peterson, 1986). Despite the complexity, the connective *but* may facilitate comprehension because it signals that a likely consequence will not occur.

Prior research has found mixed support for the facilitative effect of adversatives on comprehension. Haberlandt (1982) reported that adversatives, like causal connectives, sped up reading times. However, Caron et al. (1988) reported lower levels of recall when sentences were conjoined by the connective *but* than when the same statements were joined by either *because* or *and*. Caron et al. argued that adversatives caused subjects to elaborate more than the other connectives, but the resulting elaborations did not establish an integrated representation of the two statements. It is not surprising that readers could not integrate the statements, however, because Caron et al. used completely unrelated statements that did not contain a negation (e.g., "The priest was able to build the church, but the computer had made an error").

Experiment 2 was essentially the same as Experiment 1 except that we used the connective *but* instead of the connective *therefore*. Because the meaning of adversatives assume a disconfirmation, we also included the negation *not* in the second statement. The inclusion of the negation in the no-connective versions made this statement comparable between the conditions and allowed us to compare reading times.

We predicted that the connective conditions would lead to faster reading times across all levels of relatedness. At the high levels of relatedness, the adversative should signal the reader that a normal consequence of Statement 1 would not occur (e.g., "Joey's brother hit him again and again, but the next day his body was not covered with bruises."). In contrast, Statement 2 would not be expected in the no-connective condition because there would be no signal of the disconfirmation. At the medium and low levels of relatedness, the connective should again facilitate comprehension compared to the no-connective condition by signaling the reader to expect a disconfirmation, as implemented as a negation (e.g., "Joey went to play baseball with his brother, but the next day his body was not covered with bruises."). As for recall, we predicted that the connective versions would result in the familiar quadratic function because the negation should be consistent with the disconfirmation denoted by the adversative. Specifically, at high levels of relatedness, the connective and the negation together make the text coherent, and relatively little elaboration would be required. However, without the connective at high levels of relatedness, the reader must implicitly infer the adversative in order to make the statements coherent (e.g., "Joey's brother hit him again and again. The next day his body was not covered with bruises."). This elaboration at the high levels of relatedness should increase recall, and thus flatten the inverted-U curve for the no-connective versions.

Method

The number of subjects, procedure, and scoring were the same in Experiment 2 as in Experiment 1. As in the initial experiment, subjects appeared to be reading the sentences for comprehension; subjects answered seven of eight questions following filler texts correctly, on average.

Results

Reading Times. The reading time results are presented in Fig. 7.3. Overall, subjects read Statement 2 faster in the connective versions ($M = 3,472$ ms) than in the no-connective versions [($M = 3,657$ ms), $t(95) = 2.67$, $p < .01$]. This supports the hypothesis that the connective facilitated comprehension by signalling an expected disconfirmation.

These results were collapsed across subjects who recalled Statement 1 and those who recalled Statement 2 for the regression analyses because no differences were found between conditions with respect to the linear, quadratic, and cubic coefficients, all $ts(94) < 1.23$, $ps > .22$. Interestingly, the regression analyses found that none of the components tested were significant when the connective *but* was present, all $ts(95) < 1.52$, $ps > .13$. The regression analyses for the no-connective condition found only a significant linear component, $t(95) = 3.40$, $p < .01$. Neither the quadratic nor the cubic coefficient were significantly different from zero for the no-connective condition, $ts(95) < 1$. Unlike Experiment 1,

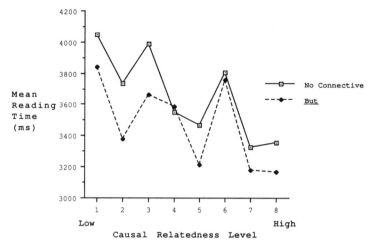

FIG. 7.3. Mean Statement 2 reading times (ms) as a function of causal relatedness level and connective condition for Experiment 2.

comparisons of the components across the connective conditions indicated that the reading-time functions did not vary for any of the components, $t(95) < 1.01$.

Recall. The recall results are presented in Fig. 7.4. The presence of a connective did not affect the overall level of recall. *T*-tests found no difference between texts that had a connective ($M = 39\%$) and those texts that had no connective ($M = 38\%$), $t(47) < 1$, for recall of Statement 1. The *t*-test was also not significant for recall of Statement 2, $t(47) < 1$ (connective $M = 24\%$, no connective $M = 25\%$).

For the regression analyses, the results for recall were collapsed across recall of Statements 1 and 2 because there were no differences between the conditions with respect to regression coefficients, all *t*s $(94) < 1.11$, *p*s $> .27$. As for the pattern of the recall scores across the levels of relatedness, we predicted that only the connective condition would show a significant quadratic trend. This prediction was confirmed by the regression analyses. For the connective versions, the linear and quadratic components significantly differed from zero, $t(95) = 5.48$, $p < .01$, and $t(95) = 2.11$, $p < .05$, respectively. The cubic coefficient for the connective condition was not significant, $t(95) < 1$. For the no-connective versions, the only component significantly different from zero was the linear component, $t(95) = 5.09$, $p < .01$. The quadratic and cubic components for the no-connective condition were not significant, ts$(95) < 1$. Comparisons of the components across the connective conditions, however, indicated that the recall functions did not vary for any of the components, ts$(95) < 1.34$. Although the inverted-U shape associated with the connective versions does not appear to be

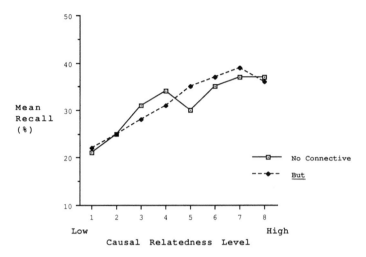

FIG. 7.4.   Mean percentage recall as a function of causal relatedness
level and connective condition for Experiment 2.

large, the slight decrease at the highest level of relatedness (Level 8) was predicted on the basis that the adversative would facilitate comprehension at the
higher levels by eliminating the need for the reader to generate an elaboration.
That is, the adversative signaled that the expected outcome in Statement 2 would
not occur.

The results of Experiment 2 indicate that the presence of an adversative
connective can affect text processing across levels of relatedness. Reading time
for the statement following the connective *but* was decreased compared to the no-
connective condition. This decrease is probably the result of subjects using the
connective as an indication of the negation to follow. As for recall, the results
found some support that the connective leads to an inverted-U function. This
function was predicted due to the negation being consistent (and therefore coherent) with the disconfirmation denoted by the adversative. The lack of an
inverted-U function for the no-connective condition was also consistent with
predictions. Without the word *but*, the reader must infer the adversative in order
to make the statements coherent. This additional elaboration was predicted to
flatten out the inverted-U curve for the no-connective versions (see Duffy et al.,
1990).

SUMMARY

We found that the type of connective influenced how readers arrive at an interpretation of a text. When the causal connective *therefore* linked the clauses, the
trend was for reading times at the lower levels of relatedness not to decrease as

much as when the connective was not present. The presence of *therefore* also led to increased overall recall of Statement 2 compared to the no-connective condition, but still resulted in the inverted-U function found in previous research that did not present a causal connective (e.g., Myers et al., 1987). This implies that, at least to some degree, readers naturally impose causality among sentence pairs. The connective *but* also altered the normal course of comprehension. Its presence decreased reading time relative to the no-connective condition, and its absence eliminated the inverted-U function for recall.

The present study was a first attempt to understand the influence of connectives on levels of causal relatedness. There is no doubt that future research is needed to clarify a number of issues raised in the present and related studies. First, the connectives used in the present study may not be representative of causal and adversative connectives. For example, perhaps another causal connective, such as *because* would result in a different pattern of results than *therefore*. Second, longer and more naturalistic texts should be examined with regard to causal relatedness. The present texts and those of other researchers (e.g., Murray, this volume) are relatively unnatural and short, consisting of only two sentences (or statements). It is possible that the impact of connectives would be different in longer and more natural texts. Third, it would be interesting to examine the effect of causal connectives on different levels of causal relatedness in expository text, because causality is often the focus of such texts (see Millis et al., 1993). Finally, the influence of negation on the effects of causal relatedness, both with and without a connective, deserves further attention. For example, the present study found that the presence of negation altered the regression functions for reading time and recall when there was no connective. Apparently subjects presented with a high-related text in this context were forced to make additional elaborations, thereby increasing recall. The importance of further understanding the role that causal relatedness plays in a variety of contexts is critical to the study of text comprehension.

ACKNOWLEDGMENTS

We would like to thank Jerry Myers for providing the experimental materials, and Brenda Davenport, Rebecca Henson, Frank Hunsaker, and Mark Siler for their assistance during the collection and scoring of the data.

REFERENCES

Beck, I. L., McKeown, M .G., Sinatra, G. M. & Loxterman, J. A. (1991). Revising social studies text from a text-processing perspective: Evidence of improved comprehensibility. *Reading Research Quarterly*, 26, 251–276.

Black, J. B., & Bern, H. (1981). Causal coherence and memory for events in narratives. *Journal of Verbal Learning and Verbal Behavior*, *20*, 267–275.

Brent, M. (1989, August). *Causal/temporal connectives: Syntax and lexicon*. Paper presented at the annual meeting of the Cognitive Science Society, Ann Arbor, MI.

Britton, B. K., Glynn, S. M., Meyer, B. J. F., & Penland, M. J. (1982). Effects of text structure on use of cognitive capacity during reading. *Journal of Educational Psychology*, *74*, 51–61.

Caron, J., Micko, H. C., & Thuring, M. (1988). Conjunctions and the recall of composite sentences. *Journal of Memory and Language*, *27*, 309–323.

Duffy, S. A., Shinjo, M., & Myers, J. L. (1990). The effect of encoding task on memory for sentence pairs varying in causal relatedness. *Journal of Memory and Language*, *29*, 27–42.

Haberlandt, K. F. (1982). Reader expectations in text comprehension. In J. F. Le Ny & W. Kintsch (Eds.), *Language and comprehension* (pp. 239–249). New York: North-Holland.

Haliday, M. A., & Hasan, R. (1976). *Cohesion in English*. New York: Longman.

Haviland, S. E., & Clark, H. H. (1974). What's new? Acquiring new information as a process in comprehension. *Journal of Verbal Learning and Verbal Behavior*, *13*, 512–521.

Hirsch, E. D. (1977). *The philosophy of composition*. Chicago: University of Chicago Press.

Keenan, J. M., Baillet, S. D., & Brown, P. (1984). The effects of causal cohesion on comprehension and memory. *Journal of Verbal Learning and Verbal Behavior*, *23*, 115–126.

Keenan, J. M., & Kintsch, W. (1974). The identification of explicitly and implicitly presented information. In W. Kintsch (Ed.), *The representation of meaning in memory* (pp. 153–166). Hillsdale, NJ: Lawrence Erlbaum Associates.

Kintsch, W., & van Dijk, T. A. (1978). Toward a model of text comprehension and production. *Psychological Review*, *85*, 363–394.

Lorch, R. F., Jr. (1989). Text signalling devices and their effects on reading and memory processes. *Educational Psychology Review*, *1*, 209–234.

Lorch, R. F., Jr., & Myers, J. L. (1990). Regression analyses of repeated measures data in cognitive research. *Journal of Experimental Psychology: Learning, Memory, and Cognition*, *16*, 149–157.

Millis, K. K., Graesser, A. C., & Haberlandt, K. (1993). The impact of connectives on the memory for expository texts. *Applied Cognitive Psychology*, *7*, 317–339.

Millis, K. K., & Just, M. A. (1994). The influence of connectives on sentence comprehension. *Journal of Memory and Language*, *33*, 128–147.

Myers, J. L., & Duffy, S. A. (1990). Causal inferences and text memory. In A. C. Graesser & G. H. Bower (Eds.), *The psychology of learning and motivation* (Vol. 25, pp. 159–173). New York: Academic Press.

Myers, J. L., Shinjo, M., & Duffy, S. A. (1987). Degree of causal relatedness and memory. *Journal of Memory and Language*, *26*, 453–465.

Noordman, L. G. M., Vonk, W., & Kempff, H. F. (1992). Causal inferences during the reading of expository texts. *Journal of Memory and Language*, *31*, 573–590.

O'Brien, E. J., & Myers, J. L. (1985). When comprehension difficulty improves memory for text. *Journal of Experimental Psychology: Learning, Memory, and Cognition*, *11*, 12–21.

Peterson, C. (1986). Semantic and pragmatic uses of 'but.' *Journal of Child Language*, *13*, 583–590.

Segal, E. M., Duchan, J. F., & Scott, P. J. (1991). The role of intercausal connectives in narrative structuring: Evidence from adults' interpretations of simple stories. *Discourse Processes*, *14*, 27–54.

Smith, R. N., & Frawley, W. J. (1983). Conjunctive cohesion in four English genres. *Text*, *3*, 347–374.

Townsend, D. J. (1983). Thematic processing in sentences and texts. *Cognition*, *13*, 223–261.

Townsend, D. J., & Bever, T. G. (1978). Interclause relations and causal processing. *Journal of Verbal Learning and Verbal Behavior*, *17*, 509–521.

Townsend, D. J., & Bever, T. G. (1983). Natural units of representation interact during sentence comprehension. *Journal of Verbal Learning and Verbal Behavior, 21*, 688–703.

Trabasso, T., & van den Broek, P. (1985). Causal thinking and the representation of narrative events. *Journal of Memory and Language, 24*, 612–630.

8 Processes of Anaphor Resolution

Stephen Dopkins
George Washington University

Johanna Nordlie
Barnard College

An anaphor is a linguistic expression that takes its meaning from material in the discourse that precedes it. Noun anaphors (e.g. pronouns or noun phrases), which will be of primary interest here, are expressions that refer to entities already present in the preceding discourse. There are at least two senses in which the meaning of an anaphor must be inferred from the preceding discourse. First, an anaphor generally does not completely specify the conceptual attributes of its referent; the referent is usually specified with greater precision earlier in the discourse. For example, a pronoun specifies only the animacy, number, and gender of its referent entity. Similarly, when a very general noun (e.g., *guy*) is used as an anaphor, it often specifies only some of the attributes of its referent. Secondly, in order to fully comprehend an anaphor's meaning, the reader or listener must recognize that statements have already been made about the referent, and that the current statement should be taken as elaborating on the referent rather than as introducing a new character.

In order to resolve an anaphor, the reader or listener must locate its antecedent in the preceding discourse. Expanding on a suggestion of Sanford (1989), we distinguish between top-down and bottom-up processes in the resolution of anaphors. In top-down processing, a term is identified as an anaphor's antecedent on the basis of the fact that the entity that it identifies is likely to have been mentioned in the context in which the anaphor occurs. The identification may reflect an imprecise expectation or a hard and fast rule. In bottom-up processing, no such predictions are involved. A term is identified as an anaphor's antecedent on the strength of a match with the anaphor. The crucial distinction is that bottom-up processes focus on information in the anaphoric expression, whereas top-down processes focus on information in the discourse prior to that expression. Most anaphors are probably resolved on the basis of both top-down and bottom-up processes. In the present discussion, however, we focus on more or less pure forms of these processes.

In this chapter we first elaborate on the distinction between top-down and bottom-up processes in the resolution of anaphors. We review some evidence concerning the importance of bottom-up processes. We then suggest that bottom-up processes of anaphor resolution may be related to more fundamental comprehension processes that monitor the recurrence of concepts in general. Finally we relate the top-down—bottom-up distinction to several other crucial distinctions.

TOP-DOWN AND BOTTOM-UP PROCESSES IN ANAPHOR RESOLUTION

The difference between top-down and bottom-up anaphoric resolution can be made clearer by means of concrete cases. One form of top-down resolution uses hard and fast syntactic rules to identify the antecedents of anaphors, or at least to narrow the field of candidates. For example, Nicol and Swinney (1989) had subjects read sentences such as: "The boxer told the skier that the doctor for the team would blame him for the recent injury". In this sentence, the anaphor *him* has three potential antecedents (*boxer, skier, doctor*). However, on the basis of syntactic constraints, only *boxer* and *skier* are viable antecedents. Using a priming paradigm, Nicol and Swinney found that syntactically viable candidates (e.g., *boxer, skier*) were activated by pronouns (as compared with neutral words), but that candidates rendered implausible by syntactic factors (*doctor* in the preceding example) were not activated.

A second form of top-down resolution uses heuristics rather than hard and fast rules to make antecedent assignments. An example of such a heuristic is the parallel function strategy: A discourse term is assigned as the antecedent for an anaphor by virtue of the fact that it holds the same grammatical role as the anaphor (Bever, 1970). Obviously, parallelism does not govern assignment in as strict a fashion as the syntactic constraints investigated by Nicol and Swinney (1989). Nevertheless the strategy does appear to operate. This was demonstrated by Grober, Beardsley, and Caramazza (1978) in a study in which subjects completed sentence fragments that ended with pronouns (e.g., "William contacted John because he _____"). By analyzing the completions, Grober et al. were able to infer subjects' biases with respect to antecedent assignment. The parallel function strategy predicted antecedent assignment in about 70% of the sentences employed. In cases where parallelism failed to predict antecedent assignment, the authors showed systematic effects of several semantic variables, such as the presence or absence of weak or strong modal auxilliary verbs (e.g., *may, must*), the semantic character of the conjunction linking the antecedent clause with the one containing the pronoun anaphor (e.g., *but, because*), and the semantic character of the main verb.

Another example of antecedent assignment on the basis of heuristic strategies involves expectations derived from the lexical features of words in the discourse. For example, Caramazza, Grober, Garvey, and Yates (1977) argued that when subjects read sentences such as, "John telephoned Bill because he wanted some information," the verb *telephoned* correctly biases the reader to expect that *John* will recur as the agent of the second clause. In contrast, if the second clause of the sentence is changed to read, "because he withheld some information," the expectation set up by the verb is violated by the pragmatics of the second clause. Caramazza et al. found that, when presented with a probe immediately after reading such sentences, subjects took longer to name the referent in sentences of the second type, even when the characters differed in gender. Caramazza et. al. argued that the first-clause verb established an expectation about the pronoun's antecedent; this assignment was tentatively made until the pragmatics of the text overruled it.

A third form of top-down anaphor resolution makes use of information concerning discourse focus. As a reader or listener moves through a discourse, he or she must maintain not only a record of the contents of the discourse, but also a sense of what information is crucial to the current discussion. This limited set of information is often called the *focus of the discourse*. In the absence of other information, the fact that a concept is in discourse focus may be taken as evidence that the concept is the antecedent of the anaphor under consideration. Garrod and Sanford (1985) demonstrated the importance of discourse focus for the resolution of anaphors. They had subjects read short stories where, in each one, there was both a main character and a secondary character. When a subsequent pronoun referred to the main character, subjects were able to locate the antecedent more quickly than when the pronoun referred to the secondary character. Note that this form of top-down resolution is slightly different than those that were described previously. In the earlier cases, assignment is made on the basis of the fact that one of the members of a limited candidate set is likely (or unlikely) to have occurred in the current context. In this case, a concept is tentatively assigned as antecedent simply on the basis of the fact that it belongs to a limited candidate set: it is the main or focal character of the discourse.

In contrast, in bottom-up anaphoric resolution an anaphor's antecedent is assigned not on the basis of prior expectations, but rather on the basis of a search that begins after the anaphor is encountered. The antecedent is sought in the memory representation of the discourse in much the same way that a word might be sought in a task requiring the recall of words from the discourse. Properties (e.g., semantic features) of the anaphor serve as cues for the retrieval of the antecedent. Cues of this type are useful for two reasons: (a) the anaphor usually bears a semantic, and sometimes (as in the case of a repeated noun) a phonological relationship, to its antecedent; and (b) the set of potential antecedents is organized in terms of these attributes. This follows from the fact that the potential antecedents are recorded in the memory representation for the discourse, which is integrated into long-term semantic memory, which in turn is organized in terms of these attributes. Thus, in attempting to locate the anaphor's anteced-ent, the reader is guided by the structure of semantic memory as well as the structure of the discourse in which the anaphor occurs. In considering bottom-up resolution, one must distinguish between the cues that can be extracted from the anaphor itself (e.g., semantic and phonological features) and the pragmatic cues that can be utilized when the anaphor is integrated within the discourse. Only the former are involved in bottom-up resolution, as we define it.

EVIDENCE FOR THE IMPORTANCE
OF BOTTOM-UP PROCESSES

Recent results from the domain of reading emphasize the importance of bottom-up processes in anaphor resolution. There is evidence, first of all, that the semantic features of anaphors are used to identify possible antecedents. Some of this evidence has been obtained with short passages in which there were few potential antecedents for the test anaphors. For example, Corbett and Chang (1983) presented sentences like, "Karen poured a drink for Emily and then she put the bottle down," and found evidence for the activation of both *Karen* and *Emily* immediately after the processing of *she*. This finding must be interpreted in the context of the findings of Chang (1980), who presented sentences like, "Bill and Mary went to the store and he bought a gallon of milk," and found evidence for the activation of *Bill* but not *Mary* following the processing of *he*. The implication of these results is that antecedents may be activated on the basis of gender features.

Further evidence for the use of semantic features has been collected using longer passages. Corbett (1984) showed that readers may activate terms that are semantically related to anaphors when searching for their antecedents. He had subjects read passages, each of which contained an anaphoric noun phrase (e.g., *frozen vegetables*) and an antecedent (e.g., *frozen asparagus*). Half of the pas-sages also contained a distracting noun phrase from the same category as spe-cified by the anaphoric phrase (e.g., *fresh corn*). Subjects were slower to read the anaphoric phrases when the distracting noun phrases were present. Corbett con-cluded that subjects in the distraction condition were activating both potential antecedents and subsequently choosing the correct one.

O'Brien, Plewes, and Albrecht (1990) provided converging support for Cor-bett's conclusion. They had subjects read long passages that were organized around pairs of semantically related concepts (e.g., plane, train), with one of the concepts for each passage occurring early in the passage and the other occurring late. The two concepts were either highly elaborated (e.g., if a character took a trip by train, a number of statements would be included describing the train trip) or minimally elaborated. Each passage ended with a statement requiring the reinstatement of either the early or the late concept (e.g., after the main character in the passage has been described as travelling first by train to one city and then by plane to another city, the passage ends with another character asking the main character how he travelled to the first city—in this case the early concept is reinstated). Immediately after finishing each passage, subjects pronounced a test word that on crucial trials was either the early or the late concept. When either the early or the late concept had been reinstated, subjects pronounced it faster, relative to a control condition in which neither concept was reinstated. O'Brien et al. (1990) concluded that this was because the reinstated concept was active in memory as a consequence of its recent reinstatement. More importantly, with respect to the present discussion, when an early concept had been reinstated, and the corresponding late concept had been highly elaborated, subjects were speeded in pronouncing the late concept as well. O'Brien et al. concluded that the late concept was active because it had been encountered in the course of a search back through the discourse for the early concept, and had briefly been considered as a possible solution to this search. They took this as evidence that concepts that are semantically related to an anaphor may be activated during the search for the anaphor's antecedent.

O'Brien and Albrecht (1991) provided more conclusive evidence that this is the case. Using a paradigm similar to that of O'Brien et al. (1990), they showed that readers in some situations activate concepts that have not even occurred in the discourse through which they are searching. They presented subjects with passages such as the one that follows, each of which was constructed around a target concept and ended with a line that prompted reinstatement of that concept. For each passage there were two possible target concepts (e.g., *skunk* and *cat*).

> Mary was driving in the country one day [when she smelled a terrific odor] [and she gazed at the setting sun as she went.] Suddenly, a small black (skunk/cat) [with a white stripe down its back] [with a long furry tail] ran in front of her car. Mary knew she couldn't stop in time. However, she hoped she had managed to miss the animal and continued on her way. After a while, she noticed she was low on gas. While at the gas station, the attendant asked her what had run in front of her car. (O'Brien & Albrecht, 1991, p. 102.)

> *Note.* The high-context version was created by including the text in the first set of brackets; the low-context version was created by using the text in the second set of brackets. The antecedent is in parentheses, with the high-related and low-related antecedent to the left and right of the slash, respectively.

In the high context condition, the context of the passage was highly supportive of one of the possible target concepts (e.g., when the sample passage reads, "Mary was driving in the country one day when she smelled a terrific odor," the concept *skunk* is highly related whereas the concept *cat* is not). In the low context condition, the context was equally supportive of the two concepts. After reading the line prompting reinstatement, subjects were required to name either the target concept or the alternative concept (that had not occurred in the passage). O'Brien and Albrecht (1991) found that the concepts that were highly related to the context in the high context condition were named more quickly in that condition than in the low context condition, even when they had not actually been mentioned in the passages (i.e., even when the animal in the sample passage had been identified as a cat, subjects were faster to pronounce *skunk* if the passage had mentioned an odor and a white stripe). The implication is that *skunk* was being considered in the antecedent search, even when it was not present in the passage. Presumably, *skunk* was activated because many of its attributes were mentioned in the passage.

Recently, Nordlie (1994) provided evidence for bottom-up processes that operate at the phonological level of representation. She showed that readers sometimes activate concepts that are phonologically related to anaphors when searching for their antecedents. For example, after reading a passage in which the last line contained the anaphor *dog* and the first line contained its antecedent *hound*, subjects were faster to recognize the adjective *black* when it was part of an intervening sentence containing the phrase *black bog* than when it was part of an intervening sentence containing *black swamp*. Thus, it appears that words that rhyme with an anaphor are activated and considered as potential antecedents.

The results of Chang (1980), Corbett and Chang (1983), Corbett (1984), O'Brien et al. (1990), O'Brien and Albrecht (1991), and Nordlie (1994) suggest that bottom-up, feature-driven memory searches play a role in anaphoric resolution. Evidently, such searches proceed through a discourse representation that is structured around the concepts of long-term semantic memory. The memory representation that records *dog* in a discourse is integrated with the representations for other concepts in semantic memory on the basis of semantic and phonological relationships. Feature-driven searches such as are implicated in these studies are bottom up in that they attempt to resolve anaphors by matching them with antecedents, without considering the larger meaning or the structure of the discourse. They treat anaphoric resolution as a problem in lexical or conceptual matching.

A MORE GENERAL PROCESS FOR DETECTING THE RECURRENCE OF CONCEPTS?

The conceptual matching that occurs in anaphoric resolution may be related to a more general process that readers use to note the recurrence of concepts of all kinds, including concepts that are not anaphorically related. It is possible that anaphoric resolution sometimes occurs as a byproduct of this more fundamental process. Garrod and Sanford (1977) provided the first hint that this might be the case when they showed that connections are often made between related concepts even when the concepts are not anaphoric. They had subjects read two-sentence passages, in each of which the second sentence contained a category name and the first sentence contained the name of either a high- or low-typical exemplar of the category (e.g., "A *bus/tank* came trundling down the hill. It nearly crushed a *vehicle*"). Subjects took longer to read the second sentence when the first sentence contained an exemplar that was atypical of the category specified in the second sentence. Garrod and Sanford interpreted this finding as a special case of the conjoint frequency effect, concluding that the exemplar presented in the first sentence was being verified as a member of the category specified in the second sentence and that this process took longer when the exemplar was a low-typical member of the category. More importantly, this verification process occurred despite the fact that both categories were marked with indefinite articles as being nonanaphors. Thus, concepts were compared with related concepts from earlier in the discourse even though there was not an anaphoric relationship between them.

To account for this phenomenon, Garrod and Sanford (1977) suggested that subjects check each noun concept in a discourse against other concepts in their memory record of the discourse to determine where the proposition containing the current concept should be stored. When a concept is semantically related to an earlier concept, but refers to a different entity, this is established through a brief comparison of the propositions associated with the two concepts. When a concept is semantically related to an earlier concept, and refers to the same entity, the proposition containing the current concept is stored with the other propositions pertaining to the entity.

Recently, Dopkins, Klin, and Myers (1993) provided support for Garrod and Sanford's account of their conceptual recurrence phenomenon. They presented subjects with passages such as those shown in the first two paragraphs that follow. Note that in the goal condition the main character has a goal (appoint a captain) that is achieved in the final sentence (the catcher is appointed captain). In the control condition, the same words are used but the goal relationship is absent. In an initial experiment, subjects recognized the goal category (*captain*) more quickly in the goal than the control condition, when queried immediately after reading the passage.

Goal version

Everybody agreed that the Wildcats had more raw talent than any other team in the league. But they were in the midst of a long losing streak. To build morale, the manager announced that he would appoint a team captain. Uncertain as to who would make the best captain, the manager sat in his office and stared at the wall. Then, a half hour before the game, the manager called the catcher into his office.

Control version

Everybody agreed that the Wildcats had more raw talent than any other team in the league. But they were in the midst of a long losing streak. To build morale, the manager announced that he would appoint a team captain. After he had released the name of the new captain, the manager sat in his office and chatted with reporters. Then, a half hour before the game, the manager sent the pitcher and catcher to warm up.

Goal version, with early mention of goal achievement concept

Everybody agreed that the Wildcats had more raw talent than any other team in the league. Their catcher had been voted most valuable player twice. But they were in the midst of a long losing streak. To build morale, the manager announced that he would appoint a team captain. Uncertain as to who would make the best captain, the manager sat in his office and stared at the wall. Then, a half hour before the game, the manager called the catcher into his office.

Control version, with early mention of goal achievement concept

Everybody agreed that the Wildcats had more raw talent than any other team in the league. Their catcher had been voted most valuable player twice. But they were in the midst of a long losing streak. To build morale, the manager announced that he would appoint a team captain. After he had released the name of the new captain, the manager sat in his office and chatted with reporters. Then, a half hour before the game, the manager sent the pitcher and catcher to warm up. (Dopkins, Klin, & Myers, 1993, pp. 79–80).

When the stories were changed in a second experiment (see the last two paragraphs of the exerpt just given) so that *catcher* was mentioned at the beginning of each story (as well as in the last sentence), *captain* was no longer more accessible in the goal condition.

The implication of these results is that subjects in the goal condition of the first experiment stored the proposition containing *catcher* with the proposition containing *captain*, on the basis of the relationship between *catcher* and *captain*. As a result, *captain* was activated immediately following reading of the last sentence of the passage. In the second experiment, subjects found a better storage site for the proposition containing *catcher*; they stored it with the earlier proposition containing *catcher*, with the result that *captain* was not activated. The key point is that there was no evidence that subjects linked *catcher* and *captain* when they did not store the proposition containing *catcher* with the proposition containing *captain*. The sensitivity of subjects to the recurrence of concepts depended on where they stored the propositions containing the current occurrences of the concepts. The key point with respect to the larger discussion is that *catcher* was not an anaphor.

HOW ARE CONCEPTUAL RECURRENCES DETECTED?

How are conceptual recurrences identified in discourse? Garrod and Sanford (1977) suggested that a check is made for each new noun term in a discourse to see if it has been used before. However, such a system would involve an enormous amount of wasted effort. Furthermore, as Nordlie (1994) pointed out, her results suggest that it is not employed. She found priming only for the adjectival modifiers of words that rhymed with anaphors. This suggests that a search for a precursor of a concept does not occur for all concepts.

How then are recurrent concepts identified? Explicit anaphors are often signalled with syntactic tags (e.g., the anaphor may be a pronoun, or it may be a definite noun phrase). But such tags are not always present for anaphors. Building on the ideas of Garrod and Sanford (1977), Nordlie (1994) suggested that the recurrence of concepts is sometimes discovered as a byproduct of the process by which words are comprehended in discourse. In order for a word to be comprehended, the long-term memory representation for its associated concept must be accessed. A concept that has already appeared in a discourse or that is related to one that has appeared can be identified as such when its memory record is accessed. The method of identification depends on whether or not the concept is exactly identical to an earlier concept. If a concept has recurred verbatim, its memory representation will be marked as having already been used in the discourse. This follows from the fact that the representation for the concept will have been used to record the statement in which the concept occurred earlier (as detailed earlier in the discussion of Garrod & Sanford, 1977). If the concept is not identical to an earlier concept but is a related term (e.g., a synonym or a superordinate category), its representation will be activated as a consequence of its links with the representation for the earlier concept, which has been activated as a consequence of its earlier use. The activation of the representation for the anaphoric concept will function as a weaker form of recurrence marker. It will be clear from the heightened activation of the concept's representation that a related concept has appeared in the discourse, making it necessary to search memory. Once this has been done, it will be possible to determine whether the current concept is an anaphor, or refers to a distinct entity.

Nordlie (1994) adduced some empirical support for her ideas from the experiment described earlier, in which activation was observed for the adjectival modifiers of words that rhymed with synonym anaphors. Nordlie concluded that the anaphors were identified provisionally as recurrent concepts when their memory records were accessed; the fact that their memory records were activated suggested that they might have occurred before in the discourse. Once a recurrent concept was provisionally identified, a search was conducted for its precursor in which the rhyming word was activated (as well, presumably, as the actual precursor). The concept was identifed as an anaphor and duly resolved as a consequence of this search.

Nordlie (1994) conducted a follow-up experiment that was identical to the aforementioned experiment except that the anaphors in her stimulus passages were outright repetitions of their antecedents. She observed no activation of the adjectival modifiers of rhyming words. Nordlie concluded that an extended search was not necessary in this case because the anaphors were identified conclusively as recurrent concepts when their memory records were accessed. It was only necessary to verify that the concepts had been used before to refer to the same entities to resolve them as anaphors.

In a third experiment, Nordlie used passages in which synonomous concepts recurred non-anaphorically. A pair of synonyms appeared in each of these passages, with the two words identifying different entities (e.g., a hound was mentioned in the first line of a passage, and a dog mentioned in the third line, and the hound and the dog were different entities). Nordlie found activation of adjectival modifiers of rhyming words in the same pattern as in her first experiment (e.g., *black* in *black bog*). Nordlie concluded that the concepts appearing in the third lines (e.g., *dog*) were identified provisionally as recurrent concepts when their memory records were accessed. Once a recurrent concept was so identifed, a search was started for its precursor, thereby activating phonologically related concepts (e.g., *bog*). When the precursor was found, the recurrent concept was evaluated to determine if it was an anaphor (and was presumably found not to be one). The key point is that the recurrence of concepts in this experiment triggered searches for precursors, even though the concepts were not anaphorically related. Nordlie concluded that the recurrence of a concept, as indicated by memory record activation, was sufficient to trigger a search for the concept's precursor, and that discovery of such recurrence relations occurred independently of the discovery of anaphoric relations.

RELATED DISTINCTIONS

If bottom-up conceptual matching processes play a substantial role in anaphoric resolution, it may be important to distinguish the processes involved in the resolution of pronoun anaphors from those figuring in the resolution of noun anaphors of other types (e.g., common and proper noun anaphors). Pronoun anaphors share fewer features with their antecedents than other noun anaphors. Furthermore, pronouns are closed-class items, and therefore may not be integrated into the rest of semantic memory the way other nouns are. Thus, there are reasons to expect that pronoun and other noun anaphors are treated differently with respect to bottom-up anaphoric processing, with bottom-up processing figuring less prominently in the resolution of pronouns. Several recent results suggest that this is in fact the case. For example, Gernsbacher (1989) presented subjects with short two-clause sentences, each of which contained two characters that were identified with proper names. The second clause of each sentence contained an anaphor that was either the name of one of the characters or a pronoun that referred to one of the characters. When the anaphor was a name, recognition latency for that name decreased, whereas latency for the other name increased. This was true when the recognition probe was presented either immediately after the anaphor was read or at the end of the sentence. When the anaphor was a pronoun, there was much less of a shift in accessibility for the names of the two characters immediately after the pronoun was read. At the end of the sentence there was still no increase in the accessibility of the name of the character to which the anaphor referred, although there was a decrease in the accessibility of the name of the other character. Gernsbacher concluded that pronouns, because they specify their referents less closely than names, are less effective than proper nouns in activating their antecedents and suppressing other potential antecedents.

Greene, McKoon, and Ratcliff (1992) found similar results with pronoun anaphors and common noun anaphors. To study the resolution of common noun anaphors (e.g., category names, as in "the man"), they used four-line passages in which the fourth line either introduced a new character or made anaphoric reference to an extant character. The passages were presented to subjects at a fixed rate, interrupted at various points by recognition probes. Subjects were faster to recognize the term to which a common noun anaphor referred following the appearance of the anaphor than following the mention of a new character. To study the resolution of pronoun anaphors, Greene et al. used passages, each of which was four lines long and contained two characters. Both characters in a given passage were introduced in the first line and one was mentioned anaphorically in the fourth line. At probe points following the appearance of a pronoun anaphor, subjects were no faster to recognize the name of its referent than the name of the other character. Greene et al. considered several explanations for the common noun advantage: the greater specificity with which the common noun anaphor identifies its antecedent (Gernsbacher's hypothesis), the greater degree of relatedness between the common noun anaphor and its antecedent, and the fact that only the common noun anaphor provides an outright repetition of its antecedent.

The present discussion suggests a slightly different account of the pronoun–noun processing difference: (a) it is necessary to access the semantic memory representations for pronouns in order to comprehend them; (b) it is necessary to access the antecedents of pronouns in order to resolve them as anaphors; (c) pronouns, because they are closed-class items, are not integrated with the rest of the concepts in semantic memory, therefore the main part of semantic memory is not accessed in comprehending pronouns; (d) it is thus more difficult to locate the antecedents for pronouns, because this requires moving from one part of semantic memory to another.

Having concerned ourselves so extensively with the distinction between top-down and bottom-up forms of anaphoric resolution, we must briefly acknowledge a related distinction—that between the mental model and propositional levels of discourse representation. The idea that a discourse is represented as a set of propositions has a long history in studies of comprehension (Kintsch & van Dijk, 1978). Recently it has been suggested that a discourse is also represented as a mental model (Johnson-Laird, 1983). For example, if a set of spatial relationships is described between three characters in a discourse (e.g., Frank is in the basement, Bob is in the attic, and Joe is in the kitchen) these spatial relationships will be represented in a spatial model.

Although it is probably not possible to draw categorical correspondences between these two levels of representation and the two forms of anaphoric processing under discussion, some relationships can be noted. Because bottom-up anaphoric resolution involves the matching of linguistic terms, it is more closely tied to the propositional level of representation. The ideas put forward earlier regarding bottom-up processes of conceptual matching assumed that a discourse is represented as a set of propositions. In so far as top-down resolution involves expectations about the mentioning of discourse entities, it is more closely tied to the mental model level of representation.

Both of these levels of representation are probably important in anaphoric resolution. Some have suggested, however (Garnham, 1987; Sag & Hankamer, 1984), that anaphors are resolved at the mental model level of representation, and that the propositional level is not consulted. In searching for a noun anaphor's referent, the reader proceeds directly to the referent, without concerning him or herself with the anaphor's linguistic antecedent. Much of the discussion with respect to the Sag and Hankamer claim has focused on distance effects (Garnham, 1987). A number of studies have shown that readers take longer to process pronoun anaphors, the further back their antecedents are in the discourse (Ehrlich & Rayner, 1983). This has been taken as evidence that the propositional level of representation is involved in anaphoric resolution. It is not easy to reconcile the preservation of a discourse's temporal dimension in a mental model representation (Garnham, 1987). In contrast, the temporal dimension is more easily accomodated in a propositional representation. The propositions of the discourse may be recorded with temporal tags reflecting their appearance in the discourse. Alternatively, the records for the propositions may be linked in memory in terms of causal relationships among the events that they describe, and these causal relationships may in turn be correlated with the temporal dimension of the discourse (Trabasso & van den Broek, 1985). Garnham (1987) showed, however, that many of the distance effects that have been reported are probably effects of focus shifting. The results that we have considered with respect to bottom-up anaphor resolution are therefore important in that they offer alternative support for the importance of the propositional level in this process. In particular, the demonstration (a) that phonological features are used in anaphor resolution and (b) that semantically-related concepts not even present in a passage can be activated in antecedent search are difficult to square with a mental-model based conception of anaphoric resolution.

In conclusion, recent results suggest that bottom-up processes are quite important in the resolution of anaphors. The end result of a discourse may be a collection of entities arranged in a mental model. Before the discourse is translated into a mental model, however, it exists as a sequential construction of words. Recent results emphasize the importance of simple relationships among the words of a discourse in anaphoric resolution.

REFERENCES

Bever, T. G. (1970). The cognitive basis for linguistic structures. In J. R. Hayes (Ed.), *Cognition and the Development of Language* (pp. 279–362). New York: Wiley.

Caramazza, A., Grober, E. H., Garvey, C., & Yates, J. (1977). Comprehension of anaphoric pronouns. *Journal of Verbal Learning and Verbal Behavior, 16*, 601–609.

Chang, F. R. (1980). Active memory processes in visual sentence comprehension: Clause effects and pronominal reference. *Memory & Cognition, 8*, 58–64.

Corbett, A. T. (1984). Prenominal adjectives and the disambiguation of anaphoric nouns. *Journal of Verbal Learning and Verbal Behavior, 23*, 683–695.

Corbett, A. T., & Chang, F. R. (1983). Pronoun disambiguation: Accessing potential antecedents. *Memory & Cognition, 11*, 283–294.

Dopkins, S. C., Klin, C., & Myers, J. L. (1993). The accessibility of information about goals during the processing of narrative texts. *Journal of Experimental Psychology: Learning, Memory, and Cognition, 19*, 70–80.

Ehrlich, S. F., & Rayner, K. (1983). Pronoun assignment and semantic integration during reading: Eye movements and the immediacy of processing. *Journal of Verbal Learning and Verbal Behavior, 22*, 75–87.

Garnham, A. (1987). Understanding anaphora. In A. W. Ellis (Ed.), *Progress in the Psychology of Language* (Vol 3., pp. 253–300). London: Lawrence Erlbaum Associates.

Garrod, S. C., & Sanford, A. J. (1977). Interpreting anaphoric relations: The integration of semantic information while reading. *Journal of Verbal Learning and Verbal Behavior, 16*, 77–90.

Garrod, S. C., & Sanford, A. J. (1985). On the real-time character of interpretation during reading. *Language and Cognitive Processes, 1*, 43–61.

Gernsbacher, M. (1989). Mechanisms that improve referential access. *Cognition, 32*, 99–156.

Greene, S. B., McKoon, G., & Ratcliff, R. (1992). Pronoun resolution and discourse models. *Journal of Experimental Psychology: Learning, Memory, and Cognition, 18*, 266–283.

Grober, E. H., Beardsley, W., & Caramazza, A. (1978). Parallel function strategy in pronoun assignment. *Cognition, 6*, 117–133.

Johnson-Laird, P. N. (1983). *Mental models: Towards a cognitive science of language, inference, and consciousness*. Cambridge, England: Cambridge University Press.

Kintsch, W., & van Dijk, T. A. (1978). Toward a model of text comprehension and production. *Psychological Review, 85*, 363–394.

Nicol, J., & Swinney, D. (1989). The role of structure in coreference assignment during sentence comprehension. *Journal of Psycholinguistic Research, 18*, 5–20.

Nordlie, J. W. (1994). *Activation of phonological information by noun anaphors*. Unpublished doctoral dissertation. Columbia University.

O'Brien, E. J., & Albrecht, J. E. (1991). The role of context in accessing antecedents in text. *Journal of Experimental Psychology: Learning, Memory, and Cognition, 17*, 94–102.

O'Brien, E. J., Plewes, P. S., & Albrecht, J. E. (1990). Antecedent retrieval processes. *Journal of Experimental Psychology: Learning, Memory, and Cognition, 16*, 241–249.

Sag, I. A., & Hankamer, J. (1984). Toward a theory of anaphoric processing. *Linguistics and Philosophy, 7*, 325–345.

Sanford, A. J. (1989). Component processes of reference resolution in discourse. In N. E. Sharkey (Ed.), *Models of cognition: A review of cognitive science* (pp. 113–140). Norwood, NJ: Ablex.

Trabasso, T., & van den Broek, P. (1985). Causal thinking and the representation of narrative events. *Journal of Memory and Language, 24*, 612–630.

9 Automatic Components of Discourse Comprehension

Edward J. O'Brien
University of New Hampshire

One of the primary goals in the study of discourse comprehension is the development of models that accurately capture the representation of text in memory and the processes that lead to that representation. A critical aspect of this process is how readers map currently processed information onto information that occurred earlier in the text. In fact, a measure of text coherence can be obtained by measuring how easily a reader can complete this mapping process.

Most current models of reading comprehension assume that readers generate at least two levels of representation of a text, a text-base representation and a situational or mental model (e.g., Johnson-Laird, 1983; Just & Carpenter, 1987; van Dijk & Kintsch, 1983). Because of limited capacity constraints, the construction of these levels of representation is assumed to be an incremental process in which text is processed over a series of cycles with only a small portion of text processed on each cycle (e.g., Garnham & Oakhill, 1992; Kintsch & van Dijk, 1978; Sanford & Garrod, 1981; van Dijk & Kintsch, 1983). Based on the reader's comprehension strategy, a subset of information is selected and maintained in focus (or active memory) to facilitate the integration or mapping of new information onto the existing representation (e.g., Fletcher, 1981, 1986). Because the ease and success of this mapping process is heavily dependent on the selection of an effective strategy for maintaining information in focus, considerable research has addressed the types of strategies that readers may use (e.g., Albrecht & O'Brien, 1993; Fletcher, 1986; Glenberg & Langston, 1992; Glenberg, Meyer, & Lindem, 1987).

The mapping process can be broken down into processes designed to establish both local and global coherence (Glenberg & Langston, 1992; Kintsch & van Dijk, 1978; McKoon & Ratcliff, 1992; O'Brien & Albrecht, 1992; van Dijk &

159

Kintsch, 1983). Local coherence involves connecting the currently processed information with the immediately preceding context (i.e., information in short-term memory, generally the previous one to three sentences). Global coherence involves establishing connections between currently processed information and information that is relevant to the currently processed information, but is no longer available in active memory (based on local coherence strategies) because it occurred much earlier in the text (e.g., McKoon & Ratcliff, 1992). In this chapter, I examine comprehension strategies and the maintenance of both local and global coherence during comprehension.

Models of comprehension differ in the degree to which they emphasize that readers establish local and global coherence (e.g., Fletcher & Bloom, 1988; Garnham, Oakhill, & Johnson-Laird, 1982; Glenberg & Langston, 1992; McKoon & Ratcliff, 1992; O'Brien & Albrecht, 1992). Several models propose that readers are primarily concerned with maintaining local coherence; readers only use global information and establish global coherence under special circumstances, such as when local coherence strategies fail (Fletcher & Bloom, 1988; Kintsch & van Dijk, 1978). For example, McKoon and Ratcliff (1992) proposed the minimalist hypothesis, which states that readers establish connections between the currently processed information and propositions that are in short-term memory. Readers will only establish connections between the currently processed information and information from long-term memory when there is a local coherence break or when global information (or world knowledge) is "readily available."

In contrast to models that emphasize the maintenance of local coherence, several other models suggest that readers routinely check and establish both local and global coherence (Garnham et al., 1982; Glenberg & Langston, 1992; O'Brien & Albrecht, 1992; Trabasso & Sperry, 1985). According to these models, readers map incoming information onto information active in memory (i.e., local processing) and onto relevant information no longer active in memory (i.e., global processing; Albrecht & O'Brien, 1993; Glenberg & Langston, 1992; O'Brien & Albrecht, 1992). For example, Sanford and Garrod (1981; Garrod & Sanford, 1988; 1990) proposed a model in which a subset of information is maintained in explicit focus and other information relevant to the discourse situation is maintained in implicit focus; incoming information is mapped onto information that is currently held in active memory (i.e., in explicit focus) and onto information that is relevant to the situation (i.e., in implicit focus).

More recently, Glenberg and Langston (1992) extended this process model to describe other discourse phenomena and incorporate general models of memory. Specifically, they have proposed that representational elements (or tokens) are maintained in focus (or foregrounded) and serve as discourse pointers to information no longer active in memory. Information that is in focus primes contextually relevant information in long-term memory through a resonance process (Gillund & Shiffrin, 1984; Hintzman, 1986; Ratcliff, 1978). Thus, when incoming text is integrated with information in focus, contextually relevant information in long-term memory is also connected to new information. In this way, new information is mapped onto relevant information in both active memory and long-term memory. As Glenberg and Langston pointed out, such a mechanism is quite powerful because it allows the reader to check and maintain coherence at both a local level (e.g., against information in focus) and a global level (e.g., against relevant information in long-term memory). This contrasts with text-base strategies that check global coherence only when local coherence strategies have failed.

Independent of whether comprehension involves processing primarily at the local level or at both the local and global level is the extent to which these processes are automatic. The remainder of this chapter is broken down into three sections. In the first section, I review evidence indicating that the retrieval of antecedent information in response to a local coherence break is generally accomplished through an automatic resonance process. In the second section, I examine evidence suggesting that this automatic resonance process takes place even when there is no local coherence break (i.e., when there is a global coherence break, or no coherence break at all). In the final section, I address how an automatic resonance process can account for several types of elaborative inferences.

LOCAL COHERENCE BREAKS

Discourse is usually written in a manner that facilitates the mapping of current information onto information that preceded it. That is, current information can usually be mapped on the information currently active in memory (i.e., in focus). However, readers occasionally encounter concepts that cannot be mapped onto the information currently in focus, but can be mapped onto information that occurred much earlier and is no longer in focus (i.e., in long-term memory). The inability to map current information onto information in focus constitutes a local coherence break. It is widely agreed that full comprehension of a text requires that the reader resolve such coherence breaks (e.g., Kintsch & van Dijk, 1978; van Dijk & Kintsch, 1983). For example, consider the following passage from O'Brien, Duffy, and Myers (1986):

Bill was late for work again. He had forgotten to set his alarm and had overslept. To top it all off, he was now behind a *bus* that was having engine trouble. As the bus pulled into a busy intersection, its engine sputtered and died. Bill shook his head in disbelief as the traffic around him came to a halt. There was an important sales meeting this morning, and he was afraid he would miss it. His boss had already warned him once about his tendency to oversleep. Bill sighed as he caught sight of a digital clock in a nearby bank window. He sat and stared at the stalled vehicle not knowing what to do. (p. 348)

When readers encounter *vehicle* in the last sentence, it is necessary for them to search long-term memory, reinstate the antecedent *bus* and map it onto *vehicle* in their representation of the passage. Although it is not necessary for a reader to complete this mapping process, failure to do so would result in an incomplete understanding and one that is different from that intended by the author.

There is considerable evidence demonstrating that readers will map an anaphor onto its antecedent, even when the antecedent is no longer active in memory (Dell, McKoon, & Ratcliff, 1983; Lesgold, Roth, & Curtis, 1979; McKoon & Ratcliff, 1980; O'Brien, 1987; O'Brien et al., 1986). It is also generally the case that when a reader initiates a reinstatement search, there is an increase in comprehension difficulty from the additional processing demanded by the text.

O'Brien (1987) proposed that the reinstatement search process is a backward parallel search starting with information currently in focus and proceeding through an integrated network. During the search, the reader accumulates two types of information: concepts from the text that match the antecedent category and information from the text that is related to the antecedent category. If the reader searches and finds the antecedent in long-term memory, the search is terminated. In contrast, a specific antecedent may be inferred if the reader has accumulated sufficient contextual information; this would also terminate the search, but at the risk of an incorrect identification of the antecedent. In either case, when a potential antecedent has been produced, it is checked against the anaphoric phrase that prompted the search to determine whether it is appropriate. If it is, the antecedent is mapped onto the anaphor and the search is terminated. If it is not appropriate given the anaphoric phrase, the reader may discard the potential antecedent and continue the search, or abandon the search, resulting in incomplete comprehension.

Although O'Brien (1987) initially described the reinstatement process as a spread of activation; subsequent findings suggest that the process is better characterized as a resonance process (Hintzman, 1986; Ratcliff, 1978). When an anaphoric phrase is encountered, it resonates with potential antecedents; the potential candidate that resonates the most or shares the greatest number of features with the anaphoric phrase will be selected (Garrod, O'Brien, Morris, & Rayner, 1990; Gernsbacher, 1989, 1990).

There are several factors that influence the resonance process including referential distance, elaboration, and general world knowledge. For example, O'Brien (1987) had subjects read passages in which the last line of the passage required reinstatement of an antecedent that occurred either early or late in a passage. In general, subjects required more time to reinstate a more distant, early antecedent than a more recent, late antecedent. Presumably, the resonance signal decays over time, making it more difficult to retrieve the early antecedent. Another possibility is that, as distance increases, the number of potential antecedents that resonate with the anaphoric phrase increases (e.g., Gernsbacher, 1990).

A closer examination of the materials from O'Brien (1987) revealed that, for a subset of the passages, readers consistently reinstated the early antecedent more quickly than the late antecedent. A subsequent rating task indicated that, for those passages in which the early antecedent was reinstated more quickly, the early antecedent was rated as significantly more important to the passage than the late antecedent; for those passages in which the late antecedent was reinstated more quickly, there was no difference in rated importance between the early and late antecedent.

O'Brien (1987) argued that the importance ratings were reflecting the degree of elaboration; early antecedents that were rated as more important than the late antecedents were more highly elaborated, producing a greater degree of interconnections and a higher probability that the antecedent was encoded. Elaboration also increases the number of possible features that can resonate with the anaphoric phrase that will facilitate mapping of the anaphor onto the antecedent by increasing the overlap between the antecedent and anaphor. (e.g., Garrod et al., 1990).

O'Brien and Myers (1987) presented indirect evidence that the degree of elaboration can facilitate the retrieval of antecedent information. They reanalyzed the passages from O'Brien (1987) using the causal analysis proposed by Trabasso and Sperry (1985) and Trabasso and van den Broek (1985) and found that the number of causal connections leading to and from an antecedent was the primary predictor of antecedent retrieval time (for similar findings see also Bloom, Fletcher, van den Broek, Reitz, & Shapiro, 1990; van den Broek, 1990).

O'Brien, Plewes, and Albrecht (1990) provided further evidence of the role of elaboration in retrieving antecedent information. They had subjects read passages that contained two possible antecedents: one occurred early in the passage and the other occurred late in the passage. For half the passages, the early antecedent was elaborated and for the other half, the late antecedent was elaborated. Consistent with O'Brien (1987), late antecedents were retrieved significantly faster than early antecedents. More importantly, elaborated antecedents were reinstated more quickly than nonelaborated antecedents. In fact, when an early antecedent was elaborated, it was reinstated more quickly than an unelaborated late antecedent.

Assuming that mapping process involves an automatic resonance between an anaphor and its antecedent, any potential antecedent that shares features with the anaphor should resonate to some degree. There is considerable evidence to suggest that this is true. For example, Corbett and Chang (1983) found that when subjects read sentences such as "Karen poured a drink for Emily and then she put the bottle down," the pronoun *she* produced activation of both potential antecedents (*Karen* and *Emily*). However, Chang (1980) found that when subjects read sentences such as "Bill and Mary went to the store and he bought a gallon of milk," the pronoun *he* activated *Bill* but not *Mary*. These two findings suggest that all possible antecedents resonate to an anaphor, but that antecedents only resonate to the extent that they share features in common with the anaphor. In the examples just cited, the pronoun only resonated with antecedents of the same gender. Stevenson (1986) provided strong support for this conclusion. She found that when subjects read sentences such as, "Joan apologized to Anne at the end of class because she regretted having caused so much trouble," both *Joan* and *Anne* become active when the pronoun *she* is encountered. However, when *Joan* is replaced with *John*, only the gender-appropriate noun *Anne* is activated.

A similar conclusion has emerged from studies that have examined the retrieval of antecedents in response to an anaphoric noun phrase. For example, Corbett (1984) had subjects read passages that contained an anaphoric noun phrase (e.g., *frozen vegetables*) and an antecedent (e.g., *frozen asparagus*). Half the passages also contained a distractor antecedent that was from the same category, as specified by the anaphoric noun phrase (e.g., fresh corn). Corbett found that the time to read an anaphoric noun phrase was significantly longer when an antecedent distractor appeared in the passage than when it did not. Consistent with the resonance metaphor, Corbett suggested that both antecedents from the category *vegetable* are accessed initially, then the correct antecedent is selected on the basis of constraining information contained in the anaphoric noun phrase. In the example described, *vegetable* would resonate with both *asparagus* and *corn*. However, *frozen* would only resonate with *asparagus*, producing a higher degree of activation on *asparagus* than *corn*, leading readers to select *asparagus* and reject *corn*.

O'Brien et al. (1990) provided further evidence that all potential antecedents resonate in response to an anaphor or anaphoric phrase. As indicated earlier, O'Brien et al. presented subjects with passages that contained two potential antecedents: One occurring early in the passage and one occurring late in the passage. One antecedent was elaborated whereas the other was not. A further manipulation was that for half of the passages, both the early and late antecedent were from the same general category whereas for the remaining half they were from different categories. Following is an example passage. We found that when the late antecedent was elaborated and the early antecedent was reinstated, both potential antecedents showed a naming time advantage over an appropriate control. That is, subjects named both potential antecedents (i.e., *church* and *barn*) equally fast following the reinstatement phrase ("what building she had been working on."). In contrast, when the two antecedents were from different categories, there was no facilitation in naming time for the late antecedent.

It was Saturday morning and Sally got up and dressed in a hurry. She knew that her mother was making blueberry pancakes and that was her favorite breakfast. Sally's mother made them every Saturday morning. As soon as breakfast was over, Sally's entire family got in the car and they went to *church*. They spent the entire morning working with all their neighbors painting and cleaning it up. After lunch, Sally had hoped to spend the afternoon playing. On her way out the front door, however, her mother stopped her and reminded her that she still had chores left to do. Reluctantly, Sally cleaned her room and dusted and vacuumed the living room. When her mother saw how much work she had gotten done though, she told Sally that she could go out and play. Sally decided to play in the *barn*. It took all of her energy to push open its great big red doors to get inside. When she did, she climbed up into its loft and she spent the next few hours jumping in the hay. From where she was playing she could see a sparrow had built a nest in one of its rafters. Sally was sorry when she heard her mother calling her for dinner. When she walked into the house, her mother sent her straight upstairs to get cleaned up and changed. By the time Sally came back downstairs, everyone was already at the table. She was happy to see that her uncle was visiting and she sat down next to him. He asked Sally what building she had been playing in (working on). (O'Brien, Plewes, & Albrecht, 1990)

Although Corbett (1984) and O'Brien et al. (1990) used two potential antecedents from the same category to determine if all potential antecedents resonate to an anaphor, a semantic relation between the anaphor and potential antecedents may not be necessary. For example consider a passage in which you learn, "Lisa worked all afternoon cleaning her room." At some other point in the passage you learn, "Lisa cleaned her car." If a subsequent anaphoric phrase requires the reader to retrieve what Lisa cleaned, both *room* and *car* should resonate even though there is no pre-existing semantic association. However, in the example just described, it is possible that the verb *clean* is what would resonate and in both cases lead to resonance of the item that was cleaned. Rizzella and O'Brien (1994) provided some evidence that the category of potential antecedents can be defined exclusively through the discourse context without any pre-existing associations:

Jimmy was playing baseball with his friend. Jimmy's friend pitched the ball to him. The ball hit Jimmy in the arm. Jimmy could not believe how much the pitch hurt. His arm muscles began to feel very sore. Jimmy knew it would hurt for days. His arm even began to turn red and swell. Because of this, Jimmy stopped playing and said he was going home. Jimmy hopped on his bike and sped down the street. Unfortunately, he turned too sharply and fell off his bike. Consequently Jimmy stood up and swept the dirt from his pants. As he was wiping his pants, Jimmy found a piece of gum in his pocket. He opened the wrapper and put the gum in his mouth. When he arrived home, his mother asked him why he was bruised. (Rizzella & O'Brien, 1994)

Rizzella and O'Brien had subjects read passages like the one presented above. Early in the passage, subjects read that Jimmy was hit in the arm with a ball. After several sentences that elaborated on this fact, subjects read a consequence sentence (i.e., "Because of this, Jimmy stopped playing and said he was going home."). Later in the passage, subjects read that Jimmy fell off his bike with the consequence that he stood up and swept the dirt off his pants. In the last sentence, subjects read, "When he arrived home, his mother asked him why he was bruised." Note that there are two possible causal antecedents for this consequence (having been hit with a ball and having fallen off his bike). However, because each of these antecedents already has a consequence, neither antecedent (*ball* or *bike*) should be active in memory (see Fletcher & Bloom, 1988). Rizzella and O'Brien (1994) confirmed that, immediately prior to the last sentence, neither potential antecedent was active. Following the last sentence, both antecedents were active, but only when the first antecedent had been elaborated; when the elaboration was removed, only the more recent antecedent was activated. This finding is consistent with O'Brien et al. (1990) in that more than one potential antecedent was activated. More importantly, there does not need to be any pre-existing relation between the potential antecedents or the anaphoric phrase; the relation can be defined exclusively by the discourse.

Given that the resonance process can result in the activation of more than one potential antecedent, it is reasonable to assume that the antecedent with the highest level of activation will be considered first. If that is the correct antecedent, then there should be little difficulty; the reader simply selects that antecedent and discards the others. However, what happens if the antecedent with the highest level of activation is an incorrect antecedent? Assuming the reader recognizes this (which may not always happen), he or she may simply discard the selected antecedent and choose another. A second possibility is that the reader does not merely discard the incorrect antecedent, but actually suppresses it. O'Brien (1987) presented some evidence indicating that incorrect antecedents are suppressed. Using a sentence verification task, I found that, for some passages, reinstatement of one antecedent increased the time necessary to verify information about an alternative antecedent.

O'Brien and Albrecht (1994) tested this directly using the materials from O'Brien et al. (1990) (see passage quoted earlier.). We found that when subjects reinstated an early antecedent, the time to verify a statement about the late antecedent was significantly slowed relative to a condition in which there was no reinstatement. However, consistent with search as a resonance process, this only occurred when the late antecedent was from the same category as the early antecedent; when the late antecedent was changed so that it was from a different category, verification times for the late antecedent were unaffected by a reinstatement of the early antecedent.

Given that the resonance process is automatic, the retrieval of potential antecedents in the presence of an anaphor should not be restricted to concepts that appeared in the discourse. That is, any concept that is semantically related to an anaphor should resonate to some degree independent of whether it occurred in the passage. In general, it should be the case that concepts related to the anaphor that appeared in the discourse will be at a somewhat higher level of activation than those that did not. Thus, readers should experience little difficulty discriminating between activated concepts that appeared in the discourse and those that did not. However, if the activation of a concept that did not appear in the passage is sufficiently high, a reader may select it as an antecedent. In fact, this is the case (O'Brien & Albrecht, 1991).

O'Brien and Albrecht (1991) presented subjects with passages such as the one that follows. Each passage contained one of two possible antecedents (e.g., *camel* or *mule*), and the last line of the passage prompted reinstatement of the target antecedent. In the high context version, the context surrounding the target antecedent was highly supportive of one of the antecedents. In contrast, in the low context version, the context was equally supportive of either antecedent. Following reinstatement, subjects were required to name either the target ante-cedent or the alternative concept. We found the time to name the high-related concept *camel* was significantly faster in the high context versions of the passage than in the low context versions. More importantly, this occurred even when the high-related concept had not appeared in the passage (i.e., the high- and low-context versions of the passage contained *mule*). This finding indicates that the resonance process is not constrained to concepts that appeared in the discourse; concepts that are semantically related to an anaphoric phrase or the context of the passage will resonate as well.

> The desert landscape was quiet until the sound of bells was heard. [Slowly a long-legged (camel/mule) with a hump on its back came galloping over the horizon.] [Slowly a large brown (camel/mule) with a pack on its back came over the hori-zon.] It was a dreadfully hot day and Howard was impressed by the animal's endurance. Howard turned and went back to work on the oil drill. One of his co-workers came up to him and asked him what he had seen near the horizon.[1]
> (O'Brien & Albrecht, 1991, p. 102)

Although this finding indicates that concepts outside the discourse will reso-nate, further evidence is needed to demonstrate that those concepts are consid-ered. So, in a subsequent experiment, we eliminated the last sentence prompting reinstatement and added two additional sentences to further background the target concept. After reading these passages, subjects responded aloud to a question that required a one-word answer that was always the target antecedent (e.g., "what came over the hill?"). When asked to respond as quickly as possible, the supportive context in the high-context passages resulted in subjects producing the high-related concept *camel* even when the passage actually contained the low-related concept *mule*. In contrast, when subjects were asked to respond as accurately as possible, they never produced the high-related concept when the passage contained the low-related concept. When asked for free recall of the passages, the highly supportive context never resulted in subjects incorrectly

---

[1]The high context and low context versions were created by using the text in the first and second set of bracket, respectively.

recalling *camel* when the passage contained *mule*. Taken together, these results indicate that activation of concepts not present in the discourse was taking place during retrieval and that under some conditions, readers can actually select an antecedent that never occurred in the passage.

Thus, when there is a local coherence break, as with anaphors or anaphoric phrases, a very consistent pattern emerges. The attempt to map an anaphor onto the correct antecedent begins with an automatic resonance process; any concept that shares features in common with the anaphoric phrase will resonate with the reader generally selecting the antecedent with the highest level of activation. Several factors can influence the level of activation: referential distance, degree of elaboration, number of competing concepts in the discourse, and context. These factors generally converge on the correct antecedent. However, as we found, these factors can also result in an initial selection of an incorrect anteced-ent (O'Brien & Albrecht, 1991; O'Brien et al., 1990).

GLOBAL COHERENCE BREAKS

Assuming that the mapping of incoming information onto the existing represen-tation involves an automatic resonance process, the mapping should take place independent of whether there is a local coherence break. An important test of the automatic resonance process in mapping incoming information is to demonstrate that readers are sensitive to global inconsistencies even when local coherence is maintained. There is increasing evidence that this is true. For example, O'Brien and Albrecht (1992) presented subjects with passages such as the following:

> As Kim stood (inside/outside) the health club she felt a rush of excitement. [Work-outs always made her feel better. Today she was particularly looking forward to the exercise class because it had been a long, hard day at work. Her boss had just been fired and she had to fill in for him on top of her own work.] She was getting anxious to start and was glad when she saw the instructor come in the door of the club. Kim really liked her instructor. Her enthusiasm and energy were contagious.[2] (O'Brien & Albrecht, 1992, p. 781)

The initial sentence placed a protagonist in a particular location (e.g., "Kim stood inside/outside the health club."). A second sentence moved the protagonist from the original location (e.g., "She decided to go outside the health club."). When the first sentence indicated that Kim was inside the health club, the second location sentence was consistent with the stated location of the protagonist. Conversely, when the first sentence indicated that Kim was outside the health

---

[2]The consistent and inconsistent conditions were created by using the words inside the parenthe-ses to the left and right of the slash, respectively. The distant conditions were created by including the information within the brackets. The second location sentence is in italics.

club, the second location sentence was inconsistent with the protagonist's stated location. The distance between the two location sentences was also varied. In the close condition, a contradiction in the stated location of the protagonist constituted a local coherence break. However, in the distant conditions, the second location sentence was always locally coherent but was inconsistent at a global level. Reading times on the second location sentence indicated that subjects noticed the contradiction in both the close and distant conditions. Despite the fact that the second location sentence was locally coherent in the distance condition, readers attempted to map information in the second location sentence onto the location information presented earlier. That is, readers were attempting to maintain coherence at a global level even when the information was locally coherent.

Albrecht and I (Albrecht & O'Brien, 1993), as well as Huitema, Dopkins, Klin, and Myers (1993) provided further evidence that the resonance process activates relevant information at a global level even when local coherence has been maintained. The passage that follows contains an example from Albrecht and O'Brien (1993). Each passage began with the introduction of a main character followed by an elaboration of some characteristic of the main character. Immediately following this, there was a shift in topic back to the story line in the introduction; the main character was mentioned and referred to throughout the remainder of the passage, but there was no reference to the elaborated characteristic until the critical sentences were encountered. In the critical sentences, the main character was described as engaging in some action that was consistent, inconsistent, or unrelated to the earlier elaboration.

Today, Mary was meeting a friend for lunch. She arrived early at the restaurant and decided to get a table. After she sat down, she started looking at the menu.

Consistent Elaboration
This was Mary's favorite restaurant because it had fantastic junk food. Mary enjoyed eating anything that was quick and easy to fix. In fact, she ate at McDonald's at least three times a week. Mary never worried about her diet and saw no reason to eat nutritious foods.

Inconsistent Elaboration
This was Mary's favorite restaurant because it had fantastic health food. Mary, a health nut, has been a strict vegetarian for ten years. Her favorite food was cauliflower. Mary was so serious about her diet that she refused to eat anything that was fried or cooked in grease.

Neutral Elaboration
This was Mary's favorite restaurant because it had a nice quiet atmosphere. Mary frequently ate at the restaurant and had recommended it to all of her friends. She especially liked the cute tables and the country style table cloths on them. It made her feel right at home.

After about ten minutes, Mary's friend arrived. It had been a few months since they had seen each other. Because of this they had a lot to talk about and chatted for over a half hour. Finally, Mary signaled the waiter to come take their orders. Mary checked the menu one more time. She had a hard time deciding what to have for lunch. *Mary ordered a cheeseburger and fries. She handed the menu back to the waiter.* Her friend didn't have as much trouble deciding what she wanted. She ordered and they began to chat again. They didn't realize there was so much for them to catch up on. (Albrecht & O'Brien, 1993, p. 1070)

For the example in the passage just given, the critical sentences are: "Mary ordered a cheeseburger and fries," and "She handed the menu back to the waiter." In the consistent version the main character, *Mary*, is described as someone who loves junk food and eats at McDonald's quite often. The action of ordering a cheeseburger is highly consistent with the earlier description of Mary's taste in food. In the inconsistent version, Mary is described as a health nut who is a strict vegetarian. Given this description, it is unlikely that Mary would be ordering a cheeseburger. Finally, in the neutral version the elaboration section provides a description of the restaurant without elaborating on some characteristic of Mary.

To ensure that the passages were locally coherent, each passage was analyzed using both the leading-edge strategy (Fletcher, 1981; Kintsch & van Dijk, 1978) and the current-state selection strategy (Fletcher & Bloom, 1988). Also local coherence was checked using the criterion proposed by McKoon and Ratcliff (1992); each pair of critical sentences along with the sentence that preceded them was checked to ensure that they could "stand on their own." That is, they could be understood without making reference to earlier parts of the passage.

Reading times on the critical sentences were significantly longer in the inconsistent versions than in either the consistent or neutral versions. Again subjects experienced comprehension difficulty in a condition in which local coherence was maintained, but global coherence was not.

In a subsequent study, Myers, O'Brien, Albrecht, and Mason (in press) extended this finding in two important ways. First, we tested for the availability of the elaborated information immediately after it was presented, after the backgrounding section, and after the critical sentences. We found that the elaborated characteristics of the protagonist were easily available immediately after it was read, as well as after the critical sentences. But it was not easily available after the backgrounding section, providing converging evidence that the increase in reading times in the inconsistent condition were a result of a coherence break at a global level and not at a local level.

Second, we changed the backgrounding section so that it backgrounded the protagonist, as well as the relevant characteristics. In this condition, we still obtained a slowdown in reading times in the inconsistent condition. However, the slowdown did not become apparent until the second critical sentence. This delay occurred presumably because the reader was forced to bring the original protagonist back into explicit focus, a process that required additional time. Once reactivated, the characteristics of the protagonist were reactivated as well. This result is important because it demonstrates that when a character is reintroduced into focus, any new information about that character must still be mapped onto earlier described characteristics.

It would be tempting to conclude that these findings provide a critical test of the minimalist hypothesis. And, in fact, if the definition of "readily (or easily) available" is constrained to information that is active in memory, they do. However, within the resonance framework, we are assuming that traces that are active in memory resonate with other active traces, as well as relevant inactive traces in the discourse model (traces with a high level of trace overlap) and relevant traces from world knowledge. It is quite reasonable to assume that inactive, but relevant trace elements will resonate and become reactivated automatically. These reactivated traces are then treated the same way currently active traces are; they are integrated into the active portion of the discourse model with little difficulty unless they introduce some sort of coherence break. Thus, these findings can be easily accommodated within the minimalist position. However, they do begin to test the limits of what is meant by readily available. They also make clear that information that is not active in memory can be readily available depending upon its relation to currently active information.

ELABORATIVE INFERENCING

There is considerable debate over the extent to which readers generate elaborative inferences; that is, inferences that go beyond the text and are not necessary to maintain coherence. One of the major problems has been the lack of agreement concerning the appropriate measures to assess elaborative inferences (Keenan, Golding, Potts, Jennings, & Aman, 1990; Keenan & Jennings, 1994; Keenan, Potts, Golding, & Jennings, 1990; McKoon & Ratcliff, 1986; in press; Potts, Keenan, & Golding, 1988).

Despite the controversy over particular measures, few researchers would argue that elaborative inferences are never drawn. A major problem is that because elaborative inferences are not necessary for comprehension, it is difficult to predict when and if an elaborative inference will be drawn or what that inference might be. Also, a conservative reader may choose to delay any inferential process until the text indicates unambiguously what the correct inference is or until it becomes necessary for comprehension. It has been suggested (O'Brien, Shank, Myers, & Rayner, 1988) that this is not an unreasonable strategy. Delaying an inference will generally do little to disrupt comprehension. But if an elaborative inference is drawn and at some later point turns out to be incorrect, the reader is likely to experience comprehension difficulty.

There may also be a more subtle reason why it has been so difficult to establish evidence of elaborative inferencing that is consistent with mapping as a resonance process. For example, consider the passage that follows from O'Brien et al. (1988). Each version of the passage contains an anaphor (e.g., *knife*) and an antecedent (either *knife* or *weapon*). In the high-context version, the preceding context was highly supportive of the weapon being a *knife*. In the low-context version, the preceding context was neutral with respect to the weapon. In all conditions, subjects needed to map the anaphor *knife* onto its antecedent (*knife* or *weapon*).

> All the mugger wanted was to steal the woman's money. But when she screamed, he [stabbed] [assaulted] her with his (knife/weapon) in an attempt to quiet her. He looked to see if anyone had seen him. He threw the knife into the bushes and ran away.[3] (O'Brien et al., 1988, p. 420)

We found that gaze durations on the anaphor were equally fast when the antecedent was direct (*knife*) in both the high- and low-context versions, as well as when the antecedent was implicit (*weapon*) in the high-context version. We argued that this occurred because subjects had drawn the inference that the weapon was a *knife*. In contrast, gaze durations on the antecedent were significantly slower in the low-context implicit condition where no inference was expected.

Garrod et al., (1990) argued that this type of elaborative inference was actually an automatic process in which the mapping was accomplished through a resonance process. For example, when the reader encounters the antecedent *knife*, a referent is introduced into the discourse model that contains the set of semantic features associated with *knife*. When the reader encounters the subsequent anaphor, the level of resonance will be quite high, facilitating the selection of the appropriate antecedent. In contrast, when the referent is introduced by using *weapon*, the degree of featural overlap is reduced, resulting in less resonance and greater time needed to resolve the subsequent anaphor.

However, consider how context can induce an automatic inference. When the referent is introduced by using *weapon*, there is already a fair degree of featural overlap between *weapon* and *knife*. A strong biasing context can further define the referent by activating additional features appropriate to *knife*. Given sufficient context, the degree of featural overlap may be equivalent to a condition in which the antecedent is introduced directly.

This interpretation fits within the spirit of the minimalist hypothesis and is consistent with some of the work McKoon and Ratcliff have done on inferencing. For example, McKoon and Ratcliff (1986) suggested that inferences are often only minimally encoded. They found that when subjects read sentences such as,

---

[3]The high- and low-context conditions were created by using the text in the first and second set of brackets. The antecedent is in parentheses with the explicit and implicit conditions to the right and left of the slash, respectively.

"The director and the cameraman were ready to shoot close-ups when suddenly the actress fell from the 14th story," a subsequent priming task showed some evidence for the activation of the concept *dead*. McKoon and Ratcliff argued that the level of priming was weak because subjects had encoded only a few of the features associated with *dead*.

Garrod et al. (1990) argued that with additional context more features associated with *dead* would be activated, leading to clearer evidence of the predicted inference. The low level of activated features would explain why McKoon and Ratcliff found weak evidence for the inference *dead* whereas others have argued that readers would be unlikely to draw that inference when so many other outcomes remain possible (e.g., Glenberg & Mathews, 1992). It would also explain why it has been so difficult to produce clear evidence of a specific elaborative inference (e.g., Potts et al., 1988; see also Murray, Klin, & Myers, 1993).

This account of many types of elaborative inferences is by no means new. For example, Garrod and Sanford (1981) demonstrated that the reading time for the sentence, "The car had recently been overhauled," was no longer when it followed, "Kent drove to London," than when it followed, "Kent took his car to London," even though only the second sentence contained an explicit antecedent. Garrod and Sanford (1981) argued that the verb *drive* introduces a referent into the discourse model that contains many of the semantic features associated with *vehicle*, thereby providing a slot into which the subsequently mentioned *car* can be mapped. Consistent with McKoon and Ratcliff (1986), the specific inference *car* was only partially encoded to the extent that it shares semantic features with the more general concept of *vehicle*.

Sanford and Garrod (1981) provided still further evidence for this type of automatic encoding of elaborative inferences. Consider the following examples:

1. "John was not looking forward to teaching math. The bus trundled slowly along the road. He hoped he could control the class today."
2. "John was on his way to school. The bus trundled slowly along the road. He hoped he could control the class today."

Sanford and Garrod found that the time to read the last sentence was faster in the first version than in the second version. They argued that the difference in reading time occurred because subjects had inferred that John was a student in the second version which then conflicted with the last sentence (see Keenan, 1992 for a similar interpretation). However, McKoon and Ratcliff (in press) recently argued that this finding is confounded by the fact that in version 1, there is information suggesting that John was a teacher, which facilitated comprehension of the last sentence in Version 1, rather than there being a conflict with the last sentence in Version 2.

Although McKoon and Ratcliff were correct in pointing out that it is not clear which version produced the effect, it must still be the case that some sort of inference was drawn. In fact, within the current framework, is likely that both interpretations are correct. Even though there is nothing in the first sentence of Version 1 that explicitly states that John is a teacher, the context would certainly activate features in world knowledge consistent with concept of teacher. These features then became a part of the discourse entity *John*. In Version 2, a higher degree of features consistent with the concept of student would be activated (it is generally students who are on their way to school) and connected to *John*. Thus, in both conditions, a partial (minimal) inference about John would have been automatically generated, producing facilitation in Version 1, and interference in Version 2.

CONCLUSION

I have argued that an automatic resonance process plays an important role in inferencing and the maintenance of coherence at both a local and global level. However, it is by no means the case that all comprehension processes are automatic. For example, the establishment of causal relations has been viewed as "the result of a complex problem-solving process" (van den Broek, 1990, p. 423). Much of the work examining the development of a mental model would be difficult to explain as involving only automatic processes (Glenberg et al., 1987; Glenberg & Langston, 1992; Glenberg & Mathews, 1992). However, consistent with the minimalist hypothesis, an appeal to conscious comprehension processes should only be made when processes assumed to be automatic cannot account for particular results.

REFERENCES

Albrecht, J. E., & O'Brien, E. J. (1993). Updating a mental model: Maintaining both local and global coherence. *Journal of Experimental Psychology: Learning, Memory, and Cognition, 19,* 1061–1070.

Bloom, C. P., Fletcher, C. R., van den Broek, P., Reitz, L., & Shapiro, B. P. (1990). An on-line assessment of causal reasoning during comprehension. *Memory and Cognition, 18,* 65–71.

Chang, F. (1980). Active memory processes in visual sentence comprehension: Clause effects and pronominal reference. *Memory & Cognition, 8,* 58–64.

Corbett, A. T. (1984). Prenominal adjectives and the disambiguation of anaphoric nouns. *Journal of Verbal Learning and Verbal Behavior, 23,* 683–695.

Corbett, A. T., & Chang, F. R. (1983). Pronoun disambiguation: Accessing potential antecedents. *Memory & Cognition, 11,* 283–294.

Dell, G. S., McKoon, G., & Ratcliff, R. (1983). The activation of antecedent information during the processing of anaphoric reference in reading. *Journal of Verbal Learning and Verbal Behavior, 22,* 121–132.

Fletcher, C. R. (1981). Short-term memory processes in text comprehension. *Journal of Verbal Learning and Verbal Behavior, 20,* 564–574.

Fletcher, C. R. (1986). Strategies for the allocation of short-term memory during comprehension. *Journal of Memory and Language, 25*, 43–58.

Fletcher, C. R., & Bloom, C. P. (1988). Causal reasoning in the comprehension of simple narrative texts. *Journal of Memory and Language, 27*, 235–244.

Garnham, A., & Oakhill, J. (1992). Discourse processing and text representation from a "Mental Models" perspective. *Language and Cognitive Processes, 7*, 193–204.

Garnham, A., Oakhill, J., & Johnson-Laird, P. N. (1982). Referential continuity and the coherence of discourse. *Cognition, 11*, 29–46.

Garrod, S., O'Brien, E. J., Morris, R. K., & Rayner, K. (1990). Elaborative inferencing as an active or passive process. *Journal of Experimental Psychology: Learning, Memory, and Cognition, 16*, 250–257.

Garrod, S., & Sanford, A. J. (1981). Bridging inferences in the extended domain of reference. In A. Baddeley & J. Long (Eds.), *Attention and performance* (Vol. 9, pp. 331–346). Hillsdale, NJ: Lawrence Erlbaum Associates.

Garrod, S., & Sanford, A. J. (1988). Thematic subjecthood and cognitive constraints on discourse structure. *Journal of Pragmatics, 12*, 519–534.

Garrod, S., & Sanford, A. J. (1990). Referential processing in reading: Focusing on roles and individuals. In D. A. Balota, G. B. Flores d'Arcais, & K. Rayner (Eds.), *Comprehension processes in reading* (pp. 465–485). Hillsdale, NJ: Lawrence Erlbaum Associates.

Gernsbacher, M. A. (1989). Mechanisms that improve referential access. *Cognition, 32*, 99–156.

Gernsbacher, M. A. (1990). *Language comprehension as structure Building*. Hillsdale, NJ: Lawrence Erlbaum Associates.

Gillund, G., & Shiffrin, R. M. (1984). A retrieval model for both recognition and recall. *Psychological Review, 91*, 1–67.

Glenberg, A. M., & Langston, W. E. (1992). Comprehension of illustrated text: Pictures help to build mental models. *Journal of Memory and Language, 31*, 129–151.

Glenberg, A. M., & Mathews, S. (1992). When minimalism is not enough: Mental models in reading, Part I. *Psycoloquy, 3*(64.2.1).

Glenberg, A. M., Meyer, M., & Lindem, K. (1987). Mental models contribute to foregrounding during text comprehension. *Journal of Memory and Language, 26*, 69–83.

Hintzman, D. L. (1986). "Schema abstraction" in a multiple-trace memory model. *Psychological Review, 93*, 411–428.

Huitema, J., Dopkins, S. E., Klin, C. M., & Myers, J. L. (1993). Connecting goals and actions during reading. *Journal of Experimental Psychology: Learning, Memory, and Cognition, 19*, 1053–1060.

Johnson-Laird, P. N. (1983). *Mental Models*. Cambridge: Harvard University Press.

Just, M. A., & Carpenter, P. A. (1987). *The psychology of reading and language comprehension*. Boston, MA: Allyn & Bacon.

Keenan, J. M. (1992). Thoughts about the minimalist hypothesis: Commentary on Garnham on reading-inference. *Psycoloquy*.

Keenan, J. M., Golding, J. M., Potts, G. R., Jennings, T. M., & Aman, C. J. (1990). Methodological issues in evaluating the occurrence of inferences. In A. Graesser & G. Bower (Eds.), *Inferences and text comprehension* (pp. 295–312). New York: Academic Press.

Keenan, J. M., & Jennings. T. M. (in press). The role of word-based priming in inference research. In R. F. Lorch, Jr., & E. J. O'Brien (Eds.), *Sources of coherence in reading*. Hillsdale, NJ: Lawrence Erlbaum Associates.

Keenan, J. M., Potts, G. R., Golding, J. M., & Jennings, T. M. (1990). Which elaborative inferences are drawn during reading? A question of methodologies. In D. Balota, G. Flores d'Arcais, & K. Rayner (Eds.), *Comprehension processes in reading* (pp. 377–402). Hillsdale, NJ: Lawrence Erlbaum Associates.

Kintsch, W., & van Dijk, T. (1978). Toward a model of text comprehension and production. *Psychological Review, 85*, 363–394.

Lesgold, A. M., Roth, S. F., & Curtis, M. E. (1979). Foregrounding effects in discourse comprehension. *Journal of Verbal Learning and Verbal Behavior*, *18*, 291–308.

McKoon, G., & Ratcliff, R. (1980). The comprehension processes and memory structures involved in anaphoric reference. *Journal of Verbal Learning and Verbal Behavior*, *19*, 668–682.

McKoon, G., & Ratcliff, R. (1986). Inferences about predictable events. *Journal of Experimental Psychology: Learning, Memory, and Cognition*, *12*, 82–91

McKoon, G., & Ratcliff, R. (1992). Inference during reading. *Psychological Review*, *99*, 440–466.

McKoon, G., & Ratcliff, R. (in press). The minimalist hypothesis: Directions for research. In C. Weaver, S. Mannes, & C. R. Fletcher (Eds.), *Discourse comprehension: Strategies and processing revisited*. Hillsdale, NJ: Lawerence Erlbaum Associates.

Murray, J. D., Klin, D. M., & Myers, J. L. (1993). Forward inferences in narrative text. *Journal of Memory and Language*, *32*, 464–473.

Myers, J. L., O'Brien, E. J., Albrecht, J. E., & Mason, R. A. (in press). Maintaining global coherence during reading. *Journal of Experimental Psychology: Learning, Memory, and Cognition*.

O'Brien, E. J. (1987). Antecedent search processes and the structure of text. *Journal of Experimental Psychology: Learning, Memory, and Cognition*, *13*, 278–290.

O'Brien, E. J., & Albrecht, J. E. (1991). The role of context in accessing antecedents in text. *Journal of Experimental Psychology: Learning, Memory, and Cognition*, *17*, 94–102.

O'Brien, E. J., & Albrecht, J. E. (1992) Comprehension strategies in the development of a mental model. *Journal of Experimental Psychology: Learning, Memory, and Cognition*, *18*, 777–784.

O'Brien, E. J., & Albrecht, J. E. (1994). *Activation and suppression of antecedents during reinstatement*. Manuscript submitted for publication.

O'Brien, E. J., Duffy, S. A., & Myers, J. L. (1986). Anaphoric inference during reading. *Journal of Experimental Psychology: Learning, Memory, and Cognition*, *12*, 346–352.

O'Brien, E. J. & Myers, J. L. (1987). The role of causal connection in the retrieval of text. *Memory & Cognition*, *15*, 419–427.

O'Brien, E. J., Plewes, P. S., & Albrecht, J. E. (1990). Antecedent retrieval processes. *Journal of Experimental Psychology: Learning, Memory, and Cognition*, *16*, 241–249.

O'Brien, E. J., Shank, D. M., Myers, J. L., & Rayner, K. (1988). Elaborative inferences during reading: Do they occur on-line? *Journal of Experimental Psychology: Learning, Memory, and Cognition*, *14*, 410–420.

Potts, G. R., Keenan, J. M., & Golding, J. M. (1988). Assessing the occurrence of elaborative inferences: Lexical decision versus naming. *Journal of Memory and Language*, *27*, 399–415.

Ratcliff, R. (1978). A theory of memory retrieval. *Psychological Review*, *85*, 59–108.

Rizzella, M. L., & O'Brien, E. J. (1994). *The effects of causality on the availability of text-based concepts*. Manuscript submitted for publication.

Sanford, A. J., & Garrod, S. (1981). *Understanding written language*. New York: Wiley.

Stevenson, R. J. (1986, August). *The time course of pronoun comprehension*. Paper presented at The Eighth Annual Conference of the Cognitive Science Society, Amherst, MA.

Trabasso, T., & Sperry, L. (1985). Causal relatedness and importance of story events. *Journal of Memory and Language*, *24*, 595–611.

Trabasso, T., & van den Broek, P. (1985). Causal thinking and the representation of narrative events. *Journal of Memory and Language*, *24*, 612–630.

van den Broek, P. (1990). The casual inference maker: Towards a process model of inference generation in text comprehension. In D. Balota, Flores d'Arcais, & K. Rayner (Eds.), *Comprehension Processes in Reading* (pp. 423–445). Hillsdale, NJ: Lawerence Erlbaum Associates.

van Dijk, T. A., & Kintsch, W. (1983). *Strategies of Discourse Comprehension*. New York: Academic Press.

10 The Role of Familiarity in Cognitive Processing

Eleen N. Kamas
Lynne M. Reder
Carnegie Mellon University

Understanding normal cognition—understanding the mechanisms underlying cognition in everyday situations—is a primary goal of cognitive science. The thesis of this chapter is that the typical modes of thinking used in everyday processes such as memory, reasoning, and question answering, involve heuristics that can be thought of as shortcuts or "sloppy matches" (or, to borrow a term from computer science, "fuzzy logic"). These short-cuts and heuristics are not an indictment of "lazy cognition"; rather, it has become clear that the only way cognition could operate is by developing heuristics that are adaptive. Given the complexities of the tasks asked of us and the knowledge base under which we must operate, it is imperative that human cognition possess tools to make short-cuts effective.

In this chapter we propose that familiarity is a measure easily computed and frequently used for judgments besides familiarity. We call this the Featural Familiarity Hypothesis. One feature of the human memory system is that it can easily confuse frequency of exposure, or familiarity, with recency of exposure. In addition, the cognitive system tends not to carefully inspect the representations in working memory to ensure a perfect match between input and what is stored in long-term memory. Gross measures of familiarity often play a role in determining the acceptability of these matches. The self-monitoring of text comprehension is an example of an area where familiarity plays a role (e.g., Maki & Berry, 1984). Another area is the role of familiarity in directing the use of question-answering strategies (e.g., Reder, 1987, 1988).

There are a number of phenomena subsumed by these areas that can be understood within our theoretical framework. That is, the illusion of comprehension, the difficulty of detecting contradictions, the inability to notice distortions

177

in questions, and spurious feelings of knowing an answer are all influenced by partial matches and use raw familiarity. In addition, we believe that analogical reasoning, judgments of liking, judgments of validity, and judgments of fame and of recognition are all influenced by the same heuristics of sloppy cognition to be described.

In this chapter, we first briefly describe several phenomena that, at a glance, appear quite disparate, but we believe are all characterized by similar cognitive heuristics. Next, we outline a quasi-mechanistic account that incorporates these principles and we attempt to show how this account can explain these phenomena. In our account, we borrow and blend ideas from Anderson (1983, 1993), Jacoby (e.g., Jacoby, Kelley, & Dywan, 1989), and Kintsch (1988); undoubtedly others have influenced us as well. What we offer is a basic framework or sketch of a model to illustrate how these principles of sloppy match and familiarity measurement can influence so much of cognition. After describing the framework, we return to the phenomena, discussing each in more detail, and showing how each can be seen as a manifestation of the simple heuristics used in most cognitive processing.

THE PHENOMENA

Feeling of Knowing

Feeling of knowing has traditionally been used to refer to the subjective experience that the answer is on the "tip of the tongue," or to estimate the likelihood of recognizing the answer on a later test when it cannot be recalled immediately. These feeling of knowing estimates are remarkably accurate (e.g., Blake, 1973; Hart, 1965; Nelson & Narens, 1990). These ratings can also be used to accurately predict such performances as exposure duration to perceive a tachistoscopically presented word, number of trials to relearn a paired associate (Nelson, Gerler, & Narens, 1984), and time to make a lexical decision (Connor, Balota, & Neely, 1992; Yaniv & Meyer, 1987).

More recent work has indicated that the feeling of knowing phenomenon is not limited to situations where there is a recall failure (Reder, 1987, 1988; Reder & Ritter, 1992). Subjects can give very rapid estimates of whether they will be able to answer a question (prior to attempting a retrieval). These estimates are surprisingly more accurate than the estimates given after a failed recall attempt. Manipulations influencing the familiarity of the terms in the question influence feeling of knowing: people erroneously think they know the answer to a question if the question terms are familiar (e.g., Costermans, Lories, & Ansay, 1992; Reder, 1987; Reder & Ritter, 1988, 1992; Schwartz & Metcalfe, 1992). Can this possibly be an adaptive and normal part of cognition? Why should the mind work this way?

Illusions of Comprehension

When students are asked to read textbook passages and then rate how well they have understood them, their judgments tend to be quite inaccurate. They are blissfully optimistic about how well they are comprehending passages in terms of future test performance (e.g., Beckett, Kestner, & White, 1989; Glenberg & Epstein, 1985, 1987; Glenberg, Sanocki, Epstein, & Morris, 1987; Maki & Berry, 1984; Maki & Serra, 1992; Pressley & Ghatala, 1988). Moreover, there seems to be little improvement at predicting test performance with practice at the task. In addition, when asked whether they have understood passages (either while reading or after the fact), they seem to be insensitive to contradictions that should make the passage incomprehensible (e.g., Epstein, Glenberg, & Bradley, 1984; Glenberg, Wilkinson, & Epstein, 1982; Otero & Kintsch, 1992). These are important aspects of text comprehension monitoring, and not just for students. Why then are people generally so poor at doing this? And why does practice not make this monitoring task easier?

The Moses Illusion

When asked, "How many animals of each kind did Moses take on the Ark?" most people will answer "Two," even when they know that Noah, not Moses, built the Ark (e.g., Bredart & Modolo, 1988; Erickson & Mattson, 1981; Reder & Cleeremans, 1990; Reder & Kusbit, 1991). This failure to notice distortions is a strong tendency, and is difficult to influence. Previous study of the correct facts does not aid in the detection of this type of distortion (Reder & Cleeremans, 1990). The failure to notice these distortions is not due to a poor encoding of the target or distorted words. If subjects are asked to repeat back the question before answering it, they will repeat the distorted term (e.g., "Moses"), not noticing it is incorrect. In addition, subjects take just as long to read the distorted term when they did not notice the distortion as when they did (Reder & Kusbit, 1991). So why is it so tough for us to notice these distortions? What is the cause of this illusion and what does it tell us about how comprehension works?

Validity Inflation

A disturbing phenomenon of human nature is that we seem to give greater credence to statements the more we hear them, regardless of whether or not they are true. That is, repeating a statement, even without any additional elaboration or support, can make people think it is true (e.g., Arkes, Hackett, & Boehm, 1989; Bacon, 1979; Gigerenzer, 1984; Hasher, Goldstein, & Toppino, 1977; Schwartz, 1982). This occurs when the entire sentence is repeated, but exact repetition of an entire statement is not required. Mere familiarity with the topic of a sentence can cause the sentence to be rated more valid than a comparable sentence on an unfamiliar topic (Begg, Armour, & Kerr, 1985). Even exposure to a word included in a sentence has been shown to increase the perceived validity of that statement (Arkes, Nash, & Joyner, 1989). This would seem to leave us vulnerable to propaganda and advertising. Why does our cognitive architecture allow us to use familiarity to judge validity?

Analogical Reasoning

When trying to solve a novel problem, people may attempt to use a previously solved problem as an example. In trying to recall a relevant past problem, the superficial similarity between the current problem and prior problems often appears to be more influential than the structural similarity of the current problem and potential analogical predecessors (e.g., Faries & Reiser, 1988; Ross, 1987, 1989a). This occurs despite the fact that structural similarity is vital for successful use of previous problem solutions (e.g., Clement & Gentner, 1991; Gentner, 1983; Ross, 1987, 1989a). Although the availability of analogs is critical to actually being able to use this form of problem solving, people seem maladaptive in how they select potential analogs.

Unconscious Uses of Memory

Jacoby and his colleagues (e.g., Jacoby, 1988; Jacoby & Kelley, 1987; Jacoby, Kelley, & Dywan, 1989) have discovered a number of interesting phenomena suggesting that memory is often used unconsciously in various tasks and judgments. For example, they have found that if subjects are exposed to nonfamous names, they are likely to false alarm and rate these same names as famous at a later time when these names are embedded among new nonfamous and famous names (Jacoby, Kelley, Brown, & Jasechko, 1989; Jacoby, Woloshyn, & Kelley, 1989). They also showed that people's ability to detect spelling errors is lessened with exposure to the incorrectly spelled form of the word (Jacoby & Hollingshead, 1990). In addition, the ability to discriminate new words from old words on a recognition test is hampered when new words are tachistoscopically (subliminally flashed) prior to the recognition judgment; that is, subjects make a lot of false alarms to such pre-exposed new words (Jacoby & Whitehouse, 1989).

These phenomena are consistent with our view of the heuristics of memory. Later in this chapter, we discuss at greater length the findings from Jacoby's lab, attempt to explicate their account of these findings, and compare and contrast these ideas with our own.

THE FEATURAL FAMILIARITY HYPOTHESIS

The phenomena just mentioned might appear to be quite disparate, with little in common but the fact that people often appear quite fallible. Why do our minds work this way? Is it really adaptive, despite appearing otherwise? Here, we offer a modest attempt to explain why these phenomena occur, using only a few key assumptions about how our cognitive architecture is organized and memory is accessed.

1. Memory is organized into a semantic network of connected ideas, with each concept and idea in memory varying in both long-term strength and short-term activation as a function of exposure. The strength of a concept is not the same as the strength of its connection to any other concept.

2. The strength of concepts and connections between concepts is fairly stable, increasing slowly each time the concept or connection is activated, and decaying slowly from disuse; activation, on the other hand, builds and decays rapidly.

3. Strength is actually the resting activation level of a concept. Therefore people can easily misattribute recent activation to long-term strength.

4. Availability of information is a function of its current level of activation. The ease with which a fact becomes active depends on its baseline strength, and how much activation it receives from a connecting link to an associated concept.

5. Retrieval from memory involves finding partial matches between the memory probe or representation in working memory and the structure in memory. Partial matches are based primarily on shared clusters of matching features, rather than features all in the exact same relationship in the probe as in memory.

6. When matching a memory probe to memory, focus of attention influences which parts of the representation will be more carefully matched. Indeed, only those elements in the focus of attention will have activation spread out from them.

For convenience, we have named these assumptions the *Featural Familiarity Hypothesis*. The first three assumptions address the structure and characteristics of memory. Consider Assumption 1, which states that memory will vary in activation and strength as a function of exposure. By this we mean that the more often a person is exposed to an idea or concept, the more activation the corresponding representation in the semantic network will receive. Each time the concept or propositional structure is activated, there is a small boost to the long-term strength or base level of activation, although the activation itself decays rapidly, as stated in Assumption 2. Strength, too, decays over time if the concept is not rehearsed or refreshed from new exposure; however, the rate of decay is much slower than for activation. Assumption 3 notes that, when inspecting memory, a person may confuse the activation of a concept with its long-term strength. Thus, a person may think that a currently active item has been stored in long-term memory when it actually has not.

The final three assumptions are concerned with the access of information in memory. Assumption 4 states that the availability of a concept depends on its strength or baseline activation, and the number and strength of connections to other concepts. These factors determine the ease of activation of the concept. The activation of a concept may be raised by exposure to the concept itself (through self-connections or feedback loops; exposure in the environment activates the concept). Alternatively, a concept may be activated by an associated concept. In this case, the amount of activation is a joint function of the target concept's base level of activation, the associated concept's strength, the strength of the connection, and the competing connections from the associated concept. A fact that is activated above a certain threshold will be available for conscious processing in working memory. This process occurs more easily for stronger traces.

Assumption 5 asserts that a complete match is not required to retrieve information from memory. The key issue is defining the criteria that determine an acceptable partial match. Obviously, the amount of overlap between the working memory representation and the long-term memory structure affects the likelihood of accepting the partial match as sufficient. The degree of acceptable overlap is primarily a function of the amount of activation arriving at the higher level structure that is being matched. In our view, this overlap is not just computed by lexical items, but also by semantic features attached to these items. It is *clusters* of activated features that are matched to the overall representation. The structural relationship among these clusters of features is rarely inspected.

Although activation is a necessary requirement for processing a memory trace, unless the trace is *in the focus of attention*, it will not be carefully inspected. Assumption 6 states that the focus of attention determines which aspects of the memory representation will be carefully matched to long-term memory structures. The task requirements partially determine the focus of attention, and thus, the portions of the representations that are matched carefully. If a portion of the probe is not in focus, activation does not spread out from its memory representation to its associates; rather, the higher level memory structure that has been activated by the constellation of features spreads activation back to the out-of-focus element to insure that it "loosely matches." In other words, if the word *dog* is part of the memory probe, but it is not in focus, then the concept *DOG* will not activate its associates, such as *BONE* and *CAT*; however, an attempt will be made to connect *DOG* to the higher level structure.

Our assumptions bear resemblance to and build on the frameworks proposed by Anderson (1983, 1993) and Kintsch (1988). Within this framework, we think that the similarities among the phenomena discussed earlier become more salient, and the mechanisms that cause them more understandable. The key ideas concern the notion of clusters of features matching to stored representations, and not focusing on a careful structural match. We articulate the Featural Familiarity Hypothesis in more detail as we use it to explain each of these phenomena.

FEELING OF KNOWING

Feeling of knowing refers to the subjective experience of feeling that the answer to a question is known. Most people have experienced this feeling in the context of a "tip of the tongue" experience, where the impression of knowing the answer is quite strong despite an inability to recall the information. Traditionally, this feeling or impression has been studied in situations where retrieval has failed, but there is no tip of the tongue state. Instead the experimenter merely asks the subjects to predict the probability of being able to recall or recognize the answer later. In this paradigm, subjects attempt to answer general knowledge questions, or recall memorized associates from a list of paired associates. If the desired information is not correctly recalled, the subject instead rates the probability of later recognition of this answer.

This classic paradigm has consistently resulted in highly accurate feeling of knowing estimates. More recently, an alternate paradigm has been developed in which people make speeded predictions of whether they would be able to retrieve the answer, prior to actually attempting to retrieve the answer. Use of this paradigm has resulted in even greater accuracy of these judgments (Reder, 1987; Reder & Ritter, 1988, 1992). That is, split-second first impressions of answerability are more accurate than the feeling of knowing judgments that occur after a retrieval failure. This is in part because there is not a restricted range of questions being measured, but other factors may also be involved.

Historically, it had been assumed that the feeling of knowing is based on a partial retrieval of the answer or at least reflected the strength of the memory trace. However, several recent studies have found that manipulations that affect the familiarity of terms in the question have a much greater impact on perceptions of ability to answer the question than those that affect the accessibility of the answer (Reder, 1987; Reder & Ritter, 1988, 1992; Schwartz & Metcalfe, 1992). For example, Reder and Ritter (1992) tested this hypothesis directly by manipulating the frequency of question parts, in this case, arithmetic problems. The more frequently the problem parts had been seen, the more likely subjects were to feel they could recall the answer, even when these problem parts had been recombined to form new problems. In addition, Schwartz and Metcalfe (1992) found that priming the question terms increased the feeling of knowing, whereas priming the answer terms had no effect on this measure.

We take as support of the Featural Familiarity Hypothesis the phenomenon that people estimate whether they can answer a question based on the perceived familiarity of the question terms as opposed to the strength of the answer. This estimation heuristic is remarkably accurate at predicting whether or not one will be able to answer a question, given the queried knowledge is not sampled. In fact, subjects are typically more accurate at predicting whether or not they know the answer to a question when they make a speeded judgment than when they make their decision by trying to answer the question. For example, Reder (1987, 1988) asked subjects to quickly predict whether they could answer questions. These subjects were more conservative than subjects asked to quickly answer the questions or respond "don't know." Subjects in both conditions correctly answered the same number of questions; however, subjects who were asked to quickly predict whether they could answer had fewer false alarms than subjects in the answer condition. In sum, when asked to rapidly judge their feeling of knowing, subjects were very good at recognizing all the questions that they could answer, and rarely thought they could answer questions that they could not. At the same time, they were more than 25% faster than the subjects who attempted to answer the questions directly. This rules out any account based on a speed-accuracy tradeoff.

In summary, although the experiments just discussed show that subjects can be made to err in their feeling of knowing judgments when question familiarity is manipulated, feeling of knowing judgments are generally excellent predictors of answerability. Why would the cognitive system develop this method of assessing whether questions can be answered? We believe this feeling of knowing process developed as it did because it provides a quick, easy, and relatively accurate estimate of the contents of memory. Retrieving an answer is much slower and more effortful than simply assessing the familiarity of the question terms. This result, that familiarity is a very useful heuristic, is indicative of the usefulness of familiarity as a cognitive tool more generally.

ILLUSIONS OF COMPREHENSION

Prediction of Test Performance

The prediction of future performance on a test based on a text passage appears at first glance to be simply the feeling of knowing judgment on a larger scale. Because people are able to accurately estimate whether they will be able to answer a question, then they should be able to predict how well they will perform on a future test based on a text. This task simply involves the added task of evaluating comprehension of the text. However, researchers have found that people are quite poor at this task, under a variety of conditions—whether they make the predictions immediately after reading or after they have had some "distance" from the material (Glenberg et al., 1987; Glenberg & Epstein, 1985). Predictions of performance on class exams are no more accurate than those given in a laboratory situation (i.e., a psychology experiment) (Beckett et al., 1989; Beckett & Kestner, 1988). People do not get better at predicting future performance on tests after having seen how poor they were initially on predicting performance. The only situation that shows any improvement is on predicting performance on a test that will be virtually the same (using the same questions) as the earlier test (Glenberg et al., 1987; Glenberg & Epstein, 1985; Maki & Serra, 1992).

There are only a few instances when subjects' estimates of future test performance are moderately accurate. Subjects who perform well on an initial test show some ability to predict their performance on a later test, whereas the poorer performing subjects show no such calibration (Maki & Berry, 1984). Another exception to the generally poor calibration of comprehension occurs when subjects who differ greatly in their knowledge in different domains make confidence judgments about comprehension across domains (Glenberg & Epstein, 1987). In such a situation, subjects predict greater comprehension and show higher performance in the domain of their expertise, resulting in significant calibration. However, these same subjects fail to show calibration when the estimates are made within a given domain, regardless of whether or not it is their domain of expertise. Maki and Serra (1992) further investigated the effects of domain familiarity on test performance predictions. Subjects' estimates of future test performance was much more accurate after reading the texts than after seeing only the title and topic of the passage. The researchers interpret this result to indicate that people have some ability to use information in the text, as well as general domain familiarity to estimate their performance on a future test. Clearly, this ability is not very good, nonetheless.

Why does the Featural Familiarity Hypothesis predict such good accuracy for prediction of feeling of knowing, but such poor accuracy for comprehension and prediction of test performance? Part of the answer is that people cannot predict what questions will appear on a test. In the case of feeling of knowing, subjects are given the question and know what they will be required to retrieve. A second reason is that the ability to recognize concepts or propositions that have been asserted is not the same as being able to answer questions that may involve conceptual integration and inferential reasoning. If subjects do not really understand the passage, they will be especially poor at predicting the types of questions that will be asked. The poor prediction may be compounded by subjects getting an illusory impression of comprehension, an issue which we now consider.

Detection of Contradictions

Another aspect of comprehension monitoring that has been studied is the detection of contradictions in a passage. Although people can easily detect nonwords and syntactic errors in passages, they are often quite poor at detecting internal contradictions, or even contradictions with well-learned prior knowledge. This has been referred to as the *illusion of knowing* (Glenberg et al., 1982). Subjects are especially vulnerable to this illusion of comprehension when the contradictory aspect of the passage must be inferred or when it is at the end of a passage, particularly a long passage (Epstein et al., 1984). Syntactically marking the contradictory information as new also reduces the detection rate (Glenberg et al., 1982).

Otero and Kintsch (1992) further explored the illusion of comprehension phenomenon. They presented subjects with passages containing contradictions, asking them to note any difficulties encountered. Subjects then recalled the passages in writing. When subjects did not detect a contradiction in the text, they often recalled only one of the two contradictory sentences, or created a plausible reason for both statements to be true. Otero and Kintsch modified Kintsch's (1988) Construction-Integration model to account for this phenomenon. The first component of this model is a construction phase, in which representations for all possible meanings of words and phrases in a sentence are activated. In the second component, the integration phase, a unified conception of the idea of a passage is created by integrating the relevant representations created in the first phase, and suppressing contradictory or irrelevant representations. Because the suppression of contradictions is a natural part of this model of comprehension, the model lends itself well to the explanation of failure to detect contradictions in a passage while claiming a good understanding.

The Otero and Kintsch model does a good job of explaining the illusion of knowing; the Featural Familiarity Hypothesis may be considered complementary to their model. As we stated earlier, the activation of a concept decays quite rapidly. In order to detect a contradiction within a passage, both of the contradictory propositions must be part of working memory at the same time. If the activation of the first concept has decayed so that it is no longer in working memory, it cannot be compared to the second, and thus, no contradiction will be noted. This account is supported by evidence that increasing the distance between the contradictory sentences decreases the likelihood that the contradictions will be detected (Epstein et al., 1984).

There are other situations, however, where contradictions are detected even when separated by many sentences. Albrecht and O'Brien (1993) found that subjects easily detected actions that violated a main character's previously described attributes. For example, in one of their stories, a character who was described as a vegetarian later ordered a hamburger for lunch. Albrecht and O'Brien assumed that concepts in the current sentence are active in working memory; they called this *explicit focus*. In addition, they assumed information pertaining to the protagonist of the story is in *implicit focus*, and thus readily available for comparison to current information. In our terms, this implicit focus would correspond to a continuing, subthreshold activation for the characteristics of the main actor. If actions related to these characteristics are mentioned or contradicted in the story, their activation will pass threshold, making the characteristics available for comparison to the current information. When people read a story or narrative text, they tend to be interested enough in the characters and events to retain this information in implicit focus, or keep it activated just below threshold. However, we do not believe this happens as frequently when processing expository texts in a psychology experiment, or in preparation for a future test.

We believe that a typical strategy, when instructions are given to "understand" an expository text in which the subject has little interest or knowledge, is to examine the local sensibility of the text. That is, the reader will evaluate the text at the word and sentence level, and not evaluate the coherence of the passage as a whole.[1] As a result, superficial filters involving lexical familiarity and syntactic acceptability are used. A focus on these superficial features of the text precludes a deeper processing of the relations between the sentences in the passage, which is necessary for the detection of the contradictions. Of course other variables such as prior knowledge of the subject matter and motivation to actually digest the content are also relevant. However, unless subjects are very motivated to make inferential connections, or are specifically told which aspects of the text to focus on, they resort to these simple strategies that focus on superficial factors such as word familiarity.

Indeed, there is evidence that many readers use primarily lexical and syntactic cues to evaluate their understanding of texts, assuming they have "understood" if the words are familiar and the sentences syntactically well formed. Baker (1985) asked subjects to identify any problems they found in comprehending some text passages, giving reasons why each was seen as a problem. Each passage contained one intentionally introduced problem, either a nonword, an internal contradiction, or a contradiction of prior knowledge. If subjects were equally sensitive to each of these types of problems, they should detect each equally often. However, consistent with the Featural Familiarity Hypothesis, lexical and syntactic problems were detected twice as often as either internal or external contradictions.

In low-verbal subjects, the tendency to rely only on lexical and syntactic understanding was even more extreme, with very few of the contradictions in the texts noted. Because these low-verbal subjects tend also to be poor readers, this focus on superficial aspects of the text could result from a lack of resources for a semantic analysis of the text. Consistent with this idea, specifically instructing subjects on the types of problems that might occur greatly improved their detection of these problems (Baker, 1985). This supports the view that people tend to focus attention at the lexical level and evaluate syntactic form rather than trying to build new structures that would be shared with previous parts of the passage or reactivate earlier portions to build deeper connections.

What does the Featural Familiarity Hypothesis have to say about the failure to detect inconsistencies? When a passage is read, the corresponding lexical ele-

---

[1]McKoon and Ratcliff (1992) recently detailed a similar account of text processing, which they call the *Minimalist theory*. They claimed that readers typically only monitor texts for local coherence. Although we believe this minimalist process occurs frequently, we do not think it is the only method used by subjects in processing texts, particularly those for which their knowledge and interest are high.

ments in memory become active. Only when the lexical items are unfamiliar is there a flag to the reader that he or she may not understand what is being said. That is, if the lexical elements in the passage match to fairly strong concepts in memory, then superficial reading does not flag a failure to comprehend. This explains why people are better calibrated across domains—they easily recognize when the terms are novel, and realize that they know nothing about it. In domains that do not seem very novel, however, readers are prone to the illusion that the passage will be well remembered because they confuse the current activation of the propositions with their long-term strength. This confusion, or misattribution, of recent activation with resting levels of activation or strength is a phenomenon that is seen in other paradigms that are also discussed in this chapter in the section on "Unconscious Uses of Memory."

In sum, we believe that comprehension monitoring is not calibrated because local activation gives a spurious sense of knowing that is inappropriate for predicting test performance: people may well not remember the facts; furthermore, fact availability, per se, may not be germane to the types of comprehension questions that are asked of the reader. Consistent with this position, people are much more calibrated at judging the correctness of answers to questions already asked than they are in the typical comprehension monitoring task (e.g., Beckett et al., 1989; Beckett & Kestner, 1988; Glenberg & Epstein, 1985, 1987; Maki, 1987). In fact, ability to predict performance on questions already answered (i.e., "How did I do?") is unrelated to predictive judgments of overall performance on an exam (i.e., "How will I do?") (Beckett et al., 1989; Maki, 1987).

THE MOSES ILLUSION

The Moses illusion has strong similarities to the failure to detect contradictions in passages. The Moses illusion is so named because people fail to notice that some elements of a question do not really belong, such as the name "Moses" in the question, "How many animals of each kind did Moses take on the Ark?" Even when warned that distortions might be present in questions to be answered, people still frequently fail to notice the distorted elements. The degree of semantic similarity between the normal term and distorted target can influence the detection of the distortion. The more closely related the distorted target was to the word it replaced, the more frequently the illusion occurred (Erickson & Mattson, 1981). Studying, or even memorizing the correct version of the queried facts before attempting to answer the questions does not aid in this detection (Reder & Cleeremans, 1990; Reder & Kusbit, 1991). Word reading times for the distorted term were not shorter (in fact, they were somewhat longer) when subjects failed to notice the distortion (Reder & Kusbit, 1991).

Increasing the salience of the inconsistent portion of a statement reduces the effect of the illusion. Bredart and Modolo (1988) created inconsistent statements with either consistent or inconsistent portions of the statements as the focus of the sentence. They used cleft sentences such as, "It was Moses who brought two animals of each kind into the ark," and, "It was two animals of each kind that Moses brought into the Ark." When the inconsistent portion of the statement was in focus, subjects noticed the discrepancy much more than when the consistent portion was in the focus. Similarly, when Baker and Wagner (1987) embedded the discrepant word in a subordinate clause, thus syntactically marking it as given information, subjects were much less likely to notice the discrepancy than when it was syntactically marked as new. These results are consistent with the findings of Hornby (1974) that people tend not to process given information as deeply as new information.

The Moses illusion can be taken as support for the Featural Familiarity Hypothesis and reinforces several of the assumptions described earlier. We assume that when a person is asked a question, processes (e.g., productions) operate to find the queried element. The speed with which the queried element can be located and given as an answer depends on the activation level of the proposition that contains the queried element. At the same time that a person is trying to answer the question, a second process is trying to monitor for distortions. If the answer is easily available, it is more difficult for a person to note the distortion and answer "can't say" before generating the otherwise correct answer. Consistent with this view, people find it significantly more difficult to detect distorted sentences (i.e., make more errors of giving the undistorted answer) when the questions contain many terms related to the knowledge structure than when there are just a few (Reder & Kusbit, 1991). In other words, the more terms in the question that are consistent with the script or knowledge structure associated with taking animals on the Ark, the harder it is to notice that Moses is the wrong term.

An important aspect of the structure of the memory representation is the number of features shared by the correct and distorted term that are also strongly associated to the script in question. For example, Moses and Noah share semantic features as biblical characters; these are the central features that relate Noah to the Ark story. Surprisingly, even the name "Jesus" can produce the illusion. In an informal survey (of the few people the authors could find that did not know of the Moses research) of the form, "I've got a quick Bible question for you: How many animals of each kind did Jesus take on the Ark?" people often failed to detect the distortion. However, we suspect that people more easily recognize the distortion once brought to their attention. We had expected a better detection rate because the concept "Jesus" has so much baseline strength and so many connections to other concepts. Apparently, the amount of strength and number of associates of the distorted element does not matter. The important factor in this illusion is that the distorted element share semantic features with the proposition and the term it is replacing.[2]

---

[2]We have sometimes thought that one would not be fooled by a substitution of a different name if one of the names is known very well; however, we note that people often substitute other family members' names when trying to retrieve one for a sentence, suggesting that lots of knowledge of an individual or concept does not make one immune to these types of errors.

Given that people fall for the illusion even when a highly familiar name such as Jesus is used as the distorted term suggests that perhaps all that matters is the amount of activation arriving at the correct memory structure. However, this cannot be the complete story, because certain types of distorted terms are very easy to detect regardless of the number of terms that activate the correct structure. For example, subjects easily recognize that "Nixon" does not belong in the Ark sentence (Erickson & Mattson, 1981). We doubt that the number of terms priming the Ark story would make much difference in how easily Nixon is detected as a distorted term. So, if the terms are totally unrelated with respect to the script that is queried, as in the case of Noah versus Nixon, the discrepancy will be noticed.

There are two key factors in understanding the Moses Illusion. The first is the apparent discrepancy between the target term and the distorted element, and the second is the activation level of the answer. This task can be viewed as one where subjects are asked to answer the question, and at the same time monitor for distortions in the question. The ease of detecting the distortion depends not only on the semantic similarity between the distorted term and the original, but also on the amount of attention that is directed at the distorted element. Whether a distortion is detected is partially a function of the speed with which the answer becomes available, and partially a function of how quickly the distorted element can be noticed. Reder (1992) had subjects study the relevant facts before answering the questions, and varied whether the answer was capitalized (e.g., "Noah took TWO animals of each kind on the ark."), the target term was capitalized (e.g., "NOAH took two animals of each kind on the ark."), or neither term was capitalized. She found that subjects were significantly less likely to notice the distortion if the answer had been capitalized during study. Previously capitalizing the target word made subjects more sensitive to the distortion, but this effect was smaller and not reliable.

A second factor that must be considered is the instructions given to the subjects. The task instructions to monitor for distortions gives more attention or processing resources to this detection process, but not enough to make the detection easy. Placing the distorted target in the focus of the statement ensures more attention is focused on it, whereas placing it in the given portion of the sentences deflects attention from it (Hornby, 1974). Only the terms in the focus of attention are compared to the memory structure. Normally the queried element is the focus of attention and the match process deflects attention from the distorted term.

We have not yet explained why a term that bears some semantic similarity might well go undetected as a distortion, but another term with no semantic similarity is almost always detected as a distortion regardless of whether or not it is in focus. Our explanation involves the notion that activation spreads *from* the distorted element *only when it is in focus*. Otherwise, activation spreads from the knowledge structure *to* the distorted element through any available connecting path. In other words, activation will spread from propositional representation of the theme of the sentence (e.g., the Ark script) to the distorted element (e.g., Moses, or Jesus, if that name is used), finding a connection through shared semantic features (e.g., Bible stories). Only when the distorted term (e.g., Moses) is in focus will activation spread from that term to its own scripts and primary associates (e.g., the Ten Commandments story becomes active), causing the mismatch to be noted. The reason people always detect unrelated terms (e.g., Nixon) as distorted is that there is no semantic similarity and therefore no connecting path between the theme of the sentence and this distorted term (e.g., between the Ark script and Nixon). Consistent with this hypothesis, when subjects studied paired associates consisting of the unrelated term and a term in the sentence (e.g., "Nixon-animals"), they often failed to detect the distorted term in the sentences (van Oostendorp & Kok, 1990).

All the research on the Moses illusion makes it clear that people can find distortions, but find this difficult if the distorted element is semantically related to the theme of the sentence. The odds of noticing the distortion are reduced by increasing the number of elements that need some kind of match (lowering the odds that the distorted element will be in focus). Why should our cognitive system be so tolerant of distortions and find it so difficult to do careful matches to memory? We believe that this partial match process enables useful communication and comprehension. Very few things that we see or hear will perfectly match the representation that we already have stored in memory. In order to answer questions, we need to be able to use an *acceptable* match. In order to understand a new situation and map it onto something we have already seen or done, we must accept slight variations. Every day, at many levels, we accept slight distortions without noticing them. We notice some and ignore them, but many we do not even realize occur. These variations also occur in our speech production; many of these variations are not errors. Our selection of lexical entries may vary from moment to moment, reflecting the wide range of options and flexibility in our means of expression. We occasionally generate slips of speech in which we substitute a semantically related element. A rigid comprehension system would have a difficult time indeed.

VALIDITY INFLATION

Validity inflation, like feeling of knowing, is a phenomenon where the familiarity of words in a statement affects a reader's judgment about that statement. For both of these phenomena, prior exposure to words that appear in the to-be-judged statement increases the illusion of relevant knowledge concerning that statement. When judging validity, subjects rate a repeated statement as more valid than a statement that has not been previously exposed (in some surreptitious task or even in the same rating task) (e.g., Hasher et al., 1977). Experiments in this paradigm have varied the delay between first exposure to a statement and its validity rating—some have been minutes, some weeks (e.g., Bacon, 1979; Schwartz, 1982). The subjects may have seen the whole sentence (e.g., Hasher et al., 1977), the topic of the sentence (Begg et al., 1985), or even just a word or two from the sentence (Arkes, Nash, & Joyner, 1989). Both college students and older adults have been tested, in both psychology labs and in their own homes (e.g., Gigerenzer, 1984; Hasher et al., 1977). Regardless of the details of the procedure, the pre-exposed sentences are consistently rated more valid than new sentences. Note that this increase in validity, although robust, is always quite small.

These data are consistent with and support the Featural Familiarity Hypothesis. That the effects occur at long delays as well as short delays suggests that the exposure is increasing long-term strength of the relevant terms, and is not just a transient priming effect. This increased strength, or higher resting activation level, means that the concepts are more easily activated to a high level, giving the illusion that (a) the statement seems very familiar (e.g., "I must have learned/heard this before") and (b) there must be a lot of knowledge stored in memory concerning the topic under discussion. In other words, propositions with perceived strength are assumed to be stored in memory, and propositions that are stored in memory are assumed to be true. Without carefully inspecting stored knowledge, this feeling of familiarity causes a person's first guess to be that he or she knows something about the seemingly familiar topic, making it seem likely to be true.

Of course, in an experiment that is designed to give irrelevant familiarity to statements that will later be judged for plausibility, such heuristics are not adaptive. On the other hand, in most everyday situations, things that we have heard many times are much more likely to be true. Typically, learning occurs through repetition, from one's own name, to the multiplication tables, to the fact that leaves turn color in autumn. Thus, the repetition-truth link is an important one. We claim, therefore, that such heuristics are adaptive, just as are the feeling of knowing heuristics. We are not claiming that this is the only method ever used to judge the truth of an assertion, just that it is a quick and simple heuristic that is employed frequently.

Sadly, it is not just in psychological experiments that there exist attempts to subvert the usefulness of this heuristic. Advertisers take advantage of this phenomenon and advertise frequently. A metro corridor in Paris may have 20 or 30 copies of the same poster—you cannot miss it and are likely to remember and be influenced by it. Of course, this is also one reason why propaganda can be so effective. A Chinese colleague informed us of a pattern that frequently occurred in Communist China: a billboard would appear with a seemingly outrageous message; after some time, the message no longer seemed so strange; finally, people accepted it as truth.

In order to deal with these frequent attempts to subvert the usefulness of a heuristic, people often develop specific strategies for situations that are likely to be suspect. When we are aware of familiarity manipulations that will give us spurious feelings of familiarity, we tend to shift our criterion for accepting the statements (e.g., Jacoby & Whitehouse, 1989; Reder, 1987). People also develop specific strategies to block the effects of familiarity in suspect situations. For example, whenever the second author of this chapter finds herself listening to an advertisement that asserts something like, "This just might be the best car on the market today," she is motivated to analyze the structure and also rehearse to herself, "This just might not be the best car on the market—what kind of claim is that?"

Clearly, people need to be able to counter these automatic effects of familiarity on validity judgments, to use other strategies in questionable situations. We tested whether requiring subjects to provide a reason for believing a statement, not just judging how valid it seems, might not discourage reliance on familiarity. As in most validity inflation experiments, subjects were asked to judge the truth of trivia statements, and we varied how often these statements were rated. Half of the subjects were required to give reasons for judging the sentence as they did for the final rating, whereas the others followed the standard paradigm. Those subjects who were required to justify their ratings did not show the usual increase in the perceived validity of the repeated statements. People can avoid being fooled by simple repetition, but this requires much more effortful processing than usual.

ANALOGICAL REASONING

When trying to solve a problem, people will often draw on previous problem solving experience, using an old problem to help solve the current one. What factors govern which problems come to mind as candidates for analogy during a problem solving attempt? We claim this analogical reminding process is governed by the same sloppy cognition that characterizes the other areas of cognition that have been discussed. That is, a problem will be retrieved for use through a partial match process, based on the similarities between the current problem and the previous problem.

When confronted with a problem, a person may be reminded of another problem because certain features of the current problem match features of the previously solved problem. Ross' (1987, 1989a) work on analogical reminding has shown that students are not very good at retrieving appropriate problems that could be used to help solve novel problems. His beginning students attempting to solve basic probability problems were often reminded of, and attempted to use, problems with surface similarities to the test problems. For example, a student trying to solve an algebra problem about boats going upstream may recall another problem about boats. However, unless the underlying structure, or principles, of the two problems are the same, the recalled problem will not be useful in finding a solution. To continue this example, the recalled boat problem may be about boats carrying passengers for pay, and a problem about airplanes flying against head winds would actually be more useful in guiding the solution of the current boat problem. As one would expect, these attempts to use problems with superficial similarities often resulted in incorrect problem solutions. Even when subjects are given problems with their solutions and told to use them as examples for solving new problems, their success at this task depends on the degree of similarity between the sample problem and the test problem (Reed, Dempster, & Ettinger, 1985).

Faries and Reiser (1988) further found that after several lessons, beginning computer programmers retrieved a mixture of superficially similar and structurally similar problems for use as analogies. These latter problems were more useful to the students in terms of number of correct solutions, than the former. Why do beginners rely so much on the surface similarities of problems? And what causes the shift toward use of more structurally similar problems apparent in the Faries and Reiser study? Evidence from several domains indicates that experts in a domain represent problems differently than novices; the experts notice structural features of the problems more readily than novices (Chi, Feltovich, & Glaser, 1981; Schoenfeld & Hermann, 1982). For instance, Chi, Feltovich, and Glaser (1981) compared physics experts and novices in a task where they were asked to sort a set of physics problems. The novices sorted the problems based on their superficial features, whereas the experts sorted them by the underlying principles. Consequently, the more experienced problem solvers were able to access structurally similar problems in the above experiments on analogical reasoning, whereas the novices had trouble seeing past the surface features.

The Featural Familiarity Hypothesis posits that reminding occurs because memory retrieval is based on partial matching to the memory probe. Thus, a superficially similar problem will be retrieved if the representation of the problem that is used to probe memory is based on surface features of the problem. A problem that matches in underlying structure, and can be successfully used in solving the current problem, will not be recalled unless the representation of the problem to be solved includes these structural elements. More experienced solvers will focus their attention on the underlying structural representation and the match will go from the underlying representation to a corresponding one in memory. Novices will focus on superficial features, and the corresponding superficial features will be activated in memory, causing a superficially related problem to be retrieved.

Others have proposed models of analogical reasoning similar to our current account. For example, Reed (1987) proposed that an analogy consists of a mapping of the nodes and relations between the two problems. This mapping may occur at any or all of the several levels of representation of the problem (e.g., at the level of the principle involved in the problems, or the frame level of the problems, or the quantity level). The success of the mapping is influenced by the isomorphic structure of the problem, and the base specificity and transparency of the relationship between the two problems. By base specificity, he means the degree to which the student understands the example problem, whereas transparency refers to how well the underlying structure of the problems can be seen to correspond. Ross (1989b) also proposed a general framework for remindings. The four components of his model are noticing an earlier problem, reconstruction of that problem and its solution, analogy from that problem and solution to the current problem, and generalization from the analogical process. His conception of noticing is much like our own: memory is probed, and what is retrieved depends on the match between this probe and the contents of memory. He also points out the tendency of novices to include only superficial aspects of the problems in their memory probes.

The task demands in analogical reasoning also influence the focus of attention, and thus, the way the problem representation is matched to memory. For example, when the task is to use a problem as an analogy, or to generate a conclusion based on an analogy, a match on surface features of the problem is less prevalent. For instance, Clement and Gentner (1991) asked subjects to make an analogy to an earlier text in order to draw conclusions from the current text. They found that the conclusions produced by subjects were based on the structure of the problems more often than on surface similarities. The task demands focused attention on the analogy itself, rather than on the use of the analogy, so that a more careful matching process is used instead of the usual sloppy match process. The sloppy match process is used primarily when the task demands direct the focus toward other portions of the problem, and not directly on those parts important for recall or the generation of an analogy.

In summary, problems are retrieved for use as analogies based on a partial match of salient features of the problem to memory. Experts and novices in a domain differ on which features are salient, with novices paying more attention to the surface features. In addition, task demands influence the focus of attention, and thus which portion of a problem is matched to memory structures. This retrieval of problems for analogical use based on superficial features is certainly not an adaptive method of problem solving. However, the data indicate that this is merely a passing phase, an artifact of learning which features of problems in a given domain are important for use in problem solving.

UNCONSCIOUS USES OF MEMORY

Jacoby (e.g., Jacoby, 1988; Jacoby & Kelley, 1987, 1992; Jacoby, Kelley, & Dywan, 1989) proposed that the unconscious use of memory affects behavior in surprising ways. If a subjective feeling of remembering does not occur, the influence of memory may be misattributed to other processes. Jacoby and his colleagues found examples of this in situations ranging from perceptual recognition (e.g., Jacoby & Dallas, 1981) to fame judgments (e.g., Jacoby, Kelley, Brown, & Jasechko, 1989; Jacoby, Woloshyn, & Kelley, 1989). The false fame effect involves asking subjects to read a list of nonfamous names. The next day, the subjects must judge the fame of a new list of names, which includes some of the previously seen nonfamous names, as well as new nonfamous names, and (new) famous names. The previously seen nonfamous names are more likely to be considered famous than the new nonfamous names. A related effect shows that subjects are misled when attempting to discriminate previously studied words from new words when a new word is flashed tachistoscopically just prior to the old/new judgment. This subliminal perception of the new word increases the chances of calling it old (Jacoby & Whitehouse, 1989). If subjects are aware of this manipulation and of the attempts to subvert their judgments, they will try to adjust their threshold to counteract the manipulation.

According to Jacoby and his colleagues, these effects are due to the familiarity of the name or word being misattributed, in one case to fame, and in the other to prior study in the experiment. Unless people consciously recollect the source of the feeling of familiarity, they will adopt the currently most plausible explanation (fame or prior exposure in the experiment). The Featural Familiarity Hypothesis is also supported by these findings. In our view, the false fame attributions occur because the name (e.g., Sebastian Weisdorf or Pearl Miller) has been activated recently. The subject detects the strength or activation of the name, and attributes this to an old, moderately strong association rather than a recent exposure. Even when the first and last names are recombined (e.g., Pearl Weisdorf and Sebastian Miller), subjects will indicate these novel names are famous (Squire & McKee, 1992). This occurs because the memory match process matches on clusters of features, and not necessarily the relation of the features to each other. Likewise, in the recognition task, the prior tachistoscopic flash elevates the activation of the word, but the subject is unaware of why it is elevated (is unaware of the flash) and therefore assumes that the familiarity must be because of a recent presentation of the word.

Jacoby has avoided mechanistic explanations involving activation or priming, preferring instead the explanatory construct *perceptual fluency*. He avoided priming types of explanations because it is known that decay of activation is rapid. In other words, he reasonably argued that priming can not account for his results, as his effects occur over long periods. We find Jacoby's explanation compatible with ours and believe that our account is satisfactory in that it can handle relatively long-term effects. Although activation decays rapidly, exposure gives a boost to the strength of the concept. Of course, low frequency words get more of a boost from a single presentation than would a high frequency word, in terms of affecting the resting level of activation. When the concept is reactivated at the next presentation, it reaches a higher level of activation and is processed faster and, in Jacoby's terms, seems more perceptually fluent. In our terms, the higher level of activation is attributed to strength or recent activation, depending on what seems most plausible in the current context.

The unconscious use of memory can also influence perceptual judgments (Jacoby, Allan, Collins, & Larwill, 1988; Jacoby & Dallas, 1981). In one experiment, subjects judged the loudness of background noise while listening to sentences read aloud. Half of the sentences that were read had been previously studied. Equivalent background noise was rated as quieter when the sentence being read aloud had been previously studied (Jacoby et al., 1988). A similar effect occurs when subjects identify words flashed tachistoscopically. If a word has been previously studied, it can be identified after a shorter exposure than that required for a new word (Jacoby & Dallas, 1981).

The Role of Focus in These Phenomena

In our previous discussions on the illusion of comprehension, feeling of knowing, and the Moses illusion, we noted that the focus of attention in a task influences which parts of the memory representation (if any) are carefully inspected.

The phenomena uncovered by Jacoby and his colleagues are sensitive to focus manipulations in a similar way. The phrase *unconscious use* of memory implies lack of attention. Jacoby means by this that subjects do not correctly attribute the source of the current high level of activation. When it is easier to hear a sentence in white noise, they do not realize it is because they have heard the sentence before—they assume that it was louder or the background noise was quieter. When subjects are not conscious of a manipulation, when the strength of the terms is not overly strong to make the connections to the source link salient (e.g., subjects do not remember where they heard the name Pearl Miller), the illusion of fame occurs; however, if they think about why the term seems familiar and make a correct attribution, there is no effect of the manipulation.

Jacoby (Jacoby, Woloshyn, & Kelley, 1989) was able to manipulate the probability of retaining source information by sometimes requiring subjects to do two tasks simultaneously. For instance, when subjects are distracted from the task of rating the fame of a list of names, by simultaneously performing another task, they are more likely to false alarm to the previously presented nonfamous names. The split of attention in this task prevents subjects from carefully examining their memories, and so they instead rely on quick estimates of the familiarity, or baseline strength, of the name. Divided attention during initial study can also affect these false impressions, in that subjects are less likely to lay down a trace of the context of presentation in the dual task situation. In our terms, the activation/strengthening occurs automatically, whether there is a secondary task or not.

Can these findings of Jacoby be considered an example of a useful adaptation of the cognitive system? We think so. As with the phenomena discussed earlier in this chapter, these findings result from heuristics used by the cognitive system to free resources for other uses. For example, in Jacoby's false fame effect, subjects are more likely to call the previously studied names famous if they are in a divided attention task (Jacoby, Woloshyn, & Kelley, 1989). In order to free the resources needed for the second task, familiarity is used as a rough measure of the fame of the name. In everyday situations when people believe it is very important not to false alarm (make false fame judgments), they will not just rely on familiarity, but also make sure that an appropriate referent for the individual can be retrieved from memory.

CONCLUSIONS

In this chapter, we have tried to illustrate that several disparate phenomena are all manifestations of some basic mechanisms that operate on memory. Our general thesis is that many of our cognitive operations are driven by familiarity based heuristics rather than careful matching operations. We have described several phenomena that use these heuristics, and have argued for the adaptiveness of these techniques in each case. We believe that the use of these heuristics extends far beyond the few instances described earlier.

In other words, we contend that everyday cognitive processing *must* be based on simple heuristics such as matching sets of features rather than exact matches, as very few tasks require exact matches. Very little that we see from one day to the next remains in the exact same shape and form as it was the last time we saw it. People wear different clothes from day to day, wear their hair in different ways, sport different facial expressions, and so on. Even concrete sculptures are seen in different light and from different perspectives. Verbal information is even less likely to be presented in the exact form in which it was stored, yet we must connect it with our stored knowledge. It only makes sense that people do sloppy, partial matches as the normal course of matching to memory.

Consistent with this view, Hintzman, Curran, and Oppy (1992) found that even with massive exposure to words, people were often unable to discriminate the singular from the plural form. Unless they had initially encoded the state of plurality as an important feature, continual exposure to the word did not improve their ability to discriminate the singular from the plural. A similar phenomenon was noted by Nickerson and Adams (1979) in that people are extremely poor at identifying the correct rendition of the common penny among foils. We see the penny every day, but our familiarity with the coin does not enable us to match features in a specific relationship. We match on familiarity of clusters of features and thus are unable to detect foils that have large numbers of the same chunks of features in slightly different configurations. Only if some of the features seem to violate our general familiarity with the stimulus do we reject that instance of it. Bransford and Franks (1971) reported another example of recognition based on familiarity with the parts and not on the specific relationships between the parts. Their subjects rated statements as old, and had higher confidence in these ratings, when the foil contained more propositional units that had been seen earlier. That is, subjects never heard a sentence containing all the propositional phrases; nonetheless, a new sentence that contained many familiar elements seemed especially familiar.

We have called the set of heuristics used by the cognitive system the Featural Familiarity Hypothesis because they operate at the level of shared features that give a sense of familiarity to an input that is matched to memory. The term *hypothesis* has two meanings here: Our speculations are essentially an hypothesis about how memory and our cognitive processes work; we also use the term *hypothesis* because our thesis about cognitive operations is that people continually make hypotheses about what they do and do not know, what they do and do not understand, based on the similarity of the input to what is already stored in memory.

ACKNOWLEDGMENTS

The work reported here was sponsored by Grant BNS-8908030 from the National Science Foundation to Lynne M. Reder, and by a National Science Foundation Graduate Research Fellowship to Eleen N. Kamas. We thank J. Anderson, K. Kotovsky, and A. Miner for commenting on earlier drafts. Order of authorship is arbitrary.

REFERENCES

Albrecht, J. E., & O'Brien, E. J. (1993). Updating a mental model: Maintaining both local and global coherence. *Journal of Experimental Psychology: Learning, Memory, and Cognition, 19,* 1061–1070.

Anderson, J. R. (1983). *The architecture of cognition.* Cambridge, MA: Harvard University Press.

Anderson, J. R. (1993). *Rules of the mind.* Hillsdale, NJ: Lawrence Erlbaum Associates.

Arkes, H. R., Hackett, C., & Boehm, L. (1989). The generality of the relation between familiarity and judged validity. *Journal of Behavioral Decision Making, 2,* 81–94.

Arkes, H. R., Nash, J. G., & Joyner, C. A. (1989). *Solving a word puzzle makes subsequent statements containing the word seem more valid.* Paper presented at the 30th Annual Meeting of the Psychonomics Society, Atlanta, GA.

Bacon, F. T. (1979). Credibility of repeated statements: Memory for trivia. *Journal of Experimental Psychology: Human Learning and Memory, 5,* 241–252.

Baker, L. (1985). Differences in the standards used by college students to evaluate their comprehension of expository prose. *Reading Research Quarterly, 20,* 297–313.

Baker, L., & Wagner, J. L. (1987). Evaluating information for truthfulness: The effects of logical subordination. *Memory & Cognition, 15,* 247–255.

Beckett, P. A., & Kestner, J. (1988). *Prediction and judgment of exam performance by college students.* Paper presented at the meetings of the Midwestern Psychological Association, Chicago.

Beckett, P. A., Kestner, J., & White, G. (1989). *Metacognitive abilities in predicting exam performance: Judging how much, what, and when you know.* Paper presented at the meetings of the Midwestern Psychological Association, Chicago.

Begg, I., Armour, V., & Kerr, T. (1985). On believing what we remember. *Canadian Journal of Behavioral Science, 17,* 199–214.

Blake, M. (1973). Prediction of recognition when recall fails: Exploring the feeling-of-knowing phenomenon. *Journal of Verbal Learning and Verbal Behavior, 12,* 311–319.

Bransford, J. D., & Franks, J.J. (1971) The abstraction of linguistic ideas. *Cognitive Psychology, 2,* 331–380.

Bredart, S., & Modolo, K. (1988). Moses strikes again: Focalization effect on a semantic illusion. *Acta Psychologica, 67,* 135–144.

Chi, M. T. H., Feltovich, P. J., & Glaser, R. (1981). Categorization and representation of physics problems by experts and novices. *Cognitive Science, 5,* 121–152.

Clement, C. A., & Gentner, D. (1991). Systematicity as a selection constraint in analogical mapping. *Cognitive Science, 15,* 89–132.

Connor, L. T., Balota, D. A., & Neely, J. H. (1992). On the relation between feeling of knowing and lexical decision: Persistent subthreshold activation or topic familiarity? *Journal of Experimental Psychology: Learning, Memory, and Cognition, 18,* 544–554.

Costermans, J., Lories, G., & Ansay, C. (1992). Confidence level and feeling of knowing in question answering: The weight of inferential processes. *Journal of Experimental Psychology: Learning, Memory, and Cognition, 18,* 142–150.

Epstein, W., Glenberg, A. M., & Bradley, M. M. (1984). Coactivation and comprehension: Contribution of text variables to the illusion of knowing. *Memory & Cognition, 12,* 355–360.

Erickson, T. D., & Mattson, M. E. (1981). From words to meaning: A semantic illusion. *Journal of Verbal Learning and Verbal Behavior, 20,* 540–551.

Faries, J. M., & Reiser, B. J. (June 1988). *Access and use of previous solutions in a problem solving situation* (CSL Report No. 29). Princeton, NJ: Princeton University, Cognitive Science Laboratory.

Gentner, G. (1983). Structure-mapping: A theoretical framework for analogy. *Cognitive Science, 7,* 155–170.

Gigerenzer, G. (1984). External validity of laboratory experiments: The frequency-validity relationship. *American Journal of Psychology, 97,* 185–195.

Glenberg, A. M., & Epstein, W. (1985). Calibration of comprehension. *Journal of Experimental Psychology: Learning, Memory, and Cognition, 11,* 702–718.

Glenberg, A. M., & Epstein, W. (1987). Inexpert calibration of comprehension. *Memory and Cognition, 15,* 84–93.

Glenberg, A. M., Sanocki, T., Epstein, W., & Morris, C. (1987). Enhancing calibration of comprehension. *Journal of Experimental Psychology: General, 116,* 119–136.

Glenberg, A. M., Wilkinson, A. C., & Epstein, W. (1982). The illusion of knowing: Failure in the self-assessment of comprehension. *Memory and Cognition, 10,* 597–602.

Hart, J. T. (1965). Memory and the feeling of knowing experience. *Journal of Educational Psychology, 56,* 208–216.

Hasher, L., Goldstein, D., & Toppino, T. (1977). Frequency and the conference of referential validity. *Journal of Verbal Learning and Verbal Behavior, 16,* 107–112.

Hintzman, D. L., Curran, T., & Oppy, B. (1992). Effects of similarity and repetition on memory: Registration without learning? *Journal of Experimental Psychology: Learning, Memory and Cognition, 18,* 667–680.

Hornby, P. A. (1974). Surface structure and presupposition. *Journal of Verbal Learning and Verbal Behavior, 13,* 530–538.

Jacoby, L. L. (1988). Memory observed and memory unobserved. In U. Neisser & E. Winograd

(Eds.), *Remembering reconsidered: Ecological and traditional approaches to the study of memory.* Cambridge, MA: Cambridge University Press.

Jacoby, L. L., Allan, L. G., Collins, J. C., & Larwill, L. K. (1988). Memory influences subjective experience: Noise judgments. *Journal of Experimental Psychology: Learning, Memory, and Cognition, 14,* 240–247.

Jacoby, L. L., & Dallas, M. (1981). On the relationship between autobiographical memory and perceptual learning. *Journal of Experimental Psychology: General, 110,* 306–340.

Jacoby, L. L., & Hollingshead, A. (1990). Reading student essays may be hazardous to your spelling: Effects of reading incorrectly and correctly spelled words. *Canadian Journal of Psychology, 44,* 345–358.

Jacoby, L. L., & Kelley, C. M. (1987). Unconscious influences of memory for a prior event. *Personality and Social Psychology Bulletin, 13,* 314–336.

Jacoby, L. L., & Kelley, C. M. (1992). A process-dissociation framework for investigating unconscious influences: Freudian slips, projective tests, subliminal perception, and signal detection theory. *Current Directions in Psychological Science, 1,* 174–179.

Jacoby, L. L., Kelley, C., Brown, J., & Jasechko, J. (1989). Becoming famous overnight: Limits on the ability to avoid unconscious influences of the past. *Journal of Personality and Social Psychology, 56,* 326–338.

Jacoby, L. L., Kelley, C. M., & Dywan, J. (1989). Memory attributions. In H. Roediger & F. Craik (Eds.) *Varieties of Memory and Consciousness: Essays in Honor of Endel Tulving* (pp. 391–422). Hillsdale, NJ: Lawrence Erlbaum Associates.

Jacoby, L. L., & Whitehouse, K. (1989). An illusion of memory: False recognition influenced by unconscious perception. *Journal of Experimental Psychology: General, 118,* 126–135.

Jacoby, L. L., Woloshyn, V., & Kelley, C. (1989). Becoming famous without being recognized: Unconscious influences of memory produced by dividing attention. *Journal of Experimental Psychology: General, 118,* 115–125.

Kintsch, W. (1988). The role of knowledge in discourse comprehension: A construction-integration model. *Psychological Review, 95,* 163–182.

Maki, R. H. (1987, May). *Metacomprehension of text: Memory predictions and confidence judgments.* Paper presented at the meeting of the Midwestern Psychological Association, Chicago.

Maki, R. H., & Berry, S. L. (1984). Metacomprehension of text material. *Journal of Experimental Psychology: Learning, Memory, and Cognition, 10,* 663–679.

Maki, R. H., & Serra, M. (1992). The basis of test predictions for text material. *Journal of Experimental Psychology: Learning, Memory, and Cognition, 18,* 116–126.

McKoon, G., & Ratcliff, R. (1992). Inference during reading. *Psychological Review, 99,* 440–466.

Nelson, T. O., Gerler, D., & Narens, L. (1984). Accuracy of feeling-of-knowing judgments for predicting perceptual identification and relearning. *Journal of Experimental Psychology: General, 113,* 282–300.

Nelson, T. O., & Narens, L. (1990). Metamemory: A theoretical framework and new findings. *The Psychology of Learning and Motivation, 26,* 125–173.

Nickerson, R. S., & Adams, M. J. (1979). Long-term memory for a common object. *Cognitive Psychology, 11,* 287–307.

Otero, J., & Kintsch, W. (1992). Failures to detect contradictions in a text: What readers believe versus what they read. *Psychological Science, 3,* 229–235.

Pressley, M., & Ghatala, E. S. (1988). Delusions about performance on multiple-choice comprehension tests. *Reading Research Quarterly, 23,* 454–464.

Reder, L. M. (1987). Strategy selection in question answering. *Cognitive Psychology, 19,* 90–138.

Reder, L. M. (1988). Strategic control of retrieval strategies. *The Psychology of Learning and Motivation, 22,* 227–259.

Reder, L. M. (1992, July). *Reading what isn't there: Further explorations of the Moses Illusion.*

Paper presented at the Belgium International Congress, Thematic Session on Inferential Processes, Brussels.

Reder, L. M., & Cleeremans, A. (1990). The role of partial matches in comprehension: The Moses illusion revisited. In A. Graesser & G. Bower (Eds.), *The Psychology of Learning and Motivation* (Vol. 25, pp. 233–258). New York, Academic Press.

Reder, L. M. & Kusbit, G. W. (1991). Locus of the Moses Illusion: Imperfect encoding, retrieval, or match? *Journal of Memory and Language, 30,* 385–406.

Reder, L. M., & Ritter, F. E. (1988, November). *Feeling of knowing and strategy selection for solving arithmetic problems.* Paper presented at the 29th annual meeting of the Psychonomics Society, Chicago.

Reder, L. M., & Ritter, F. E. (1992). What determines initial feeling of knowing? Familiarity with question terms, not with the answer. *Journal of Experimental Psychology: Learning, Memory and Cognition, 18,* 435–451.

Reed, S. K. (1987). A structure-mapping model for word problems. *Journal of Experimental Psychology: Learning, Memory, and Cognition, 13,* 124–139.

Reed, S. K., Dempster, A., & Ettinger, M. (1985). Usefulness of analogous solutions for solving algebra word problems. *Journal of Experimental Psychology: Learning, Memory, and Cognition, 11,* 106–125.

Ross, B. H. (1987). This is like that: The use of earlier problems and the separation of similarity effects. *Journal of Experimental Psychology: Learning, Memory, and Cognition, 13,* 629–639.

Ross, B. H. (1989a). Distinguishing types of superficial similarities: Different effects on the access and use of earlier problems. *Journal of Experimental Psychology: Learning, Memory, and Cognition, 15,* 456–468.

Ross, B. H. (1989b). Remindings in learning and instruction. In S. Vosniadou & A. Ortony (Eds.), *Similarity and analogical reasoning* (pp. 438–469). New York: Cambridge University Press.

Schoenfeld, A. H., & Hermann, D. J. (1982). Problem perception and knowledge structure in expert and novice mathematical problem solvers. *Journal of Experimental Psychology: Learning, Memory, and Cognition, 8,* 484–494.

Schwartz, B. L., & Metcalfe, J. (1992). Cue familiarity but not target retrievability enhances feeling-of-knowing judgments. *Journal of Experimental Psychology: Learning, Memory and Cognition, 18,* 1074–1083.

Schwartz, M. (1982). Repetition and rated truth value of statements. *American Journal of Psychology, 95,* 393–407.

Squire, L. R., & McKee, R. (1992). Influence of prior events on cognitive judgments in amnesia. *Journal of Experimental Psychology: Learning, Memory and Cognition, 18,* 106–115.

Van Oostendorp, H., & Kok, I. (1990). Failing to notice errors in sentences. *Language and Cognitive Processes, 5,* 105–113.

Yaniv, I., & Meyer, D. E. (1987). Activation and metacognition of inaccessible stored information: Potential bases for incubation effects in problem solving. *Journal of Experimental Psychology: Learning, Memory, and Cognition, 13,* 187–205.

11

The Role of Co-Occurrence, Coreference, and Causality in the Coherence of Conjoined Sentences

Charles R. Fletcher
Susan T. Chrysler
Paul van den Broek
Jennifer A. Deaton
Charles P. Bloom
University of Minnesota

Virtually all models of discourse understanding share the assumption that successful comprehension results in a mental representation that includes both the events described in a text and the relationships among those events. Unfortunately, that is where the consensus ends. Some models suggest that discourse events are tied together by causal relationships (e.g., Black & Bower, 1980; Schank, 1975; Trabasso & Sperry, 1985; van den Broek, 1990). Others emphasize the role of coreference, assuming that two events are connected if they involve the same objects or participants (e.g., Kintsch & van Dijk, 1978; van Dijk & Kintsch, 1983). Finally, models of both types often assume that two events must co-occur in a reader's short-term memory before a connection between them can be encoded in long-term memory (e.g., Fletcher & Bloom, 1988; Kintsch & van Dijk, 1978; van den Broek, 1990; van Dijk & Kintsch, 1983).

The research reported here was designed to evaluate the hypothesis that co-occurrence, coreference, and causality all contribute to the coherence of a discourse. This hypothesis is illustrated by the three sentences in Table 11.1 and their semantic network representations shown in Fig. 11.1. If the hypothesis is true, then Sentence 11.1a is "coherent" even though it describes two seemingly unrelated events. It is coherent because the context that the events share provides a connection between them in a reader's long-term memory (as illustrated by Fig. 11.1a). The hypothesis also suggests that Sentence 11.1b is "more coherent" than the first sentence. It depicts two events that are connected via both the context and the shared referent *cow* (Fig. 11.1b). Finally, if the hypothesis is true then Sentence 11.1c is the "most coherent" sentence in this set. It describes events that are related by means of their common context, the shared referent *cow*, and a

203

TABLE 11.1
Example Materials From Experiment 1

(a)	The receptionist named the ship and the cow kicked over the bucket. (Co-occurrence)
(b)	The receptionist named the cow and the cow kicked over the bucket. (Coreference)
(c)	The receptionist startled the cow and the cow kicked over the bucket. (Causality)

direct causal connection (Fig. 11.1c). Intuition suggests that these claims are obviously (perhaps even trivially) true, but an examination of the psychological literature shows that they cannot be taken for granted.

As suggested earlier, the co-occurrence of two events in a reader's short-term memory is treated as a necessary, but insufficient, condition for coherence in many models of discourse comprehension. Thus, Kintsch and van Dijk (1978) assumed that two events must co-occur in short-term memory and share a referent to be associated in long-term memory, whereas van den Broek (1990) assumed that they must co-occur in short-term memory and be causally related. Yet contemporary models of human learning and memory (e.g., McClelland & Rumelhart, 1985; Raaijmakers & Shiffrin, 1981) suggest that co-occurrence by itself should be sufficient for the formation of a connection between two events in long-term memory. This suggestion is supported by a series of computational experiments carried out in our laboratory. Fletcher, van den Broek, and Arthur (in press) created a computer model (based on Raaijmakers & Shiffrin, 1981) that

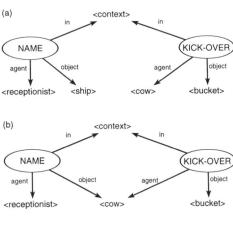

FIG. 11.1. Semantic network representations (based on Norman & Rumelhart, 1975) of conjoined clauses related by: (a) co-occurrence only, (b) co-occurrence plus coreference, (c) co-occurrence, coreference, and causality.

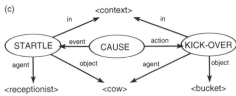

simulates the flow of ideas through a reader's short-term memory as a simple narrative text is first read and then recalled. The free recall protocols generated by this model were more like those of a group of college student subjects when links were created between all ideas that co-occurred in short-term memory during comprehension, regardless of the semantic relationships between them. One goal of the present research is to determine empirically if co-occurrence, in the absence of more meaningful semantic relationships, contributes to the coherence of a discourse.

Kintsch and van Dijk's (1978; Kintsch, 1988; van Dijk & Kintsch, 1983) model of discourse comprehension is, without a doubt, one of the most successful models in cognitive psychology. Among other things, it predicts how a text will be recalled (Kintsch & van Dijk, 1978, Miller & Kintsch, 1980), how it will be summarized (Kintsch & Kozminsky, 1977), the contents of think-aloud protocols generated during reading (Fletcher, 1986), and text differences in readability (Miller & Kintsch, 1980; Fletcher, 1986). Because this model assumes that discourse events are related through shared referents, its success provides indirect support for the claim that coreference contributes to the coherence of a discourse. More direct evidence was offered by McKoon and Ratcliff (1980). They presented subjects with simple stories followed by a probe recognition task. Subjects were able to verify that a probe word had occurred in one of these texts more quickly when the immediately preceeding probe was from the same text. More importantly, the degree of facilitation increased as the referential distance between the two test words decreased. As an example, after reading the text in Table 11.2, subjects responded to the probe word *countryside* more quickly if the preceeding probe was *pesticides* (1 referential step away) rather than *insects* (4 referential steps away). This result appears to offer strong support for the claim that coreference contributes to coherence. Unfortunately, by the criteria normally used to identify causal connections (Trabasso, van den Broek, & Suh, 1989) the pattern of referential links observed in Table 11.2 is completely confounded with the pattern of causal links. This raises the possibility that results that have been taken as evidence that coreference contributes to the coherence of a discourse are actually due to causal connections. This possibility was explored by Trabasso and van den Broek (1985), who examined the relationship between referential connectivity, causal connectivity, and the memorability of statements from

TABLE 11.2
An Example Story From McKoon and Ratcliff (1980, Adapted From Table 4)

The crops drew insects.
The insects troubled the farmer.
The farmer surveyed the fields.
The fields needed pesticides.
The pesticides troubled the crows.
The crows fouled the countryside.

simple narrative texts. They found that statements with many referential connections were recalled better than statements with fewer referential connections. But when the effects of causal connections on memorability were removed using multiple regression, the influence of coreference was eliminated. A second goal of the experiments described here is to determine if coreference, independent of causality, contributes to the coherence of a discourse.

At least two lines of research imply that causal connections contribute to the coherence of a discourse. Unfortunately, both sets of results are ambiguous. First, experiments on the comprehension of narrative texts have shown that story events with many causal connections are recalled better (Fletcher & Bloom, 1988; Trabasso & van den Broek, 1985), retrieved from memory more quickly (O'Brien & Myers, 1987), and judged more important (Trabasso & Sperry, 1985; van den Broek, 1988) than otherwise similar events with fewer causal connections. These results are usually interpreted as evidence that causality is the primary source of coherence in narrative discourse. But Kintsch (1992) showed that a model which assumes only referential connections between the events in a story can reproduce these effects. Second, experiments using a cued recall paradigm (Keenan, Baillet, & Brown, 1984; Myers, Shinjo, & Duffy, 1987) suggest that the strength of association between a pair of sentences depends on the causal relationship between them. After subjects have studied materials such as those in Table 11.3, the probability that one sentence will elicit the other in a cued recall task increases as we move from the weakest causal relationship (Table 11.3a) to a moderate causal relationship (Table 11.3c), then declines again for the strongest causal connection (Table 11.3d). One explanation for this result is that cued recall performance is determined by two factors; total study time (which decreases as causal relatedness increases) and the probability that a causal connection is perceived. This explanation is consistent with the claim that causal connections contribute to coherence. However, Duffy, Shinjo, and Myers (1990) showed that a third factor is a better predictor of cued recall performance in this task, the time required to generate an event that intervenes between the first and second sentence. This suggests that performance is best for Sentences 3c because

TABLE 11.3
Example Materials From Myers, Shinjo, and Duffy (1987, p. 462)

(a)	Tony sat under a tree reading a good book. Tony walked home, soaking wet, to change is clothes. (Low related)
(b)	Tony met his friend near a pond in a park. Tony walked home, soaking wet, to change his clothes.
(c)	Tony had a fight with his friend near a pond. Tony walked home, soaking wet, to change his clothes.
(d)	Tony's friend suddenly pushed him into a pond. Tony walked home, soaking wet, to change his clothes. (High related)

subjects are more likely generate an elaborative inference, thus creating a more richly interconnected representation. Because the inferred events are likely to share referents with the explicitly presented events, the relationship between causal relatedness and cued recall probability cannot be interpreted as evidence that causal connections have a direct influence on coherence. A third goal of the research reported here is to determine empirically if causality contributes to the coherence of a discourse in the absence of elaborative inferences.

Because most discourse is so richly interconnected, it is difficult to isolate the connection between just two events. To circumvent this problem, the experiments reported here were performed with conjoined sentences that describe a single pair of events (an example is shown in Table 11.1). If subjects are prevented from generating elaborative inferences as they read these materials, the probability that the second event is recalled when the first is given as a retrieval cue provides a direct measure of the coherence between them (see, e.g., Keenan et al., 1984; Myers et al., 1987). If the first event provides an effective retrieval cue even when the events have no relationship beyond their co-occurrence in the sentence (as in Table 11.1a), the claim that co-occurence contributes directly to coherence will be supported. If a shared referent, in the absence of a causal relationship (illustrated by Table 11.1b), improves cued-recall performance, the claim that coreference contributes to coherence will be supported. Finally, if performance when the events are both referentially and causally related (as in Table 11.1c) exceeds performance when the only relationship is coreference, the claim that causality contributes to coherence will be supported.

EXPERIMENT 1

The goal of this experiment was to examine the effects of co-occurrence, coreference, and causal coherence on cued recall of conjoined sentences in the absence of elaborative inferences. Two steps were taken to prevent such inferences. First, all materials were modeled after Duffy, Shinjo, and Myers' (1990) "high related" or "low related" conditions (see Table 11.3). These researchers found that subjects required, on average, more than 40 s to generate explicit elaborations in these conditions. Second, each conjoined sentence was presented at a controlled rate of 10 s or less, far short of the times observed by Duffy and her colleagues. To insure the success of these manipulations, two presentation rates were used. Any effects due to elaboration (a time and resource consuming process) should be magnified at the slower rate.

Method

Subjects.   Subjects for this experiment were 60 undergraduate psychology students from the University of Minnesota who received course credit for their participation.

Materials.   The primary materials for this experiment were 30 triplets of sentences. An example is shown in Table 11.1. Each sentence included two conjoined clauses and the second clause was the same for the three sentences in each set. Within sets, the semantic relationship between the clauses differed across sentences. In one sentence the clauses were related only by virtue of their co-occurrence. In another sentence the two clauses were referentially coherent. Finally, each set included a sentence where the clauses were both referentially and causally coherent.

An additional 19 sentences were used as fillers. Each of these sentences was similar in syntactic and semantic structure to the test sentences.

Design and Procedure.   Upon entering the laboratory, subjects were seated in front of an IBM PC equipped with a response box and a millisecond timer. Following instructions, seven blocks of trials were presented. The first block consisted entirely of filler items and was included to familiarize subjects with the procedure. Each of the remaining blocks included five test items and two fillers. The order of these blocks was determined at random for each subject. During each block, seven sentences were presented one at a time. Half of the sentences were presented for 250 ms per word and the remaining half for 500 ms per word. After all seven sentences had been presented, subjects were shown the first clause from each test sentence and asked to write down the associated second clause. Upon completing this task subjects pressed a button to initiate the next block of trials.

This experiment employed a within subjects design in which three degrees of semantic relatedness (co-occurrence, coreference, and causal coherence) were orthogonally crossed with two presentation rates (250 ms or 500 ms per word). The response measure was the probability of correctly recalling the second clause of a sentence given the first clause as a cue. Each subject was tested on five items from each condition, one from each set of related sentences. The selection of items from each set was counterbalanced across subjects.

Results and Discussion

A subject's response was scored as correct if it included the main proposition from the second clause; (KICK-OVER AGENT:COW OBJECT:BUCKET) in the example shown in Table 11.1. The strict scoring criterion recommended by both Bovair and Kieras (1985) and Turner and Greene (1978) was employed. The results are shown in Fig. 11.2.

A series of four planned, nonorthogonal comparisons was made using the Bonferroni t procedure (Kirk, 1982, pp. 106–109). With four comparisons at $\alpha = .05$, the critical difference between means was .11 ($MSe = .03$) in an analysis by subjects and .08 ($MSe = .02$) in an analysis by items. By these criteria, the difference between the co-occurrence and coreference conditions was reliable at

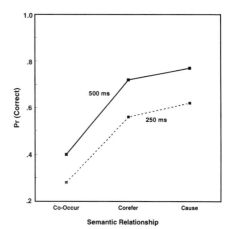

FIG. 11.2. Probability of a correct cued recall response in Experiment 1 as a function of semantic relationship and presentation rate.

both presentation rates. In contrast, the difference between the coreference and the causal coherence conditions was not significant at either rate. Repeated measures analysis of variance reveals a significant difference between presentation rates, $F(1,59) = 32.21$, $p < .001$, $MSe = .05$ by subjects and $F(1,29) = 28.36$, $p < .001$, $MSe = .03$ by items. Also note that the 95% confidence interval around each of the six condition means lies above zero.

Five conclusions emerge from this experiment. First, co-occurrence in a sentence is sufficient to create a link between two clauses in memory. Second, the effect of co-occurrence increases with study time. Third, coreference increases the degree of association between co-occurring clauses. Fourth, and perhaps most surprisingly, in the circumstances created by this experiment, causal coherence has no impact on the degree of association between two clauses in memory. Fifth, and last, the similar pattern of results across presentation rates suggests that our attempt to control elaborations was successful.

EXPERIMENT 2

The primary goal of this experiment was to determine why causal coherence had no impact on cued recall performance in Experiment 1. We consider two possibilities. The first, suggested by the results of Duffy et al. (1990), is that causal connections have no impact on the mental representation of discourse in the absence of elaborations. A second possibility is that causal connections must be explicitly encoded in order to have an effect. To distinguish between these alternatives, half of the subjects in this experiment were instructed to "try to figure out how the event described by the first clause in each sentence might have caused the event described by the second clause." The remaining subjects received the same instructions used in Experiment 1. If causal connections have no impact on coherence in the absence of elaborations, both groups should replicate the results observed in Experiment 1. But if causal connections need to be explicitly encoded, subjects receiving the modified instructions should perform better in the causal coherence condition than in the coreference condition.

Method

Subjects.   Subjects for this experiment were 24 University of Minnesota undergraduate and graduate psychology students who received course credit for their participation.

Materials.   Fifteen of the conjoined sentence sets from Experiment 1 were used again in this experiment.

Design and Procedure.   For half the subjects, the procedure was similar to Experiment 1. The instructions given these subjects encouraged them to study each sentence carefully in order to maximize their performance on the cued recall test. For the remaining subjects, the instructions were modified. They were encouraged to determine how the first clause of each sentence might have caused the second clause. Following these instructions, the procedure used in Experiment 1 was followed for both groups of subjects except that all sentences were presented for 500 ms per word and the cued recall test was administered after all items had been presented.

This experiment used a 2 × 3 mixed design. The two types of instructions (recall vs. causal) were manipulated between subjects whereas semantic relatedness (co-occurrence vs. coreference vs. causal) was manipulated within subjects.

Results and Discussion

The results of this experiment are summarized in Fig. 11.3. Again, four planned comparisons were evaluated using the Bonferroni procedure. With $\alpha = .05$ the critical difference between means was .18 ($MSe = .03$) in an analysis by subjects and .15 ($MSe = .03$) in an analysis by items. By these criteria, the recall instructions produced the same pattern of results observed in Experiment 1. Performance in the referential coherence condition exceeded the co-occurrence condition, but did not differ from the causal coherence condition. The causal instructions, in contrast, led to different results. Referential coherence still led to better cued recall performance than co-occurrence, but performance in the causal coherence condition exceeded performance in the referential coherence condition. These results suggest that causal connections do make the mental representation of a sentence more coherent, but only if they are afforded by the materials and explicitly encoded. Similar results have been reported by Caron, Micko, and Thüring (1988). These researchers found that composite sentences conjoined by *because* are recalled better than otherwise identical sentences conjoined by *and*.

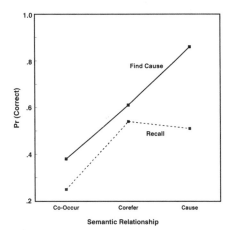

FIG. 11.3. Probability of a correct cued-recall response in Experiment 2 as a function of semantic relationship and instructions.

EXPERIMENT 3

The previous experiment shows that causal connections improve cued recall performance when subjects are instructed to encode them. We have interpreted this result as evidence for a more coherent representation in memory, but this interpretation is permissable only if we rule out the possibility that instructions to encode causal connections influence retrieval performance rather than encoding. This could happen if, for example, subjects generated plausible consequences of each retrieval cue and occasionally hit upon close associates to a target clause. To address this posibility, this experiment included a group of subjects who received recall instructions initially, but were told just prior to the cued recall task that many of the sentences described pairs of causally related events. They were encouraged to use this fact to improve their cued recall performance. If instructions to encode causal connections alters performance only at the time of retrieval, the performance of these subjects should be indistinguishable form the causal instruction group in Experiment 2. However, if instructions to encode causal connections influence only the initial encoding of each sentence, the new instructional group should exhibit the same pattern of results observed with recall instructions in the first two experiments (see, e.g., Bransford & Johnson, 1972).

Method

Subjects.   The participants in this experiment were 45 University of Minnesota undergraduate students who received $5 each in return for their participation.

Materials.   All 30 sets of conjoined sentences plus two of the filler sentences from Experiment 1 were used again in this experiment.

Design and Procedure. Upon entering the laboratory, all subjects were told that they would be shown a series of conjoined sentences on a computer monitor. They were also told that a cued recall test would follow in which they would be asked to provide the second clause of each sentence given the first clause as a cue. In addition, 15 subjects (the causal before group) were told that they could enhance their performance by trying to think of how the first clause in each sentence might have caused the second clause. Following these instructions, each subject was shown one filler sentence followed by 30 test sentences in a random order, then one more filler sentence. This entire sequence was repeated three times to avoid floor effects on the cued recall test. Each subject was presented with ten sentences from each semantic relatedness condition, one from each set of three related sentences. The selection of items from each set was counter-balanced across subjects. The presentation rate for this experiment was 250 ms per word.

After each sentence was presented three times, all subjects were given instruc-tions for the cued recall task. Subjects from the causal before group and an additional 15 subjects (the causal after group) were told that in many of the sentences the first clause described the cause of the second clause. They were encouraged to use this fact to improve their cued recall performance. The re-maining subjects (the recall group) were told only to write down the second clause associated with each retrieval cue. All subjects were then given a test booklet containing the first clause of each test sentence (in a random order) along with enough space for them to write down the associated second clause.

This experiment used a 3 × 3 mixed design. Instructions (recall vs. causal before vs. causal after) were varied between subjects whereas semantic related-ness (co-occurrence vs. coreference vs. causal) was manipulated within subjects.

Results and Discussion

The results of this experiment are summarized in Fig. 11.4. The Bonferroni t procedure was used to evaluate six planned, nonorthogonal comparisons. The critical difference between means was .12 ($MSe = .02$) in an analysis by subjects and .11 ($MSe = .03$) in an analysis by items. By these criteria, the same pattern of results was observed in the recall and causal after conditions; coreference produced better cued recall than co-occurrence, and the same level of perfor-mance as the causal coherence condition. In the causal before condition, per-formance in the coreference condition was better than performance in the co-occurrence condition but worse than performance in the causal coherence condition. Because causal coherence aided cued recall in the causal before group but not in the causal after group, we conclude that the primary influence of causal coherence on cued recall performance occurs at encoding rather than at the time of retrieval.

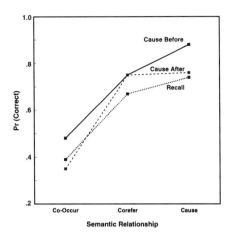

FIG. 11.4. Probability of a correct cued-recall response in Experiment 3 as a function of semantic relationship and instructions.

EXPERIMENT 4

This experiment had two goals. The first was to examine the generality of of our previous results by examining a new set of experimental materials (adapted from Duffy et al., 1990). The second was to test the possibility that the cued recall difference between the coreference and causal conditions that we have observed when subjects are instructed to encode causal connections results from elaborations rather than direct causal connections. This test is facilitated by Duffy, Shinjo, and Myers' materials, which include sentences with strong causal connections (similar to our causally related sentences) and sentences with intermediate strength causal connections. Duffy and her colleagues found that subjects need significantly more time to generate explicit elaborations when the sentences are related by a strong causal connection. As a result, if the difference we have observed between our coreferential and causal sentences is due to elaborations, cued recall for sentences with intermediate strength causal connections should exceed cued recall for sentences with strong causal connections. But if this difference is the result of direct causal connections stored in long-term memory, cued recall for sentences with intermediate strength causal connection should be less than (or perhaps equal to) cued recall for sentences with strong causal connections.

Method

Subjects. Subjects for this experiment were 24 undergraduate psychology students from the University of Minnesota who received course credit in return for their participation.

Materials.   The primary materials for this experiment were 28 sets of four related sentences adapted from Myers et al. (1987; Duffy et al., 1990). An example is shown in Table 11.4. As with the materials used in Experiments 1 and 2, each sentence consisted of two clauses conjoined with *and*. Within each set, the second clause was the same for all four sentences. Within each set, the first clause of one sentence was related to this second clause only by virtue of their co-occurrence. For a second sentence, the two clauses were referentially, but not causally, related. For the remaining sentences the clauses were both referentially and causally coherent. These sentences differed, however, in the strength of their causal connections. Duffy et al. (1990) showed that subjects can easily (and quickly) generate elaborations in response to the sentences whose clauses are linked by causal connections of intermediate strength, but find it difficult (and slow) to do so for the sentences whose clauses are linked by a strong causal connection.

An additional 36 sentences were used as fillers. These sentences were similar in structure and coherence to the test sentences.

Design and Procedure.   In this experiment all subjects were instructed to look for causal connections between clauses to facilitate their perfomance on the cued recall task. The sentences were presented in eight blocks of trials at a rate of 250 ms per word. A cued recall test on four items followed each block. The first block included only filler sentences, the remaining blocks included four test sentences and four fillers in a random order. All subjects were tested on seven sentences from each level of semantic relatedness (co-occurrence vs. coreference vs. intermediate causal vs. strong causal), one sentence from each set of four sharing the same last clause. The selection of items from each set was counter-balanced across subjects.

Results and Discussion

The results of this experiment are shown in Fig. 11.5. The Bonferroni *t* proce-dure was used to evaluate three planned, nonorthogonal comparisons. With α =

TABLE 11.4
Example Materials From Experiment 4

(a)	Ed was bored with working for his father, and Tony walked home, soaking wet, to change his clothes. (Co-occurrence)
(b)	Tony sat under a tree reading a good book, and he walked home, soaking wet, to change his clothes. (Coreference)
(c)	Tony had a fight with his friend near a pond, and he walked home, soaking wet, to change his clothes. (Intermediate causality)
(d)	Tony's friend suddenly pushed him into a pond, and he walked home, soaking wet, to change his clothes. (Strong causality)

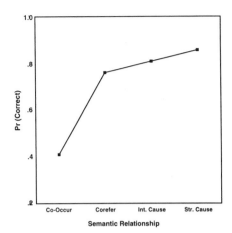

FIG. 11.5. Probability of a correct cued-recall response in Experiment 4 as a function of semantic relationship.

.05 the critical difference between means was .11 (*MSe* = .03) in an analysis by subjects and .10 (*MSe* = .03) in an analysis by items. By these criteria, referential coherence led to better cued recall performance than co-occurrence, and strong causal coherence led to better performance than referential coherence. This replicates the results of Experiments 2 and 3. The intermediate and strong causal conditions were not reliably different from one another, suggesting that the difference between the coreferential and causal conditions is not due to elaborations.

GENERAL DISCUSSION

One goal of the research reported here was to determine if the co-occurrence of two discourse events in a reader's short-term memory is sufficient (not just necessary) for those events to be linked in long-term memory. Across four experiments, the cued recall probability for the second clause of a sentence that was neither referentially nor causally related to the first clause ranged from a low of .25 to a high of .48. One explanation for this finding is that subjects occasionally recall the target clause of a co-occurrence sentence in isolation, then pair it with the correct retrieval cue by chance. If this interpretation is correct, the hit rate in the co-occurrence condition (the probability of pairing a target clause with the correct retrieval cue) should not exceed the intrusion rate (the probability of pairing a target clause with the wrong retrieval cue). An examination of the data reveals that this is not the case. Within the co-occurrence condition the intrusion rates range from .03 to .07, and in no case are they reliably greater than zero. This suggests that subjects are able to form efffective connections in long-term memory between co-occurring discourse events that are neither referentially nor causally related. This finding is consistent with contemporary models of human learning and memory and suggests that an important source of coherence has been overlooked by most discourse comprehension researchers.

A second goal of this research was to determine if coreference contributes to the coherence of a discourse. All four experiments suggest that it does. When the two clauses of a conjoined sentence refer to a common person or object, cued recall improves substantially. Moreover, the influence of coreference in these experiments was unaffected by presentation rate and processing instructions, suggesting that it occurs automatically. This finding is consistent with Kintsch and van Dijk's (1978) well-known model of discourse comprehension along with its intellectual descendents (e.g., Fletcher & Bloom, 1988; Kintsch, 1988; van Dijk & Kintsch; 1983).

The third and final goal of this research was to find out if causal connections improve the coherence of a discourse. Across experiments, cued recall performance was enhanced by causal connections when subjects were specifically instructed to look for causal links between the first and second clause of each sentence. In the absence of such instructions, causal connections had no impact. This suggests that causality contributes to coherence if and only if it is afforded by the discourse (McDaniel & Einstein, 1989) and intentionally encoded. This is perhaps the most surprising outcome of this research.

It is certainly resonable to question whether the results of these experiments generalize to meaningful texts. To find out, we reanalyzed data from a free recall study reported by Fletcher and Bloom (1988). Subjects in this experiment read and recalled eight short narrative texts. From each of these texts, we selected three pairs of clauses. The clauses in each pair were adjacent in the text but seperated by a sentence boundary. One pair of clauses from each text corresponded to our co-occurrence condition, they were neither referentially nor causally related. A second pair corresponded to our coreference condition, both clauses referred to the same person or object but neither could be interpreted as causing the other. The third pair from each text corresponded to our causal coherence condition, they referred to the same person or object and the first clause could be easily interpreted as causing the second clause. We then examined the conditional probability of recalling the second clause in each pair given that the first clause was recalled. Performance across subjects was .35 in the co-occurrence condition, .73 in the coreference condition, and .92 in the causal coherence condition. These results are similar to those observed in Experiments 2, 3, and 4 when subjects were explicitly instructed to look for causal connections within each sentence. This is noteworthy because numerous researchers (e.g., Fletcher & Bloom, 1988; Trabasso & Sperry, 1985; van den Broek, 1990) have argued that readers make a conscious attempt to encode causal relations during narrative comprehension. Our reanalysis of Fletcher and Bloom's (1988) data support this claim and, together with Experiments 2–4, suggest that causal connections do enhance the coherence of narrative discourse.

Why is it that causal connections have to be intentionally encoded whereas referential connections do not? One possible answer was suggested by van Dijk and Kintsch (1983; see also Fletcher, in press). These researchers argued that the meaning of a discourse is represented at two distinct "levels" in a reader's memory. The more superficial level, the propositional textbase, represents the meaning of a text per se. It consists of the individual propositions conveyed by the text along with the connections among those propositions. It is constructed automatically and is, therefore, relatively unaffected by a reader's goals. The deeper level of representation is referred to as the situation model. It is constructed by combining prior knowledge with the information in the textbase to construct the same kind of representation that would result from direct experience with the situation described by the text. Unlike the propositional textbase, it requires controlled processing and is sensitive to a reader's goals. This suggests that referential connections are encoded in the propositional textbase whereas causal connections are (optionally) encoded in the situation model. If this is true, the effects of causal structure on the comprehension and recall of narrative discourse might not generalize to other genres where readers are less likely to ask themselves, "Why did this happen?" as they read each sentence.

ACKNOWLEDGMENTS

This research was supported in part by the Center for Research in Learning, Perception, and Cognition at the University of Minnesota, and by grant MH42468–01 to Charles R. Fletcher. We are grateful to Bob Lorch for his comments on an earlier draft of this chapter.

REFERENCES

Black, J. B., & Bower, G. H. (1980). Story understanding as problem solving. *Poetics, 9*, 223–250.

Bovair, S., & Kieras, D. E. (1985). A guide to propositional analysis for research on technical prose. In B. K. Britton & J. B. Black (Eds.), *Understanding expository text* (pp. 315–362). Hillsdale, NJ: Lawrence Erlbaum Associates.

Bransford, J. D., & Johnson, M. K. (1972). Contextual prerequisites for understanding: Some investigations of comprehension and recall. *Journal of Verbal Learning and Verbal Behavior, 11*, 717–726.

Caron, J., Micko, H. C., & Thüring, M. (1988). Conjunctions and the recall of composite sentences. *Journal of Memory and Language, 27*, 309–323.

Duffy, S. A., Shinjo, M., & Myers, J. L. (1990). The effect of encoding task on memory for sentence pairs varying in causal relatedness. *Journal of Memory and Language, 29*, 27–42.

Fletcher, C. R. (1986). Strategies for the allocation of short-term memory during comprehension. *Journal of Memory and Language, 25*, 43–58.

Fletcher, C. R. (in press). Levels of representation in memory for discourse. In M.A. Gernsbacher (Ed.), *Handbook of psycholinguistics*. New York: Academic Press.

Fletcher, C. R., & Bloom, C. P. (1988). Causal reasoning in the comprehension of simple narrative texts. *Journal of Memory and Language, 27*, 235–244.

Fletcher, C. R., van den Broek, P., & Arthur, E. J. (in press). A model of narrative comprehension and recall. In B.K. Britton & A.C. Graesser (Eds.), *Models of understanding text*. Hillsdale, NJ: Erlbaum.

Keenan, J. M., Baillet, S. D., & Brown, P. (1984). The effects of causal cohesion on comprehension and memory. *Journal of Memory and Language, 23,* 115–126.

Kintsch, W. (1988). The role of knowledge in discourse comprehension: A construction integration model. *Psychological Review, 95,* 163–182.

Kintsch, W. (1992). How readers construct situation models for stories: The role of syntactic cues and causal inferences. In A.F. Healy, S. Kosslyn, & R.M. Shiffrin (Eds.), *Essays in honor of William K. Estes* (pp. 261–278). Hillsdale, NJ: Lawrence Erlbaum Associates.

Kintsch, W., & Kozminsky, E. (1977). Summarizing stories after reading and listening. *Journal of Educational Psychology, 69,* 491–499.

Kintsch, W., & van Dijk, T. A. (1978). Toward a model of text comprehension and production. *Psychological Review, 85,* 363–394.

Kirk, R. E. (1982). *Experimental design: Procedures for the behavioral sciences*. Monterey, CA: Brooks/Cole.

McClelland, J. L., & Rumelhart, D. E. (1985). Distributed memory and the representation of general and specific information. *Journal of Experimental Psychology: General, 114,* 159–188.

McDaniel, M. A., & Einstein, G. O. (1989). Material appropriate processing: A contextualistic approach to reading and studying strategies. *Educational Psychology Review, 1,* 113–145.

McKoon, G., & Ratcliff, R. (1980). Priming in item recognition: The organization of propositions in memory for text. *Journal of Verbal Learning and Verbal Behavior, 19,* 369–386.

Miller, J. R., & Kintsch, W. (1980). Readability and recall of short prose passages: A theoretical analysis. *Journal of Experimental Psychology: Human Learning and Memory, 6,* 335–354.

Myers, J. L., Shinjo, M., & Duffy, S. A. (1987). Degree of causal relatedness and memory. *Journal of Memory and Language, 26,* 453–465.

Norman, D. A., & Rumelhart, D. E. (Eds.). (1975). *Explorations in cognition*. San Francisco: Freeman.

O'Brien, E. J., & Myers, J. L. (1987). The role of causal connections in the retrieval of text. *Memory & Cognition, 15,* 419–427.

Raaijmakers, J. G. W., & Shiffrin, R. M. (1981). Search of associative memory. *Psychological Review, 88,* 93–134.

Schank, R. (1975). The structure of episodes in memory. In D. G. Bobrow & A. M. Collins (Eds.), *Representation and understanding: Studies in cognitive science* (pp. 237–272). New York: Academic Press.

Trabasso, T., & Sperry, L. L. (1985). Causal relatedness and importance of story events. *Journal of Memory and Language, 24,* 595–611.

Trabasso, T., & van den Broek, P. (1985). Causal thinking and the representation of narrative events. *Journal of Memory and Language, 24,* 612–630.

Trabasso, T., van den Broek, P., & Suh, S. Y. (1989). Logical necessity and transitivity of causal relations in stories. *Discourse Processes, 12,* 1–25.

Turner, A., & Greene, E. (1978). Construction and use of a propositional text base. *JSAS Catalogue of Selected Documents in Psychology*. (Ms. No. 1713)

van den Broek, P. (1988). The effects of causal relations and hierarchical position on the importance of story statements. *Journal of Memory and Language, 27,* 1–22.

van den Broek, P. (1990). The causal inference maker: Towards a process model of inference generation in text comprehension. In D. A. Balota, G. B. Flores d'Arcais, & K. Rayner (Eds.), *Comprehension processes in reading*. Hillsdale, NJ: Lawrence Erlbaum Associates.

van Dijk, T. A., & Kintsch, W. (1983). *Strategies of discourse comprehension*. New York: Academic Press.

12 Explanatory Inferences and Other Strategies During Comprehension and Their Effect on Recall

Tom Trabasso
Soyoung Suh
Paula Payton
Rachna Jain
The University of Chicago

Jerry Myers (1990), in reflecting upon the heavy reliance on *recall* to assess text comprehension, urged, along with others (e.g., Frederiksen, 1985) that we study the processes that occur during rather than after reading. These processes, he argued, should be studied close in time to their operation but separate from those that occur in retrieval. It is fitting, therefore, in a volume dedicated to Jerry Myers, that we report studies that follow his advice.

We address two questions in this chapter. The first is: What do readers do in trying to understand a text while they read it? This question is concerned with Myers' directive to investigate processes that occur during comprehension. The second question is: Does what readers do during reading affect their subsequent access and use of the information that was contained in the text? This question retains the previous interest in the use of text recall, not as a measure of comprehension, but as an assessment of the effect of the comprehension processes that occurred during reading. We assume that during reading, the reader tries to construct a functional memory representation of the text. What the reader does during reading, then, should influence what is remembered after reading. In addition to answering these questions, we investigated whether what is done during reading and what is retained depends on individual and developmental differences in comprehension processes, and/or differences in the degree to which texts allow such processing to occur.

COMPREHENSION AND RECALL

Several studies of text recall have shown a correlation between what is remembered and what people are *hypothesized* to do during comprehension. The hypothesized processes may be inferred from discourse analysis of a text. The proper- ties of a text representation identified by this means predict the degree of recall of the text (Trabasso, Secco, & van den Broek, 1984). For example, the stronger a causal relationship or the greater number of causal relations that a sentence has to other sentences, the better the retention of its content (Keenan, Baillet, & Brown, 1984; Myers, Shinjo, & Duffy, 1987; Omanson, 1982; Trabasso et al., 1984; Trabasso & van den Broek, 1985). This correlation suggests that readers inte- grate sentences by making causal inferences between them during reading. The integration could be established by constructing connections between the concep- tualizations that underlie each of the sentences (Schank, 1975). These links would later be used in retrieval to access a conceptualization via activation of another conceptualization. The more connections that a sentence has, the more likely it is that the sentence would be accessed by activation of a related sen- tence, and the more likely it would be recalled. However, these studies demon- strate a correlation between the potential inferences that could be made on a particular text, as revealed by the discourse analysis, and recall of its clauses. It should be possible to find more direct evidence on how readers integrate sen- tences during comprehension, and whether the observed integration is predictive of later retrieval.

SHORT-TERM MEMORY AND COMPREHENSION

There is also reason to believe that a relationship should exist between text recall and hypothesized processes that occur in short-term memory during reading. For example, in Kintsch and van Dijk's (1978) model, propositions are retained and linked by rules in a short-term memory buffer. Propositions are cycled through the buffer during reading. Propositions that reside the longest in the buffer receive the most attention, have the greatest strength, have the largest number of connections to other propositions, and should be the best recalled. Although this particular processing model received empirical support in predicting recall (Fletcher, 1986), Fletcher and Bloom (1988) found that models that connected sentences by causal relations in short-term memory were better predictors of recall than ones that used the proposition rules of Kintsch and van Dijk (1978). Regardless of the kinds of links that are made, the evidence is mainly based on a correlation between hypothesized comprehension processes and recall. Again, more direct evidence on what occurs during reading comprehension is required.

COMPREHENSION DURING READING

In recent times, considerable attention has focused on word recognition and sentence parsing processes, measured in real time, under the assumption that these processes underlie comprehension. McKoon and Ratcliff (1990 a, 1990b) and Keenan and her colleagues (Keenan, Golding, Potts, Jennings, & Aman, 1990a; Keenan, Potts, Golding, & Jennings, 1990b), respectively, provide comprehensive reviews of the methods and issues in this kind of online processing. As it turns out, the variety of methods developed to isolate word recognition and syntactic processing are not without problems. In studies of lexical decision making, word naming, word and sentence reading time, and other real-time measures, particular attention is given to the control for word associations and to guarding against possible processes that happen because of testing and not during reading. This problem, called *context checking* (Forster, 1981) occurs where readers fit the target or test probe to the context after the processing of interest has been completed. The context checking problem extends to the study of inferences during reading. This problem requires controls such as matching for content or locating the tests at points where context checking predicts a different pattern of findings than those predicted by a theory of comprehension and inference making (Suh & Trabasso, 1993). Context checking has been used to discredit claims that inferences are made during comprehension. McKoon and Ratcliff (1992), in commenting on the relationships between causal inferences identified by discourse analysis (e.g., Trabasso et al., 1984; Trabasso & van den Broek, 1985), suggested that such inferences were made at retrieval rather than during comprehension. The present studies test this claim by assessing inferences during comprehension and whether they predict retrieval.

Two of the methodological reviews mentioned previously, one by McKoon and Ratcliff (1990a) and one by Keenan et al. (1990a) appeared in an edited volume by Balota, Flores d'Arcais, and Rayner (1990). Half of this volume was devoted to investigations using reaction time during reading to assess word recognition and within-sentence processing. Curiously, none of these kinds of online studies investigated possible relations of processing during reading to postreading measures such as question answering or recall (Trabasso, 1992). Rather, the concern of these investigators over the past decade has been with the experimental isolation of processes rather than with what they accomplish and how they might relate to other measures of comprehension. The relationship between these kinds of online processes with comprehension, a word used in the Balota et al. (1990) volume title, remains a matter of faith.

One problem with online measures of processing of inferences during *comprehension* is the assumption that the probes used to assess the making of an inference at a particular point during reading may not match the inference that is actually made (Suh & Trabasso, 1993). The sentence, "The actress fell from the 14th story" may lead to the inference that she hit the ground rather than that she died. The use of *dead* as a probe by McKoon and Ratcliff (1986) may have mismatched the inference made and yielded misleading negative results. Another problem is that although the target word or sentence may match what is being thought about, these probes severely restrict the content of thinking that can be assessed. In contrast, *verbal protocol* methods such as questioning, thinking-aloud, or open generation can provide us with the informational content accessible to the person as he or she tries to understand a text (Ericsson, 1988; Ericsson & Simon, 1984). The expressed content provides outcome data from which one can infer comprehension processes. Finally, what is observed in verbal protocols during reading may predict what one retains from one's understanding of the text (Suh & Trabasso, 1993; Trabasso & Suh, 1993).

Verbal protocols obtained during reading can test whether people make the inferences that one thinks they should based upon one's intuitions or upon a more rigorous discourse analysis of a text (Magliano & Graesser, 1991; Suh & Trabasso, 1993; Trabasso & Suh, 1993). Verbal protocols can provide data that serve as norms to predict online performance on word or sentence recognition tests designed to probe inferences during reading. Convergent validation of intuitions, discourse analysis, verbal protocols, and online performance gives one greater faith in a theory than do findings on studies that employ only one performance measure such as priming. Convergent evidence approaches include the use of questioning to provide verbal protocol data (Long & Golding, 1993; Long, Golding, & Graesser, 1992; Long, Golding, Graesser, & Clark, 1990; Magliano, Baggett, Johnson, & Graesser, 1993), word association production norms (Sharkey & Sharkey, 1992), and think-aloud protocols during reading by one group of subjects to predict priming during online processing of the same texts by a different group of subjects (Suh & Trabasso, 1993; Trabasso & Suh, 1993).

In order to find out what information a person can access in trying to understand a text, one can ask questions as the reader tries to comprehend each sentence. Graesser and his colleagues have made extensive use of questions to expose inferences in this way (Graesser, 1981; Graesser & Black, 1985; Graesser & Clark, 1985; Graesser, Haberlandt, & Kozumi, 1987; Long, Golding, Graesser, & Clark, 1990; see also Lehnert, 1978, for a taxonomy of questions and their role in revealing inferences). In particular, they asked why, how, and what happens next; when, where, and other kinds of questions on events, states, and actions. Why, how, and what-happens-next questions are most revealing of inferences about events and actions because the answers to these questions integrate information between sentences rather than requiring a search for information within them (Trabasso, van den Broek, & Liu, 1988). These integrative, explanatory questions entail knowledge of causality, particularly that involving human intentions, goals, plans, procedural descriptions, and causal consequences. All of these are important to understanding events and actions as they occur in text and in real life events.

Rumelhart (1991) also used questioning methods to study understanding of sentences as they are read. He was able to trace the changes in hypotheses that occur over the course of reading the text. In his data, subjects constructed hypotheses and situation models about who, when, where and what was happening. These findings are quite similar to those of Collins, Brown, and Larkin (1980) who examined how subjects constructed and revised mental models of text while thinking aloud about sentences one at a time. Stein and Levine (1989,

1990) and Stein and Trabasso (1989) also used online questioning procedures during the reading of episodes to investigate emotional understanding in terms of the events that affect goals, and the plans that follow from changes in the status of goals.

Another method for studying comprehension during reading is to allow the reader to think aloud during the reading of each sentence. The think-aloud method was successfully pioneered by Newell and Simon (1972) in their well known studies of human problem solving. A comprehensive discussion of the use of verbal protocols is found in Ericsson and Simon (1984) and a specific review of these methods in reading comprehension is found in Ericsson (1988).

Of particular interest is the use of think aloud methods in investigating comprehension during reading. Among the first studies are those by Waern (1979) and Guindon (1980, 1981). Waern (1979) compared verbalization of thoughts during versus after the reading of a paragraph of text. Although more verbalization occurred during than after reading, the content of what was verbalized did not differ. Guindon (1980, 1981) examined inferences under thinking aloud versus retrospective conditions. The number of inferences generated was about the same in the two conditions, as was the comprehension of stories as measured by answers to questions and recall. Similarly, Fletcher (1986) found that subjects who thought aloud and subjects who read normally did not differ in what they included in their summaries of a text.

Olson and his colleagues (Olson, Duffy, & Mack, 1980, 1984; Olson, Mack, & Duffy, 1981) evaluated the merits of protocol analysis in reading comprehension. They carried out systematic analyses of the inferences that occur in think-aloud protocols during reading of narrative and expository texts. In their studies, subjects read one sentence at a time and thought aloud about each one as they read and tried to comprehend it. They were explicitly instructed to make inferences or to elaborate, to report on connections between the present sentence and prior ones, to make predictions on what might occur, and to comment on what they felt was the role of the current sentence in the overall organization of the text. In line with these instructions, the subjects frequently made reference to antecedent information, inferences, and predictions during reading. Olson et al. (1984) validated their verbal protocol data against reading time measures. Of interest is their finding that think-aloud inferences accounted for about 4% to 5% of the variance in the normal reading times for sentences.

The verbal methods, especially those involving questions or explicit requests to process information in particular ways while thinking aloud, may affect the comprehension processes that one observes. The instruction to think aloud may force deeper and richer processing of the material than one would ordinarily obtain with normal reading. However, Waern's (1979), Guindon's (1980, 1981), and Fletcher's (1986) comparisons on recall, postreading comprehension, or summaries indicate that there was no positive benefit to having thought aloud as compared to normal reading. In order to minimize the effect of concurrent thinking aloud on processing, Suh and Trabasso (1993) and Trabasso and Suh (1993) argued for using instructions to think aloud during reading with minimal direction so as to reveal what subjects do when they try to understand a text and not force the processing to be of a certain kind. At the same time, the think-aloud studies indicate that this methods may be more sensitive to certain kinds of inferences over others. Explanatory and predictive inferences on goals, actions, and outcomes seem to occur more frequently in thinking aloud about narrative text or newspaper stories (Fletcher, 1986; Guindon, 1980, 1981; Olson et al., 1984). Referential, part/whole, categorical, and other kinds of inferences may be less apparent or only indirectly observed by these techniques. Real-time or online methods may be more sensitive to these kinds of low level inferences.

We adopted the think-aloud method in our studies for a variety of reasons. First, we assumed, as is commonly believed (Ericsson & Simon, 1984; Olson et al., 1984), that thinking aloud would reveal the content of information available to working memory during the comprehension of sentences. Second, the content of the protocols should be less directed by allowing the subjects to think aloud and by giving them less specific instructions than those used by Olson et al. (1984) and Fletcher (1986), and by not using questions as was done by Rumelhart (1991) and Graesser (1981). We wanted to allow the readers as much freedom as possible to express whatever content was available to them as they tried to comprehend the text. We also wanted them to be as free as possible as to how they processed the text. In this way we hoped to reveal which contents they thought about and how they thought about them as they tried to understand the text.

EXPERIMENTS

We shall report data from three experiments that bear directly on what occurs during comprehension and how what occurs during comprehension predicts recall. Two experiments involved having third-grade children or adults think aloud as they read narrative texts, one sentence at a time, under the instruction to try to understand what it was that they were reading and then to tell us about their understanding. No other instructional goal was given to the subjects. In thinking aloud about their understanding, we hoped to find evidence for how readers constructed a coherent representation of a text during reading. Two of the experiments involved asking the subjects to recall the same texts. These experiments provided the retention data that could be predicted from knowledge of what people did during comprehension as revealed in the think-aloud protocols.

As Schank (1986) speculated, a coherent construction of a text could be achieved by explanation and prediction of events. Translating this into the present context, in order to achieve explanatory coherence, subjects would have to find purposes, reasons, causes for, and make predictions based on causal consequences of the current event. These operations should occur in working memory while the subject tries to understand the focal sentence in reading through the text. If purposes, reasons, and causes are to be used as explanations that integrate sentences, the current sentence would have to be held in working memory, and information from long-term memory would have to be activated and accessed, either from a representation of the text that has been constructed thus far or from relevant world knowledge.

Causal explanations have been termed *backward inferences* by van den Broek (1990) and van den Broek, Fletcher, and Risden (1993). Predicting consequences would constitute *forward-going inferences* (van den Broek, 1990) or *elaborative inferences* (McKoon & Ratcliff, 1986). When the latter successfully predict what occurs in the text, they, along with explanatory inferences, could serve to integrate the current focal sentence with other sentences and with stable knowledge structures. The construction of an integrated, coherent representation of a text, while it is read, would lead to better recall. Conceptualizations of the sentences would thus be linked into a text representation through operations in working memory. In retrieval, the activation of one conceptualization would lead to the activation and retrieval of other conceptualizations. Hence, those subjects who integrate sentences through explanation or those texts that allow more explanatory integration would lead to greater recall of the sentences contained in the text.

The think-aloud data and materials for Experiment 1 came from a dissertation study by Suh (1989; see Suh & Trabasso, 1993, for thinking-aloud data on references to goals as explanations, and their validation against online, recognition-priming data of goal-based inferences). The stories were written according to the constraints on categories and relations imposed by goal failure or goal success (hierarchical or sequential) representations generated from the causal network model of Trabasso, van den Broek, and Suh (1989).

There were three episodes in each story. In the first episode, the protagonist's main goal was either attained or not, leading to a related or unrelated second goal that was attained. Each story was identified by the main protagonist's name. The first and second goals of the main protagonist were: Betty (give a birthday present; knit a sweater), Bill (regain eyesight, find a magic waterfall), Fred (attain a passing math grade, organize a study group), Ivan (kill a giant, learn to be a swordsman), Jimmy (attain a bicycle, earn money), Mickey (find food, make a hole in a wall), William (become a king, kill a brother), and Jane (lose weight, learn racquetball). The length of the stories ranged from 13 to 18 sentences with a mean of 15 sentences. The eight pairs of stories are contained in Suh (1989) and are available upon request from the first author.

In Suh's study, eight students at The University of Chicago each read eight different stories, one sentence at a time. The instructions were to try to understand the sentence in the context of its story, and to tell us about his or her understanding. Because each story had one of two possible structures based upon a goal success or failure in the first episode, there were 16 stories in all. Each subject read four different goal success stories and four different goal failure stories. The structure of the stories was counterbalanced over subjects. Following is an example of a goal failure (hierarchical) story, called the Betty Story:

> Once there was a girl named Betty.
> One day, she found that her mother's birthday was coming soon.
> Betty really wanted to give her mother a present.
> She went to the department store.
> She found that everything was too expensive.
> Betty could not buy anything for her mother.
> She felt sorry.
> Several days later, Betty saw her friend knitting.
> Betty was good at knitting.
> She decided to knit a sweater.
> She selected a pattern from a magazine.
> She followed the instructions in the article.
> Finally, Betty finished a beautiful sweater.
> She pressed the sweater.
> She folded the sweater carefully.
> She gave the sweater to her mother.
> Her mother was excited when she saw the present.
> (Suh, 1989, p. 86)

A second study, called Experiment 2, was carried out in order to obtain recall data on adult subjects. An independent group of 16 students at The University of Chicago each read, normally and silently, eight different (four goal success and four goal failure) versions of the sixteen total that were used in Experiment 1. After reading a story, each subject rated it on a 7-point scale of coherence. Each subject recalled, in turn, four stories after reading and rating each story, and came back 2 days later and recalled the remaining four stories. The rating and recall of all 16 versions and their orders were counter-balanced over the subjects.

For Experiments 1 and 2, we report data from analyses of the operations observed during thinking aloud, and on the relationship of these strategies to long-term retention obtained 2 days later. Our interest in delayed rather than immediate recall rests on the assumption that the delayed recall is a better measure than immediate recall of the effect of integration of the text content during comprehension. The reader is referred to Suh and Trabasso (1993) for studies on goal references in Experiment 1 and their relation to recognition priming during reading, to Trabasso and Suh (1993) for data on the effects of comprehension in Experiment 1 on immediate and delayed recall, and to Trabasso, Suh, and Payton (1994) for the relation between goal inferences during comprehension and coherence ratings by adult subjects in Experiment 2.

Experiments 1 and 2 constitute a between-subjects design where different subjects thought-aloud during comprehension or recalled the texts. These experiments allowed the evaluation of differences between stories but not of individual differences between subjects in comprehension and in recall. In Experiment 3, think-aloud data on 20 third-grade children (average age was 9 years) were obtained in a within-subject design. Here the same subjects thought aloud and recalled the same stories, and allowed the study of individual differences in strategies used during comprehension and the amount recalled. In Experiment 3, each subject read three of the stories used in Experiments 1 and 2 (Jimmy, Betty, and John). The children each thought aloud under the same conditions of Experiment 1 during comprehension of the first and third stories. During the reading of the second story, they answered questions. The question-answering data are not reported here. The subjects then were asked to recall the first and third stories. The data of interest, then, are those on thinking aloud during the first and third stories, and on the recall of these same stories.

Strategies During Comprehension

The think-aloud procedure in Experiments 1 and 3 yielded a rich set of data. Adult subjects in Experiment 1 averaged 2.99 clauses whereas the third-graders in Experiment 3 averaged 3.87 clauses in thinking about their understanding of each sentence.

Trabasso and Suh (1993) identified four types of strategies or what they called, *mental operations*, that were used by the adult subjects in understanding sentences. The operations all pertained to and were constrained by the content of the focal sentence: (a) maintaining the focal sentence, (b) explaining it, (c) associating to it, and (d) predicting its consequences. Tables 12.1 and 12.2 show examples of these operations from adult and child protocols of Experiments 1 and 3, respectively. The examples from adults and children are both shown in order to indicate their similarity.

When these subjects maintained the current focal sentence, they either repeated it verbatim or paraphrased it so as to preserve its meaning, and they frequently embedded it in an explanation. In Tables 12.1 and 12.2 (Section 1, "Maintain") subjects maintained the current sentence by making minor changes or additions of the original text. They explained the current sentence in one of three ways. First (Section 2A, "Explain, Retrieve Text Only"), they retrieved information from a sentence or sentences that occurred earlier in the text and gave this retrieved information as a reason or reasons for the information in the current sentence. The respective examples give a condition (expensive) or a goal (earn money) as reasons from the text for an failed outcome (not able to buy anything) or an attempt (asking for a job). Second, they elaborated world knowledge and used this information as a reason or reasons for the current event (Section 2B, "Explain, Retrieve and Elaborate"). The adult subject explained the failed outcome (merchandise was too expensive) by a set of circumstances (children don't have much money), whereas the child subject explained a successful

TABLE 12.1
Think-Aloud (TA) Operations On Current Sentence: Experiment 1, Adult Readers

---

1.   MAINTAIN

Story: Once there was a girl named Betty.
TA: "There's a young female person whose name is Betty."

2.   EXPLAIN

  A.   Retrieve Text Only

Story: Betty found that everything was too expensive.
Story: Betty could not buy anything for her mother.
TA: "This was because everything was so expensive."

  B.   Retrieve Text and Elaborate

Story: Betty found that everything was too expensive.
TA: "This is Betty discovering that on her childhood budget, she really has not the money necessary to buy the kind of gift that she wants to give to her mother."

  C.   Elaborate Only

Story: One day, Betty found that her mother's birthday was coming soon.
TA: "Most children eventually discover that their parent's birthday is around the corner or somebody tells them."

3.   ASSOCIATE

Story: One day, Betty found that her mother's birthday was coming soon.
TA: "I imagine Betty kind of young."

4.   PREDICT

  A.   Event in Text

Story: Betty found a pretty purse.
TA: "She is gonna ask how much it was or buy it."

  B.   Event not in Text

Story: Several days later, Betty saw her friend knitting.
TA: "This could put ideas in Betty's mind that she could learn how to knit."

---

outcome (attaining a bike) by goal plans of action (earning money through a job and going to a department store to purchase the goal object). Third, they both retrieved and elaborated in order to explain the current event (Section 2C, "Explain and Elaborate Only"). Here, subjects added relevant information from world knowledge that went beyond the text. The adult subject explains an initiating event (discovering a birthday date) by the means by which this could occur (someone tells the person). The child subject explains how an initiating event (seeing something) occurred by describing the actions and conditions that enable it to occur (riding along the street).

The subjects associated to the current sentence by adding to it, but what was added did not provide reasons or conditions for the occurrence of the current sentence's content (Section 3, "Associate"). Both subjects associated an age with the protagonist. Subjects also made predictions of future events that reflected causal or conditional inferences about consequences of the event in the current sentence (Section 4, "Predict"). In prediction, the events sometimes actually occurred later in the story (Section 4, "Predict, Event in Text"). The subjects both inferred possible outcomes from attempts (finding a purse was a prelude to buying it, and walking to the second floor was a prelude to locating a goal object). In each case, the text supported a forward-going inference. Predictions about events were made but they did not occur in the text (Section 4, "Predict,

TABLE 12.2
Think-Aloud (TA) Operations On Current Sentence: Experiment 3, Nine-Year-Old Readers

1.   MAINTAIN

Story: Jimmy spoke to his mother.
TA: "Jimmy asked his mother."

2.   EXPLAIN

     A.   Retrieve Text Only

Story: Jimmy wanted to earn some money.
Story: Jimmy asked for a job at a nearby grocery store.
TA: "Jimmy wanted to earn some money so he asked for a job at a nearby grocery store."

     B.   Retrieve and Elaborate

Story: Jimmy wanted to buy a bike.
Story: Jimmy bought a new bike.
TA: "Jimmy wanted a new bike. He went to a grocery store where he was selling a lot of groceries so he got a lot of money for it and then he went to a department store and he saw a new bike and bought it."

     C.   Elaborate Only

Story: One day, Jimmy saw his friend Tom riding a new bike.
TA: "Maybe, um, he was just riding his bike along the street or something."

3.   ASSOCIATE

Story: Once there was a boy named Jimmy.
TA: "He was a teenager."

4.   PREDICTION

     A.   Event in Text

Story: Jimmy walked to the second floor.
TA: "It might be where the bikes are."

     B.   Event not in Text

Story: Jimmy wanted to earn some money.
TA: "He might like work for people in the garden or something."

Note. When these subjects maintained the current focal sentence, they either repeated it verbatim or paraphrased.

Event Not in Text"). The adult subject inferred that an initiating event (seeing a friend doing something) could cause a goal (learn how to knit). This was done before the adult subject found out that the protagonist was already skilled at knitting. The child subject inferred a goal plan (working as a gardener) as a means to achieve a goal (earning money). This was done before the subject found out that the protagonist went to a grocery store and asked for a job.

When subjects explained something, they attempted to provide the conditions, reasons or circumstances that caused or enabled it to occur. These explanations met the criterion of logical necessity (negative counter-factual of the form, if not-A, then not-B) argued for by the philosopher Mackie (1980) and applied by Trabasso and his colleagues (Trabasso, Secco, & van den Broek, 1984; Trabasso & Sperry, 1985; Trabasso & van den Broek, 1985; Trabasso, van den Broek, and Suh, 1989) in evaluating the existence of a causal relation between two events in narrative texts. Tables 12.1 and 12.2 provide several situated examples where the current sentence is a necessary condition for what they expect to occur. For example, on the unfulfilled predictions, if Betty did not find a purse, she would not have asked how much it cost or bought it. If Jimmy did not want a job, he would not have worked for someone in a garden.

In order to assess the degree of occurrence of each of these four types of operations, and to compare younger and the older readers, the total number of clauses across subjects and stories were counted for Experiments 1 and 3. Then, the proportion of total clauses for each category was determined. Table 12.3 summarizes these proportions for the adult and child subjects.

The Function of Mental Operations During Comprehension

If subjects are constructing a functional, mental representation of the text, what role do these operations play? They all involve relationships between information in the current sentence and either world knowledge or information in other sentences. To integrate the sentences of the text with one another, three operations appear to be important: maintaining, retrieving and explaining, and predicting. Through these operations, the present sentence is related to events from the past and/or to future text. These three operations constituted 83% of the clauses uttered in thinking aloud by adults. In the children's protocols, they constituted 78%. Associating information from the current sentence with information stored about the world does not seem to facilitate integration of the text representation. We now turn to the examination of the co-occurrence of these operations by subjects and on texts.

Correlation of Operations

Integration of the conceptualizations that underlie the sentences being read can occur by maintaining the current sentence, retrieving information from the text,

TABLE 12.3
Distribution of Strategies

	Percentage of Total Clauses	
Straategy	Adults	Children
1. Maintain	24	39
2. Explain		
A. Retrieve	19	22
B. Retrieve-Elaborate	17	6
C. Elaborate	9	4
3. Associate	17	22
4. Predict		
A. in Text	2	6
B. not in text	12	2

For adult subjects, explaining constituted 45% of the clauses. This was followed by maintaining (24%), associating (17%), and predicting (14%). The 9-year-olds followed a similar pattern except that they maintained (39%) more than they explained (32%), and they associated (22%) more and predicted less (8%) than did the adults (14%). The 9-year-olds were more accurate in predicting what was going to occur than the adult readers.

Statistical comparisons are not made on these data. Only two (hierarchical) stories were used for the children whereas sixteen were used for adults.

and/or activating world knowledge to explain its occurrence, and drawing implications or predictions for future events. The pair-wise correlations between retrieving, explaining, associating and predicting were found for each of kind of reader. To calculate these correlations, the total frequencies of explaining, retrieving, maintaining, and associating/predicting were found for each of 8 stories and multiplied by 2 versions, which equals 16 stories over the eight adult subjects in Experiment 1. For Experiment 3, the same frequencies were found across the two stories for each of the 20 children. Thus, the correlations among operations are first, by stories for Experiment 1, and second, by subjects for Experiment 3. Figure 12.1 summarizes the findings.

Figure 12.1 shows that for stories, the strategies of explaining and retrieving text information were positively correlated with maintaining the current sentence ($p < .05$) However, when subjects maintain, explain, or retrieve, they do not tend to associate or predict. These negative correlations did not, however, reach statistical significance. Figure 12.1 shows that the pattern of data found on stories were replicated in Experiment 3 on children. All correlations for the children in Fig. 12.1 were significant at the .05 level except for the relationship between maintaining and associating/predicting ($p = .11$). The pattern of findings on correlations among the operations thus held over both subjects and stories.

We examined the *reliability* of individual differences on the children's data since the children thought about the sentences in each of two stories. Correlations between the subject's operations during the first and third stories were found.

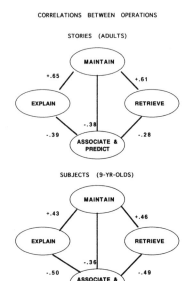

CORRELATIONS BETWEEN OPERATIONS

FIG. 12.1.   Correlations of mental operations.

The dependent measures were the respective relative frequencies of explaining, maintaining, associating, predicting, or recalling. Of these, three correlations reached significance at the .05 level: explaining ($r = .73$), maintaining ($r = .58$), and recalling ($r = .79$). Associating and predicting were not reliable within subjects (the respective r's were .37 and .06). Thus, reliable individual differences were found across stories in some comprehension strategies and in recall. We now examine whether there is a relationship between what was done during comprehension and what is recalled.

Relationships Between Mental Operations During Comprehension and Retention of Text

With respect to question on the relationship between comprehension and recall, our expectations were as follows. Those subjects who integrate sentences during comprehension should retain them better than those subjects who do not. Similarly, those stories that allow sentences to be integrated should be retained better than those stories that do not. To test these hypotheses, we examined correlations between the frequency of occurrence of the operations with retention of the text, both by individuals and by stories.

In using correlation methods, we apologize to Jerry Myers (1990) has argued for experimental over correlation methods in studies of text. However, there are occasions when the best or perhaps the only way to explore data is to do correlation analyses. Correlation analysis is especially useful when the text properties covary and when one wishes to examine whether there are individual or text differences (Kieras & Just, 1984).

In order to assess the correlation between what occurred during comprehension and what was remembered, we carried out multiple regression analyses on the number of each kind of operation and the number of sentences recalled for the 16 stories of Experiments 1 and 2, and by the 20 children of Experiment 3. Recall that Experiments 1 and 2 followed a between-subjects design of having independent groups of adults think-aloud or recall the same stories. Experiment 3 had the same group of children think aloud and recall the same two stories.

The variables of explaining, maintaining, and associating and predicting were entered into a regression analysis. For stories read and recalled by adults, the percentage of variance accounted for in recall by this four-factor model was 52% $[F(3,12) = 4.32, p < .05]$. For the children, it was 41% $[F(3,16) = 3.66, p < .05]$. In a stepwise regression, only the explaining variable was significant. For the stories on adult subjects, explaining accounted for 45% of the variance; for the children, explaining accounted for 31%, $[F(1,14) = 11.31, p < .01; F(1,18) = 8.20, p < .01]$.

Explanation and prediction were assessed further as measures of integration by individual subjects. Recall that the prediction data (see Table 12.3) showed that the children were more accurate in their predictions than were the adults. In a multiple regression analysis, 54% of the variance $[F(2,17) = 9.80, p < .01]$ was accounted for in recall for children by the variables of explaining and predicting. In a stepwise regression, explaining accounted for 31% of the variance $[F(1,18) = 8.20, p < .01]$ The prediction variable accounted for an additional 22% of the variance $[F(2,17) = 9.80, p < .01]$. These data constitute the best evidence that backward and forward inferences during reading comprehension integrate information into a coherent, functional, memory representation.

Individual differences in explaining a story and recalling the same or a different story were further studied on the children's data. The explain-recall correlation within the first story, within the third story, between the first and third stories, and between the third and first stories were found. The four correlations were significant and virtually identical $(r = .51, p < .01)$. This means that what a child does by way of explanation predicts what that child remembers for the same story or across stories. The latter finding is important because different stories are used on the same subjects. It did not matter whether we used explaining the content of first story to predict memory of the content of the third story or explaining the content of the third story to predict the recall of the content of the first story. The within story data indicate that the stories that invoked more integrative activities are the stories that are better recalled.

DISCUSSION AND CONCLUSIONS

The three experiments, taken together, show that people attempt to understand narrative texts by striving for coherence in their interpretation of what they read. This coherence is explanatory in nature (Schank, 1986) and uses both backward and forward causal inferences to integrate sentence information. The inferences are backward (van den Broek, 1990) in that they serve to retrieve prior text and/or elaborate world knowledge in order to explain the current, focal sentence. The focal sentence is also maintained and embedded within an explanation. Other inferences are forward in nature (van den Broek, 1990) and are used to predict future events based upon causal consequences or implications of the current sentence. The explanations and predictions reflect knowledge of necessary relations. The cause of or reasons for what is being explained are necessary in the circumstances. Likewise, what is being explained is necessary in the circumstances for the predictions that are made. For texts and for individual subjects, the operations of maintaining, explaining, and retrieving were positively correlated among themselves. These operations apparently facilitated the integration of sentences over segments of the text during reading, and they were predictive of successful recall.

Because the operations were observed to occur in the think-aloud protocols, the information used in them is assumed to be accessible to subjects during reading. This accessibility suggests that the integration of information occurred in working memory. The correlation of retrieval, explanation, and maintenance found with texts and individual subjects suggests that the correlated operations occupied working memory at the same time. Trabasso and Suh (1993) analyzed the operations that occurred on 10 out of 16 stories (134 out of 235 sentences) in Experiments 1. The average intercorrelation of retrieval, explanation, and maintenance for the sentences was positive ($r = .30, p < .01$). The average intercorrelation of these three variables with associating was negative ($r = -.17, p < .01$). These data replicate the pattern found in the analysis given earlier for stories and individuals. They indicate that retrieval, explanation, and maintenance are invoked by the same sentences, and provide stronger evidence that the operations actually co-occur in working memory. More complete analyses on sentence operations will be reported in the future.

These data suggest that operations that occur during comprehension result in a more coherent memory representation and better long-term recall. The correlation between what occurs during encoding, as revealed by the think-aloud protocols, with what is recalled indicates that the prior findings by Trabasso and his colleagues (Trabasso et al., 1984; Trabasso & van den Broek, 1985) on causal chain and causal relations and recall were not merely retrieval effects as claimed by McKoon and Ratcliff (1992). The data, however, suggest that explanatory inferences are "strategic" and motivated, as also claimed by McKoon and Ratcliff

(1992). That does not, however, detract from their importance as comprehension strategies. Our findings suggest that the strategies we have identified are important to constructing coherent interpretations of text and have consequences for long-term retention of what is read and understood. Most readers read for a purpose, and that purpose is to understand and learn from what they read.

The regularity of the strategies that were revealed by the think-aloud data appears to validate this verbal method for assessing what occurs during the comprehension of a text. The data indicate that subjects have access to the contents of what they are thinking about during comprehension, consistent with the claims of Ericsson and Simon (1984) and Ericsson (1988). We inferred strategies used by subjects from the content available and expressed by the subjects. The processes that underlie these strategies were not directly observable nor were they accessible to the subjects. That fact that people cannot access processes (Nisbit & Wilson, 1977) does not detract from the use of think-aloud data to infer such processes or their outcomes such as strategies. The use of think-aloud data in this way is consistent with the use of performance measures to accomplish the same goal. The think-aloud data also support the arguments by Magliano and Graesser (1991) for the use of verbal protocols to assess inferences during comprehension as a part of a convergent-methods strategy of investigation.

The findings on individual differences in strategic processing suggest that subjects who use them may also be more efficient in processing information in working memory during comprehension. Trabasso and Suh (1993) found that explaining, maintaining, and retrieving predicted faster reading times for individual sentences. Daneman and Carpenter's (1980, 1983) working-memory span test assumes that subjects are more efficient in integrating information between sentences. They found a correlation between working memory capacity and the making of pronominal inferences at varying distances across sentences in the surface text or in resolving inconsistencies within sentences. Whitney, Ritchie, and Clark (1991) found that differences in performance on the same working-memory span test also correlated with differences in ability to make predictive inferences. Singer, Andrusiak, Reisdorf, and Black (1992) found that differences in a similar working-memory span test predicted differences in bridging causally related ideas, over and above differences in vocabulary. They interpreted their findings in terms of access of relevant knowledge during comprehension.

The promise of the present set of studies is that the strategies revealed by think-aloud methods during comprehension require access of knowledge from prior text and from other sources, as well as integration of sentences prior to and subsequent to the current one. We hope to examine whether the occurrence of the strategies predict, a priori, measures of working memory span as well as individual differences in pronominal resolution, answering questions, or bridging inferences.

ACKNOWLDGMENTS

This research was supported by grants from the Spencer Foundation, the Smart Foundation, and Grant HD 25742 from the National Institute of Child Health and Human Development. Paula Payton and Rachna Jain were supported by Irving B. Harris Fellowships thorough the Harris Center for Developmental Studies.

REFERENCES

Balota, D. A., Flores d'Arcais, G. B., & Rayner, K. (1990). (Eds.), *Comprehension processes in reading* (pp. 9–32). Hillsdale, NJ.: Lawrence Erlbaum Associates.

Collins, A., Brown, J. S., & Larkin, K. M. (1980). Inference in text understanding. In R. J. Spiro, B. C. Bruce, & W. F. Brewer (Eds.), *Theoretical issues in reading comprehension* (pp. 385–407). Hillsdale, NJ: Lawrence Erlbaum Associates.

Daneman, M., & Carpenter, P. (1980). Individual differences in working memory and reading. *Journal of Verbal Learning and Verbal Behavior, 19*, 450–466.

Daneman, M., & Carpenter, P. (1983). Individual differences in integrating information between and within sentences. *Journal of Experimental Psychology: Learning, Memory, and Cognition, 9*, 561–584.

Ericsson, K. A. (1988). Concurrent verbal reports on text comprehension: A review. *Text, 8*, 295–235.

Ericsson, K. A., & Simon, H. A. (1984). *Protocol analysis: Verbal reports as data*. Cambridge, MA: MIT Press.

Fletcher, C .R. (1986). Strategies for the allocation of short-term memory during comprehension. *Journal of Memory and Language, 25*, 43–58.

Fletcher, C. R., & Bloom, C. P. (1988). Causal reasoning in the comprehension of simple narrative texts. *Journal of Memory and Language, 27*, 235–244.

Forster, K. I. (1981). Priming and the effects of sentence and lexical contexts on naming time: Evidence for autonomous lexical processing. *Quarterly Journal of Experimental Psychology, 33a*, 465–495.

Frederiksen, C. H. (1985). Cognitive models and discourse analysis. In C. R. Cooper & S. Greenbaum (Eds.), *Written communication annual. Vol. 1: Linguistic approaches to the study of written discourse* (pp. 227–267). Beverly Hills, CA: Sage.

Graesser, A. C. (1981). *Prose comprehension beyond the world*. New York: Springer-Verlag.

Graesser, A. C., & Black, J. B. (Eds.),(1985). *The psychology of questions*. Hillsdale, NJ: Lawrence Erlbaum Associates.

Graesser, A. C., & Clark, L. F. (1985). *Structures and procedures of implicit knowledge*. Norwood, NJ: Ablex.

Graesser, A. C., Haberlandt, K., & Kozumi, D. D. (1987). How is reading time influenced by knowledge based inferences and world knowledge? In B. K. Britton & S. M. Glynn (Eds.), *Executive control processes in reading?* Hillsdale, NJ: Lawrence Erlbaum Associates.

Guindon, R. (1980). *Inferences in story comprehension*. Unpublished master's thesis, University of Toronto.

Guindon, R. (1981). *Use of verbal reports to study inferences in text comprehension*. Paper presented at the Cognitive Science Conference, University of California at Berkeley.

Keenan, J. M., Baillet, S. D., & Brown, P. (1984). The effects of causal cohesion on comprehension and memory. *Journal of Verbal Learning and Verbal Behavior, 23*, 115–126.

Keenan, J. M., Golding, J. M., Potts, G. R., Jennings, T. M., & Aman, C. J. (1990). Methodological issues in evaluating the occurrence of inferences. In A. C. Graesser & G. H. Bower (Eds.), *Inferences and text comprehension* (pp. 295–312). Orlando, FL: Academic Press.

Keenan, J. M., Potts, G. R., Golding, J. M., & Jennings, T. M. (1990). Which elaborative inferences are drawn during reading? A question of methodologies. In D. A. Balota, G. B. Flores d'Arcais, & K. Rayner (Eds.), *Comprehension processes in reading* (pp. 377–402). Hillsdale, NJ: Lawrence Erlbaum Associates.

Kieras, D. E., & Just, M. A. (Eds.), (1984). *New Methods in Reading Comprehension Research.* Hillsdale, NJ.: Lawrence Erlbaum Associates.

Kintsch, W., & van Dijk, T. A. (1978). Toward a model of text comprehension and production. *Psychological Review, 85*, 363–394.

Lehnert, W. G. (1978). *The process of question answering.* Hillsdale, NJ: Lawrence Erlbaum Associates.

Long, D. L., & Golding, J. M. (1993). Super-ordinate goal inferences: Are they automatically encoded during comprehension? *Discourse Processes, 15*, 55–74.

Long, D. L., Golding, J. M., & Graesser, A. C. (1992). A test of the online status of goal-related inferences. *Journal of Memory and Language, 31*, 634–647.

Long, D. L., Golding, J. M., Graesser, A. C., & Clark, A. C. (1990). Goal, event, and state inferences: An investigation of inference generation during story comprehension. In A. C. Graesser & G. H. Bower (Eds.), *Inferences and text comprehension* (pp. 89–102). Orlando, FL: Academic Press.

Mackie, J. L. (1980). *The cement of the universe: A study of causation.* Oxford: Clarendon.

Magliano, J. P., Baggett, W. B., Johnson, B. K., & Graesser, A. C. (1993). The time course of generating causal antecedent and causal consequence inferences. *Discourse Processes, 16*, 35–54.

Magliano, J. P. & Graesser, A. C. (1991). A three-pronged method for studying inference generation in literary text. *Poetics, 20*, 193–232.

McKoon, G., & Ratcliff, R. (1986). Inferences about predictable events. *Journal of Experimental Psychology: Learning, Memory and Cognition, 12*, 82–91.

McKoon, G., & Ratcliff, R. (1990a). Dimensions of inference. In A. C. Graesser & G. H. Bower (Eds.), *Inferences and text comprehension* (pp. 313–328). Orlando, FL: Academic Press.

McKoon, G., & Ratcliff, R. (1990b). Textual inferences: Models and measures. In D. A. Balota, G. B. Flores d'Arcais, & K. Rayner (Eds.), *Comprehension processes in reading* (pp. 403–422). Hillsdale, NJ: Lawrence Erlbaum Associates.

McKoon, G., & Ratcliff, R. (1992). Inference during reading. *Psychological Review, 99*, 440–466.

Myers, J. L. (1990). Causal relatedness and text comprehension. In D. A. Balota, G. B. Flores d'Arcais, & K. Rayner (Eds.), *Comprehension processes in reading* (pp. 361–376). Hillsdale, NJ: Lawrence Erlbaum Associates.

Myers, J. L., Shinjo, M., & Duffy., S. D. (1987). Degree of causal relatedness and memory. *Journal of Memory and Language, 26*, 453–465.

Newell, A., & Simon, H. A. (1972). *Human problem solving.* Englewood Cliffs, NJ: Prentice-Hall.

Nisbit, R. E., & Wilson, T. D. (1977). Telling more than we can know: Verbal reports on mental processes. *Psychological Review, 84*, 231–259.

Olson, G. M., Duffy, S. A., & Mack, R. L. (1980). Applying knowledge of writing conventions to prose comprehension and composition. In W. E. McKeatchie (Ed.). *Learning, cognition & college teaching* (pp. 67–84). San Francisco: Jossey-Bass.

Olson, G. M., Duffy, S. A., & Mack, R. L. (1984). Thinking-out-loud as a method for studying real-time comprehension processes. In D. Kieras & M. Just (Eds.), *New methods in the study of immediate processes in comprehension* (pp. 253–286). Hillsdale, NJ: Lawrence Erlbaum Associates.

Olson, G. M., Mack, R. L., & Duffy, S. A. (1981). Cognitive aspects of genre. *Poetics, 10*, 283–315.

Omanson, R. C. (1982). An analysis of narratives: Identifying central, supportive and distracting content. *Discourse Processes, 5*, 195–224.

Rumelhart, D. E. (1991). Understanding understanding. In W. Kessen, A. Ortony, & F. Craig (Eds.), *Memories, thoughts, and emotions: Essays in honor of George Mandler* (pp. 257–275). Hillsdale, NJ: Lawrence Erlbaum Associates.

Schank, R. C. (1975). The structure of episodes in memory. In D. G. Bobrow & A. M. Collins (Eds.), *Representation and understanding: Studies in cognitive science*. New York: Academic Press.

Schank, R. C. (1986). *Explanation patterns: Understanding mechanically and creatively* (pp. 237–272). Hillsdale, NJ: Lawrence Erlbaum Associates.

Sharkey, A. J. C., & Sharkey, N. E. (1992). Weak contextual constraints in text and word priming. *Journal of Memory and Language, 31*, 543–572.

Singer, M., Andrusiak, P., Reisdorf, P., & Black, N. (1992). Individual differences in bridging inference processes. *Memory & Cognition, 20*, 539–548.

Stein, N. L., & Levine, L. (1989). The causal organization of emotion knowledge: A developmental study. *Cognition and Emotion, 3*, 343–378.

Stein, N. L., & Levine, L. (1990). Making sense out of emotional experience: The representation and use of goal-directed knowledge. In N. L. Stein, B. Leventhal, & T. Trabasso (Eds.), *Psychological and biological approaches to emotion* (pp. 45–74). Hillsdale, NJ: Lawrence Erlbaum Associates.

Stein, N. L., & Trabasso, T. (1989). Children's understanding of changing emotional states. In P. Harris & C. Saarni (Eds.), *The development of emotional understanding* (pp. 50–77). New York: Cambridge University Press.

Suh, S. (1989). *Converging evidence for causal inferences during comprehension*. Unpublished doctoral dissertation, The University of Chicago.

Suh, S., & Trabasso, T. (1993). Inferences during online processing: Converging evidence from discourse analysis, talk-aloud protocols, and recognition priming. *Journal of Memory and Language, 32*, 279–301.

Trabasso, T. (1992). Review of "Comprehension Processes in Reading," edited by D. A. Balota, G. B. Flores d'Arcais & K. Rayner. *Language and Speech, 34*, part 2, 195–205.

Trabasso, T., Secco, T., & van den Broek, P. (1984). Causal cohesion and story coherence. In H. Mandl, N. L. Stein, & T. Trabasso (Eds.), *Learning and comprehension of text* (pp. 83–111). Hillsdale, NJ: Lawrence Erlbaum Associates.

Trabasso, T., & Suh, S. (1993). Understanding text: achieving explanatory coherence through on-line inferences and mental operations in working memory. *Discourse Processes, 16*, 3–34.

Trabasso, T., & Sperry, L. (1985). Causal relatedness and importance of story events. *Journal of Memory and Language, 24*, 595–611.

Trabasso, T., Suh, S., & Payton, P. (1994). Explanatory coherence in understanding and thinking about events. In M. Gernsbacher & T. Givon (Eds.), *Coherence in conversational interaction*. Hillsdale, NJ: Lawrence Erlbaum Associates.

Trabasso, T., & van den Broek, P. (1985). Causal thinking and the representation of narrative events. *Journal of Memory and Language, 24*, 612–630.

Trabasso, T., van den Broek, P. W., & Liu, L. (1988). A model for generating questions that assess and promote comprehension. *Question Exchange, 2*, 25–38.

Trabasso, T., van den Broek, P., & Suh, S. (1989). Logical necessity and transitivity of causal relations in the representation of stories. *Discourse Processes, 12*, 1–25.

van den Broek, P. (1990). The causal inference maker: Towards a process model of inference generation in text comprehension. In D. A. Balota, G. B. Flores d'Arcais, & K. Rayner (Eds.), *Comprehension processes in reading* (pp. 423–446). Hillsdale, NJ: Lawrence Erlbaum Associates.

van den Broek, P., Fletcher, C. R., & Risden, K. (1993). Investigations of inferential processes in reading: A theoretical and methodological integration. *Discourse Processes, 12*, 169–180.

Waern, Y. (1979). *Thinking aloud during reading: A descriptive model and its application* (Tech. Rep. No. 546). Stockholm: University of Stockholm, Department of Psychology.

Whitney, P., Ritchie, B. G., & Clark, M. B. (1991). Working-memory capacity and the use of elaborative inferences in text comprehension. *Discourse Processes, 14*, 133–145.

13 Causal Validation and Causal Comprehension

Murray Singer
University of Manitoba

One theme in the study of discourse processes is that comprehension depends on the understander's detection of local and global coherence relations in a message. No global text characteristic has received more scrutiny in this regard than the causal relations underlying a message. One reason for this is that causal structure is a characteristic that transcends genre, pertaining to narrative and expository text alike (Black, 1985; Trabasso, Secco, & van den Broek, 1984).

There are a variety of devices that may be used to signal causation in a text, such as causal conjunctions. It is striking, therefore, that many text causal relations are implicit. Consider the story sequence, "Androclus, the slave of a Roman consul stationed in Africa, ran away from his brutal master." It is plain that Androclus ran away because he disliked being a slave, even though no explicit signal of causality appears. Indeed, in some circumstances, the use of causal conjunctions has no measurable impact (Singer, 1986).

As a result, causal inferences have been subjected to careful inspection, particularly those that bridge (Haviland & Clark, 1974) the current text idea to what has preceded. Consider the sequence, "Tony's friend suddenly pushed him into a pond, He walked home, soaking wet, to change his clothes" (Myers, Shinjo, & Duffy, 1987, p. 462). A complete understanding of the second sentence requires the bridging inference that Tony was wet because he was pushed into the pond. Evidence that converges from online and memory measures indicates that causal bridging inferences frequently accompany comprehension (e.g., Black & Bern, 1981; Keenan, Baillet, & Brown, 1984; Myers et al., 1987; Potts, Keenan, & Golding, 1988; Singer & Ferreira, 1983; Trabasso & Sperry, 1985).

A basic assumption in this field is that bridging inferences are based upon the general knowledge of the reader. A central goal of the present project has been to

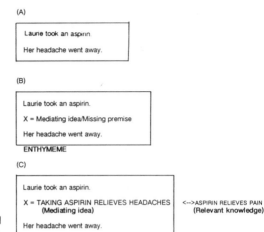

FIG. 13.1. Validation model analysis of a causal sequence.

subject that assumption to direct testing. More fundamentally, this work was designed to evaluate a model that specifies, in greater detail than prior analyses, the mental processes of bridging inference, with particular emphasis on causal bridges.

The Validation Model of Bridging Inferences

The validation model (Singer, Halldorson, Lear, & Andrusiak, 1992; Singer, Revlin, & Halldorson, 1990) may be outlined with reference to the sequence, "Laurie took an aspirin, Her headache went away," shown in Figure 13.1a. The evidence favoring online bridging inference computation suggests that, upon reading this sequence, the understander infers that the first event caused the second. However, according to the *validation model*, this inferential bridge must be validated with reference to relevant world knowledge before it is accepted by the reader. To achieve this, the reader first must identify a fact that when combined with the idea that Laurie took an aspirin, accounts for her headache going away. It is as though the reader constructs a mental *enthymeme*: that is, a syllogism with a missing premise. The missing premise "mediates" the explicit ideas. Figure 13.1b outlines the enthymeme.

As shown in Figure 13.1c, a tentative solution to the enthymeme is derived from the text ideas, yielding a proposition such as "TAKING ASPIRIN RE-LIEVES HEADACHES."[1] Then, this solution must be compared to world

---

[1]The abstract concepts and propositions that underlie words and messages are shown in all capitals.

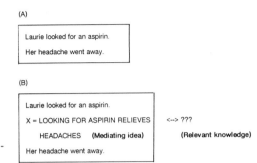

FIG. 13.2.   Validation model analysis of a temporal sequence.

knowledge. For the present example, the mediating fact is supported by that knowledge.

Consider, in contrast, the processing of a temporal sequence (e.g., Black & Bern, 1981) such as, "Laurie looked for an aspirin, Her headache went away." The sequence must be subjected to validation, because the reader does not know a priori whether or not the antecedent idea will turn out to be a satisfactory cause of the outcome. Figure 13.2 shows that a mediating idea is again computed for this sequence. The particular relevant knowledge that this mediating idea engages is uncertain. Therefore, the outcome of validating a temporal sequence is variable. First, causal search might be terminated when a criterion of duration is exceeded (Anderson, 1976, p. 268). Second, the reader might elaborate new ideas to mediate otherwise puzzling causal sequences. Indeed, people seem quite adept at doing this. For example, after reading sequences such as, "The floor was dirty because Sally used the mop," people later incorrectly recognized inference statements that might plausibly link the clauses, such as, "The mop was dirty" (Bransford & Johnson, 1973). Third, and furthermore, ideas that mediate temporal sequences might invoke the same validating knowledge as a corresponding causal sequence. Having read, "Laurie looked for an aspirin, Her headache went away," one might decide that Laurie had found and taken some aspirin.

The validation model has generated numerous testable hypotheses concerning causal bridging inferences. The rest of this chapter is organized as follows. First, evidence supporting a basic prediction of the validation model is presented. Second, some alternate interpretations of the evidence are considered. Third, the status of validating knowledge in the resulting text representation is evaluated. Fourth, several corollaries of validation processing are inspected. Finally, the relationship between the validation model and other theories of causal text processing are examined.

VALIDATION OF CAUSAL BRIDGING INFERENCES

A basic test of the validation model was performed using materials such as set (1).

(1) a. Laurie took an aspirin. Her headache went away.

b. Laurie looked for an aspirin. Her headache went away.

c. Do aspirins relieve headaches?

The subjects read either the causal sequence (1a) or the control temporal sequence (1b). The first and second sentence of such sequences will be called the *antecedent* and the *outcome*, respectively. After an interval of 2.5 seconds, all subjects viewed question (1c). This question queries the knowledge that was hypothesized to validate the mediating fact of the causal sequence. The mediating fact of the temporal sequence, in contrast, is posited to engage either no knowledge, different knowledge, or, with small probability, the same knowledge. Therefore, it was predicted that people would need less time to answer (1c) after reading the causal sequence than the temporal sequence.

In this experiment and most of the others, alternatives such as (1a) and (1b) were randomly cycled across different lists so that each subject viewed each item in one condition; and, across lists, each item appeared once in each condition. Over 60% of the stimuli were filler items that presented "no" questions about general knowledge and "yes" and "no" questions about passage details. The subjects read the sentences in a self-paced fashion on computer-controlled monochrome monitors. Answers were registered using the keys either of response panels or computer keyboards. All effects were evaluated alternately treating subjects and items as the random variable, and using a criterion of $\alpha = .05$. Exceptions to these features are noted later.

Consistent with the main prediction, answer times of 2,174 ms and 2,373 ms were measured in the causal and the temporal conditions, respectively (Singer et al., 1992, Experiment 1).[2] Furthermore, this outcome was measured in the frame of reference of another familiar result. That is, an important online index of bridging inference has been that people need more time to read about the far effects of text causes than about near effects (Keenan et al., 1984; Myers et al., 1987; cf. McKoon & Ratcliff, 1980a). The causal and temporal sequences in (1) are comparable to exemplars of Myers et al.'s nearest and furthest degrees of causal relatedness, respectively. Consistent with the previous findings, reading time for, "Her headache went away" was 311 ms faster in the causal than the temporal condition.

---

[2]In all of the experiments, the condition mean answer times and error rates were positively correlated, discounting the possibility of speed accuracy trade offs.

244

We next set out to evaluate the answer time prediction using longer texts (Singer et al., 1992, Experiment 2). Causal (and corresponding temporal) sequences such as, "Mark poured (placed) the bucket of water on (by) the fire, The fire went out," were embedded in passages of seven sentences. After each passage, the subject answered six randomly ordered questions, including the experimental item, "Does water extinguish fire?" Answer time for these questions was 156 ms faster in the causal condition than the temporal condition. The reading time for the second sentences of the experimental sequences was likewise 271 ms faster for causal items. The results were viewed as strongly supporting the validation model.

ALTERNATIVE EXPLANATIONS

Although the joint profile of the reading time and answer time results supported the validation hypothesis, several counterexplanations of the data were considered. First, the *priming* hypothesis states that, even though the wording was very similar in the causal and temporal antecedents (McKoon & Ratcliff, 1986; Potts et al., 1988), the questions might have been primed more by the causal words. Second, the *context checking* interpretation is that the causal answer time advantage is due to greater compatibility between the question and the causal passage than its temporal counterpart (e.g., Forster, 1981; McKoon & Ratcliff, 1986; Potts et al., 1988). According to this view, the causal advantage reflects retrieval processes rather than online inference processing.

To address both priming and context checking, Singer et al. (1992) conducted a control experiment in which the causal outcome sentences were deleted from sets such as (1). That is, the subjects simply read "Laurie took/looked-for an aspirin," and then answered, "Do aspirins relieve headaches?" This procedure should preserve any priming advantage that accrues from the causal antecedent sentence. Likewise, insofar as the entire contextual difference between causal and temporal *passages* is due to the antecedent sentence, the one-sentence control ought to sustain context checking. In contrast, the validation model predicts that no causal advantage should be detected using the control procedure. Given only the antecedent sentence, the reader does not have to construct a bridging inference. Therefore the "relevant" world knowledge should not be invoked. Consistent with this analysis, the control procedure abolished the answer time advantage of the causal condition.

According to a third counterexplanation, the processes of comprehending the temporal outcome sentence spill over into the answering phase, yielding slow temporal answering times. However, *spillover* is refuted by the results of the experiment that used passages of seven sentences. As discussed earlier, those passages were followed by random sequences of six questions, including two experimental questions. Because of the lengthy and unpredictable interval between an experimental sequence and its question, the causal answer time advantage could not have been due to spillover.

These three counterexplanations were also addressed by some of the data of Singer et al. (1990) and by the inspection of validation processing using a priming procedure (Halldorson & Singer, 1992). The application of the priming procedure is considered next.

INTEGRATING VALIDATING KNOWLEDGE
AND TEXT REPRESENTATION

Support for the validation model raises the question of whether the relevant, validating knowledge is integrated with the text representation. McKoon and Ratcliff (1988) asked a comparable question about the knowledge that supports elaborative inferences (in contrast to bridging inferences). Their subjects read series, each of which consisted of several brief passages followed by a list of test statements. Item (2) illustrates an experimental passage in one series.

> (2) The child psychologist watched the infant play with her toys. The little girl found a tomato to roll across the floor with her nose.

Sequence (2) emphasizes the shape of tomatoes. Postreading judgments revealed that passage sentences (e.g., "The child psychologist . . .") and relevant facts (e.g., "Tomatoes are round") mutually primed one another. Following the basic rationale of this priming procedure (McKoon & Ratcliff, 1980b), the authors concluded that the relevant knowledge was integrated with the passage representation.

Halldorson and Singer (1992) applied McKoon and Ratcliff's priming procedure to the question of whether validating knowledge is integrated with text representation. In one experiment, the subjects read series consisting of one experimental and two filler passages. Table 13.1 provides an example.

The experimental passage appeared either in a causal or a temporal version. Each series of three passages was followed by a fixed random sequence of four filler questions plus an experimental pair of questions consisting of a prime and a target. The target queried the knowledge hypothesized to validate the bridge between the causal antecedent and outcome (e.g., "Do bullets kill animals?"). There were three alternative priming questions: the same passage outcome, a different passage outcome, and a numerical question (see Table 13.1).

If validating knowledge is integrated with text ideas, then the outcome question, "Did the deer die?" should prime the question about the validating knowledge. However, this should occur only in the causal condition. As a result, answer time for the knowledge question should be faster in the causal condition than the temporal condition.

TABLE 13.1
Sample Materials Used to Investigate the Integration of Validating Knowledge and Text Ideas

---

A Series of Three Passages

The hiker shot/examined the injured deer. (causal/temporal)
The deer died.

Laurie's cousin lent her a hundred dollars.
Laurie bought some flowers.

The goat chewed on the rope.
The rope broke.

Prime-Target Question Pairs

Did the deer die? (same passage)
Do bullets kill animals?

Did Laurie buy some flowers? (different passage)
Do bullets kill animals?

Does two plus six equal eight? (numerical)
Do bullets kill animals?

Note. The passages were presented in a fixed random order.

Table 13.2 shows the results. Answer time was significantly faster in the causal than the temporal condition with same- and different-passage primes, but not with numerical primes. The same-prime result supports the validation hypothesis. The causal-temporal difference in the different prime effect was analogous to a result measured by McKoon and Ratcliff (1988). Their explanation states that, for the present study, the prime from the different passage does not remove the subject from the "retrieval context" of the series of three experimental passages. As a result, there is a causal answer time advantage even with different-passage primes. The numerical prime, in contrast, changes the retrieval context. General knowledge still permits "Do bullets kill animals?" to be answered correctly, but the causal answer time advantage is not significant with the numerical prime.

We interpreted these results to indicate that the validating knowledge was integrated with the text ideas. This conclusion, in turn, raises new questions about the resulting representation. To cite one example, after reading "The hiker shot the injured deer, The deer died," the reader might incorrectly recognize the inferential test statement, "A bullet killed the deer" (Bransford & Johnson, 1973). In contrast, it seems unlikely that false alarms would be observed for "Bullets kill animals." We are conducting further studies to probe this issue and other relationships between integrated text ideas and relevant knowledge.

The priming outcome provided further evidence against a context-checking interpretation of the inference validation results. First, the mutual priming of text

TABLE 13.2
Priming Experiment: Answer Times (in msec) as a Function of Condition and Prime Type

| Condition | Prime | | |
	Same	Different	Numerical
Causal	1,885	1,999	2,128
Temporal	2,003	2,082	2,174
Differences	128*	83*	46

*p < .05.

ideas is considered to reflect encoding processes rather than retrieval processes (McKoon & Ratcliff, 1980b). Second, the causal answer time advantage in the different-prime condition is inconsistent with context checking. This is because the different prime should not activate the paragraph with which the test question is hypothetically more compatible (McKoon & Ratcliff, 1988, p. 338).

COROLLARIES OF THE VALIDATION MODEL

The validation model has been a fruitful source of predictions concerning the processing of causal bridging inferences. This section evaluates several predictions, with reference to empirical evidence.

Validating Consistent and Inconsistent Causal Sequences

The validation model was initially evaluated using consistent causal sequences. In ordinary circumstances, however, causes do not always produce their expected outcomes. One might well encounter a text sequence such as "Mark poured the bucket of water on the fire, The fire grew hotter." In the present case, the fire might have been too great for a bucket of water to have much impact. Like consistent sequences, inconsistent ones must be subjected to validation. Indeed, if validation could be applied only to consistent sequences, it would be a pointless exercise.

Figure 13.3 shows that, according to the validation model, the comprehension of inconsistent causal sequences proceeds much in the same way as causal sequence validation. To understand "Mark poured the bucket of water on the fire, The fire grew hotter," the reader must identify an idea that, when coupled with the fact that Mark poured water on the fire, accounts for the fire going out. Figure 13.3b indicates that the reader might compute mediating ideas such as "WATER FEEDS FIRE" or "WATER IS COMBUSTIBLE." The comparison of

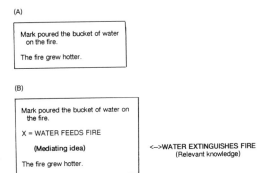

FIG. 13.3. Validation model analysis of an inconsistent sequence.

these ideas with general knowledge readily reveals them to be false, resulting in the reader's judgment that the sequence is unusual or inconsistent.

For the present example, validation processing invokes the same knowledge as the corresponding consistent sequence, namely, "WATER EXTINGUISHES FIRE." Perhaps counterintuitively, this leads to the prediction that understanding the consistent and inconsistent sequences will both facilitate the same relevant fact. That prediction (Singer, 1993) was inspected using materials such as Set (3):

(3) a. Mark poured the bucket of water on the bonfire. The bonfire went out. (consistent)

b. Mark placed the bucket of water by the bonfire. The bonfire burned hotter. (temporal)

c. Mark poured the bucket of water on the bonfire. The bonfire burned hotter. (inconsistent)

d. Does water extinguish fire?

Sequences (3a), (3b), and (3c) were consistent,[3] temporal, and inconsistent, respectively. In the experiment, the subject performed self-paced reading of the sentences of one version, and then answered Question (3d). Question (3d) probes the knowledge posited to validate the consistent and inconsistent sequences. Therefore, it was predicted that answer time would be slower in the temporal condition than in the others.

The comparison of consistent and inconsistent sequences prohibited using identical second sentences in all three conditions. Because the main new hypothesis was that answer time would be slower in the temporal than the inconsistent condition, the materials were constructed so that those versions had identical second sentences.

---

[3]The consistent sequences were simply the causal sequences of the prior experiments.

TABLE 13.3
Mean Correct Answer Times and Reading Times (in msec) in Experiments Examining
Validation Model Corollaries

| | | Measure | |
| | | | |
Experiment	Condition	Final Sentence Reading Time	Answer Time
Consistency	Consistent	1,905	2,131
	Temporal	2,132	2,331
	Inconsistent	2,333	2,153
Causal	Near causal	1,766	2,027
distance	Far causal	1,932	2,058
	Temporal	2,181	2,131
Backward	Causal forward	–	1,810
sequences	Temporal forward	–	2,028
	Causal backward	–	1,775
	Temporal backward	–	1,947
Moderate text	Motive	1,861	1,956
distance	Temporal	1,879	2,150
	Explicit	2,314	1,905
Greater text	Motive	1,818	1,938
distance	Temporal	1,909	2,060

The top panel of Table 13.3 shows that the temporal answer times exceeded the consistent and inconsistent ones, which were about equal. This outcome clearly supported the validation analysis. The pattern for second sentence reading time, also shown in Table 13.3, was different: Temporal reading time was slower than consistent, but faster than inconsistent. The slow inconsistent reading times suggest that the processes associated with detecting causal inconsistency are time consuming. In spite of this, the validating fact was equally facilitated in the consistent and inconsistent conditions. Finally, the slow inconsistent reading times also indicate that the answer time profile did not result from the spillover of temporal reading time into the answering phase.

Degrees of Causal Distance

The impact of causal relatedness upon the computation of bridging inferences has received careful examination. In fact, systematic inspection has revealed that outcome reading time increases monotonically with decreasing causal related-ness over at least four degrees of causal connection (Keenan et al., 1984; Myers et al., 1987). This suggests that it is more demanding to bridge a text effect to a far cause than a near one.

The validation model was applied to the problem of detecting connections as a function of causal relatedness (Singer et al., 1992, Experiment 3). The subjects viewed either antecedent (4a), (4b), or (4c), followed by outcome (4d); and then answered question (4e):

(4)   a. The hiker shot the deer. (near causal antecedent)
      b. The hiker aimed at the deer. (far causal antecedent)
      c. The hiker examined the deer. (temporal antecedent)
      d. The deer died. (outcome)
      e. Do bullets kill animals?

In the previous experiments, Sentences (4a), (4c), and (4d) functioned as the (near) causal antecedent, the temporal antecedent, and the outcome, respectively. The new antecedent, (4b), bears a causal relationship with (4d); but one which, compared with (4a), is more distant in nature. In spite of this, the causal path between (4b) and (4d) overlaps that between (4a) and (4d). In particular, like the near causal sequence, the far causal sequence (4b)–(4d) suggests that the deer was shot. Therefore, the validation model specifies that the knowledge that bullets may kill animals ought to be invoked both in the near and far causal conditions. This yields the prediction that answer time for (4d) will be approximately equal in the near and far causal conditions, but slower in the temporal conditions.

This prediction dissociated the answer time and second sentence reading time measures for this task. This is because the findings of Keenan et al. (1984) and Myers et al. (1987) strongly suggested that reading time would increase monotonically with causal distance.

The results, shown in the second panel of Table 13.3, supported these predictions. Reading time was faster for near causal outcomes than far causal outcomes, and was slowest for temporal outcomes. Most importantly, contrasts revealed that, although answer time was not statistically distinguishable between the near and far causal conditions, those conditions were jointly faster than temporal answer time.

This outcome suggests several conclusions. First, even the inferences that bridge only modestly related causes and effects are subjected to validation. Second, if the inferential bridging path between a far cause and its effect partially coincides with a near cause–effect path, some common validating knowledge will be invoked.

Third, causal distance or relatedness refers to at least two subtly different dimensions. Consider Set (5).

(5)   a. Patty's husband died suddenly from a heart attack.
      b. Patty's husband found an error in her check book.
      c. She became hysterical and needed a sedative.

Alternate antecedents (5a) and (5b) represented causal relatedness Levels 1 and 2 out of four levels (1 = strongest) in Myers et al.'s (1987) study. It is apparent that (5b) is a weaker cause of (5c) than is (5a), but there is no overlap between paths (5b)–(5c) and (5a)–(5c). In contrast, aiming at the deer and shooting the deer (set 4) do lie on a common path. "Aiming" is the weaker cause because it is more remote from the deer's demise. These two meanings of causal distance should be distinguished in research of this type.

Validating Forward and Backward Causal Sequences

Although causes always chronologically precede their effects (Trabasso, van den Broek, & Suh, 1989), discourse is not constrained to preserve this order. Writers employ flashback and other narrative devices for stylistic reasons. Therefore, the sequence, "Ken fell down, He stepped on a banana peel," might well appear in a text. Furthermore, it does not seem likely that the surface order will disguise the underlying causality of the sequence.

Forward sequences and corresponding backward chronological sequences were constructed, as illustrated by the set in Table 13.4 (Singer et al., 1992, Experiment 4). Each set also included a question that probed the knowledge posited to validate the inference linking the sentences of the forward causal condition. According to the validation model, because the sentences of the backward sequences will co-occur in working memory, the reader will detect their causal relatedness, and subject the link to validation. Therefore, a causal answer time advantage for "Are banana peels slippery?" will appear in the backward condition as well as the forward condition.

In the experiment, each sentence appeared for 3.5 seconds (and hence reading times were not measured), and the question was presented. As shown in the third panel of Table 13.3, the forward and backward conditions yielded significant causal answer time advantages of 218 ms and 172 ms, respectively. Accordingly, the validation model was supported. Intriguingly, answer times were marginally ($p < .20$) faster in the backward than the forward condition. It is speculatively suggested that bridging the backward sequences requires a greater degree of inferential elaboration than is necessary for the forward sequences (Duffy, Shinjo, & Myers, 1990).

TABLE 13.4
Forward and Backward Causal Sequences

Ken stepped on the banana peel. He fell down.	(causal forward)
Ken jumped over the banana peel. He fell down.	(temporal forward)
Ken fell down. He stepped on the banana peel.	(causal backward)
Ken fell down. He jumped over the banana peel.	(temporal backward)
Are banana peels slippery?	

Validating Motive Bridging Inferences

The initial evaluation of the validation model focused predominantly on causal inferences, because they contribute in an essential way to the meaning of narrative and nonnarrative texts alike. Scrutiny of literary texts, however, reveals that coherence more often turns upon the motives of narrative characters than upon physical causes. Causal analyses of text have, in fact, examined both physical and motivational causation. Causes, goals, and motives may "enable" the events and reactions described in a text (Graesser, 1981; Schank & Abelson, 1977; Trabasso et al., 1989). Intentional actions must be inferentially bridged to characters' motives, much as physical outcomes are linked to antecedent causes. Therefore, some predictions of the validation model have been tested with reference to motive bridging inferences.

Validating Motive Bridging Inferences: Moderate Text Distance.   In addition to applying the validation model to motive bridges, the next experiment added two new features to the investigation. First, the main comparison in the previous experiments was between the causal inference condition and the temporal condition. Certainly, the causal answer time advantage constitutes evidence of inferential activity (e.g., Long, Golding, & Graesser, 1992). An even stronger test of inference processing, however, involves comparing the status of inferred ideas with corresponding explicit ideas (e.g., Singer, 1980). The next experiment (Singer, 1994, Experiment 3) compared implicitly and explicitly expressed motives.

Second, the actions (outcomes) and their antecedent motives were separated by the moderate text distance of two sentences. The reader's ability to inferentially bridge text intervals is inherently interesting. Furthermore, it has taken on special theoretical significance. The minimal inference hypothesis (McKoon & Ratcliff, 1992) states that an inference will reliably accompany comprehension only if it either contributes to local coherence or is based on readily available relevant information. A clear tenet of minimalism is that if a text is locally coherent, causal inferences that traverse more than one intervening sentence will not be drawn (McKoon & Ratcliff, 1992, p. 441). The materials are illustrated by Set (6):

(6) a. Valerie left (early for the birthday party/the birthday party early).

b. She headed north on the freeway.

c. She exited at Antelope Drive.

d. She spent an hour shopping (for a present) at the mall.

e. Do birthday parties involve presents?

Sentences (6a) and (6d) defined the experimental conditions, and were separated by (6b) and (6c). In (6a), *early for the party* and *party early* appeared in the motive and temporal conditions, respectively. The knowledge underlying (6e) was viewed as relevant to shopping before but not after the party. Therefore, as usual, faster motive than temporal answer times for (6e) were predicted. Minimal inference, in contrast, predicts no answer time difference, because passage (6) is referentially coherent and the global motive inference traverses two intervening sentences.

In the third, explicit, version of the passage, the hypothetically validating knowledge was stated more directly, usually in the (d) sentence. For the present example, the phrase *for a present* was simply added to the outcome sentence of the *motive* sequence. This modification indicated why Valerie was shopping. If the knowledge that validates a motive bridging inference is activated as much as an explicit idea, then answer time should be about equal in the explicit and motive conditions.

The answer times, as well as the final sentence (sentence d) reading times, appear in the fourth panel of Table 13.3. The temporal answer times were the slowest, and the motive and explicit answer times were statistically indistinguishable from one another. This finding is a powerful one in several respects. First, it extends the validation analysis to motive bridging inferences. Second, the answer time profile suggests that validating knowledge and explicit text ideas are activated to a similar degree. It would have been neither surprising nor inconsistent with validation had the answer times merely ordered the conditions as explicit, motive, and temporal. The similarity of the motive and explicit condition answer times strongly supports the engagement of validating ideas.

Third, the answer time pattern supports the validation model rather than the minimal inference view. Minimal inference predicts no answer time difference between the motive and temporal conditions, because the motive bridges under investigation spanned two intervening sentences in a referentially coherent passage.

Actions and their distant motives could be inferentially linked either if the motive were maintained in working memory across the text distance, or if it were reinstated upon the detection of the intentional action. For the present example, the current state strategy (Fletcher & Bloom, 1988) favors the latter alternative. It states that the most recent causal chain event with causal antecedents and no consequences will be retained for further processing. Because (6a) has the causal impact of enabling (6b), it should be deleted from working memory. According to this analysis, the bridging of (6d) and (6a) requires the reinstatement of (6a). There is accumulating evidence that antecedent motives and goals must be reinstated to working memory in order to be inferentially linked to their distant outcomes (Bloom, Fletcher, van den Broek, Reitz, & Shapiro, 1990; Dopkins, Klin, & Myers, 1993; Trabasso & Suh, 1993).

The final sentence (e.g., 6d) reading times were slowest in the explicit condition, and about equal in the motive and temporal conditions. The slow explicit reading times are attributed to the addition of phrases such as *for a present* to the motive outcome sentences. The similar reading times in the other two conditions may reflect the fact that their validation processing was similar. The temporal sequences, of course, would have invoked different validating facts, such as, for set (6), "people enjoy shopping" (Singer, 1994).

Validating Motive Bridging Inferences: Greater Text Distance.   The text distance between the antecedent and outcome sentences of the previous experiment only barely exceeded the minimalist (McKoon & Ratcliff, 1992) criterion. In a more stringent test, passages were next constructed in which the antecedent and outcome were five displays apart: There were four intervening complex clauses, comprising two to four sentences. Set (7) illustrates the materials:

(7)   a. Valerie left (early for the birthday party/the birthday party early).

b. She checked the contents of her purse.

c. She backed out of the driveway.

d. She headed north on the freeway.

e. She exited at Antelope Drive.

f. She spent an hour shopping at the mall.

g. Do birthday parties involve presents?

The subjects performed self-paced reading of either the motive or temporal version of the passage. Answer time was 122 ms faster in the motive condition than in the temporal condition (see the bottom panel of Table 13.3). This outcome is inconsistent with the minimalist prediction. In particular, it indicates that readers inferentially link distant text ideas even under the condition of local coherence (see also Dopkins et al., 1993; O'Brien & Albrecht, 1992; Trabasso & Suh, 1993; van den Broek & Lorch, 1993). Finally, unlike the previous experiment, the motive reading times were faster than the temporal reading times.

VALIDATION AND THE CAUSAL ANALYSIS OF TEXT

A complete treatment of the validation model requires the identification of its relation to other features of the causal processing of text. Causal analysis is a prominent manifestation of the understander's construction of text situation models (van Dijk & Kintsch, 1983). Causal analysis may be even more fundamental than has previously been stressed. For example, support for the current state strategy (Bloom et al., 1990; Fletcher & Bloom, 1988) suggests that causal processing is intrinsically involved in the dynamic allocation of working memory resources during reading.

Elaborating upon the analysis of Singer et al. (1992), it is proposed that there are several subtly different facets of causal text processing. First, causal analysis is initiated by the appearance of a physical effect or its motivational counterpart, an intentional action. Second, a search is conducted for candidate causes. Third, the causal force of the candidates is evaluated. Fourth, tentative cause–effect bridges must be validated.

Identifying Effects

Text causal relations may be explicitly signaled by devices including causative (e.g., *so*) and adversative (e.g., *although*) conjunctions, and causal verbs, such as *strengthen* (Clark & Clark, 1977). Even in the absence of such signals, however, the reader will readily detect intentional actions (e.g., "Valerie spent an hour shopping at the mall") and changes in physical state (e.g., "the glacier melted"). Several theorists have characterized causal analysis in text comprehension and problem solving as being driven by state changes (Cheng & Holyoak, 1985; Graesser, 1981; Trabasso et al., 1989). A rationale for this proposal is provided by the principle of "effort after meaning," according to which a prevailing goal of the reader is to construct globally coherent representations of the situations described by the text (Graesser, Singer, & Trabasso, in press). Causal situations figure centrally in this endeavor.

Causal Search

The detection of effects is proposed to initiate the search for candidate causes. To be accessed, the cause must either currently reside in, or be reinstated to, working memory. Plausible causes have a high probability of residing in working memory, for at least two reasons. First, antecedent causes may be retained in working memory by virtue of their recency and importance (Kintsch & van Dijk, 1978). Second, the most recent causal chain event with an antecedent but no effect is posited to be retained in working memory for further processing (Fletcher & Bloom, 1988).

If no cause appears in working memory, then one must be reinstated from the reader's memory of prior text ideas (Kintsch & van Dijk, 1978; Lesgold, Roth, & Curtis, 1979). Two mechanisms of reinstatement are the spread of activation along pathways of the text representation, and pattern matching between the effect and its antecedent cause (Graesser et al., in press; O'Brien, 1987; O'Brien, Plewes, & Albrecht, 1990). In an experimental comparison of these alternatives, subjects encountered sentences such as "Cathy's friend asked what she had bought at the bakery," toward the end of a passage (O'Brien, 1987). After the passage, the subjects were timed as they named test items shown on the screen. The items included possible referents of the anaphoric phrase *what she had bought at the bakery*. The naming times indicated that the subjects reinstated a distant referent, *pie*, without reinstating a closer text distractor, *doll*, which Cathy had bought for her daughter. O'Brien concluded that readers execute a backward parallel search for anaphoric referents in causal representations. The activation of referents is also influenced by their semantic structure and degree of elaboration in the text (Corbett, 1984; Corbett & Chang, 1983; O'Brien et al., 1990). Although these studies have inspected anaphoric resolution in causal networks, comparable processes may characterize causal search in those networks (Dopkins et al., 1993; Singer, in press).

Causal Force

Among the semantic properties of antecedent causes that may regulate their activation by later effects are the causal criteria of sufficiency and of "necessity in the circumstances" (Trabasso et al., 1989; Trabasso & van den Broek, 1985; van den Broek, 1990). In a general manner, this proposal is supported by the fact that memory for text ideas and importance ratings of those ideas are consistently higher for (a) ideas on the main causal chain of a message than those in dead-ends, and (b) for text ideas bearing numerous causal interconnections with other text ideas (Graesser, Robertson, Lovelace, & Swinehart, 1980; Omanson, 1982; Trabasso et al., 1984; Trabasso, & Sperry, 1985).

It is unlikely that the application of these causal criteria is independent of, or serial to, the processes of causal search discussed in the previous section. More plausibly, the criteria affect the extent to which backgrounded text ideas are activated by detected text outcomes during causal search.

Validating Causal Bridges

Once a tentative cause–effect bridge has been identified, it must be validated, as described earlier. To recapitulate, the reader first combines the effect and cause in an incomplete mental syllogism. The solution of the syllogism is a mediating idea that, when coupled with the cause, accounts for the effect. Validation occurs when the mediating idea is supported by relevant knowledge in long-term memory.

The evidence presented in this chapter supports the validation analysis. Answer time consistently reflected the privileged status of the knowledge that was posited to validate the mediating premise of the syllogism. However, validation does not always entail confirmation. Rather, for temporal and inconsistent sequences, the validating knowledge denies the existence of a causal connection between antecedent and outcome.

Caution is necessary in any proposal that validation follows causal search. Therefore, *facet* of causal processing is a more prudent characterization of validation than *stage*. On the one hand, it stands to reason that a candidate cause must be found before its link to an effect may be validated. On the other, it is difficult to strongly deny, at this stage of research, that validation can definitively be distinguished from the assessment of the causal force of a text antecedent.

CONCLUSIONS

The present results suggest conclusions about the validation model, its corollaries, related formulations, and new paths of investigation. With regard to the basic model, perhaps the most important derived finding is that validating knowledge is integrated with the text representation (Halldorson & Singer, 1992). The quality of the relationships among text ideas and validating knowledge will require further inspection.

The validation analysis and experimental results bear on the minimal inference hypothesis (McKoon & Ratcliff, 1992) in at least two ways. First, the data suggest that causal processing is a regular feature of text understanding. Ostensively, this is not inconsistent with the minimalist hypothesis: McKoon and Ratcliff (1992, p. 441) agreed that local coherence may be preserved on the basis of causal relations. However, their proposal appears to contradict the minimalist denial that readers regularly construct text situation models. Causal representations constitute high-level situation models (Trabasso et al., 1989). McKoon and Ratcliff did not explain why local coherence is supported by causal relations if the reader is not engaged in deriving the causal situation.

Second, two experiments revealed that, even with locally coherent texts, readers validate motive bridging inferences that traverse two to four intervening sentences. Because these distances exceed the minimalist criterion, this outcome is inconsistent with the minimalist hypothesis.

The relationship between validation and more general comprehension theories remains to be explored. For example, the causal text analysis of the previous section can be cast in terms of the construction–integration model (Kintsch, 1988). At the construction stage, a set of candidate causes is relatively automatically activated by a detected effect. Ideas associated with the effect by virtue of other semantic relations are also accessed. During integration, the candidate set would be winnowed by the application of causal criteria (Trabasso et al., 1989) and of validation processes. Indeed, Kintsch and Welsch (1991) already used construction–integration to simulate the integration of text ideas and the knowledge relevant to elaborative inferences.

Numerous promising paths of investigation still lie ahead. In one investigation, the impact of people's reading span and tendency to access pertinent knowledge (Singer, Andrusiak, Reisdorf, & Black, 1992) was examined in the realm of validation processing. This may reveal systematic differences in the extent to which readers engage in bridging inference validation.

ACKNOWLEDGMENTS

This research was funded by Research Grant OGP9800 from the Natural Sciences and Engineering Research Council of Canada. I would like to thank Bob

Lorch for his editorial suggestions about the chapter. I am grateful to Penny Macmillan, Susan Larson, and Kathryn Ritchot, each of whom conducted one or more of these experiments.

REFERENCES

Anderson, J. R. (1976). *Language, memory, & thought.* Hillsdale, NJ: Lawrence Erlbaum Associates.

Black, J. B. (1985). An exposition on understanding expository text. In B. Britton & J. Black (Eds.), *Understanding expository text* (pp. 249–267). Hillsdale, NJ: Lawrence Erlbaum Associates.

Black, J. B., & Bern, H. (1981). Causal inference and memory for events in narratives. *Journal of Verbal Learning and Verbal Behavior, 20,* 267–275.

Bloom, C. P., Fletcher, C. R., van den Broek, P., Reitz, L., & Shapiro, B. P. (1990). An on-line assessment of causal reasoning during comprehension. *Memory & Cognition, 18,* 65–71.

Bransford, J. D., & Johnson, M. K. (1973). Considerations of some problems of comprehension. In W. Chase (Ed.), *Visual information processing* (pp. 383–438). New York: Academic Press.

Cheng, P. W., & Holyoak, K. J. (1985). Pragmatic reasoning schemas. *Cognitive Psychology, 17,* 391–416.

Clark, H. H., & Clark, E. V. (1977). *Psychology and language.* New York: Harcourt Brace.

Corbett, A. (1984). Prenominal adjectives and the disambiguation of anaphoric nouns. *Journal of Verbal Learning and Verbal Behavior, 23,* 683–695.

Corbett, A. T., & Chang, F. R. (1983). Pronoun disambiguation: Accessing potential antecedents. *Memory & Cognition, 11,* 283–294.

Dopkins, S., Klin, C., & Myers, J. L. (1993). Accessibility of information about goals during the processing of narrative texts. *Journal of Experimental Psychology: Learning, Memory and Cognition, 19,* 70–80.

Duffy, S. A., Shinjo, M., & Myers, J. L. (1990). The effect of encoding task on memory for sentence pairs varying in causal relatedness. *Journal of Verbal Learning and Verbal Behavior, 29,* 27–42.

Fletcher, C. R., & Bloom, C. P. (1988). Causal reasoning in the comprehension of simple narrative texts. *Journal of Memory and Language, 27,* 235–244.

Forster, K. I. (1981). Priming and the effects of sentence and lexical contexts on naming time: Evidence for autonomous lexical processing. *Quarterly Journal of Experimental Psychology, 33A,* 465–495.

Graesser, A. C. (1981). *Prose comprehension beyond the word.* New York: Springer.

Graesser, A. C., Robertson, S. P., Lovelace, E. R., & Swinehart, D. M. (1980). Answers to why-questions expose the organization of story plot and predict recall of actions. *Journal of Verbal Learning and Verbal Behavior, 19,* 110–119.

Graesser, A. C., Singer, M., & Trabasso, T. (in press). Constructing inferences during narrative text comprehension. *Psychological Review.*

Halldorson, M., & Singer, M. (1992, November). *Integration of inference-validating knowledge and text representation.* Paper presented at the meeting of the Psychonomic Society, St. Louis.

Haviland, S. E., & Clark, H. H. (1974). What's new? Acquiring new information as a process in comprehension. *Journal of Verbal Learning and Verbal Behavior, 13,* 512–521.

Keenan, J. M., Baillet, S. D., & Brown, P. (1984). The effects of causal cohesion on comprehension and memory. *Journal of Verbal Learning and Verbal Behavior, 23,* 115–126.

Kintsch, W. (1988). The role of knowledge in discourse comprehension: A construction-integration model. *Psychological Review, 95,* 163–182.

Kintsch, W., & van Dijk, T. A. (1978). Toward a model of text comprehension and production. *Psychological Review, 85*, 363–394.

Kintsch, W., & Welsch, D. M. (1991). The construction-integration model: A framework for studying memory for text. In W. Hockley & S. Lewandowsky (Eds.), *Relating theory and data: Essays on human memory in honor of Bennet B. Murdock*. Hillsdale, NJ: Lawrence Erlbaum Associates.

Lesgold, A. M., Roth, S. F., & Curtis, M. E. (1979). Foregrounding effects in discourse comprehension. *Journal of Verbal Learning and Verbal Behavior, 18*, 291–308.

Long, D. L., Golding, J. M., & Graesser, A. C. (1992). A test of the on-line status of goal-related elaborative inferences. *Journal of Memory and Language, 31*, 634–647.

McKoon, G., & Ratcliff, R. (1980a). The comprehension processes and memory structures involved in anaphoric reference. *Journal of Verbal Learning and Verbal Behavior, 19*, 668–682.

McKoon, G., & Ratcliff, R. (1980b). Priming in item recognition: The organization of propositions in memory for text. *Journal of Verbal Learning and Verbal Behavior, 19*, 369–386.

McKoon, G., & Ratcliff, R. (1986). Inferences about predictable events. *Journal of Experimental Psychology: Learning, Memory, and Cognition, 12*, 82–91.

McKoon, G., & Ratcliff, R. (1988). Contextually relevant aspects of meaning. *Journal of Experimental Psychology: Learning, Memory, and Cognition, 14*, 331–343.

McKoon, G., & Ratcliff, R. (1992). Inference during reading. *Psychological Review, 99*, 440–466.

Myers, J. L., Shinjo, M., & Duffy, S. A. (1987). Degree of causal relatedness and memory. *Journal of Verbal Learning and Verbal Behavior, 26*, 453–465.

O'Brien, E. J. (1987). Antecedent search processes and the structure of text. *Journal of Experimental Psychology: Learning, Memory, and Cognition, 13*, 278–290.

O'Brien, E. J., & Albrecht, J. E. (1992). Comprehension strategies in the development of a mental model. *Journal of Experimental Psychology: Learning, Memory, and Cognition, 18*, 777–784.

O'Brien, E. J., Plewes, P. S., & Albrecht, J. E. (1990). Antecedent retrieval processes. *Journal of Experimental Psychology: Learning, Memory, and Cognition, 16*, 241–249.

Omanson, R. C. (1982). The relation between centrality and story category variation. *Journal of Verbal Learning and Verbal Behavior, 21*, 326–337.

Potts, G. R., Keenan, J. M., & Golding, J. M. (1988). Assessing the occurrence of elaborative inferences: Lexical decision versus naming. *Journal of Memory and Language, 27*, 399–415.

Schank, R. C., & Abelson, R. (1977). *Scripts, plans, goals, and understanding*. Hillsdale, NJ: Lawrence Erlbaum Associates.

Singer, M. (1980). The role of case-filling inferences in the coherence of brief passages. *Discourse Processes, 3*, 185–201.

Singer, M. (1986). Answering yes–no questions about causes. *Memory & Cognition, 14*, 55–63.

Singer, M. (1993). Causal bridging inferences: Validating consistent and inconsistent sequences. *Canadian Journal of Experimental Psychology, 47*, 340–359.

Singer, M. (1994). *Constructing and validating motive bridging inferences*. Manuscript submitted for publication.

Singer, M. (in press). Discourse inference processes. In M. Gernsbacher (Ed.), *Handbook of psycholinguistics*. New York: Academic Press.

Singer, M., Andrusiak, P., Reisdorf, P., & Black, N. (1992). Individual differences in bridging inference processes. *Memory & Cognition, 20*, 538–548.

Singer, M., & Ferreira, F. (1983). Inferring consequences in story comprehension. *Journal of Verbal Learning and Verbal Behavior, 22*, 437–448.

Singer, M., Halldorson, M., Lear, J. C., & Andrusiak, P. (1992). Validation of causal bridging inferences. *Journal of Memory and Language, 31*, 507–524.

Singer, M., Revlin, R., & Halldorson, M. (1990). Bridging-inferences and enthymeme. In A. Graesser & G. Bower (Eds.), *The psychology of learning and motivation* (Vol. 25, pp. 35–51). New York: Academic Press.

Trabasso, T., Secco, T., and van den Broek, P. (1984). Causal cohesion and story coherence. In

H. Mandl, N. Stein, & T. Trabasso (Eds.), *Learning and comprehension of text* (pp. 83–111). Hillsdale, NJ: Lawrence Erlbaum Associates.

Trabasso, T., & Sperry, L. L. (1985). Causal relatedness and importance of story events. *Journal of Memory and Language, 24*, 595–611.

Trabasso, T., & Suh, S. (1993). Understanding text: Achieving explanatory coherence through on-line inferences and mental operations in working memory. *Discourse Processes, 16,* 3–34.

Trabasso, T., & van den Broek, P. (1985). Causal thinking and the representation of narrative events. *Journal of Memory and Language, 24*, 612–630.

Trabasso, T., van den Broek, P., & Suh, S. Y. (1989). Logical necessity and transitivity of causal relations in stories. *Discourse Processes, 12*, 1–25.

van den Broek, P. (1990). The causal inference maker: Towards a process model of inference generation in text comprehension. In D. Balota, G. Flores d'Arcais, & K. Rayner (Eds.), *Comprehension processes in reading* (pp. 423–445). Hillsdale, NJ: Lawrence Erlbaum Associates.

van den Broek, P., & Lorch, Jr., R. F. (1993). Network representations of causal relations in memory for narrative tests: Evidence from primed recognition. *Discourse processes, 16*, 75–98.

van Dijk, T. A., & Kintsch, W. (1983). *Strategies of discourse comprehension.* New York: Academic Press.

14 Goal Processing and the Maintenance of Global Coherence

Jason E. Albrecht
University of Massachusetts

Edward J. O'Brien
University of New Hampshire

Any complete account of the reading process must describe the online comprehension processes and the resulting memory representation. One type of processing that plays a significant role in comprehension is causal processing (Keenan, Baillet, & Brown, 1984; van den Broek, 1990). There is substantial evidence demonstrating that the ease of comprehension and the resulting memory representation depend greatly on the extent to which readers can detect and establish causal relations in the text (Keenan et al., 1984; Myers, Shinjo, & Duffy, 1987; van den Broek, 1990). Building on this work, more recent research has focused on the degree to which readers establish these relations at local and global levels (e.g., McKoon & Ratcliff, 1992).

In this chapter we suggest that readers routinely check incoming information against recently processed information and more global, discourse-relevant information in an attempt to maintain both local and global coherence (e.g., Albrecht & O'Brien, 1993; O'Brien & Albrecht, 1992). The process model proposed by Glenberg and Langston (Albrecht & O'Brien, 1993; Myers, O'Brien, Albrecht, & Mason, in press; O'Brien & Albrecht, 1992; Sanford & Garrod, 1981) is described and extended to include processing of goal-based information. In much of this discussion, the goals that are referred to are the goals of the protagonist. An implicit assumption of much of the causal reasoning work is that readers adopt the perspective of the protagonist. In the final section of the chapter, we provide some evidence suggesting that readers do not always adopt the perspective of the protagonist.

CAUSAL RELATIONS

The research that has examined the role of causal reasoning in comprehension views reading as a problem solving process in which the reader attempts to establish causal connections between text-based units from the opening event of a narrative to the final outcome (Fletcher & Bloom, 1988; Trabasso & Sperry, 1985; Trabasso & van den Broek, 1985). The resulting representation has been characterized as a causal network in which text-based units are connected on the basis of causal dependencies (e.g., Trabasso & Sperry, 1985). The number of causal connections leading to and from a causal unit and the role of the causal unit in the causal chain of events are good predictors of memory performance (e.g., O'Brien & Myers, 1987; van den Broek & Trabasso, 1986). Van den Broek and Lorch (1993) provided additional support for a causal network representation. They found that idea units that were hypothesized to be connected to goal-based units served as effective episodic primes, regardless of whether the goal and prime were adjacent in the surface structure. Van den Broek (1990) suggested that the additional connections leading to and from goal information are generated because goals often provide necessary and sufficient conditions for actions that occur later in the narrative.

Although this view of causal processing has been successful in describing memory performance, it does not describe comprehension processes within limited memory constraints (e.g., Fletcher, 1981, 1986). Thus, it is not clear if readers generate all of the causal connections that are predicted to be made (e.g., Fletcher & Bloom, 1988). Recent attempts to describe the construction of the memory representation within the constraints of limited memory capacities have varied in their emphasis on maintaining global coherence (Albrecht & O'Brien, 1993; Fletcher & Bloom, 1988; Garnham, Oakhill, & Johnson-Laird, 1982; Glenberg & Langston, 1992; Kintsch & van Dijk, 1978; McKoon & Ratcliff, 1992; Trabasso & van den Broek, 1985). Several models predict that readers are primarily concerned with maintaining local coherence and only attempt to establish global coherence when there is a disruption in local processing or when global information is "readily available" (e.g., McKoon & Ratcliff, 1992). Other models predict that readers routinely attempt to establish both local and global coherence even when there are no local coherence breaks (e.g., Albrecht & O'Brien, 1993). Because of the different emphasis on global processing, these models make different predictions about when and how readers access global information, including goal-based information.

STRATEGIES EMPHASIZING LOCAL COHERENCE

Fletcher and his colleagues (Bloom, Fletcher, van den Broek, Reitz, & Shapiro, 1990; Fletcher & Bloom, 1988) proposed the current-state selection strategy,

264

which describes the role of causal processing during comprehension within the constraints of the limited memory capacities. Based on this strategy, readers maintain in working memory the most likely causal antecedent without a causal consequence. On subsequent cycles, readers attempt to find and connect a causal consequence to the causal antecedent in working memory (Bloom et al., 1990; Fletcher & Bloom, 1988; Fletcher, Hummel, & Marsolek, 1990). If a causal consequence is found, comprehension proceeds smoothly and the next causal antecedent without a consequence becomes the focus of working memory.

The current-state strategy proposes no special status for goal information (Fletcher & Bloom, 1988; van den Broek, 1990). However, because of the emphasis on maintaining local coherence, there are few conditions under which readers are predicted to access to goal-based information. The strategy predicts that readers should have access to goal information when it is involved in local processing (i.e., when the goal is the most likely causal antecedent without a causal consequence; Fletcher & Bloom, 1988). Readers should also have access to goal information when it is reinstated. Reinstatement of goal information is predicted to occur when there is a local coherence break that requires goal information to re-establish coherence (Fletcher & Bloom, 1988; McKoon & Ratcliff, 1992) and when a goal-satisfying statement is encountered (Bloom et al., 1990; van den Broek, 1990).

Recent research has clearly demonstrated that local coherence breaks are sufficient to initiate reinstatement and reactivation of global goal information (McKoon & Ratcliff, 1992). However, it is less clear whether such coherence breaks and reinstatement processes are necessary to provide access to global goal information. Several recent results have indicated that readers access global information, including information about goals, even when the texts were locally coherent (Albrecht & O'Brien, 1993; Huitema, Dopkins, Klin, & Myers, 1993; Suh & Trabasso, 1993). This finding suggests that readers not only focus on maintaining local coherence but that readers also routinely attempt to establish global coherence. The strategies that emphasize the maintenance of both local and global coherence provide a way to describe goal processing that leads to slightly different predictions about the status of goal information during comprehension.

STRATEGIES EMPHASIZING BOTH LOCAL AND GLOBAL COHERENCE

Generally, the strategies that emphasize the maintenance of both local and global coherence also emphasize processes involved in the development of a mental-model level of representation; readers use linguistic, pragmatic, and world knowledge to construct a representation of the situation described by the text (Albrecht & O'Brien, 1993; Garnham, Oakhill, & Johnson-Laird, 1982; Glenberg & Langston, 1992; Glenberg, Meyer, & Lindem, 1987).[1] The discourse model represents the characters being discussed, the properties of these characters, and the relations among these characters, as well as the events and situations being discussed and the relations among the events and situations (Glenberg et al., 1987; Webber, 1988b).

Like local coherence strategies, strategies describing the maintenance of both local and global coherence must also take into account the reader's limited memory capacities. Several researchers (Albrecht & O'Brien, 1993; Garrod & Sanford, 1988, 1990; Glenberg & Langston, 1992; Sanford & Garrod, 1981; van Dijk & Kintsch, 1983) have proposed a process model that maintains the memory limitations of local coherence strategies but also provides a mechanism that allows access to discourse-relevant information during comprehension. These researchers have proposed that active memory can be partitioned into two focused sections: explicit focus and implicit focus. In explicit focus, readers maintain tokens representing explicitly mentioned information. Because of memory constraints, only a limited number of tokens can be maintained active at any one time. However, the tokens serve a second function: they also point to discourse-relevant information stored in long-term memory (i.e., implicit focus). These discourse pointers provide access to relevant information that was mentioned earlier in the text and unmentioned information that was implied by the text. Accessibility of information in implicit focus depends on maintaining the relevant tokens in explicit focus. When tokens in explicit focus are removed or backgrounded, there is a decrease in accessibility of the information that the backgrounded token pointed to (Glenberg & Langston, 1992; Myers et al., in press).

Within this model, comprehension is described as a process of mapping new information onto tokens in explicit focus and the relevant information in implicit focus. The mapping process involves two components. One component is an automatic resonance process in which new information in conjunction with information in explicit focus serve as a memory probe to activate relevant discourse information (Myers et al., in press; O'Brien, this volume). The second component involves checking and integrating the incoming information with information activated via the resonance process (see Myers et al., in press; O'Brien, this volume, for a more detailed discussion of the mapping process). Through this mapping process, readers are able to maintain both local and global coherence (Albrecht & O'Brien, 1993). The success and ease of the mapping process depends on the information in focus and the incoming information. If there is a large degree of overlap between incoming information and information in focus, the reader should have access to all of the information needed to establish coherence. However, if there is a low degree of overlap between the incoming information and information in focus, the reader may be required to reinstate information that is no longer in focus (Myers et al., in press).

There is an increasing amount of data supporting this process model (Albrecht & O'Brien, 1993; Glenberg & Langston, 1992; Glenberg & Mathews, 1992; Myers et al., in press; O'Brien & Albrecht, 1992). However, the model and empirical support have focused on only one part of the discourse model, namely, the representation of the characters, their properties, and relations. We attempt to extend the general process model to describe processing of events including goal-based information. However, in order to do so, we must first provide a brief background about events and relations among events, which draws on Webber's (1988b) discussion about tense as an anaphor. Then we discuss goal processing within the focus model and review evidence that is consistent with this model.

DISCOURSE MODELS AND GOAL PROCESSING

Webber (1988b; Moens & Steedman, 1988) suggested that readers interpret a narrative episode (or event) as having a preparatory phase, a culmination, and a consequence phase. A culmination is, " . . . an event which the speaker views as punctual or instantaneous, and as accompanied by a transition to a new state of the world" (Moens & Steedman, 1988, p. 16). The preparatory phase includes those events leading up to the culmination and the consequence phase contains the new state resulting from the culmination (Moens & Steedman, 1988). Any one of these phases may be composed of several sentences (Moens & Steedman, 1988). Readers use world knowledge, knowledge about causality, and the prior discourse to determine whether an action is an antecedent, culmination, or consequence.

Webber (1988b) also assumed that readers focus most of their attention on only one "entity" within the episode structure at any one time. This is referred to as temporal focus and is designed to capture the online processing constraints and the natural movement of readers' (or listeners') attention from event to event during comprehension of narratives. There are several similarities between the functions of temporal focus and discourse focus (as discussed by Sidner, 1983a, 1983b), however, Webber discussed them separately, noting that discourse focus is concerned with tracking characters in the text and temporal focus is designed to track events. It seems obvious that temporal focus and discourse focus are closely related and probably interact. However, to simplify the discussion, we describe temporal focus using texts that maintain the same discourse focus throughout the entire passage. Later, we review existing data that begin to address the potential interaction between temporal and discourse foci.

When new information is processed, it is interpreted with respect to the developing discourse model that not only establishes the situation currently discussed, but also provides a point of reference with which to interpret the current event. The point of reference is the point in time that is "talked about" (Moens & Steedman, 1988; Reichenbach, 1947; Webber, 1988a, 1988b). This point is established through verb tense and the events in the prior discourse (Reichenbach, 1947).[2] Narratives are written in the simple past tense, which establishes the point of reference as some time in the past. However, some events that are described fall outside of the established point of reference. For example, events that proceed the point of reference are described using the past perfect construction.

To illustrate how episode structure, temporal focus, and point of reference work, consider the following pairs of sentences.

(1a)   The magician needed to find an assistant from the audience.

(2a)   While he paced around the stage, he looked out into the crowd.

(1b)   The magician quickly found an assistant from the audience.

(2b)   While he paced around the stage, he looked out into the crowd.

(1c)   The magician quickly found an assistant from the audience.

(2c)   While he had paced around the stage, he had looked out into the crowd.

In the first sentence pair, the magician is looking for an assistant. In the second sentence (2a), the event of walking around the stage is consistent with the previously established point of reference and therefore implies that walking around the stage took place after (or simultaneously with) the event in the first sentence. This situation can be described using the event structure and tense as depicted in Fig. 14.1a (following the notation of Moens & Steedman, 1988 and Webber, 1988b). In this figure, the action of looking for an assistant is viewed as a preparatory action and the actions in the second sentence can be understood as attempts or actions leading to the culminating event (finding an assistant). In

---

[2]A complete discussion of tense as an anaphor is beyond the scope of this chapter. However, central to this idea is Reichenbach's (1947) description of the structure of tensed clauses. Reichenbach proposed that a tensed clause provides three pieces of temporal information: the point of speech, the point of the event, and the point of reference. The point of speech provides information about when the utterance was spoken with respect to the here and now. The point of the event is the time when the event took place. The point of reference is the time that is "talked about." It is the point of reference that gives tensed clauses their anaphoric nature; when readers interpret the current clause against the previous information, they are checking the reference point of the current clause against the reference point generated by the prior discourse. For a more complete discussion of these concepts, see Reichenbach (1947), Webber (1988b), and Moens and Steedman (1988).

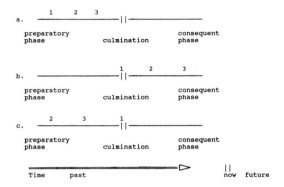

FIG. 14.1. Diagram of events as a function of event structure and verb tense. Note that the numbers on the line represent the clauses from Sentences 1 and 2.

these simple texts, temporal focus moves from clause to clause. By the end of the second sentence, the third clause would be in temporal focus.[3]

In the second sentence pair, the magician has already found an assistant and therefore this event is considered a culminating event. In the second sentence (2b), the event of walking around the stage is consistent with the previously established point of reference and therefore implies that walking around the stage took place subsequent to finding an assistant. As with the first sentence pair, this situation is depicted in Fig. 14.1b in terms of the event structure and tense. Now at the end of this sentence pair, the temporal focus is in the consequent phase and moving away from the previous culminating event.[4]

Finally, consider the third sentence pair. The first sentence is the same as in second example pair (i.e., a culminating event). However in sentence (2c), the past perfect construction indicates that the event of walking around the stage took place prior to the established point of reference, sentence (1c). This indicates that walking around the stage was an event prior to the event of finding an assistant and is considered a preparatory action. Figure 14.1c depicts this situation in terms of event structure and tense. In this case, there is a backward movement in temporal focus to a point prior to the culminating event.[5]

---

[3]As used here with these simple texts, temporal focus is consistent with Fletcher and Bloom's (1988) current-state selection strategy.

[4]Without a more complete context, it is difficult to unambiguously label clauses/sentences as preparatory, culmination or consequences. Thus, in (2b), Clause 3 may be considered part of the consequence phase or as a component of a preparatory phase of a new episode.

[5]In the examples, we assumed that temporal focus will follow from clause to clause. However, it is an empirical question as to exactly when readers detect an embedded segment of text and thus shift temporal focus. For example, it is not completely clear whether readers will shift temporal focus when they encounter the first past perfect construction. Instead, they may recognize the event as prior

Using Webber's ideas about tense as anaphor, the model describing the maintenance of local and global coherence can be extended to include the processing of goal-based information. Just as we suggested that readers maintain tokens representing the main character(s) in explicit focus, readers may also maintain tokens representing actions or events in explicit focus (this is the equivalent of Webber's temporal focus). These tokens represent the content and the current point of reference and point to discourse-relevant information in implicit focus, which includes the point of reference established by the previous discourse, previously mentioned information, and implied but unmentioned information. The pointed-to information is influenced and restricted by episode structure and the point of reference. That is, although the main character may participate in several actions, readers should have greater access to those events and actions relevant to the current event/episode than events and actions from previous episodes.

Incoming information about subsequent events is mapped onto the information in explicit focus, which resonates with and updates the information in implicit focus. The mapping process requires readers to check the plausibility of the content and temporal features of the new information against the existing discourse model. As noted earlier, the accessibility of information in implicit focus depends on the tokens in explicit focus; the removal of a token from explicit focus reduces accessibility of the previously pointed-to information.

The processing of goal information fits nicely within this general framework. An unsatisfied goal statement often specifies the start of a process that is likely to culminate later in the story. Following an unsatisfied goal statement, new information generally continues the story and describes attempts to achieve the goal. As long as there has been no shift in the discourse, it is likely that readers will maintain event information in explicit focus which will point to discourse-relevant information in implicit focus, including unsatisfied-goal information and other preparatory actions. By mapping new information onto information in explicit focus, readers can establish relations between incoming information and unsatisfied-goal information in implicit focus. More importantly, this suggests that when readers encounter new information that is relevant to the goal, such as a goal-satisfying statement, readers do not have to complete a high-level reinstatement search (Bloom et al., 1990; van den Broek, 1990). Instead, unsatisfied goal information is accessed as a by-product of completing the mapping process.

---

to the current point of reference but wait to see if the subsequent event continues the embedded segment or returns to the point of reference established by the previous discourse (see Webber, 1988b). In the extended examples presented in Table 14.1, the embedded segment is clearly marked by the use of the past perfect in most all of the postgoal sentences. With more explicit cues, it is likely that readers would shift temporal focus immediately. For example, "He recalled an event several years ago . . . " provides a very specific time in the past and is likely to produce a shift in temporal focus.

The situation with satisfied-goal statements is slightly different. A satisfied-goal statement describes the culmination of a process. Assuming that there is no shift in verb tense, goal information should be accessible during the first few cycles (i.e., while it is still in explicit focus), but accessibility should decrease as new information is processed. The reduction in accessibility is due to a combination of the episode structure and the forward progression of narrative texts. The information in explicit focus points to the culminating event, but as incoming information is processed the temporal focus moves forward and further away from the previous goal information. This increases the likelihood that a new episode will begin and reduces the probability that the previously satisfied goal will be referred to again.

However, we are not suggesting that unsatisfied goals are always maintained in implicit focus or that satisfied goals are never maintained in implicit focus. Rather, we are proposing that mapping and shifting focus depend on the information in explicit focus, the incoming information, and the degree to which these pieces of information can be integrated. Accessibility of unsatisfied-goal information in implicit focus may decrease if information from the current cycle introduces a new goal (e.g. Huitema et al., 1993). Similarly, accessibility of satisfied-goal information may be sustained by a shift in verb tense. To illustrate the second point, consider the different versions of the passage in Table 14.1 (modified from Dopkins, Klin, & Myers, 1993).

First, consider the unsatisfied-goal/no shift in verb tense condition. The passage in Table 14.1 contains an unsatisfied goal statement that is followed by several sentences that maintain the same verb tense as the goal statement (i.e., the simple past tense). In this passage, there are two factors that facilitate the mapping process and increase the likelihood that readers will maintain the unsatisfied-goal information in implicit focus: the content of the continuation sentences and the point of reference established by the verb tense of the continuation sentences.

For example, after reading that the captain has begun looking for a thief, the subsequent sentences about walking around the office and looking through reports are completely consistent with the goal of beginning an investigation to catch a thief. Maintaining the same verb tense also facilitates mapping because it provides the reader with a point of reference against which to establish the time sequence of the actions. That is, by maintaining the simple past tense, all of the described actions took place at some definite time in the past; the only information that the reader has about the sequence of these events is the order in which the actions are presented. Thus, pacing around the office took place after the captain began the investigation. The resulting representation is one in which the reader is uncertain about the outcome of the goal and the postgoal information is mapped onto this unsatisfied goal information. This situation is similar to the situation depicted in Fig. 14.1a. Readers should have relatively easy access to

TABLE 14.1
Sample Passage Varying Goal Satisfaction and the Verb Tense of Postgoal Information

Part of Passage	Passage
Introduction	The luxury liner was preparing for its weekly cruise. The captain completed a last minute check to ensure that the ship was set for the trip. After all of the passengers has checked in and settled into their rooms, the captain returned to his office. A few hours after departing, some passengers stopped by the captain's office to report missing valuables.
Unsatisfied goal	The captain began an investigation in order to catch the thief.
Satisfied goal	The captain conducted an investigation and caught the thief.
No shift in verb tense	The captain paced around his office and then went about his business. He picked up several recent reports off of the filing cabinet. The captain satdown at his desk and looked through the reports. After carefully examining each of them, he walked out on the deck.
Shift in verb tense	The captain had paced around his office and then had gone about his business. He had picked up several recent reports off of the filing cabinet. The captain had sat down at his desk and had looked through the reports. After carefully examining each of them, he had walked out on the deck.

the goal concept because it is part of the situation that is currently described by the text. Using passages like these, Albrecht (1993) provided some support for this prediction.

Consider the situation that is described by the text when there is a satisfied goal and no shift in the verb tense. In this condition, the content of the continuation sentences is consistent with the completion of the goal (i.e., having already caught the thief). Furthermore, the verb tense of the subsequent sentences makes it unlikely that the subsequent sentences would be understood as preparatory actions taken to achieve the goal. That is, the goal statement describes the captain's action in the past tense (i.e., "The captain conduct*ed* an investigation and *caught* the thief") and the subsequent sentences also describe the captain's actions in the simple past tense. This provides a cue to the reader that all of these actions (i.e., catching the thief, pacing around the office, looking through reports, etc.) took place at a definite time in the past. The only information that the reader has about the sequence of events is the order in which they are presented in the text. Thus, the sequence of events suggests that pacing around the office occurred after catching the thief and was in no way related to the achievement of the goal. In this case, the satisfied goal describes the culminating event and the tense of the verbs in the postgoal sentences continue the natural forward progression of the narrative that in the discourse situation is moving away from the goal-related event. This situation is depicted in Fig. 14.1b. This type of situation should reduce accessibility of goal information. Using passages like the one in Table 14.1, Albrecht (1993) provided some support for this prediction.

Finally, consider the case where there is a satisfied-goal statement and a shift in the verb tense of the postgoal sentences.[6] The satisfied-goal statement describes the completion of the goal. In the immediately subsequent sentences, there is a shift in verb tense from simple past tense to the past perfect tense. By shifting tense, the sentences immediately after the goal statement describe actions as having occurred prior to the culminating event in the satisfied-goal statement. In this way, the sentences subsequent to the goal statement can be understood as actions taken to achieve the goal or elaborate on the completion of the goal. Thus, the captain paced around his office and looked through the reports prior to or as a means to achieving the goal. In this case, the shift in verb tense immediately after the goal statement describes events as occurring before the established point of reference, which should be sometime prior to the completion of the goal. It seems likely that readers would map the postgoal sentences onto the satisfied goal. This situation is depicted in Fig. 14.1c. In this situation, the process model described earlier predicts that readers should maintain information about the satisfied goal in implicit focus.

EMPIRICAL SUPPORT

One prediction of the model is that readers should access global goal information even when the text is locally coherent. Recent research investigating goal processing has provided some support for this prediction. For example, Huitema et al. (1993) had subjects read passages that contained an unsatisfied-goal statement (e.g., "Mark would have to improve his mind"). Several sentences later, a goal satisfying statement was presented that was consistent (e.g., picking out a history book) or inconsistent (e.g., picking out a comic book) with the originally stated goal. In contrast to the predictions of local coherence strategies, Huitema et al. found that readers took considerably longer to read the goal-satisfying sentence when it was inconsistent with the original goal. These results are consistent with the hypothesis that readers maintain unsatisfied goal information in implicit focus and make contact with this information in the process of establishing coherence.

---

[6]With the present example, combining an unsatisfied goal statement and the past-perfect-continuation sentences generates an anomalous passage. After stating that the captain began an investigation to catch the thief, shifting verb tense produces an ambiguity. Presumably this is because there is no definite time in the past with which to interpret the postgoal statements.

Huitema et al. (1993) also demonstrated that introducing a subordinate goal can reduce accessibility of more superordinate goal information. According to the focus model, the reduced accessibility to superordinate goal information is due to a shift in temporal focus. When a subordinate goal is introduced, readers maintain tokens representing events relevant to the subordinate goal in explicit focus, which point to discourse relevant information about the subordinate goal and the respective preparatory actions. The focus on subordinate goal information reduces the accessibility of information about superordinate goals in implicit focus. Thus, reference to the superordinate goal should take longer to complete because readers have to re-establish the context for the backgrounded superordinate goal.

When an episode is interrupted, such as the case when an unsatisfied subordinate goal is nested within an unsatisfied superordinate goal, readers may cache (Webber, 1988b) or buffer (Bower & Morrow, 1990) the superordinate goal for resumption later. The extent to which readers resume superordinate goals following the completion of subordinate goals seems to depend on the relation between the goals. For example, if achievement of the subordinate goal is seen as a necessary means toward achieving the superordinate goal, then completion of the subordinate goal may result in a quick and immediate resumption of the superordinate goal. Suh and Trabasso (1993) provided evidence consistent this claim. In contrast, if there is weaker dependence between the subordinate and superordinate goals, then readers may postpone resumption of the superordinate goal until the author cues such a shift back to the original goal.

As noted earlier, temporal focus and discourse focus (i.e., components of explicit focus) are closely related. However, there have been no direct comparisons between them. Previous research investigating global processing of goal information has maintained a consistent discourse focus, whereas the work investigating global processing of characters has maintained the same situation throughout the narrative. Further research directly addressing the similarities, differences, and interactions between temporal focus and discourse focus is needed. Viewing processing in this way raises several interesting issues such as the necessary and sufficient conditions for re-establishing previously backgrounded information to temporal focus and discourse focus. Myers et al. (in press) demonstrated that simply re-introducing a previously backgrounded character is sufficient to re-establish the properties of that character in implicit focus. However, it is less clear what would be required to re-establish the context of a previously backgrounded goal.

PERSPECTIVES AND GOALS

The goals that have been discussed are the goals of the protagonist. Because narratives are often written around a main character, it is often assumed that readers adopt the perspective and the goals of the protagonist (e.g., Morrow,

Bower, & Greenspan, 1989; Morrow, Greenspan, & Bower, 1987). Although many results are consistent with this assumption (e.g., Black, Turner, & Bower, 1979; Morrow et al., 1987, 1989), much of this evidence is also consistent with strategies based on other nonprotagonist perspectives. Recently, Albrecht, O'Brien, and Myers (1993) directly tested the assumption using versions of simple narrative texts adapted from passages used by Dopkins, Klin, and Myers (1993). Table 14.2 presents an example passage from Albrecht et al.

In the unsatisfied-goal versions of the passage, the captain's goal is to catch the thief. In the satisfied-goal versions, the passage states that the captain has already caught the thief. The last sentence of each passage introduces a new character. In the potential-inference versions, the last sentence introduces a new character who may serve as a potential instantiation of the goal category. The potential inference in the first passage is that the purser is the thief (e.g., " . . . the captain had the purser brought to his office"). In the no potential-inference versions, the last line introduces the new character but provides a context that reduces the likelihood of connecting the new character to the goal character. In these versions, the likelihood of identifying the purser as the thief is greatly reduced (e.g., " . . . the captain had the purser write a report on the case").

If readers adopt the perspective of the protagonist, they presumably focus on the protagonist's thoughts, actions, and goals (Morrow et al., 1987, 1989). A reader identifying with the protagonist should attempt to relate each new action to the goal when it has not yet been satisfied; there is no reason to do the same

TABLE 14.2
Example Passage From Albrecht, O'Brien, and Myers (1993): Experiments 1 and 2

Part of Passage	Passage
Introduction	While strolling on the deck after dinner, the captain noticed that the atmosphere on the luxury liner was getting tense. Several valuable items had disappeared from the cabins.
Unsatisfied goal statement	When he heard about the problem, the captain began an investigation in order to nab the theif.
Satisfied goal statement	When he heard about the problem, the captain held an investigation and quickly nabbed the theif.
Potential inference statement	After two days of considering the evidence, the captain had the purser brought to his office.
No potential inference statement	After two days of reviewing the evidence, the cap[tain had the purser write a report on the case.

Note. The four conditions were created by crossing goal satisfaction and potential inference. Adapted from Dopkins, Klin, and Myers (1993). Reprinted by permission.

when the goal is no longer operative. As a consequence, the goal category should be recognized more quickly following unsatisfied-goal statements than following satisfied-goal statements. Assuming that any action of the protagonist is relevant to an unsatisfied goal, this effect of goal satisfaction should be present in both the potential- and no potential- inference conditions. Furthermore, there should be no effect of the type of inference. From the viewpoint of the protagonist, if the goal has been satisfied, there is no reason to attempt to relate either final sentence to the goal. If the goal has not been satisfied, any action is potentially relevant and should result in reactivation of the goal.

Alternatively, readers may adopt their own perspectives. In that case, the goal is operative for the reader in both the unsatisfied- and satisfied-goal conditions. Although the captain knows who the thief is in the satisfied-goal condition, the reader does not. The predictions following from the assumption of a reader-centered perspective are just the opposite of those that follow from the assumption of a protagonist-centered perspective: the status of the goal should have no effect, but a final sentence that provides a potential inference should lead to reactivation of the goal and thus faster recognition of the goal category.

Albrecht et al. (1993) found that subjects adopted the perspective and goals of the protagonist only when they were explicitly instructed to do so. When readers were given no special instructions, they adopted a reader-centered perspective. These results are important because they demonstrate that, given the same set of facts (i.e., text base), different information will be focused on depending on the perspective that readers have adopted.

CONCLUSIONS

There is a growing body of evidence suggesting that readers attempt to establish both local and global coherence. In this chapter, we have attempted to extend the process model proposed by Glenberg and Langston (1992; Albrecht & O'Brien, 1993; O'Brien & Albrecht, 1992) to include processing of goal-based information. In doing so, we provide an account that emphasizes the importance of the temporal relations between events as well as the semantic content of the events. There are several recent results that are consistent with the extended model. Furthermore, by describing goal processing, several questions about the relation between discourse focus and temporal focus are raised. By investigating how these components influence one another, a better understanding of comprehension of narrative texts may be achieved.

REFERENCES

Albrecht, J. E. (1993). *Accessibility of goal information in a mental model*. Unpublished doctoral dissertation, University of New Hampshire.

Albrecht, J. E., & O'Brien, E. J. (1993). Updating a mental model: Maintaining both local and global coherence. *Journal of Experimental Psychology: Learning, Memory, and Cognition, 19*, 1061–1070.

Albrecht, J. E., O'Brien, E. J., & Myers, J. L. (1993). *The role of perspective in the accessibility of information about goals during the processing of narrative texts.* Unpublished manuscript.

Black, J. B., Turner, E., & Bower, G. H. (1979). Point of view in narrative comprehension and memory. *Journal of Verbal Learning and Verbal Behavior, 18* 187–198.

Bloom, C. P., Fletcher, R. C., van den Broek, P., Reitz, L., & Shapiro, B. P. (1990). An on-line assessment of causal reasoning during comprehension. *Memory & Cognition, 18*, 65–71.

Bower, G. H., & Morrow, D. G. (1990, January). Mental models in narrative comprehension. *Science*, pp. 44–48.

Dopkins, S., Klin, C., & Myers, J. L. (1993). The accessibility of information about goals during the processing of narrative texts. *Journal of Experimental Psychology: Learning, Memory, and Cognition 19*, 70–80.

Fletcher, C. R. (1981). Short-term memory processes in text comprehension. *Journal of Verbal Learning and Verbal Behavior, 20*, 564–574.

Fletcher, C. R. (1986). Strategies for allocation of short-term memory during comprehension. *Journal of Memory and Language, 25*, 43–58.

Fletcher, C. R., & Bloom, C. P. (1988). Causal reasoning in the comprehension of simple narrative texts. *Journal of Memory and Language, 27*, 235–244.

Fletcher, C. R., Hummel, J. E., & Marsolek, C. J. (1990). Causality and the allocation of attention during comprehension. *Journal of Experimental Psychology: Learning, Memory, and Cognition, 16*, 233–240.

Garnham, A., Oakhill, J., & Johnson-Laird, P. N. (1982). Referential continuity and the coherence of discourse. *Cognition, 11*, 29–46.

Garrod, S., & Sanford, A. (1988). Thematic subjecthood and cognitive constraints on discourse structure. *Journal of Pragmatics, 12*, 519–534.

Garrod, S., & Sanford, A. (1990). Referential processing in reading: Focusing on roles and individuals. In D. A. Balota, G. B. Flores d'Arcais, & K. Rayner (Eds.), *Comprehension processes in reading* (pp. 465–484). Hillsdale, NJ: Lawrence Erlbaum Associates.

Glenberg, A. M., & Langston, W. E. (1992). Comprehension of illustrated text: Pictures help to build mental models. *Journal of Memory and Language, 31*, 129–151.

Glenberg, A. M., & Mathews, S. (1992). When minimalism is not enough: Mental models in reading comprehension. *Psycoloquy, 3(64)* reading-inference-2.1.

Glenberg, A. M., Meyer, M., & Lindem, K. (1987). Mental models contribute to foregrounding during text comprehension. *Journal of Memory and Language, 26*, 69–83.

Huitema, J. S., Dopkins, S., Klin, C., & Myers, J. L. (1993). Connecting goals and actions during reading. *Journal of Experimental Psychology: Learning, Memory, and Cognition, 19*, 1053–1060.

Keenan, J. M., Baillet, S. D., & Brown, P. (1984). The effects of causal cohesion on comprehension and memory. *Journal of Verbal Learning and Verbal Behavior, 23*, 115–126.

Kintsch, W., & van Dijk, T. A. (1978). Toward a model of text comprehension and production. *Psychological Review, 85*, 363–394.

McKoon, G., & Ratcliff, R. (1992). Inference during reading. *Psychological Review, 63*, 81–97.

Moens, M., & Steedman, M. (1988). Temporal ontology and temporal reference. *Computational Linguistics, 14*, 15–28.

Morrow, D. G., Bower, G. H., & Greenspan, S. E. (1989). Updating situation models during narrative comprehension. *Journal of Memory and Language, 24*, 304–319.

Morrow, D. G., Greenspan, S. E., & Bower, G. H. (1987). Accessibility and situation models in narrative comprehension. *Journal of Memory and Language, 26*, 165–187.

Myers, J. L., O'Brien, E. J., Albrecht, J. E., & Mason, R. A. (in press). Maintaining global coherence during reading. *Journal of Experimental Psychology: Learning, Memory, and Cognition.*

Myers, J. L., Shinjo, M., & Duffy, S. A. (1987). Degree of causal relatedness and memory. *Journal of Memory and Language*, *26*, 453–465.

O'Brien, E. J., & Albrecht, J. E. (1992). Comprehension strategies in the development of a mental model. *Journal of Experimental Psychology: Learning, Memory, and Cognition*, *18*, 777–784.

O'Brien, E. J., & Myers, J. L. (1987). The role of causal connection in the retrieval of text. *Memory & Cognition*, *15*, 419–427.

Reichenbach, H. (1947). *Elements of symbolic logic*. New York: Macmillan.

Sanford, A. J., & Garrod, S. C. (1981). *Understanding written language*. New York: Wiley.

Sidner, C. (1983a). Focusing and discourse. *Discourse Processes*, *6*, 107–130.

Sidner, C. (1983b). Focusing in the comprehension of definite anaphora. In M. Brady & R. Berwick (Eds.), *Computational Models of Discourse* (pp. 267–330). Cambridge, MA: MIT Press.

Suh, S., & Trabasso, T. (1993). Inferencing during reading: Converging evidence from discourse analysis, talk-aloud protocols, and recognition priming. *Journal of Memory and Language*, *32*, 279–300.

Trabasso, T., & Sperry, L. L. (1985). Causal relatedness and importance of story events. *Journal of Memory and Language*, *24*, 595–611.

Trabasso, T., & van den Broek, P. (1985). Causal thinking and the representation of narrative events. *Journal of Memory and Language*, *24*, 612–630.

van den Broek, P. (1990). Causal inferences and the comprehension of narrative texts. In A. C. Graesser & G. H. Bower (Eds.), *The psychology of learning and motivation* (Vol. 25, pp. 175–196). Orlando, FL: Academic Press.

van den Broek, P., & Lorch, R. F., Jr. (1993). Network representations of causal relations in memory for narrative texts: Evidence from primed recognition. *Discourse Processes*, *16* 75–98.

van den Broek, P., & Trabasso, T. (1986). Causal networks versus goal hierarchies in summarizing texts. *Discourse Processes*, *9*, 1–15.

van Dijk, T. A., & Kintsch, W. (1983). *Strategies of discourse comprehension*. Orlando, FL: Academic Press.

Webber, B. L. (1988a). Foreword. *Computational Linguistics*, *14*, 1–2.

Webber, B. L. (1988b). Tense as discourse anaphor. *Computational Linguistics*, *14*, 61–73.

15 Integration of Topic Information During Reading

Robert F. Lorch, Jr.
University of Kentucky

The focus of this chapter is on the processing of topical information in expository text. Because expository text is organized around semantically related topics, topic information is a potentially critical focus for the integration of information in expository text (Britton, in press; Kieras, 1980; Kintsch & van Dijk, 1978). First, it provides a context for the integration of subordinate information (Lorch, 1993). For example, if the paragraph topic is the eating habits of orangutans, then the sentence, "Meals are a solitary activity for orangutans" is likely to be interpreted as emphasizing the nature of an orangutan's meal. If the topic is social interactions of orangutans, the emphasis of the same sentence is likely to be interpreted as the solitary activity of taking a meal. Second, text topics must be integrated with one another if the reader is to adequately represent the macrostructure of the text. If readers fail to determine how text topics relate to preceding topics, then their text representations will consist of a sequence of unrelated structures corresponding to the distinct text topics (cf. Gernsbacher, Hargreaves, & Beeman, 1989; Gernsbacher, Varner, & Faust, 1990). The specific question of interest in this study is: Do readers use topic information as a context for the integration of subsequent, related topic information?

There is considerable empirical evidence suggesting that readers integrate subordinate information with respect to the relevant superordinate topic as they read. Subordinate statements are read more quickly if the relevant topic sentence is presented in the paragraph-initial sentence than if it is not presented (Kieras, 1978). In addition, reminding readers of the relevant paragraph topic facilitates resumption of reading after an interruption (Lorch, 1993). Finally, several studies demonstrate that readers organize their recall of text content around the topic of the text (Kieras, 1981; Kozminsky, 1977; Perfetti & Goldman, 1975; Schallert, 1976).

The issue of whether readers integrate new topics with previous text topics on-line has received less attention, but has been addressed in one series of studies. The relevant finding is that reading times on topic-introducing sentences depend on the relationship of the new topic to the immediately preceding text topic; the new topic sentence is more quickly comprehended if it is directly, rather than indirectly related to the preceding topic (Lorch, Lorch, Gretter, & Horn, 1987; Lorch, Lorch, & Matthews, 1985; Lorch, Lorch, & Mogan, 1987). Although this finding is certainly consistent with the hypothesis that readers attempt to integrate new topics with prior topics, it is not conclusive support for the hypothesis. A slow down in reading indicates some additional processing is taking place, but does not pinpoint the nature of the additional processing.

To determine whether readers find a prior text topic a useful context for the integration of a new topic, a paradigm introduced by Glanzer and his colleagues (Fischer & Glanzer, 1986; Glanzer, Fischer, & Dorfman, 1984) was employed in the current investigation. In this task, subjects read a sentence at a time while their reading times are recorded. At specific points in the text, reading is interrupted and subjects perform a distractor task (e.g., counting backwards by 3's) for 30 s. Following the distractor task, subjects resume reading. Reading time on the first new sentence following the interruption ("target sentence") is examined as a function of the type of cue subjects are presented concerning what they had been reading before the interruption. For example, subjects might be given no information about what they had been reading, or they might be reminded of the relevant paragraph topic, or they might be reminded of the last sentence they had read before interruption. The logic of the procedure is that a subject's reading time on the target sentence should depend on the extent to which the cue reinstates context needed to integrate the new information into the subject's existing text representation. The more effectively the cue reinstates relevant context, the faster reading time should be on the target sentence. In the present investigation, readers were occasionally interrupted just before a new topic sentence was to be presented. In the critical condition, the cue presented upon completion of the distractor task was a reminder of the topic sentence of the paragraph the subject had been reading when interrupted. If the topic of the last paragraph is a useful context for integrating the new paragraph topic, reading times on the new topic sentence should be faster in this topic-cue condition than in an appropriate baseline condition (i.e., no reminder of recent text content).

EXPERIMENT 1

Subjects in the first experiment read three, nine-paragraph texts while their reading times were recorded on four target sentences embedded in each of the texts. The target sentences were always paragraph-initial sentences introducing a new text topic and the new topic was always directly related to the topic of the immediately preceding paragraph. Immediately before three of the target sentences, subjects were interrupted without warning and required to perform addition problems for 30 s. When the distractor task was completed, subjects resumed reading after: (a) rereading the initial, topic sentence of the paragraph they had been reading (topic cue); (b) rereading the last sentence they had read before the interruption (local cue): or (c) receiving no reminder of what they had been reading (no cue). In the fourth condition, there was no interruption of reading before the target sentence (continuous).

Reading times in the topic-cue condition were of primary interest. If comprehension of a new topic sentence entails integrating the new topic with a prior related topic, then reading times should be faster in the topic-cue condition than in the no-cue condition. The continuous condition was included to determine the lower limit on reading times for the target sentences. The local-cue condition was included because Glanzer et al. (1984) found that this condition greatly facilitated resumption of reading when subjects read single topic, eight-sentence texts. In the same study, topic cues provided no facilitation whatsoever. This pattern of findings has been interpreted as demonstrating that readers integrate new information only with respect to the local context (Glanzer et al., 1984; McKoon & Ratcliff, 1992). Thus, the local-cue condition was included to determine whether readers presented with a long, multiple-topic text also integrate new information only with respect to the immediate, local context.

Finally, two different comprehension tests were employed following reading. In one condition, subjects performed a verification task in which they were tested for recognition of paraphrased statements from the text. This task placed a relatively low demand on readers to integrate information across sentences. In the second condition, subjects were required to write an outline of the text after reading. Relative to the verification task, this task required more attention to, and integration of, topic information in the text. This manipulation was included in the experimental design to examine whether the processing task might affect use of topic cues. If the integration of new topics with prior text topics is a strategic reading behavior employed only when the reading task demands such integration, then topic cues might facilitate reading in the outline condition but not the verification condition. An alternative possibility is that topic cues will facilitate reading in both task conditions. This would occur if readers routinely integrate subordinate information with topic information when they read multiple topic texts for comprehension.

Method

Subjects.   Subjects were 98 volunteers from introductory psychology classes at the University of Kentucky. The data of one subject were lost due to experimenter error and the data of another subject were excluded because the subject took notes while reading.

Materials.   The materials consisted of a brief practice text and two versions of each of three experimental texts. The practice text was 25 sentences long and discussed Daguerre's discovery of a photographic development process. The experimental texts were between 65 and 79 sentences long and were titled: "The Great Apes"; "A Comparison of Two Countries"; and "A Comparison of Two Children's Games."

The experimental texts all had the same topic structure. Each text began with an introductory paragraph that gave an overview of the organization of the text. The introductory paragraph was followed by eight paragraphs discussing four attributes of each of the two major text topics. For example, the "Apes" text discussed the habitat, social structure, communication methods, and eating habits of chimpanzees and orangutans. All texts were organized by attributes, alternating between the two major topics (e.g., chimpanzees and orangutans). The two versions of a given text differed only in the order of discussion of the two major topics. The purpose of this manipulation was to double the number of target sentences to increase the power of tests of effects against item variability.

For each of the experimental texts, the initial sentence of each of the eight attribute paragraphs introduced the topic of the paragraph and stated the main idea (i.e., expressed the most superordinate proposition of the paragraph). These topic sentences served as the target sentences in the experiment (i.e., the sentences for which reading times were of interest). In a given version of an experimental text, only four of the target sentences were of interest; namely, the topic sentences introducing an attribute of the second-discussed topic. For example, in the "Apes" text that always discussed a given attribute first for chimpanzees and then for orangutans, the four targets were the sentences introducing the four paragraphs on orangutans. Target sentences across the three texts were between 38 and 52 characters long, although the range of sentence lengths within the same text was no more then 5 characters.

In addition to the texts, sentences were constructed for the verification task. For the practice text, four true and four false statements were constructed. For each of the experimental texts, eight true and eight false statements were constructed. For the experimental texts, all statements were assertions regarding the four attributes discussed in the texts. Half of the statements paraphrased information presented in the text and half contradicted information presented in the text. Half of the statements were about one of the major topics and half were about the other topic. The same set of verification sentences was used for both versions of each experimental text.

Procedure.   Subjects were instructed that they would read four short texts on different topics and would be tested after each text. Subjects in the outline condition were informed that they would write an outline after each text; subjects in the verification condition were informed that they would be required to answer some true-false questions after each text. Subjects were also instructed in the computer-controlled procedure for reading texts and were told that they would occasionally be interrupted and asked to perform simple math problems for a short period of time.

When a subject understood the procedure, the practice text was presented by an Apple 2e computer. Each time the subject pressed the spacebar, the current sentence was erased and the next sentence was presented. The computer recorded the reading time for each sentence. Immediately before the 20th sentence of the practice text, reading was interrupted and the instructions for the addition problems were presented. Pairs of two-digit numbers were randomly generated by the computer, one at a time. The subject computed the answer for each problem (use of paper and pencil was allowed), then entered the answer on the computer. After 30 s of addition problems, the computer informed the subject that the reading task would be resumed. The subject pressed the spacebar twice and received the message, "Press the spacebar twice when you want to see the next sentence of the text, then continue reading as before." When the spacebar was pressed twice, the message was erased and the 20th sentence appeared. Thereafter, each press of the spacebar erased the current sentence and presented the next sentence, as before.

When the practice text was completed, subjects were instructed in the testing procedure. Subjects in the verification condition were told that they would be presented a series of statements based on the text they had just read. They were told to decide for each one whether it was true or false. They pressed a key marked "Yes" (the "0" key) to respond "true" and a key marked "No" (the "1" key) to respond "false." The computer recorded response latencies and accuracy for each statement.

Subjects in the outline condition were instructed in the outlining procedure, but were not asked to provide an outline for the practice text, in the interest of saving time. The subjects were provided with a sample outline and asked to read it over and ask questions if they did not understand the procedure. Subjects were required to provide a handwritten outline for each of the experimental texts and were informed of this requirement after completing the practice text.

The procedure for the experimental texts was analogous to that for the practice text except that reading was interrupted three times for each of the experimental texts. For one of the interruptions, the procedure was identical to that described for the practice text. That is, when the subject was instructed to resume reading the experimental text, no information was provided concerning what the subject had been reading at the time of interruption (no-cue condition).

For another of the interruptions, the subject was reminded of the information in the last sentence before the interruption (local-cue condition). For example, if the subject was reading the "Apes" text and was interrupted before the target sentence introducing the orangutan's habitat, the subject was informed, "Recall that you were last reading that trees provide chimpanzees with safety from most predators." This message was presented after the message to press the spacebar to see the next sentence of the text, so it was the last message the subject saw before being presented the target sentence.

Finally, for the other interruption, the subject was reminded of the topic sentence of the paragraph that was being read at the time of interruption (topic-cue condition). The procedure was identical to that for the local-cue condition except for the information that was presented immediately before the target sentence. For the example of the target sentence on the orangutan's habitat, the topic cue was, "Recall that you were last reading about why chimpanzees find the plains to be an ideal place to live."

For a given subject and text version, one of the target sentences was assigned to the continuous condition (i.e., no interruption before the target), one was assigned to the no-cue condition, one was assigned to the local-cue condition, and one was assigned to the topic-cue condition. Across subjects, each target of a given text version was assigned equally often to the four cue conditions using a Latin square. There were two different sets of target sentences corresponding to the two different versions of each experimental text.

Results and Discussion

The data of interest were the reading times on the target sentences in the reading task; the data from the verification and outlining tasks were not analyzed. All scores exceeding three standard deviations above the relevant condition mean were deleted from the data set (1.2%). Because the pattern of significant effects was the same for tests against subject and item variability, only the tests against subject variability are reported. All reported results are significant at the .05 level unless noted otherwise.

The mean reading times are reported as a function of condition in Table 15.1. These data were analyzed using a mixed-factors analysis of variance with a between-subjects factor of task (verification or outline) and a within-subjects factor of cue (continuous, topic, local, no cue). In addition, planned orthogonal contrasts were computed using the Bonferroni procedure to control family-wise error rate at the .05 level.

Table 15.1 shows faster reading times in the verification condition than in the outline condition; $F(1,94) = 8.69$, $MSe = 2.058$. This result is consistent with our previous findings (e.g., Lorch et al., 1985) and it validates the *a priori* assumption that the outline task places more emphasis than the verification task on attention to topic information.

Table 15.1 also shows an effect of the cue on reading times; $F(3,282) = 12.94$, $MS_e = 0.309$. The nature of the cue effect is that: (a) subjects were faster to read target sentences if they were not interrupted than if they were interrupted in their reading, $t(282) = 5.27$; (b) subjects were faster to read targets following an interruption if they received some kind of information about what they had been reading than if they received no reminder, $t(282) = 3.29$; but (c) it did not matter what type of reminder they received—they were equally fast to read the target whether they received a topic or local cue, $t(282) < 1$. These findings

TABLE 15.1
Mean Reading Times (s) on Target Sentences in Experiment 1 as a Function of Cue
and Processing Task

	Cue				
Task	Continuous	Topic	Local	No Cue	Mean
Verification	2.059	2.399	2.349	2.547	2.338
Outline	2.532	2.688	2.819	3.040	2.770
Mean	2.295	2.544	2.584	2.793	2.554

demonstrate that both the topic and local cues provided useful contexts for the integration of the subsequent topic sentences.

Although topic cues appeared to facilitate reading of target sentences somewhat more in the outline task than in the verification task, there was no statistical evidence of an interaction of task with cue, $F < 1$. The similar pattern of cue effects suggests that readers' strategies for integrating new topic information into their text representations were the same for the two processing tasks.

The hypothesis that readers integrate new topics with prior text topics as they read explains why reminding readers of the last text topic facilitated processing of the new, related topic. However, this hypothesis does not explain why reminding readers of the last statement they read facilitated processing of the new topic sentence just as much as presenting a topic cue. There are two possible reasons for the similar facilitatory effects of the topic and local cues. One possibility is the local cues may have led readers to reinstate the paragraph topic because these cues were generally directly subordinate to the topic and frequently explicitly mentioned the topic. For example, the local cue from the paragraph about chimpanzees' use of hand signals to communicate was, "Recall that you were last reading that scientists have identified gestures that chimpanzees use to request food and affection." If local cues effectively reinstated topic information, then they would be expected to act like topic cues with respect to their effects on processing of new topic sentences.

The second potential reason that topic and local cues had similar facilitatory effects is that the baseline for assessing the cue effects may have been inappropriate. It could be that the specific information provided by the topic and local cues was not used as a context for integrating targets; rather, these conditions simply prepared readers better to resume the reading task. In the no-cue condition, subjects were returned rather abruptly to the target sentence; they were warned that they would resume reading the text when they pressed the spacebar, but they may still have been attending to the addition task they had just completed. In the topic and local-cue conditions, reading the cue may have effectively redirected their attention to the reading task before they were actually presented the target.

Experiment 2 was conducted to evaluate these two possible accounts of the pattern of cue effects observed in Experiment 1.

EXPERIMENT 2

The design of the second experiment was basically the same as the first experiment, but a change was made in the texts and in one of the cue conditions. The experimental texts were slightly modified so that the last sentence of each paragraph did not present information that was directly subordinate to the topic of the paragraph. For example, the last sentence of the paragraph on why chimpanzees find the plains to be an ideal habitat was, "Branches and grasses are used to make nests." Similarly, the paragraph on the orangutan's habitat in the dense rain forests ended with the sentence, "Fruit is a very important source of food." Because the cues in the local-cue condition were paraphrases of paragraph-ending sentences, this change should have resulted in local cues that did not readily lead to a reinstatement of the paragraph topic. Thus, if the facilitatory effects of local cues in Experiment 1 were based on a reinstatement of topic information, local cues should produce less facilitation than topic cues in Experiment 2.

The other change in Experiment 2 was that the no-cue condition of Experiment 1 was replaced by a general-cue condition. Instead of returning directly to the reading task after completion of the distractor task, readers were reminded of which superordinate topic was relevant at the point of interruption. For example, if the paragraph they had been reading concerned the chimpanzees' habitat, the cue was, "Recall that you were last reading about chimpanzees." This cue should help readers redirect their attention to the reading task, but it does not provide the specific topic (chimpanzees' habitat) that constitutes the most appropriate context for understanding the subsequent target sentence introducing the topic of the orangutans' habitat. Thus, if the reason for the facilitatory effects of topic and local cues in Experiment 1 was that the cues better prepared subjects to resume reading, then the facilitation should be reduced or eliminated in Experiment 2. However, if the facilitation in Experiment 1 was due to the contextual information provided by topic and local cues, reading times in Experiment 2 should be faster in the topic and local-cue conditions than in the general-cue condition.

Method

Subjects.   Subjects were 97 volunteers from introductory psychology courses at the University of Kentucky, including one subject whose data were deleted for failure to follow instructions.

Materials.   The materials consisted of the verification sentences, the practice text, and revised versions of the experimental texts of Experiment 1. The revisions of the experimental texts consisted of rewriting the paragraph-ending sentences so that they were not directly subordinate to the topic sentences of their respective paragraphs. Rather, the sentences were usually "dead-end" elaborations of the immediately preceding sentence in the paragraph. As stated earlier, the intent of the revisions was to render the local cues less effective reminders of the paragraph topic relative to the local cues of Experiment 1.

Procedure. The procedure was identical to that of Experiment 1 with the exception of the change from the no-cue condition to the general-cue condition. Subjects in Experiment 1 received no information about what they had been reading following an interruption in the no-cue condition; whereas, subjects in Experiment 2 were reminded of the superordinate topic that was current at the time of interruption in the general-cue condition (e.g., "Recall that you were last reading about chimpanzees.").

Results and Discussion

Reading times exceeding three standard deviations above the condition mean were deleted from all analyses (1.3%). The results are summarized in Table 15.2. The data were analyzed as in Experiment 1.

A comparison of Tables 15.1 and 15.2 demonstrates that Experiment 2 replicated the findings of Experiment 1 in all respects. Subjects read target sentences more quickly in the verification task than in the outlining task, $F(1,94) = 6.80$, $MSe = 2.314$. Reading times varied systematically as a function of the cue condition, $F(3,282) = 6.73$, $MSe = 0.538$, and the effect of the cue manipulation was similar for the verification and outline tasks, $F(3,282) < 1$ for the interaction. The effect of the cue manipulation was the same as observed in Experiment 1: (a) subjects were faster to read target sentences if they were not interrupted than if they were interrupted, $t(282) = 3.29$; (b) subjects were faster to read target sentences if they received a topic or local cue than if they received a general cue, $t(282) = 2.96$; but (c) there was no reliable difference in reading times following topic versus local cues, $t(282) < 1$.

The findings of Experiment 2 demonstrate that the facilitatory effects of topic

TABLE 15.2
Mean Reading Times (s) on Target Sentences in Experiment 2 as a Function of Cue
and Processing Task

	Cue				
Task	Continuous	Topic	Local	General	Mean
Verification	2.283	2.324	2.446	2.591	2.411
Outline	2.517	2.780	2.826	3.139	2.816
Mean	2.400	2.552	2.636	2.865	2.613

and local cues found in Experiment 1 were not due simply to the cues helping readers make the transition back to reading after doing an addition task. Like the topic and local-cue conditions, the general-cue condition of Experiment 2 provided subjects with some reminder of what they had been reading in the text, so all three conditions should have been equally effective in signaling the return to the reading task. A major difference between the three conditions involving interruption was that the topic and local cues provided specific information concerning what the subject had recently been reading, whereas the general cues provided only the most general reminder. Thus, the effectiveness of the topic and local cues seems due to their providing an effective context for the integration of the target sentences into readers' text representations.

Despite the changes from Experiment 1 to Experiment 2 in the relationship of the local cues to the paragraph topic, the local cues were again nearly as effective as the topic cues with respect to aiding processing of topic sentences. It is unclear why the local cues were so effective. The information contained in the local cues generally should not have constituted an effective context for understanding the subsequent topic sentence because the two sentences were relatively unrelated. One possible explanation is that subjects used local cues to reconstruct the context prior to being interrupted. According to this account, the specific information contained in the local cues was an effective cue for such reconstruction, whereas the general information contained in the general cues could not effectively guide such reconstruction because the superordinate topic was associated with too much of the text content. Thus, although the revisions of the materials in Experiment 2 were intended to make the local cues ineffective as reminders of the paragraph topic, the revisions may have been unsuccessful. This possibility is considered further in the general discussion. An alternative explanation is tested in Experiment 3.

EXPERIMENT 3

In the first two experiments, subjects were consistently faster to resume reading if they were reminded of the topic sentence or the last sentence before interruption than if they were given no information or provided only the relevant superordinate topic. Although these findings may reflect that subjects use the topic and local cues to facilitate the integration of the target sentence into their text representations, an alternative possibility is that subjects initiated the construction of an entirely new representation after each interruption (Gernsbacher et al., 1989; Gernsbacher et al., 1990). According to this hypothesis, comparing the topic and local-cue conditions with the no-cue and general-cue conditions amounts to comparing conditions where a context is provided for integrating the target information with conditions where no context is provided. If this explanation is correct, then the first two experiments simply do not address the issue of how readers employ topic information to construct an integrated text representation.

Subjects in Experiment 3 read the target sentences of Experiment 2 embedded in lists of unrelated sentences. Subjects either were not interrupted (continuous condition) or were interrupted before reading the target sentence. If they were interrupted, the first sentence following the interruption was either: the topic sentence of the paragraph from which the target sentence was extracted (topic-cue); the sentence that would have preceded the target in the original text (local-cue); or a sentence that provided the superordinate topic that would have been active at the point of interruption of the text used in Experiment 2 (general-cue). In all three conditions involving interruption, the second sentence following interruption was the target sentence. If subjects in the first two experiments were integrating target sentences only with respect to the cues after an interruption, then the cue effects observed in Experiments 1 and 2 should be observed in Experiment 3. However, if subjects in the initial two experiments were integrating the target sentences into a coherent text representation, then there should be no cue effects in Experiment 3 because subjects were not presented a coherent text to process.

Method

Subjects. Subjects were 48 volunteers from introductory psychology classes at the University of Kentucky.

Materials. The materials consisted of a practice text and three experimental texts. Each text was a list of unrelated sentences consisting of both factual statements (e.g., "Golf was invented in Scotland") and statements about fictional characters, places, or events (e.g., "Winters in Pruvak are cold and windy"). The practice text was 23 sentences long and was interrupted once. The experimental texts were equal in length to the experimental texts of Experiment 2 and each was interrupted three times.

There were four target sentences embedded in each of the three experimental texts. The target sentences were identical to the target sentences used in Experiment 2 and they were embedded in their respective texts in the same serial positions as the target sentences in the texts of Experiment 2. As in Experiment 2, there were two sets of experimental texts differing only in the target sentences used (i.e., a different set of 12 target sentences was used in the two sets of texts).

Each target sentence was assigned to a cue condition. Sentences assigned to the continuous condition were preceded by an unrelated sentence. Sentences assigned to the topic-cue condition were preceded by the topic sentence associated with the target in the experimental text of Experiment 2. Similarly, sentences assigned to the local-cue condition were preceded by the sentence that would have preceded it in the corresponding text of Experiment 2. Sentences assigned to the general-cue condition were preceded by a sentence that asserted a category membership relation involving the superordinate topic that would have been relevant in the corresponding text of Experiment 2. For example, if the target sentence concerned orangutans, the general cue that preceded it was the sentence, "Chimpanzees are a type of animal." In all three conditions involving interruption, the first sentence presented after the distractor task was the cue sentence and the second sentence presented was the target sentence.

In addition to the texts, sentences were constructed for the verification task. There were 8 sentences constructed for the practice text and 16 sentences constructed for each experimental text. Half of the sentences had appeared in the associated text and half had not appeared in the text, but the two types of sentences were otherwise indistinguishable.

Procedure.   The procedure for the reading task was analogous to that of Experiment 2 except for changes in instructions because of the differences in the texts across the two experiments. There was no condition analogous to the outline condition of the previous experiments. All subjects were told that they would be presented lists of unrelated statements and that they were to read them in preparation for a "yes–no test of your memory for the sentences." Subjects were told not to try to memorize the sentences word for word, but to read the sentences for understanding. In conditions where subjects were interrupted, they were told to resume reading after the addition task. Unlike Experiments 1 and 2, the first statement they saw upon returning to the reading task was not of the form, "Recall that you had been reading that. . . ." Rather, they were simply presented the sentence appropriate to the interruption condition when they pressed the spacebar to resume the reading task.

All subjects performed a verification test after each text. The task was to decide as quickly as possible for each sentence whether it had appeared in the list of unrelated sentences that had just been presented. In all other respects, the procedures for Experiment 3 were identical to those for Experiment 2.

Results and Discussion

Reading times exceeding three standard deviations above the condition mean were deleted from all analyses (0.9%). Mean reading times for the four experimental conditions are presented in the top row of Table 15.3, along with the results from the verification condition of Experiment 2 for comparison.

The top row of Table 15.3 shows that the pattern of reading times in Experiment 3 was quite different from that found in Experiments 1 and 2. There was an effect of the cue manipulation, $F(3,72) = 4.85$, $MSe = 0.270$, but its nature was different from that of the earlier experiments. As in the earlier experimenters, reading times were faster if reading was continuous rather than interrupted, $t(72) = 3.66$. However, reading times were no faster if subjects were provided a topic or local cue than if subjects received a general cue, $t(72) < 1$. The magnitude of the difference between the two informative cues and the general cue was greater in the verification condition of Experiment 2 (.206 s) than in the verification condition of Experiment 3 (−.075 s), $t(144) = 2.06$.

TABLE 15.3
Mean Reading Times (s) on Target Sentences in Experiment 3 and the Verification Condition of
Experiment 2

			Cue		
Format	Continuous	Topic	Local	General	Mean
List (E3)	2.570	2.951	2.873	2.837	2.837
Story (E2)	2.283	2.324	2.446	2.591	2.411

The topic and local cues facilitated processing of target sentences when subjects read coherent texts (Experiments 1 and 2), but not when subjects read an incoherent text (Experiment 3). This contrast between the findings of Experiment 3 and those of Experiments 1 and 2 supports the conclusion that the topic and local cues of the first two experiments facilitated readers in their attempts to integrate new topic sentences into their text representations.

GENERAL DISCUSSION

The findings of this study are easily summarized. When subjects resumed reading after being interrupted while reading coherent text, processing of the new topic sentence was facilitated if they were reminded of either the paragraph topic or the last sentence read before interruption. In addition, the facilitatory effects of topic and local cues were the same regardless of whether subjects read to prepare for a verification test or to write an outline of the text. These findings support two broad conclusions. First, reminding readers of a paragraph's topic sentence or of the last sentence read reinstates contextual information that helps the readers to integrate the new topic sentence into their existing text representations. Second, the processes by which readers integrate new topic information into their text representations are not very task specific. The verification and outlining tasks place very different emphases on topic information, as indicated by the much slower reading times on topic sentences in the outlining task; however, the effects of the cue manipulation were very similar for the two tasks.

The focus of this study was on the function of prior topic information as a context for the integration of new topic information. Specifically, I have argued that in order to adequately represent the structure of a text, a reader must systematically identify new text topics as they are introduced and relate them appropriately to prior text topics. According to this hypothesis, topic cues facilitated processing of new topic information by reinstating an appropriate context for the integration of the new topic. However, the hypothesis does not account for the finding that reminding readers of the last sentence read before interruption facilitated processing of the new topic sentence almost as much as reminding readers of the previous paragraph's topic. In fact, it is not at all clear why local cues in Experiment 2 facilitated processing of the subsequent topic sentence. For instance, why should the information that the subject had been reading that "branches and grasses are used to make nests" facilitate processing of the sentence, "Orangutans make their home in dense rain forests"? One potential explanation of the effects of local cues is that subjects used the local cues to retrieve the relevant paragraph topics despite my attempts in Experiment 2 to write texts that would minimize this possibility. Because the experimental texts were quite coherent and relatively simple in content, subjects might still have been able to retrieve the relevant topic given a local cue.

There is a way to test this hypothesis using the data from Experiment 2. If subjects used local cues to retrieve topic information, then they should have spent more time processing local cues than topic cues before signaling that they were ready to resume reading. In fact, subjects did spend more time processing local cues (8.27 s) than topic cues (7.86 s), $t(188) = 1.96$, $p < .05$, 1 tailed. Although the experiment was not designed to test this issue, the results are consistent with the suggestion that subjects used local cues to recover topic information. If subjects did use local cues in this way, that would explain why local cues were as effective as topic cues in facilitating the processing of new topic sentences.

The present study demonstrates that readers find the previous text topic a useful context for understanding a sentence introducing a new, related text topic. Previous studies have shown that the speed with which readers process a topic sentence depends on the ease with which the new topic can be related to the immediately preceding text topic (E. Lorch et al. 1987; Lorch et al., 1985; R. Lorch et al., 1987). Together, these findings support the hypothesis that experienced readers relate new topics to prior topics as they encounter the new topics while reading. However, although the findings are consistent with the hypothesis, they do not provide definitive support for it. The hypothesis states that readers retrieve information about prior text topics upon encountering a new text topic, then connect the new topic appropriately into their representations of the text's topic structure (Lorch et al., 1985). There are two implications of this claim that require further investigation. First, a test is needed of whether readers retrieve prior text topics in the course of processing a new topic sentence. One approach to this issue would be to use a probe procedure to test whether prior related topics are active during the time the new topic sentence is being processed (Fischer & Glanzer, 1986; Trabasso & Suh, 1993). Another approach might be to use talk-aloud protocols to identify how readers relate topic sentences to prior text (e.g., Trabasso, Suh, Payton, & Jain, this volume). Second, a test is needed of whether related text topics are, in fact, represented as connected in readers' text representations. A possible approach to this question is to use a priming procedure to examine text memory (e.g., van den Broek & Lorch, 1993).

Let me conclude by noting that this is one of the few chapters in this book that directly concerns reading of expository text. Most research on text processing has examined comprehension of narrative, and for good reason. The availability of successful theories of narrative representation has greatly facilitated research on how readers construct text representations (e.g., Dopkins, Klin, & Myers, 1993) and subsequently retrieve information from their representations (e.g., O'Brien & Myers, 1987). Many of the reading processes involved in understanding narrative are surely involved in understanding exposition. It is also likely that models of how readers process aspects of narrative that are relatively specific to that genre will prove to be adaptable as models of how readers process parallel aspects of exposition. For example, models of processing of goal information (e.g., Trabasso & Suh, 1993) in narrative may share important features with models of processing of topic information in exposition. However, expository text differs in important ways from narrative text. Narrative has a goal-outcome macrostructure and a relatively tight, linear microstructure based heavily on causal relations (Trabasso, Secco, & van den Broek, 1984). Expository text is hierarchically organized around topics that vary in their relationships (Meyer, 1985); thus, the structure of exposition is less constrained than that of narrative. Given these differences in how narrative and expository texts are structured, it seems likely that processing of expository text will differ in systematic ways from processing of narrative text (Einstein, McDaniel, Owen, & Cote, 1990; McDaniel, Einstein, Dunay, & Cobb, 1986). It is important to study reading of expository text in its own right.

REFERENCES

Britton, B. K. (In press). Understanding expository text: Building mental structures to induce insights. In Morton A. Gernsbacher (Ed.), *Handbook of psycholinguistics*. New York: Academic Press.

Dopkins, S., Klin, C., & Myers, J. L. (1993). Accessibility of information about goals during the processing of narrative texts. *Journal of Experimental Psychology: Learning, Memory, and Cognition, 19*, 70–80.

Einstein, G. O., McDaniel, M. A., Owen, P. D., & Cote, N. C. (1990). Encoding and recall of texts: The importance of material appropriate processing. *Journal of Memory and Language, 29*, 566–581.

Fischer, B., & Glanzer, M. (1986). Short-term storage and the processing of cohesion during reading. *Quarterly Journal of Experimental Psychology, 38A*, 431–460.

Gernsbacher, M. A., Hargreaves, D. J., & Beeman, M. (1989). Building and accessing clausal representations: The advantage of first mention versus the advantage of clause recency. *Journal of Memory and Language, 28*, 735–755.

Gernsbacher, M. A., Varner, K. R., & Faust, M. E. (1990). Investigating differences in general comprehension skill. *Journal of Experimental Psychology: Learning, Memory, and Cognition, 16*, 430–445.

Glanzer, M., Fischer, B., & Dorfman, D. (1984). Short-term storage in reading. *Journal of Verbal Learning and Verbal Behavior, 23*, 467–486.

Kieras, D. E. (1978). Good and bad structure in simple paragraphs: Effects on apparent theme, reading time, and recall. *Journal of Verbal Learning and Verbal Behavior, 17*, 13–28.

Kieras, D. E. (1980). Component processes in the comprehension of simple prose. *Journal of Verbal Learning and Verbal Behavior*, *20*, 1–23.

Kieras, D. E. (1981). Topicalization effects in cued recall of technical prose. *Memory & Cognition*, *9*, 541–549.

Kintsch, W., & van Dijk, T. A. (1978). Toward a model of text comprehension and production. *Psychological Review*, *85*, 363–394.

Kozminsky, E. (1977). Altering comprehension: The effect of biasing titles on text comprehension. *Memory & Cognition*, *5*, 482–490.

Lorch, E. P., Lorch, R. F., Jr., Gretter, M. L., & Horn, D. G. (1987). On-line processing of topic structure by children and adults. *Journal of Experimental Child Psychology*, *43*, 81–95.

Lorch, R. F., Jr. (1993). Integration of topic and subordinate information during reading. *Journal of Experimental Psychology: Learning, Memory, and Cognition*, *32*, 1071–1081.

Lorch, R. F., Jr., Lorch, E. P., & Matthews, P. D. (1985). On-line processing of the topic structure of a text. *Journal of Memory and Language*, *24*, 350–362.

Lorch, R. F., Jr., Lorch, E. P., & Mogan, A. M. (1987). Task effects and individual differences in on-line processing of the topic structure of a text. *Discourse Processes*, *10*, 63–80.

McDaniel, M. A., Einstein, G. O., Dunay, P. K., & Cobb, R. E. (1986). Encoding difficulty and memory: Toward a unifying theory. *Journal of Memory and Language*, *25*, 645–656.

McKoon, G., & Ratcliff, R. (1992). Inference during reading. *Psychological Review*, *99*, 440–466.

Meyer, B. J. F. (1985). Prose analysis: Purposes, procedures, and problems. In B. K. Britton & J. B. Black (Eds.), *Understanding expository text: A theoretical and practical handbook for analyzing explanatory text* (pp. 11–64). Hillsdale, N. J.: Lawrence Erlbaum Associates.

O'Brien, E. J., & Myers, J. L. (1987). The role of causal connections in the retrieval of text. *Memory & Cognition*, *15*, 419–427.

Perfetti, C. A., & Goldman, S. R. (1975). Discourse functions of thematization and topicalization. *Journal of Psycholinguistic Research*, *4*, 257–271.

Schallert, D. L. (1976). Improving memory for prose: The relationship between depth of processing and context. *Journal of Verbal Learning and Verbal Behavior*, *15*, 621–632.

Trabasso, T., Secco, T., & van den Broek, P. (1984). Causal cohesion and story coherence. In H. Mandl, N. L. Stein, & T. Trabasso (Eds.), *Learning and comprehension of text* (pp. 83–111). Hillsdale, N. J.: Lawrence Erlbaum Associates.

Trabasso, T., & Suh, S. (1993). Using talk-aloud protocols to reveal inferences during comprehension of text. *Discourse Processes*, *16*, 3–34.

van den Broek, P. W., & Lorch, R. F., Jr. (1993). Network representations of causal relations in memory for narrative texts: Evidence from primed recognition. *Discourse Processes*, *16*, 75–98.

16

Inference Generation During the Comprehension of Narrative Text

Arthur C. Graesser
Eugenie L. Bertus
Joseph P. Magliano
Memphis State University

A complete theory of text comprehension must provide an explanatory account of inference generation. The theory should furnish decisive predictions about what inferences are generated, the conditions under which they are generated, and the timecourse of generating them. The theory should also be able to specify the resulting memory representation and the processes that participate in its construction. During the last 20 years, dozens of hypotheses and models of inference generation have been tested in the fields of cognitive psychology and discourse processing (e.g., Balota, Flores d'Arcais, & Rayner, 1990; Graesser & Bower, 1990; Graesser & Kreuz, 1993; Kintsch, 1993; Magliano & Graesser, 1991; McKoon & Ratcliff, 1992; Singer, 1988, in press; Whitney, 1987). Unfortunately, these extensive research efforts have not converged on a mature theory that would receive widespread consensus. There still are numerous models of inference generation that researchers are seriously pursuing. In this chapter, we present our own theory of inference generation and attempt to reduce the set of theoretically plausible alternatives.

The focus in this chapter is on narrative text and knowledge-based inferences. When readers comprehend narrative text, they construct a referential *situation model* (or mental model) of what the text is about. A situation model is a cognitive representation of the people, setting, actions, and events that are explicitly mentioned or suggested by the text (Glenberg, Meyer, & Lindem, 1987; Johnson-Laird, 1983; Kintsch, 1988; Morrow, Greenspan, & Bower, 1987; van Dijk & Kintsch, 1983). It is normally assumed that readers generate knowledge-based inferences when they construct these situation models. When an adult reads a novel, for example, several classes of knowledge-based inferences are potentially constructed: the spatial setting and layout, character traits, the knowledge and beliefs of characters, properties of objects, the goals and plans that motivate character actions, the manner of executing actions, the causes of anomalous events, expectations about future episodes in the plot, attitudes of the writer, appropriate emotional reactions of the reader, and so on. Although all of these classes of inferences could be potentially generated after an extensive analysis of a novel, only a subset of these inferences are normally generated online during the initial reading of the text. One of our objectives is to identify those classes of inferences that are normally generated online rather than offline (i.e., generated during a later retrieval task but not during comprehension).

We propose a constructionist theory that decisively predicts which knowledge-based inferences are constructed online during narrative comprehension. Many of the components and assumptions of the constructionist theory are compatible with contemporary psychological theories in discourse processing: the existence of reader goals, multiple levels of text representation, multiple memory stores (short-term and working memory vs. long-term memory), multiple information sources, focal attention, constraint satisfaction, and achievement of local coherence. The most distinctive property of the proposed constructionist theory is that it embraces the principle of "effort after meaning" (Bartlett, 1932; Berlyne, 1949, 1971; Stein & Trabasso, 1985). As articulated by Berlyne, the "ability to see external phenomena endowed with meaning is one of the main functions of both perceptual processes and the pursuit of knowledge" (Berlyne, 1949, p. 192). This effort-after-meaning principle is elaborated with three specific assumptions:

The reader goal assumption: The reader constructs a meaning representation that addresses the reader's goals.

The coherence assumption: The reader attempts to construct a meaning representation that is coherent at both local and global levels.

The explanation assumption: The reader attempts to explain why actions, events, and states are mentioned in the text.

As is discussed later, these three assumptions furnish decisive predictions about what knowledge-based inferences are constructed online. Alternative hypotheses, models, and theories of comprehension do not make the same predictions.

This chapter has three sections. The first section clarifies the scope of knowledge-based inferences and presents some example inferences in the context of a story. The second section presents the assumptions and predictions of the constructionist theory, as well as alternative theoretical positions. The third section summarizes the empirical evidence for the constructionist theory.

WHAT IS A KNOWLEDGE-BASED INFERENCE?

Given that we are focusing on knowledge-based inferences, it is important to define these classes of inferences. Knowledge-based inferences are constructed whenever knowledge structures from long-term memory are activated and a subset of this information is encoded as inferences in the meaning representation of the text. The meaning representation consists of both the textbase model and the referential situation model (Kintsch, 1988; van Dijk & Kintsch, 1983). Some of the activated knowledge structures are generic packages of world knowledge such as scripts, frames, stereotypes, or schemata (Bower, Black, & Turner, 1979; Graesser & Clark, 1985; Mandler, 1984; Rumelhart & Ortony, 1977; Schank & Abelson, 1977). These generic knowledge structures are triggered by particular content words, combinations of content words, and interpreted text constituents. Generic knowledge structures that are very familiar (e.g., RESTAURANT, FATHER) are automatized, so much of its content is activated in working memory at little cost to available cognitive processing resources (Graesser & Clark, 1985; Kintsch, 1988, 1993). World knowledge structures may be specific rather than generic. A specific knowledge structure refers to a particular experience, a text, or a previous excerpt from the text that is being comprehended. Compared to generic knowledge structures, it takes more time and processing resources to access and reconstruct information from a specific knowledge structure (because it is not overlearned and automatized).

A knowledge-based inference may be directly copied or inherited from a world knowledge structure (either generic or specific) when the text is comprehended. In this case, the process of incorporating it into the meaning representation of the text places relatively light demands on processing resources in working memory. Alternatively, a novel knowledge-based inference may be constructed after several cognitive cycles of searching memory and accumulating knowledge from multiple information sources in an incremental fashion (Just & Carpenter, 1992). The construction of a novel knowledge-based inference should place a larger burden on working memory. A lazy or hasty reader would not bother constructing such an inference online. In some cases, there is a temporary activation of information in a knowledge structure, but this information does not end up being incorporated in the meaning representation for the text. These transient activations are not considered knowledge-based inferences because they are not instantiated as part of the representation in long-term memory.

Some examples of knowledge-based inferences are presented in Table 16.1. While reading the story of "The Czar and his Daughters," the reader eventually attempts to comprehend the explicit action *A dragon kidnapped the daughters*. Several classes of knowledge-based inferences are potentially generated at that point, as illustrated in Table 16.1 and defined as follows.

TABLE 16.1
The Czar Story and Example Inferences

The Czar and his Daughters

Once there was a Czar who had three lovely daughters. One day the three daughters went walking in the woods. They were enjoying themselves so much that they forgot the time and stayed too long. A Dragon kidnapped the three daughters. As they were being dragged off they cried for help. Three heroes heard their cries and set off to rescue the daughters. The heroes came and fought the dragon and rescued the maidens. Then the heroes returned the daughters to their palace. When the Czar heard of the rescue, he rewarded the heroes.

Inferences when comprehending "The dragon kidnapped the daughter"

SUPERORDINATE GOAL: *The dragon wanted to eat the daughters.*
SUBORDINATE GOAL/ACTION: *The dragon grabbed the daughters.*
CAUSAL ANTECEDENT: *The dragon saw the daughters.*
CAUSAL CONSEQUENCE: *Someone rescued the daughters.*
CHARACTER EMOTION: *The daughters were frightened.*
STATE: *The dragon has scales.*

Superordinate goal: The inference is a goal that motivates an agent's intentional action.

Subordinate goal/action: The inference is a goal, plan, or action that specifies how an agent's intentional action is achieved.

Causal antecedent: The inference is on a causal chain (bridge) between the current explicit action, event, or state and the previous passage context.

Causal consequence: The inference is on a forecasted causal chain, unfolding from the current explicit action, event, or state. These include physical events and new plans of agents, but not emotions.

Character emotion: The inference is an emotion experienced by a character in response to an event, action, or state.

State: The inference is an ongoing state, from the time frame of the story plot, that is not causally linked to the episodes in the plot. These inferences include character traits, properties of objects, and spatial relationships among entities.

These inferences obviously do not exhaust the classes of potential knowledge-based inferences. These were selected because researchers have investigated these inferences empirically and because the status of these inferences discriminates alternative theoretical positions.

There is an important distinction between *text-connecting* inferences and *extratextual* inferences. Text-connecting inferences establish a link (i.e., relational arc) between the current clause being comprehended and a previous explicit constituent in the text. The inference being constructed is the connective link. Anaphoric inferences consist of one type of text-connecting inference. An anaphoric inference is constructed when a noun or pronoun in the text refers to a previous noun, proposition, clause, or excerpt in the text. For example, the pronoun *they* in the third sentence in Table 16.1 refers to *the daughters* mentioned in the second sentence; the text-connecting inference is: "*they* refers to *the daughters.*" Another type of text-connecting inference specifies the type of conceptual relation between two explicit propositions in the text (e.g., Proposition A causes Proposition B; Proposition A is the motive for Proposition B). In the case of extratextual inferences, however, the inference is a proposition that is not explicitly mentioned in the text. All of the example inferences in Table 16.1 are extratextual inferences. These inferences are copied or derived from the content of the generic and specific knowledge structures associated with the text. It should be noted that some extratextual inferences are needed to establish text coherence, whereas others are elaborative inferences that are not necessary for constructing a coherent text representation. This chapter concentrates on the extratextual inferences rather than text-connecting inferences.

Several classes of inferences are not knowledge-based inferences. Knowledge-based inferences do not include symbolic expressions that are derived from systems of domain-independent formal reasoning, such as propositional calculus, predicate calculus, or theorem proving (Newell & Simon, 1972; Rips, 1990). These logic-based inferences are normally a struggle to derive and are therefore offline, although some logic-based inferences are generated under particular processing conditions (Lea, O'Brien, Fisch, Noveck, & Brain, 1990). Knowledge-based inferences do not include quantitative and statistical inferences that are derived from formulas and quantitative procedures (Kahneman, Slovic, & Tversky, 1982). These quantitative inferences also are difficult to derive, as everyone knows who has taken a course in mathematics or statistics. Finally, knowledge-based inferences do not include linguistic inferences at the syntactic level.

Given that world knowledge structures furnish knowledge-based inferences, it is critical to make sure that readers have an adequate amount of world knowledge in tests of whether these inferences are generated online. The researcher needs to validate that the inferences could be generated by the designated reader population if the readers had sufficient time to make the inferences. Researchers have sometimes collected verbal protocols from readers during comprehension in order to validate that the readers could potentially generate the inferences under investigation. In think-aloud tasks, the reader expresses whatever comes to mind as each explicit clause is comprehended (Ericsson & Simon, 1980; Olson, Duffy, & Mack, 1984; Suh & Trabasso, 1993; Trabasso & Suh, 1993). In question answering tasks, the reader answers particular questions about each clause, such as "why," "how," and "what happens next" (Graesser, 1981; Graesser & Clark, 1985; Graesser, Robertson, & Anderson, 1981). In question-asking tasks, the reader asks questions that come to mind while reading each clause (Collins, Brown, & Larkin, 1980; Olson, Duffy, & Mack, 1985). These verbal protocols expose potential knowledge-based inferences that can be used as test items in subsequent studies. There is some assurance that the inference could be made, that the reader population has the prerequisite world knowledge, and that the inference is expressible in language. Magliano and Graesser (1991) advocated a "three-pronged method" that coordinates: (a) the collection of verbal protocols to expose potential inferences, (b) theories of discourse processing that make predictions about inference generation, and (c) the collection of online temporal measures during reading to assess whether a class of inferences is truly made online. An application of the three-pronged method is presented later in this chapter.

THEORETICAL POSITIONS THAT OFFER PREDICTIONS ABOUT INFERENCE GENERATION

This section presents some alternative theoretical positions that make specific claims about which knowledge-based inferences are generated online. We focus primarily on the six inference categories that are illustrated in Table 16.1. In order to simplify matters, each class of inferences is assigned to either an online status or an offline status. We acknowledge that there is a probabilistic continuum between online and offline. The continuum can be attributed to fluctuations in reading ability, reading goals, text materials, samples of inferences, experimental tasks, and so on. The continuum may also be explained by the possibility that inferences are instantiated to some degree rather than all-or-none (Gernsbacher, 1990; Kintsch, 1988; Sharkey & Sharkey, 1992). Technically speaking, when we say that inference Class A is online and Class B is offline, our intention is to claim that Class A inferences have a higher likelihood of being generated than Class B inferences.

There are some theoretical components and assumptions that are widely accepted by researchers in discourse processing and cognitive psychology. These are embraced by virtually any theory of inference generation. These components and assumptions are listed here; Graesser, Singer, and Trabasso (1993) discussed these assumptions in more detail.

1. *Multiple information sources.* Several information sources contribute to the generation of inferences during comprehension: the explicit text, background world knowledge structures, goals of the reader, and the pragmatic context of a communicative exchange.

2. *Surface code and textbase vs. situation model.* These three levels of cognitive representation are achieved as a result of comprehension (Kintsch, 1988; Kintsch, Welsh, Schmalhofer, & Zimny, 1990; van Dijk & Kintsch, 1983). The surface code preserves the exact wording and syntax of a clause. The textbase contains the explicit text propositions in a form that preserves meaning and a small number of inferences that are needed to establish local text coherence. The referential situation model is described earlier.

3. *Multiple memory stores.* There are three memory stores: short-term memory (STM), working memory (WM), and long-term memory (LTM). The current clause being processed is held in a passive STM buffer that preserves the surface code. WM is an active work space for processing text; it preserves the meaning of approximately two to three sentences prior to the current clause, plus very important information earlier in the text. LTM is a vast storehouse of generic knowledge structures, specific knowledge structures, and interpreted segments of the current text that do not reside in STM or WM. Note that researchers disagree about the exact boundary between STM and WM; unfortunately, they sometimes use the two constructs interchangeably.

4. *Focus of attention.* Readers actively construct a small subset of information in their conscious, focal attention. Metaphorically, this component is analogous to a mental camera that scans the constructed mental scenario and zooms in on particular characters, character actions, spatial regions, unusual events, novel information, and other hot spots throughout the course of comprehension. Our construal of focal attention adopts Mandler's (1985) theoretical claims about consciousness: (a) it is an active construction rather than a product of passive activations of knowledge, (b) it is limited in capacity, and (c) it cannot be reduced to the memory and processing functions of STM and WM. Focal attention is akin to the mind's eye (Kosslyn, 1980), the discourse focus (Grosz, Joshi, & Weinstein, 1983), and the explicit focus (Sanford & Garrod, 1981).

5. *Learning and automaticity.* Degree of learning influences the accessibility of knowledge structures and information units within the knowledge structures. A knowledge structure is more quickly and successfully accessed to the extent that it is overlearned through repetition. When a knowledge structure is automatized, its content is wholistically accessed and activated as a single chunk, at little cost to the processing resources in working memory (Just & Carpenter, 1992; LaBerge & Samuels, 1974).

6. *Convergence and constraint satisfaction.* Both explicit information and inferences receive more activation to the extent that they are activated by several information sources (i.e., there is convergence) and they satisfy the conceptual constraints imposed by multiple information sources (Graesser & Clark, 1985; Kintsch, 1988; O'Brien, Shank, Myers, & Rayner, 1988). A passive, activation-based inference is formed when it receives a sufficient amount of positive activation from multiple information sources, and negative inhibitory activation from few (if any) information sources.

Once again, these six components and assumptions are comparatively uncontroversial because they are embraced by most contemporary theories of text comprehension.

This section examines six theoretical positions that make distinctive predictions about the online status of the knowledge-based inferences. The constructionist theory is the primary theoretical position that we endorse. The alternative positions are an explicit textbase position, a minimalist hypothesis, a current-state selection strategy, a prediction-substantiation model, and a promiscuous inference generation position. These theoretical positions make different predictions about the online status of the six classes of knowledge-based inferences under consideration. The predictions are summarized in Table 16.2. The rationale for these predictions are provided in the remainder of this section.

Constructionist Theory

The distinctive property of the constructionist theory resurrects the effort-after-meaning principle (Bartlett, 1932; Berlyne, 1949, 1971; Stein & Trabasso, 1985). This principle asserts that comprehenders attempt to construct meaning out of text, social interactions, and perceptual input. As mentioned earlier, this vague but essentially correct principle is empowered by three specific assumptions: the reader goal assumption, the coherence assumption, and the explanation assumption. It is important to emphasize that the effort-after-meaning principle involves an *effort*, not necessarily an *achievement*. There are many conditions that would prevent a reader from constructing a message that is coherent, that

TABLE 16.2
Predictions of Six Theoretical Positions Regarding the On-Line Status of Six
Classes of Inferences

Theoretical Position	Class of Inference					
	Causal Antecedent	Causal Consequence	Superordinate Goal	Subordinate Goal/Action	State	Character Emotion
Explicit text base						
Minimalist hypothesis	X*					
Current-state selection strategy	X		X			
Constructionist theory	X		X			X
Prediction-substantiation model	X	X	X			X
Promiscuous inference generation	X	X	X	X	X	X

*Cells with an "X" signify the class of inferences is normally generated on-line. Cells without an "X" signify inferences are not normally constructed on-line.

explains all of the explicit text, and that addresses the reader's goals. If the reader devotes no effort, no inferences will be drawn. A coherent message will not be drawn if the text is choppy, incoherent, and pointless. Few if any inferences will be drawn if the reader lacks prerequisite background knowledge structures.

Satisfaction of Reader Goals.   The process of reading is partially governed by reading goals (Britton & Glynn, 1987). The goals may be ill-defined and general, such as when an adult reads a newspaper to become informed about current events, or reads a short story to be entertained. Alternatively, the reader's goals may be very specific. For example, the reader might read a newspaper in order to determine whether a company is going bankrupt. The reader might read a short story in order to form a mental picture of the spatial setting. According to the reader goal assumption, the reader is persistent in attempting to satisfy these goals during comprehension and during inference generation. Consequently, readers generate inferences that address the reader's goals. Without this assumption, reader goals might get lost in the shuffle among multiple information sources (i.e., text, world knowledge structures, pragmatic context).

The reader goal assumption does not offer any distinctive predictions about which inferences are normally generated during comprehension. Any one of the six classes could potentially be generated online, depending on the reader's goals. For example, if the reader has a specific goal to gain a vivid mental picture of the spatial setting and to track locations of objects, then spatial state inferences would be constructed online even though these inferences take considerable time and effort to generate (Mani & Johnson-Laird, 1982; Morrow, Bower, & Greenspan, 1989), and even though they are not normally generated when reading naturalistic stories for entertainment (Zwaan & van Oostendorp, 1993). None of the classes of inferences would be generated online if the reader had a shallow goal to proofread the text for spelling errors. The predictions in Table 16.2 are based on the condition in which the reader has a general goal to comprehend the meaning of the text, but not a specific goal to focus on any particular level.

Local and Gobal Coherence.   Readers attempt to build a coherent meaning representation at both local and global levels. Of course, a reader might abandon such an attempt if the reader regards the text as incoherent (Roberts & Kreuz, 1993). The claim that readers attempt to establish local coherence is not particularly controversial. Local coherence refers to structures and processes that organize elements, constituents, and referents of adjacent clauses, or of short sequences of clauses that co-occur in WM. More specifically, readers link noun and pronoun arguments in the current clause with explicit arguments and propositions in the previous text (Duffy & Rayner, 1990; Kintsch & van Dijk, 1978; McKoon & Ratcliff, 1992; O'Brien, Duffy, & Myers, 1986; O'Brien & Albrecht, 1991). Connectives (i.e., *and, or, because, so*) play a major role in linking adjacent clauses and clauses co-occurring in WM (Halliday & Hasan, 1976;

Mann & Thompson, 1986; Millis, Graesser, & Haberlandt, 1993). Local coherence is sometimes established by inferring causal chains and relations between clauses that co-occur in WM; the process of inferring these causal chains and relations takes additional processing time to complete (Bloom, Fletcher, van den Broek, Reitz, & Shapiro, 1990; Haberlandt & Bingham, 1978; Keenan, Baillet, & Brown, 1984; Myers, Shinjo, & Duffy, 1987). The causal antecedent inferences in Tables 1 and 2 are the only inferences that are needed to establish local text coherence.

Global coherence involves both (a) the organization of local chunks of information into higher order chunks and (b) the linking of an incoming clause to a clause or excerpt much earlier in the text (i.e., in LTM, but no longer in STM and WM). Researchers in text linguistics, artificial intelligence, psychology, and education have developed detailed theories of global coherence in narrative (Dyer, 1983; Lehnert, 1981; Mandler, 1984; van Dijk & Kintsch, 1983). For example, a narrative may be organized at a global level by a REVENGE structure: Characters A and B have a positive bond; Character C harms Character B for unjustifiable reasons; subsequently, Character A harms Character C. Readers presumably infer these higher order, global themes during comprehension, but there is very little empirical research that has evaluated that possibility (see Seifert, McKoon, Abelson, & Ratcliff, 1986). In contrast, there is empirical support for the claim that an incoming clause is linked to a causally related event or goal that is much earlier in the text (i.e., 2 above). These distant causal linkages are achieved even under conditions in which local coherence is intact and when the earlier clause is outside of WM (Dopkins, Klin, & Myers, 1993; Suh & Trabasso, 1993; van den Broek & Lorch, 1993).

Superordinate goals and character emotions are two classes of inferences that are important in the global thematic structures that organize narrative (Dyer, 1983; Lehnert, 1981; Stein & Levine, 1991). Emotions and main goals are the central components of Lehnert's plot unit analysis, Dyer's "thematic affect units," and Stein & Levine's analysis of children's narrative. For example, negative emotions occur when the main goals of characters are blocked by other characters or by unexpected events in the world. Positive emotions occur when difficult goals are accomplished and when a character unexpectedly obtains a valued resource. Cognitive theories of emotion have emphasized the systematic relationships between goals and emotions (Mandler, 1976). The constructionist theory predicts that superordinate goals and character emotions are normally generated online because the reader attempts to achieve global coherence.

Explanation.   Readers attempt to explain why episodes in text occur and why the author explicitly mentions particular information in the message. Thus, explanation is a central component of understanding (Schank, 1986). When viewed from the standpoint of question-driven models of comprehension (Collins, Brown, & Larkin, 1980; Schank, 1986), comprehension is guided by "why" questions rather than other types of questions (i.e., "how," "what happens next," "where," "when," etc.). The reasons that characters perform intentional actions include their superordinate goals and the causal antecedents that trigger these goals (Graesser, Lang, & Roberts, 1991; Lehnert, 1978). Explanations of involuntary events include their causal antecedents (Graesser et al., 1991; Schank, 1986). Given that people have a natural proclivity to explain input, readers are expected to generate online the superordinate goal inferences and causal antecedent inferences.

The importance of explanation in understanding has been proposed by theorists both inside and outside of psychology. Explanation plays a central role in causal theories of narrative comprehension (Black & Bower, 1980; Trabasso & Suh, 1993; Trabasso & van den Broek, 1985; van den Broek, 1990; van den Broek & Lorch, 1993), in theories of causal attribution in social psychology (Hastie, 1983; Hilton, 1990; Pennington & Hastie, 1986; Read, 1987), and theories of planning and mundane reasoning in artificial intelligence (Mooney, 1990; Schank, 1986).

A pragmatic level of explanation must also be considered in the comprehension process. A reader might wonder why an author would bother mentioning some information and construct some explanation for it. Readers follow the Gricean postulate that whatever the author expresses is relevant and important (Grice, 1975; Roberts & Kreuz, 1993). In a mystery novel, for example, the reader might puzzle over why the author would bother mentioning that a women always carried white gloves in her purse. The reader might either construct a tentative explanation or be on the lookout for the subsequent plot to explain it.

To summarize, the constructionist theory predicts that three classes of inferences are normally generated online when narrative is read for understanding: causal antecedents, character emotions, and superordinate goals. Causal antecedent inferences are constructed in an effort to explain explicit actions and events, to establish local coherence, and to provide global coherence. Superordinate goal inferences are generated to explain explicit actions and to establish global coherence. Character emotions play an important role in establishing global coherence.

There is indeed justification for constructionist theory's prediction that the other classes of inferences are *not* normally generated online. These other classes are elaborative inferences that are not needed to explain the explicit information or to establish coherence. The subordinate goals/actions embellish the details of how intentional actions are executed. The states embellish details about people, objects, locations, and other static entities. If these details were important, the author would have explicitly mentioned them in the narrative. Causal consequence inferences are not normally constructed online because there are too many alternative hypothetical plots that could be forecasted and most of these would end up being erroneous when the full story is known (Graesser, 1981; Graesser & Clark, 1985; Kintsch, 1988; Potts, Keenan, & Golding, 1988). It also takes substantial cognitive resources to construct a forecasted hypothetical plot (Johnson-Laird, 1983). The only condition in which a consequence is forecasted is if it is highly constrained by context and very few (if any) alternative consequence chains would causally unfold (Murray, Klin, & Myers, 1991), as specified by Assumption 6 earlier in this section.

Explicit Textbase Position

The explicit textbase reigned supreme in early psychological theories of comprehension (Kintsch, 1974; Kintsch & van Dijk, 1978; Mandler & Johnson, 1977). Researchers did not greet inferences with enthusiasm in their attempts to create coherent representations of the explicit information. An inference was introduced as a patch to preserve coherence. They were to be used sparingly. Now that inferences have received more attention in cognitive psychology and discourse processing, this explicit textbase position is perhaps a strawman. This position predicts that none of the classes of inferences in Tables 1 and 2 are normally generated online.

The explicit textbase position appears to have some validity for expository texts on topics in which the reader has a small amount of world knowledge (Britton, Van Dusen, Glynn, & Hemphill, 1990). When there is skimpy world knowledge, there is little or no foundation for readers to construct knowledge-based inferences. Writers of expository text frequently assume (mistakenly) that readers can fill in the missing information and establish coherence. Britton et al. (1990) reported that recall for expository text can dramatically improve when this missing information is made explicit in revisions of expository texts. Narrative is a different kettle of fish, however. Compared to expository text, narrative text has a much closer correspondence to everyday experiences in which people perform actions in pursuit of goals, people encounter obstacles to goals, and people experience emotions (Britton & Pelligrini, 1990; Bruner, 1986; Nelson, 1986; Schank, 1990). There is a richer inventory of background knowledge in the case of narrative text, so knowledge-based inferences are more prevalent in this genre.

Minimalist Hypothesis

McKoon and Ratcliff (1989, 1992) proposed this hypothesis to account for those inferences that are automatically (vs. strategically) encoded during comprehension. According to this position, the only inferences that are encoded automatically during reading are "those that are based on easily available information, either from explicit statements in the text or from general world knowledge, and those that are required to make statements in the text locally coherent" (Mckoon & Ratcliff, 1992, p. 440). Therefore, causal antecedent inferences should be the only class (in Tables 16.1 and 16.2) generated automatically.

McKoon and Ratcliff never proposed an adequate definition of automaticity so it is difficult to evaluate this position. They inappropriately equated automatic processes with quick processes. Contemporary theories of automaticity (Logan, 1985; Schneider & Shiffrin, 1977) stipulated that an automatic process needs to satisfy multiple criteria: (a) once started, the process runs to completion, (b) the process can be executed simultaneously with another task without any degradation of performance on the automatic task, and (c) there is minimal reliance of focal attention to execute the process. None of the inferences in Tables 1 and 2 would be encoded automatically if they had to meet all of these criteria. Of course, if none of the inferences met these criteria, automaticity would be a poor selection of a processing threshold for investigating inferences. In any case, McKoon and Ratcliff never offered any rigorous test of whether inferences are automatically encoded, so the status of such a claim is an open question. We would argue, for example, that "understanding" is a more suitable processing threshold than automaticity for a theory of inference generation (also, see Schank, 1986).

The minimalist hypothesis does offer the general prediction that causal antecedent inferences should receive the highest strength of encoding and have the highest likelihood of being generated online. This is the only class of inferences that is needed for local text coherence. This is the only class of inference that would be consistently generated; the other five classes are strategic inferences, which, by definition, are only probabilistically encoded during comprehension.

Current-State Selection Strategy

This is a strategic model of narrative comprehension that specifies the process of constructing causal connections between explicit clauses (Bloom et al., 1990; Fletcher & Bloom, 1988). The strategy augments Kintsch's early model of comprehension (Kintsch & van Dijk, 1978), which relied heavily on argument repetition as a foundation for establishing local text coherence. The current-state selection strategy is very similar to van den Broek's causal inference maker model (van den Broek, 1990; van den Broek & Lorch, 1993).

According to the current-state selection (CSS) strategy, the reader's attention is focused on a small set of clauses in STM after each sentence is read. Comprehension is fast when there is a causal or noncausal connection between this information in STM (i.e., the current state) and information in the sentence that follows. Local coherence is directly established when such a connection can be found. If and only if no such connection can be found, then the reader attempts to establish coherence by reinstating relevant explicit information from previous text segments in LTM. It should be noted that these time-consuming reinstatement searches are executed only when there is a break in local coherence. When a reinstatement search is successful, the reader connects the incoming sentence to a causal antecedent or a main goal (i.e., a superordinate goal) of a character that was explicitly mentioned earlier in the text. Sometimes the reinstatement search is unsuccessful and the reader must wait for subsequent text to ascribe meaning to the current clause.

The CSS strategy predicts that extratextual inferences may be constructed whenever there is a break in local coherence. Two classes of inferences are generated online under these conditions, namely causal antecedents and superordinate goals. The CSS predicts that the other four classes are not generated online.

Prediction-Substantiation Model

This model asserts that reading is expectation driven in addition to being explanation driven. Readers generate expectations about future occurrences in the plot and these expectations guide the interpretation of clauses in a top-down fashion (Bower et al., 1979; DeJong, 1979; Dyer, 1983; Schank & Abelson, 1977). Expectations are formulated when a higher order knowledge structure is activated, such as a script or theme. If a story activates a RESTAURANT script, for example, and the text mentions that a character ordered some food, then the reader expects that the character will subsequently be served food, eat, and pay the bill. If the story activates a revenge theme when the text states that Character C murders Character B, then the reader might form the expectation that Character A (the friend of B) will harm Character C. The reading time for a clause is facilitated if it matches a prior expectation and slows down if it clashes with the expectation (Bower et al., 1979). When an irrelevant or inconsistent clause occurs, there is an expectation failure and the reader attempts to explain the atypical input.

As specified in Table 16.2, this prediction-substantiation model predicts that four classes of inferences are generated online. This model asserts that readers forecast future plots that would causally unfold from the current clause. Therefore, causal consequences should be generated online. As discussed earlier, character emotions and superordinate goals play a central role in the higher order thematic structures that are activated during comprehension. Therefore, these classes of inferences should be generated online. Finally, causal antecedent inferences should be generated in order to explain why incoming actions and events occur.

Promiscuous Inference Generation

This extreme position asserts that all classes of inferences are generated online as long as the reader has the prerequisite world knowledge. The reader builds a complete, lifelike situation model by fleshing out all of the details about the characters, props, spatial layout, actions, events, and so on. The meaning representation would be a high-resolution mental videotape of the narrative, along with exhaustive information about the mental states of the characters and the pragmatic exchange between author and reader. This is perhaps a strawman because no one has seriously advocated it. However, it is interesting to point out that McKoon and Ratcliff (1992) mistakenly claimed that a constructionist theory would embrace such a position.

EMPIRICAL EVIDENCE FOR THE CONSTRUCTION OF KNOWLEDGE-BASED INFERENCES

Researchers in cognitive psychology and discourse processing have debated over the proper measures and experimental designs for testing whether inferences are generated online (Graesser & Bower, 1990; McKoon & Ratcliff, 1989; Potts et al., 1988; Singer, 1988, 1991). There does not appear to be a perfect measure and task. Instead, there are trade-offs, with each enjoying some benefits and some shortcomings. An adequate dependent measure taps processes that occur during comprehension. Therefore, recall and summarization tasks do not furnish appropriate measures. An ideal task collects response times in order to track the time course of various cognitive processes. Time-based measures include self-paced reading times for text segments, gaze durations on words in eye-tracking studies, lexical decision latencies on test words (i.e., whether a test string is a word or nonword), naming latencies on test words, latencies to judge whether test statements interspersed within a text are true or false, and speeded recognition judgments under a deadline procedure. We also advocate a three-pronged method that coordinates (a) the collection of verbal protocols that expose candidate inferences, (b) the collection of time-based behavioral measures to test which inferences are online, and (c) theory (Magliano & Graesser, 1991).

This section reviews the empirical evidence that tests the six theoretical positions with respect to the six classes of inferences in Tables 1 and 2. We first focus on studies that used time-based behavioral measures, but not necessarily the three-pronged method. We subsequently report some studies that did use the three-pronged method. As will be seen, the available evidence supports the constructionist theory rather than the five alternative theoretical positions.

Evidence From Studies Using Time-based Behavioral Measures

The constructionist theory predicts that three of the six inference classes in Table 16.2 are normally generated online during text comprehension: causal antecedents, superordinate goals, and character emotions. There is empirical support for these predictions in the case of causal antecedents (Bloom et al., 1990; Fletcher & Bloom, 1988; Graesser, Haberlandt, & Koizumi, 1987; Magliano, Baggett, Johnson, & Graesser, 1993; McKoon & Ratcliff, 1986, 1989; Myers et al., 1987;

Potts et al., 1988; Singer, Halldorson, Lear, & Andrusiak, 1992; van den Broek & Lorch, 1993), superordinate goals (Bloom et al., 1990; Dopkins et al., 1993; Graesser et al., 1987; Long & Golding, 1993; Long, Golding, & Graesser, 1992; Long, Golding, Graesser, & Clark, 1990; Suh & Trabasso, 1993), and character emotions (Gernsbacher, Goldsmith, & Robertson, 1992).

In contrast, the constructionist theory predicts that the following inferences are not normally generated during comprehension: causal consequences, subordinate goals/actions, and states. Once again, however, these inferences might be generated if the reader has a specific goal to generate a particular class of inferences or if an inference is highly predictable by virtue of convergence and constraint satisfaction (see Assumption 6 presented earlier). Available empirical evidence supports the constructionist theory in the case of causal consequences (Graesser et al., 1987; Magliano et al., 1993; McKoon & Ratcliff, 1986, 1989; Potts et al., 1988; Singer & Ferreira, 1983), subordinate goals/actions (Long & Golding, 1993; Long et al., 1990; Long et al., 1992), and states (Long et al., 1990; Seifert, 1990; Seifert, Robertson, & Black, 1985). Instrumental inferences are conceptually similar to the subordinate goals/actions in the sense that the use of an instrument (i.e., object, part of body, resource) is part of the subplan of executing an action. For example, when presented the explicit sentence "John pounded the nail," the instrumental inference would be *with a hammer* (which has the same meaning as the subordinate action description *John used a hammer*). The constructionist theory predicts that these instrumental inferences are not generated online and available empirical evidence supports this prediction (Corbett & Dosher, 1978; McKoon & Ratcliff, 1981; Singer, 1979, 1980).

The central argument is that the constructionist theory predicts the exact subset of inferences that are generated online and the conditions under which they are generated. In contrast, accurate predictions are not delivered by the alternative theoretical positions (see Table 16.2).

Evidence From Studies Using the Three-Pronged Method

Graesser and his colleagues have used the three-pronged method to investigate extratextual inferences during the comprehension of short narrative texts (Graesser et al., 1987; Long & Golding, 1993; Long et al., 1990; Long et al., 1992; Magliano et al., 1993). The texts included the Czar story in Table 16.1 and three stories of comparable length that were investigated by other researchers. They tested five of the six inferences under focus in this chapter. The exception was character emotions (but see Gernsbacher et al., 1992, for evidence supporting the generation of these inferences).

One prong of the three-pronged method addresses theory. The alternative theoretical positions offer different predictions about the online status of these five classes of inference (see previous section). It should be noted that the current-state selection strategy and the constructionist theory offer equivalent predictions with respect to the five classes of inferences examined in this subsection. These two theories will be contrasted at the end of this subsection.

A second prong of the three-pronged method involves the collection of verbal protocols. Graesser and his colleagues collected question-answering protocols while readers comprehended the stories clause by clause. After reading each clause (that referred to an action, event, or state), the subjects answered questions about the clause. One group answered a "why" question, a second group answered a "how" question, and a third group answered a "what happens next" (WHN) question. The question categories were selected to extract particular classes of extratextual inferences. Available research has established that "why," "how," and WHN questions are selective in extracting particular inferences (Graesser et al., 1991; Graesser et al., 1981). "Why" questions expose superordinate goals and causal antecedents; "how" questions expose subordinate goals/actions and causal antecedent events; WHN questions expose causal consequences. States are exposed by more than one of these question categories and can be distinguished by content.

A *constructive history chart* was prepared for each of the inferences that was elicited by the question-answering protocols. The chart identified which explicit clauses in the text elicited a particular inference, the type of question that elicited it, and the proportion of subjects who mentioned the inference in the question-answering protocols. The point in the story where an inference first emerged was particularly informative. In fact, all experiments that collected time-based measures tested an inference when it first emerged in the situation model, as manifested in the question-answering protocols.

Whenever Graesser and his colleagues compared the online status of classes of inferences, they always equated the classes of inferences on the proportion of subjects who generated the inferences in the question-answering task. The selection of inference test words also ensured that classes of inferences were equated on a number of extraneous measures, such as word length, word frequency, and word class (i.e., nouns and verbs vs. adjectives). Long et al. (1992) contrasted superordinate goals and subordinate goals; the generation likelihoods in the question–answer (Q/A) tasks did not significantly differ for the two groups of inferences (.31 vs. .26). Magliano et al.'s (1993) comparison of causal antecedents and consequences equated the two classes of items on generation likelihood (.39 vs. .32). Long et al.'s (1990) comparison of causal antecedent events and states once again equated the two classes of inferences on generation likelihood in the Q/A task (.22 vs. .22).

These generation likelihoods would appear to be low or modest rather than high. However, Graesser (1981) reported that generation likelihoods are rarely above .50 for these classes of inferences and that inferences with modest generation likelihoods are regarded as true by most subjects (as long as an inference is generated by two or more subjects). Graesser (1981) collected verification ratings for explicit story statements and the inferences generated by 2 or more out of 10 people in the Q/A task. The verification ratings were extremely high for the inferences (almost as high as the explicit statements) and generation likelihood scores did not significantly predict verification ratings for the inference items. An inference with a modest generation likelihood is probably constructed online by most comprehenders, but only a subset of the comprehenders can articulate the inference in the Q/A task. It is not the case that most comprehenders regard these inferences as false; such an interpretation would be incompatible with the results of the verification rating studies (Graesser, 1981).

A third prong of the three-pronged method involved the collection of lexical decision latencies or naming latencies for test words during the comprehension of the stories. Debra Long conducted three studies that contrasted superordinate goals and subordinate goals/actions. In a study by Long et al. (1992), a test word was presented 500 ms after each sentence in a story was read. The subjects were instructed to say the test word aloud as quickly as possible. The test word was sometimes a word that came from a superordinate goal (e.g., *eat* after reading "the dragon kidnapped the daughters" in the Czar story, see Table 16.1) and sometimes a word from a subordinate goal/action (e.g., *grab*). Once again, these goals were new inferences constructed for the first time in the story by the explicit target actions (e.g., "the dragon kidnapped the daughters"). There was also a control condition in which the superordinate and subordinate inferences were named in an unrelated passage context. Therefore, an "inference activation score" could be computed for each test word by subtracting the naming latency of the word in the inference context from the naming latency of the same word in an unrelated context. This computation of inference activation scores has been used by other researchers who have collected lexical decision latencies to study inference processing (Kintsch, 1988; Sharkey & Sharkey, 1992; Till, Mross, & Kintsch, 1988). Long et al. (1992) reported significantly higher inference activation scores for superordinate goal words than for subordinate goal/action words, which in turn were essentially zero. Long et al. reported a similar pattern of data when lexical decisions were collected instead of naming latencies. The activation scores showed the following pattern for the lexical decision data: superordinate goal > subordinate goal/action > 0. The results of Long's investigations of superordinate and subordinate goals are compatible with the constructionist theory and incompatible with most of the alternative theoretical positions.

In another study, Long and Golding (1993) reported that superordinate goals were very quickly constructed (within 700 ms) in the case of fast readers with good comprehension. In contrast, inference activation scores were essentially zero in the following conditions: (a) subordinate goals/actions for all readers and (b) superordinate goals for readers who are not fast, good comprehenders. There was precise control over reading time by implementing a rapid serial visual presentation (RSVP) rate of 250 ms per word. There was precise control over the time course of inference activation by imposing a short, 250-ms, stimulus onset asynchrony (SOA) between the final word of the clause and the test word. Given that fast readers had a naming latency of approximately 600 ms and that the SOA was 250 ms, the superordinate goals were generated by these readers within 850 ms. If we assume that 150 of the 850 ms consisted of motor response time, then the superordinate goal inferences were generated within 700 ms for these subjects. McKoon and Ratcliff (1986, 1989, 1992) proposed that speed is a sufficient criterion for defining whether inferences are generated automatically. According to their definition of automaticity, these superordinate goal inferences are automatically encoded by fast readers, but not by slow readers.

Joe Magliano and his colleagues tested whether causal antecedent and causal consequence inferences are generated online (Magliano et al., 1993). Magliano also determined the time course of their activation. The passages were the same texts as those investigated by Long. Magliano et al. manipulated inference category (causal antecedent vs. causal consequence), RSVP rate (250 ms vs. 400 ms), and SOA interval (250 ms, 400 ms, 600 ms, vs. 1200 ms). Lexical decision latencies were collected on test items after each sentence, following the same procedure as the studies presented earlier. The results indicate that there was a threshold of 400 ms after stimulus presentation (either RSVP or SOA) before causal antecedents were generated online. That is, activation scores were above zero only in the cells where the RSVP rate was 400 ms and the SOA was 400 ms or higher (mean activation score = 13 ms); when either the RSVP rate or the SOA interval was only 250 ms, the activation scores were consistently negative (mean scores = −28). In contrast, the causal consequence inferences were not generated online. Their activation scores were nearly always negative (mean score = −23). The meaning of the negative activation scores was addressed in the Magliano et al. (1993) study, but is not elaborated in this chapter (see also Lorch, Balota, & Stamm, 1986). The results of the study by Magliano et al. (1993) were compatible with the constructionist theory's predictions that causal antecedent inferences are generated online whereas causal consequences are not normally generated online.

Studies using the three-pronged method have revealed that state inferences are not generated online. Long et al. (1990) compared causal antecedent event inferences with state inferences in a study that collected lexical decision latencies. Latencies were shorter for test words that referred to causal antecedent event inferences than those referring to state inferences. Graesser et al. (1987) collected word-reading times using a moving window method and focused on the reading times for end-of-clause words. It was assumed that inferences are generated primarily at end-of-clause words, following the results of previous research (Haberlandt & Graesser, 1985; Just & Carpenter, 1980; Kintsch & van Dijk, 1978). Graesser et al. (1987) found that end-of-clause reading times were predicted by the number of new goal inferences and causal antecedent event inferences that were constructed during the comprehension of the clause, but not by the number of state inferences.

In summary, Graesser and his colleagues' research on extratextual inferences using the three-pronged method is compatible with the predictions of the constructionist theory (and also the current-state selection strategy). Superordinate goals and causal antecedents are generated online, whereas subordinate goals/actions, causal consequences, and states do not tend to be generated online. These results are not consistent with the predictions of the explicit textbase position, the minimalist hypothesis, the prediction-substantiation model, and the promiscuous inference generation position.

The constructionist theory and CSS strategy make identical predictions about the five classes of inferences that we have examined in this section. However, two additional empirical findings support the constructionist theory rather than the CSS strategy. One finding is that character emotion inferences are generated online. Gernsbacher et al. (1992) collected naming latencies for emotion words that were interspersed in a story. For example, one story involved a main character stealing money from a store where his best friend worked and later learning that his best friend had been fired. Guilt is presumably generated online when this story is comprehended. The test words for the naming task were either an appropriate emotion (i.e., guilt) or an inappropriate emotion (e.g., pride). Gernsbacher et al. (1992) reported that the naming latencies were shorter for the appropriate emotion than for the inappropriate emotion. Patterns of sentence reading times were also consistent with the claim that character emotion inferences are generated online. A second finding that is consistent with the constructionist theory, but not the CSS strategy, addresses global text-connecting inferences. The CSS strategy predicts that an incoming clause is causally connected to a causal antecedent or a main goal that was mentioned much earlier in the text under one condition: When there is a break in local coherence. These distant causal connections shout not be made if local coherence is intact (according to the CSS strategy). In contrast, the constructionist theory predicts that global causal connections are formed even when local coherence is intact. Recent evidence supports the constructionist theory (Albrecht & O'Brien, 1993; Dopkins et al., 1993; O'Brien & Albrecht, 1992; Singer, in press; Suh & Trabasso, 1993; van den Broek & Lorch, 1993).

CLOSING COMMENTS

A rigorous, scientific understanding of knowledge-based inferences has been one of the major gaps in contemporary psychological theories of comprehension. We believe that the three-pronged method will provide the rigor and analytical detail for developing a mature theory of inference generation. The method coordinates the collection of verbal protocols, the collection of time-based behavioral measures, and discourse theories that make decisive predictions about inference generation. This chapter has illustrated how the three-pronged method was applied to the study of inference generation during narrative comprehension. The best theoretical position was a constructionist theory that embraced an effort-after-meaning principle. The constructionist theory fared better than five alternative theoretical positions when we examined available empirical findings.

We hope that researchers will continue to pursue the mysteries of world knowledge, inferences, and deep comprehension. We now have the methodological tools to investigate this murky arena—we didn't 10 years ago. It is fitting to offer a quote from the first book that Graesser published 12 years ago (Graesser, 1981)

> Many experimental psychologists have shied away from some challenging questions about comprehension. For example, many researchers have studied the representation and memory of explicit content, but relatively few researchers have tried to investigate how inferences are incorporated into the memory representations. Ironically, most of the mysteries, mechanisms, and marvels of prose comprehension reside in the tacit knowledge that exists beyond the word. A risky journey into the deep conceptual jungles may be preferable to a safe sojourn so skittishly skirting the borders. (pp. 273–274)

It is also fitting to acknowledge Jerome Myers as one of the few researchers who has explored these jungles and unraveled some of the mysteries.

ACKNOWLEDGMENTS

This research was funded by contracts awarded to Arthur C. Graesser by the Office of Naval Research (N00014-88-K-0110 and N00014-90-J-1492). We would like to thank Bill Baggett for his help throughout many portions of this project.

REFERENCES

Albrecht, J. E., & O'Brien, E. J. (1993). Updating a mental model: Maintaining both local and global coherence. *Journal of Experimental Psychology: Learning, Memory, and Cognition, 19*, 1061–1070.

Balota, D. A., Flores d'Arcais, G. B., & Rayner, K. (Eds.). (1990). *Comprehension processes in reading.* Hillsdale, NJ: Lawrence Lawrence Erlbaum Associates Associates.

Bartlett, F. C. (1932). *Remembering: A study in experimental and social psychology.* Cambridge, MA: Cambridge University Press.

Berlyne, D. E. (1949). "Interest" as a psychological concept. *British Journal of Psychology, 39*, 184–195.

Berlyne, D. E. (1971). *Aesthetics and psychobiology.* New York: Appleton-Century-Crofts.

Black, J. B., & Bower, G. H. (1980). Story understanding as problem-solving. *Poetics, 9*, 223–250.

Bloom, C. P., Fletcher, C. R., van den Broek, P., Reitz, L., & Shapiro, B. P. (1990). An online assessment of causal reasoning during comprehension. *Memory and Cognition, 18*, 65–71.

Bower, G. H., Black, J. B., & Turner, T. J. (1979). Scripts in memory for text. *Cognitive Psychology, 11*, 177–220.

Britton, B. K., & Glynn, S. M. (1987). *Executive control processes in reading.* Hillsdale, NJ: Lawrence Erlbaum Associates.

Britton, B. K., & Pelligrini, A. D. (1990). *Narrative thought and narrative language.* Hillsdale, NJ: Lawrence Erlbaum Associates.

Britton, B. K., van Dusen, L., Glynn, S. M., & Hemphill, D. (1990). The impact of inferences on instructional text. In A. C. Graesser & G. H. Bower (Eds.), *Inferences and text comprehension* (pp. 53–70). New York: Academic Press.

Bruner, J. (1986). *Actual minds, possible worlds.* Cambridge, MA: Harvard University Press.

Collins, A. M., Brown, J. S., & Larkin, K. M. (1980). Inferences in text understanding. In R. J. Spiro, B. C. Bruce, & W. F. Brewer. (Eds.), *Theoretical issues in reading comprehension* (pp. 385–404). Hillsdale, NJ: Lawrence Erlbaum Associates.

Corbett, A. T., & Dosher, B. A. (1978). Instrument inferences in sentence encoding. *Journal of Verbal Learning and Verbal Behavior, 17*, 479–491.

DeJong, G. (1979). Prediction and substantiation: A new approach to natural language processing. *Cognitive Science, 3*, 251–273.

Dopkins, S., Klin, C., & Myers, J. L. (1993). Accessibility of information about goals during the processing of narrative texts. *Journal of Experimental Psychology: Learning, Memory, and Cognition, 19*, 70–80.

Duffy, S. A., & Rayner, K. (1990). Eye movements and anaphor resolution: Effects of antecedent typicality and distance. *Language and Speech, 33*, 103–119.

Dyer, M. G. (1983). *In-depth understanding: A computer model of integrated processing for narrative comprehension.* Cambridge, MA: MIT Press.

Ericsson, K. A., & Simon, H. A. (1980). Verbal reports as data. *Psychological Review, 87*, 215–251.

Fletcher, C. R., & Bloom, C. P. (1988). Causal reasoning in the comprehension of simple narrative texts. *Journal of Memory and Language, 27*, 236–244.

Gernsbacher, M. A. (1990). *Language comprehension as structure building.* Hillsdale, NJ: Lawrence Erlbaum Associates.

Gernsbacher, M. A., Goldsmith, H. H., & Robertson, R. R. (1992). Do readers mentally represent character's emotional states? *Cognition and Emotion, 6*, 89–112.

Glenberg, A. M., Meyer, M., & Lindem, K. (1987). Mental models contribute to foregrounding during text comprehension. *Journal of Memory and Language, 26*, 69–83.

Graesser, A. C. (1981). *Prose comprehension beyond the word.* New York: Springer-Verlag.

Graesser, A. C. & Bower, G. H. (Eds.). (1990). *Inferences and text comprehension.* New York: Academic Press.

Graesser, A. C., & Clark, L. F. (1985). *Structures and procedures of implicit knowledge.* Norwood, NJ: Ablex.

Graesser, A. C., Haberlandt, K., & Koizumi, D. (1987). How is reading time influenced by knowledge based inferences and world knowledge. In B. K. Britton & S. M. Glynn (Eds.), *Executive control processes in reading* (pp. 217–252). Hillsdale, NJ: Lawrence Erlbaum Associates.

Graesser, A. C., & Kreuz, R. J. (1993). A theory of inference generation during text comprehension. *Discourse Processes, 16*, 145–160.

Graesser, A. C., Lang, K. L., & Roberts, R. M. (1991). Question answering in the context of stories. *Journal of Experimental Psychology: General, 120*, 254–277.

Graesser, A.C., Robertson, S.P., & Anderson, P.A. (1981). Incorporating inferences in narrative representations: A study of how and why. *Cognitive Psychology*, *13*, 1–26.

Graesser, A. C., Singer, M., & Trabasso, T. (1993). *A constructionist theory of inference generation during narrative text comprehension.* Manuscript submitted for publication.

Grice, H. P. (1975). Logic and conversation. In P. Cole & J. L. Morgan (Eds.), *Syntax and semantics: Vol. 3 Speech acts* (pp. 41–58). New York: Academic Press.

Grosz, B. J., Joshi, A. K., & Weinstein, S. (1983). Providing a unified account of definite noun phrases in discourse. *Proceedings of the 21st Annual Meeting of the Association of Computational Linguistics*, 44–50.

Haberlandt, K., & Bingham, G. (1978). Verbs contribute to the coherence of brief narratives: Reading related and unrelated sentence triplets. *Journal of Verbal Learning and Verbal Behavior*, *17*, 419–425.

Haberlandt, K., & Graesser, A.C. (1985). Component processes in text comprehension and some of their interactions. *Journal of Experimental Psychology: General*, *114*, 357–374.

Halliday, M. A. K., & Hasan, R. (1976). *Cohesion in English.* London: Longmans.

Hastie, R. (1983). Social inference. *Annual Review of Psychology*, *34*, 511–542.

Hilton, D. J. (1990). Conversational processes and causal explanation. *Psychological Bulletin*, *107*, 110–119.

Johnson-Laird, P. N. (1983). *Mental models.* Cambridge, MA: Harvard University Press.

Just, M. A., & Carpenter, P. A. (1980). A theory of reading: From eye fixations to comprehension. *Psychological Review*, *87*, 329–354.

Just, M. A., & Carpenter, P. A. (1992). A capacity theory of comprehension: Individual differences in working memory. *Psychological Review*, *99*, 122–149.

Kahneman, D., Slovic, P., & Tversky, A. (1982). *Judgments under uncertainty: Heuristics and biases.* Cambridge, MA: Cambridge University Press.

Keenan, J. M., Baillet, S. D., & Brown, P. (1984). The effects of causal cohesion on comprehension and memory. *Journal of Verbal Learning and Verbal Behavior*, *23*, 115–126.

Kintsch, W. (1974). *The representation of meaning in memory.* Hillsdale, NJ: Lawrence Erlbaum Associates.

Kintsch, W. (1988). The role of knowledge in discourse comprehension: A constructive-integration model. *Psychological Review*, *95*, 163–182.

Kintsch, W. (1993). Information accretion and reduction in text processing: Inferences. *Discourse Processes*, *16*, 193–202.

Kintsch, W., & van Dijk, T. A. (1978). Toward a model of text comprehension and production. *Psychological Review*, *85*, 363–394.

Kintsch, W., Welsch, D., Schmalhofer, F., & Zimny, S. (1990). Sentence memory: A theoretical analysis. *Journal of Memory and Language*, *29*, 133–159.

Kosslyn, S. M. (1980). *Image and mind.* Cambridge, MA: Harvard University Press.

LaBerge, D., & Samuels, S. J. (1974). Toward a theory of automatic information processing in reading. *Cognitive Psychology*, *6*, 293–323.

Lea, R. B., O'Brien, D. P., Fisch, S. M., Noveck, I. A., & Brain, M. D. S. (1990). Predicting propositional logic inferences in text comprehension. *Journal of Memory and Language*, *29*, 361–387.

Lehnert, W. G.. (1978). *The process of question answering.* Hillsdale, NJ: Lawrence Erlbaum Associates.

Lehnert, W. G. (1981). Plots units and narrative summarization. *Cognitive Science*, *5*, 283–331.

Logan, G. D. (1985). Toward an instance theory of automatization. *Psychological Review*, *95*, 492–527.

Long, D. L., & Golding, J. M. (1993). Superordinate goal inferences: Are they automatically generated during comprehension? *Discourse Processes*, *16*, 55–73.

Long, D. L., & Golding, J. M., & Graesser, A. C. (1992). The generation of goal related inferences during narrative comprehension. *Journal of Memory and Language. 5*, 634–647

Long, D. L., Golding, J. M., Graesser, A. C., & Clark, L. F. (1990). Goal, event, and state inferences: An investigation of inference generation during story comprehension. In A. C. Graesser & G. H. Bower (Eds.), *Inferences and text comprehension* (pp. 89–102). New York: Academic Press.

Lorch, R. F., Balota, D. A., & Stamm, E. G. (1986). Locus of inhibition effects in the priming of lexical decisions: Pre- or postlexical access? *Memory and Cognition, 14*, 95–103.

Magliano, J. P., Baggett, W. B., Johnson, B. K., & Graesser, A. C. (1993). The time course of generating causal antecedent and causal consequence inferences. *Discourse Processes, 16*, 35–53.

Magliano, J. P., & Graesser, A. C. (1991). A three-pronged method for studying inference generation in literary text. *Poetics, 20*, 193–232.

Mandler, G. (1976). *Mind and emotion*. New York: Wiley.

Mandler, G. (1985). *Cognitive psychology: An essay in cognitive science*. Hillsdale, NJ: Lawrence Erlbaum Associates.

Mandler, J. M. (1984). *Stories, scripts, and scenes: Aspects of schema theory*. Hillsdale, NJ: Lawrence Erlbaum Associates.

Mandler, J. M., & Johnson, N. S. (1977). Remembrance of things parsed: Story structure and recall. *Cognitive Psychology, 9*, 111–151.

Mani, K., & Johnson-Laird, P. N. (1982). The mental representation of spatial descriptions. *Memory & Cognition, 10*, 181–187.

Mann, W. C., & Thompson, S. A. (1986). Relational propositions in discourse. *Discourse Processes, 9*, 57–90.

McKoon, G., & Ratcliff, R. (1981). The comprehension processes and memory structures involved in instrumental inferences. *Journal of Verbal Learning and Verbal Behavior, 20*, 271–286.

McKoon, G., & Ratcliff, R. (1986). Inferences about predictable events. *Journal of Experimental Psychology: Learning, Memory, and Cognition, 12*, 82–91.

McKoon, G., & Ratcliff, R. (1989). Semantic associations and elaborative inferences. *Journal of Experimental Psychology: Learning, Memory, and Cognition, 15*, 326–338.

McKoon, G., & Ratcliff, R. (1992). Inference during reading. *Psychological Review. 99*, 440–466.

Millis, K., Graesser, A. C., & Haberlandt, K. (1993). The impact of connectives on memory for expository texts. *Applied Cognitive Psychology, 7*, 317–339.

Mooney, R. J. (1990). *A general explanation-based learning mechanism and its application to narrative understanding*. San Mateo, CA: Kaufman.

Morrow, D. G., Bower, G. H., & Greenspan S. L (1987). Accessibility and situation models in narrative comprehension. *Journal of Memory and Language, 26*, 165–187.

Morrow, D., Bower, G., & Greenspan, S., (1989). Updating situation models during narrative comprehension. *Journal of Memory and Language, 28*, 292–312.

Murray, J. D., Klin, C. M., & Myers, J. L. (1991, November). *Forward inferences about specific events during reading*. Paper presented at the 32nd Annual Meeting of Psychonomic Society, San Francisco, CA.

Myers, J. L., Shinjo, M., & Duffy, S. A. (1987). The role of causal relatedness and memory. *Journal of Memory and Language, 26*, 453–465.

Nelson, K. (1986). *Event knowledge: Structure and function in development*. Hillsdale, NJ: Lawrence Erlbaum Associates.

Newell, A., & Simon, H. A. (1972). *Human problem-solving*. Englewood Cliffs, NJ: Prentice-Hall.

O'Brien, E. J., & Albrecht, J. E. (1991). The role of context in accessing antecedents in text. *Journal of Expreimental Psychology: Learning, Memory, and Cognition, 17*, 94–102.

O'Brien, E. J., & Albrecht, J. E. (1992). Comprehension strategies in the development of a mental mode. *Journal of Expreimental Psychology: Learning, Memory, and Cognition, 18*, 777–785.

O'Brien, E. J., Duffy, S. A., & Myers, J. L. (1986). Anaphoric inference during reading. *Journal of Experimental Psychology: Learning, Memory, and Cognition, 12*, 346–352.

O'Brien, E. J., Shank, D. M., Myers, J. L., & Rayner, K. (1988). Elaborative inferences during reading: Do they occur online? *Journal of Experimental Psychology: Learning, Memory, and Cognition, 14*, 410–420.

Olson, G. M., Duffy, S. A., & Mack, R. L. (1984). Thinking-out loud as a method for studying real-time comprehension processes. In D. E. Kieras & M. A. Just (Eds.), *New methods in the study of immediate processes in comprehension* (pp. 253–286). Hillsdale, NJ: Lawrence Erlbaum Associates.

Olson, G. M., Duffy, S. A., & Mack, R. L. (1985). Question asking as a component of text comprehension. In A. C. Graesser & J. B. Black (Eds.), *The psychology of questions* (pp. 219–226). Hillsdale, NJ: Lawrence Erlbaum Associates.

Pennington, N., & Hastie, R. (1986). Evidence evaluation in complex decision making. *Journal of Personality and Social Psychology, 52*, 288–302.

Potts, G. R., Keenan, J. M., & Golding, J. M. (1988). Assessing the occurrence of elaborative inferences: Lexical decision vs. naming. *Journal of Memory and Language, 27*, 399–415.

Read, S. J. (1987). Constructing causal scenarios: A knowledge structure approach to causal reasoning. *Journal of Personality and Social Psychology, 52*, 288–302.

Rips, L. J. (1990). Reasoning. *Annual Review of Psychology, 41*, 321–354.

Roberts, R. M., & Kreuz, R. J. (1993). Nonstandard discourse and its coherence. *Discourse Processes, 16*, 451–464.

Rumelhart, D. E., & Ortony, A. (1977). The representation of knowledge in memory. In R. C. Anderson, R. J. Spiro, & W. E. Montague (Eds.), *Schooling and the acquisition of knowledge* (pp. 99–136). Hillsdale, NJ: Lawrence Erlbaum Associates.

Sanford A. J., & Garrod, S. C.(1981). *Understanding written language: Explorations in comprehension beyond the sentence*. New York: Wiley.

Schank, R. C. (1986). *Explanation patterns: Understanding mechanically and creatively*. Hillsdale, NJ: Lawrence Erlbaum Associates.

Schank, R. C. (1990). *Tell me a story: A new look at real and artificial memory*. New York: Scribner's.

Schank, R. C., & Abelson, R. (1977). *Scripts, plans, goals and understanding: An inquiry into human knowledge structures*. Hillsdale, NJ: Lawrence Erlbaum Associates.

Schneider, W., & Shiffrin, R. M. (1977). Controlled and automatic human information processing: I. Detection, search, and attention. *Psychological Review, 84*, 1–66.

Seifert, C. M. (1990). Content-based inferences in text. In A. C. Graesser & G. H. Bower (Eds.), *Inferences and text comprehension* (pp. 103–122). New York: Academic Press.

Seifert, C. M., McKoon, G., Abelson, R. P., & Ratcliff, R. (1986). Memory connections between thematically similar episodes. *Journal of Experimental Psychology: Learning, Memory, and Cognition, 12*, 220–231.

Seifert, C. M., Robertson, S. P., & Black, J. B. (1985). Types of inferences generated during reading. *Journal of Memory and Language, 24*, 405–422.

Sharkey, A. J. C., & Sharkey, N. E. (1992). Weak contextual constraints in text and word priming. *Journal of Memory and Language, 31*, 543–572.

Singer, M. (1979). Process of inference in sentence encoding. *Memory and Cognition, 7*, 192–200.

Singer, M. (1980). The role of case-filling inferences in the coherence of brief passages. *Discourse Processes, 3*, 185–201.

Singer, M. (1988). Inferences in reading. In M. Daneman, G. E. Mackinnon, & T. G. Waller (Eds.), *Reading Research: Advances in Theory and Practice.* (pp. 177–219). New York: Academic Press.

Singer, M. (1991). Independence of question-answering strategy and searched representation. *Memory and Cognition, 19*, 189–196.

Singer, M. (in press). Discourse inference processes. In M. Gernsbacher (Ed.), *Handbook of psycholinguistics*. San Diego, CA: Academic Press.

Singer, M., & Ferreira, F. (1983). Inferring consequences in story comprehension. *Journal of Verbal Learning and Verbal Behavior*, *22*, 437–448.

Singer, M., Halldorson, M., Lear, J. C., & Andrusiak, P. (1992). Validation of causal bridging inferences in discourse understanding. *Journal of Memory and Language*, *31*, 507–524.

Stein, N. L., & Levine, L. J. (1991). Making sense out of emotion: The representation and use of goal-structured knowledge. In W. Kessen, A. Ortony, & F. I. M. Craik (Eds.), *Memories, thoughts, and emotions: Essays in honor of George Mandler* (pp. 295–322). Hillsdale, NJ: Lawrence Erlbaum Associates.

Stein, N. L., & Trabasso, T. (1985). The search after meaning: Comprehension and comprehension monitoring. *Applied Developmental Psychology*, *2*, 33–58.

Suh, S. Y., & Trabasso, T. (1993). Inferences during reading: Converging evidence from discourse analysis, talk-aloud protocols and recognition priming. *Journal of Memory and Language*, *32*, 279–300.

Till, R. E., Mross, E. F., & Kintsch, W., (1988). Time course of priming for associate and inference words in a discourse context. *Memory and Cognition*, *16*, 283–298.

Trabasso, T., & Suh, S. Y. (1993). Using talk-aloud protocols to reveal inferences during comprehension of text. *Discourse Processes*, *16*, 283–298.

Trabasso, T., & van den Broek, P. (1985). Causal thinking and the representation of narrative events. *Journal of Memory and Language*, *24*, 612–630.

van den Broek, P. (1990). Causal inferences and the comprehension of narrative text. In A. C. Graesser & G. H. Bower (Eds.), *Inferences and text comprehension* (pp. 423–446). New York: Academic Press.

van den Broek, R., & Lorch, R. F. (1993). Network representations of causal relations in memory for narrative texts: Evidence from primed recognition. *Discourse Processes*, *16*, 75–98.

van Dijk, T. A., & Kintsch, W.(1983). *Strategies of discourse comprehension*. New York: Academic Press.

Whitney, P. (1987). Psychological theories of elaborative inferences: Implications for schema-theoretic views of comprehension. *Reading Research Quarterly*, *22*, 299–310.

Zwaan, R. A., & van Oostendorp, H. (1993). Do readers construct spatial representations in naturalistic story comprehension? *Discourse Processes*, *16*, 125–143.

17 The Role of Background Knowledge in the Recall of a News Story

Walter Kintsch
Marita Franzke
University of Colorado

It is well established that knowledge has strong effects on text comprehension and memory (e.g. Beck, Omanson, & McKeown, 1982; Moravcsik & Kintsch, 1993; Pearson, Hanson, & Gordon, 1979; Schneider, Körkerl, & Weinert, 1989, 1990; Spilich, Vesonder, Chiesi, & Voss, 1979), on learning (Eylon & Reif, 1984), and on writing (Perfetti & McCutchen, 1987). But knowledge is a very general term. The question addressed here is what kind of knowledge affects which aspect of comprehension. Our target article is an actual news story about a recent political event of some complexity. In order to understand it, a reader needs both general and special knowledge. General knowledge is knowledge about the language and the world that is widely shared among members of a culture. Specifically, in the present case it is general knowledge about war and warfare, armies, sieges, guerrillas, governments, and so on. Special knowledge, on the other hand, varies more widely among people, depending on their exposure to a certain topic. In the present case, this is the civil war in Sri Lanka. We selected subjects who knew next to nothing about this special topic and provided them with either full, partial or no background information before we asked them to read and recall the target article. The target article contains both information that should be understandable on the basis of general knowledge alone and information for which special background knowledge is necessary. Note that the distinction between general and special knowledge is not the same as that between semantic and episodic memory: both may have semantic as well as episodic components.

The result of comprehension is a mental representation of the text. It is often useful to distinguish different types of relationships in this structure. On the one hand, there are the relations that are directly derived from the text. For instance, suppose two propositions are linked in the mental representation because they were linked by a sentence connective in the text, or one proposition is subordinated to another because the latter was marked in the text by some linguistic cue as the superordinate. Van Dijk and Kintsch (1983) called these text-base relations. In general, text-base relations can be constructed by the comprehender on the basis of general linguistic and general world knowledge. Text-base relations comprise only part of the comprehender's mental representation, however. In addition, the mental structure contains situation model relations that were not explicitly cued by the text but are derived from the comprehender's knowledge about the situation described in the text (van Dijk & Kintsch, 1983). These are often labeled as *inferences*, though the use of that term can be more confusing than helpful (Kintsch, 1993). Thus, two propositions that were not explicitly linked in the text may be related in the situation model because the comprehender knows that one is a consequence of the other. In another case, two propositions may be subordinated because the comprehender knows that one is a specification of the other, even though there are no linguistic cues in the text. Special knowledge about the domain of the text is usually required for the construction of the situation model. Comprehension, thus, involves a delicate interplay between processes relying on general knowledge and processes requiring special domain knowledge. Depending on the availability of the requisite domain knowledge, as well as on task constraints, the mental representation that a comprehender constructs will be based more on text-base or on situation model relations.

The present experiment explores how subjects with various degrees of special background knowledge are able to recall a news story, parts of which require special knowledge for comprehension and parts of which should be understandable even without it. The theoretical considerations sketched earlier lead us to expect an interaction effect between background knowledge and different sections of the news report.

METHOD

Subjects

Fifty-one paid subjects participated in the experiment. The subjects were undergraduates from the University of Colorado and were randomly assigned to one of three experimental conditions. Eighteen subjects each participated in the full-and partial-knowledge conditions, and 15 in the no-knowledge condition. Subjects were screened for preknowledge of the subject covered in the textual material, which led to the exclusion of one potential subject who had taken a class on this topic.

Design and Material

There were three experimental conditions that varied the amount of background reading subjects received before the last experimental session, which was identical for all groups. In general, subjects in the full-knowledge group received the most complete information about the topic, subjects in the partial-knowledge group received systematically impoverished background information, and subjects in the no-knowledge group received no information before reading the final text. The texts used to introduce these experimental manipulations are described here.

As our topic, we chose the civil war in Sri Lanka because it satisfied several constraints: First, the situation was a true political sequence of events that had been reported about in the news media. Hence we could use actual magazine articles as our experimental material. Secondly, we could expect that the topic would be unfamiliar to college students, so that confounding effects of already existing background knowledge could be avoided. However, it could be assumed that our subjects would have general schematic knowledge about civil wars or wars in general that would allow them to comprehend the articles in a general way. And finally, the political motives and the events in the Sri Lanka civil war were complex enough, so that the lack of specific background information was likely to lead to a loss of comprehension.

The following core events summarize the political situation in Sri Lanka that served as the content of the experimental materials: Sri Lanka's population mainly consists of two groups of people, the majority, which are Sinhalese, and a minority, the Tamils. The Tamils, who originally migrated to Sri Lanka from South India, have formed an independence movement after a change in the Sri Lankan Government deprived them of their political and economical privileges. The Indian Government has supported the Tamil Independence movement because of the Tamils' Indian descent, by providing arms and training to the militant arm of the movement, the guerrilla group The Tigers of Tamil Eelam. This political involvement lead India into intervening in the Sri Lankan civil war, by showing open humanitarian support for the Tamils against the Sri Lankan Government. India's subsequent attempt to enforce a settlement in the role of a peace keeper has failed, however. This has forced the Indian army to fight the very people it set out to protect.

Experimental Texts.   All experimental texts were adapted versions of previously published magazine articles. Text 1 was adapted from *The New Yorker*, Text 2 form *The New York Times Magazine*, and Texts 3 and 4 from *Newsweek*. Subjects in the full- and partial knowledge conditions read Text 1, and different versions of Text 2 and Text 3 that were edited to provide varying degrees of background information about the Sri Lankan conflict. All subjects (including the no-knowledge group) read Text 4, which reported on the peace treaty and India's war against the Tamil guerrillas. Text 1 was the same for the full-knowledge and partial-knowledge subjects groups. It informed about the history and political situation of Sri Lanka in general terms up to the current conflict. Text 2 reported about a specific event, a terrorist attack on the Sri Lankan prime minister and following retaliations on Tamils. Text 2 also contained a comprehensive explanation of the history and causes of the atrocities between the fighting parties. The full-knowledge group read this long version of Text 2. The partial-knowledge group received a version in which parts of the text explaining the causal development of the conflict were not included. The text was slightly edited to preserve coherence. Text 3 described a subsequent terrorist attack from the continuing civil war and its consequences: the war of the Sri Lankan government against the Tamils and India's humanitarian intervention. It also included a section that elaborated on the reasons for India's involvement in the conflict. Again, subjects in the full-knowledge group read the full version of the text, whereas subjects in the partial-knowledge group received a shortened version, which did not include the section about India's political reasons for intervening. Text 1 was comprised of 1,279 words, Texts 2 and 3 contained 1,092 and 942 words, respectively, in the full version, and 598 and 536 words, respectively in the shortened version.

All subjects read the same magazine article (Text 4) on the last day. This article (892 words) contained a description of the most recent developments in the conflict at the time. It summarized the terms of a peace treaty, talked about the difficulties in enforcing the treaty, and reported an attack of the Indian army on the Tamils.

Text 4 was analyzed into idea units corresponding to propositional schemata as discussed in van Dijk and Kintsch (1983). Propositional schemata are more global units than atomic propositions, containing optional modifiers and circumstantial information. These units were arranged in a five-level hierarchy, as shown in Fig. 17.1. The top node in the hierarchy included the title of the text, "The Siege of Jaffna," as well as the highest level summary of the text, "India intervenes in Sri Lanka's civil war." The next level of the hierarchy marked a major subdivision: the first part of the text was concerned with the complex political situation between the governments of India and Sri Lanka and the Tamil rebels. This is referred to as the *politics part* in the analysis of the data. It contained an enumeration of the conditions of the peace treaty that had been worked out in an effort to end the war, as well as a discussion of the shortcomings of the political negotiations. This part of the text contained 17 propositional schemata. In the second part of the text, the Indian attack on the Tamil stronghold Jaffna was described, which is subsequently be referred to as the *war part* of the text. This description comprised about two thirds of the text and contained 38 idea units. These two parts of the text were further subdivided into subtopics that correspond to the nodes at Level 3 in the text hierarchy. For example, in the

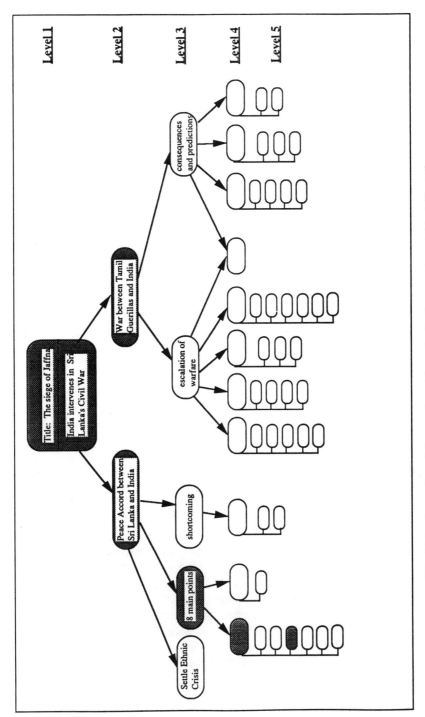

FIG. 17.1.   An outline of the text-base hierarchy for the experimental text (Text 4).

325

politics part of the text, one node at this third level included the propositional schema for " the accord had eight major points." At this level, three idea units were identified for the politics part and two for the war part. The idea units at Level 4 further subdivided the text into content-specific paragraphs. An Example is the node, *some points were included to satisfy the Tamils*. Single statements containing the lowest level detail made up the Level 5 idea units in the analysis. Extending our example, one of the propositional schemata at this level was *general amnesty for Tamil militants*. The given examples are represented as highlighted nodes in Fig. 17.1.

Procedure

Subjects participated in the experiment individually. For the subjects in the full- and partial-knowledge conditions, the experiment was extended over four 1-hour sessions on four consecutive days. Subjects in the no-knowledge condition came in on one day only . On the first day, subjects in the full- and partial-knowledge conditions read Text 1. On the two following days, the respective versions of Texts 2 and 3 were given to subjects in these two conditions. Subjects in the full-knowledge group read the full version of these two texts and subjects in the partial-knowledge group read the shorter, edited versions. On the last day, all subjects read Text 4. This text that was given to all experimental groups. On all days, subjects were told to read each text only once, but carefully, and to make sure that they understood it as well as possible. After reading Text 4, all subjects completed two tasks unrelated to this chapter. Finally, subjects were asked to recall the texts in writing as well as they could. They were given a limit of 10 minutes for recall.

RESULTS

Scoring

The breakdown of Text 4 into propositional units (text propositions, as defined in van Dijk & Kintsch, 1983, chap. 4) and their hierarchical structure was used as the basis for scoring the recall protocols. For each subject, a yes–no decision was made whether each unit was or was not expressed in the recall protocol and whether it was expressed correctly or misrepresented. For example, a protocol statement scored as correct representation of the summary propositional state-ment in Level 1 of the hierarchy was, "The Indian government has intervened with the civil war that is going on in Sri Lanka." A recall statement scored as incorrect would misrepresent an important part of the propositional unit. For example, "India helped organize a peace accord between Sinhalese and Tamil groups," would be scored as incorrect, because of the misrepresentation of the

Sri Lankan government as Sinhalese group. The number of correct propositional units minus those that were incorrect was used as a recall score.[1] In each condition, 10% of the total recall was incorrect. In addition, the number of elaborations each subject made was recorded, and it was noted whether the elaboration was correct or incorrect. The number of correct elaborations minus those that were incorrect was used as an elaboration score. Metastatements, which appeared in the protocols (i.e., statements that referred to the process of recall itself), were relatively rare. Only 13% of the subjects provided metastatements, consequently metastatements were disregarded in the analysis.

Reproductive Recall

For the reproductive recall, total proportional recall scores were calculated for each subject and four defined parts of the hierarchy. Recall was scored by text part (war vs. politics) and by level in the hierarchy (high vs. low). Levels 1–3 in Fig. 17.1 were counted as high-level recall, whereas Levels 4–5 were counted as low-level, detailed recall. Proportional recall scores were derived by dividing the total recall per text part by the maximum number of propositional units in that part of the text. For the politics-related, high-level text part there were four possible idea units; for the politics-related, low-level part there were 13 idea units. For the war-related part of the text there were 3 high-level and 35 low-level idea units. The proportional recall scores are presented in Table 17.1. Two mixed 2 (high vs. low level) × 2 (war vs. politics) × 3 (group) ANOVAs were performed on the total and proportional recall scores. The two analyses led to similar conclusions. Here, the analysis on the proportional data is reported, because it makes comparisons across text parts more meaningful. A set of planned comparisons was conducted also, which tested for more specific group effects. Specifically, we tested whether the full-knowledge group produced higher proportional recall scores than the partial- and no-knowledge groups, and whether the scores of the partial-knowledge group differed from scores of the no-knowledge group.

There were statistically significant differences between the overall proportional recall scores of the three groups of subjects. On the average, subjects recalled 27.5% of the idea units in the full-knowledge condition, 25% in the partial-knowledge condition, and 21% in the no-knowledge condition, $F(2,48) = 6.07$, $p < .05$. Planned comparisons showed that this effect was due to a marginally significant difference between the full-knowledge group and the average of the other two groups, $F(1,48) = 3.99$, $p < .06$. There was no statistically significant difference between the partial- and no-knowledge groups. Furthermore, there were interesting differences among the three conditions in what subjects recalled.

There are 17 idea units (propositional schemata) in Text 4 belonging to the

---

[1]Just looking at the number of correctly recalled units leads to basically the same conclusions.

politics portion of the text and 38 belonging to the war portion. The average proportional recall of idea units was significantly higher for the Politics part. Subjects recalled 28% of the politics units and 16% of the war units, $F(1,48) = 27.43$, $p < .01$. The effects of level (text hierarchy) were as expected: significantly more higher order units (Levels 2 and 3) were recalled than lower order units (Levels 4 and 5). Specifically, 29% of the higher order units were recalled versus 20% of the lower order units, $F(1, 48) = 11.12$, $p. < .01$.

The three experimental conditions differed significantly in the proportion of idea units reproduced from the two parts of the text, war versus politics, $F(2,48) = 6.207$, $p < .05$. This interaction is shown in Fig. 17.2. Whereas recall was approximately equal among the three groups for the war-related portion of the text, there were large differences in how well the politics part of the text was recalled. This interaction is due mainly to a significant difference between the full-knowledge subjects and the average of the other two groups, $F(1,48) = 4.36$, $p < .05$. Subjects who were given full background information recalled more from that part of the text than subjects who were given incomplete or no background information.

The locus of the recall deficit for the low- and no-information conditions can be further specified by considering the level $\times$ part interaction. This interaction was statistically significant, $F(1,48) = 86.92$, $p < .001$, and is shown in Table 17.1. Here we see that for the relatively abstract politics part of the text, a higher proportion of high-level idea units were reproduced than low-level units. This was quite different for the more concrete, familiar, war-related part of the text, where most of the recall consisted of lower level detail. The triple interaction

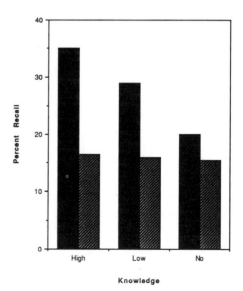

FIG. 17.2. Percent recall (correct minus incorrect propositions as percentage of total possible) of the politics- (solid bars) and war-related parts (shaded bars) of the text for subjects with different knowledge back-

TABLE 17.1
The Average Proportion of Propositional Units Reproduced as a function of the Level in the Text Hierarchy From the Two Parts of the Text, War and Politics, for Readers With Full, Partial, or no Knowledge Background

Text Part		
Group	High-Level Statements	Low-Level Statements
Politics		
High knowledge	50%	20%
Low knowledge	44%	14%
No knowledge	35%	5%
War		
High knowledge	12%	21%
Low knowledge	9%	23%
No knowledge	7%	24%

with of this effect with group failed to reach statistical significance, $F(2,48) = .59, p > .40$.

Elaborative Recall

On the average, there were 2.7 elaborations per subject in the recall protocols, with no significant differences between groups. That is, elaborations were produced irrespective of knowledge. However, the elaborations made by the subjects with background information tended to be more correct than the elaborations made by the subjects without knowledge. The average elaboration scores (correct minus incorrect elaborations) were 1.9, 1.1, and .01 for the full-, partial-, and no-knowledge conditions. However, these differences were not statistically reliable, $F(2,48) = 1.20$, because they depended heavily on the performance of a few subjects. Many subjects produced only a few elaborations, irrespective of condition.

DISCUSSION

The effects of background knowledge on the ability to reproduce a news article are quite complex. It is not simply the case that subjects with more background recall more. The total amount of recall—reproductive as well as elaborative—was not widely different in the three background conditions. Subjects in all knowledge conditions elaborated. However, subjects who lacked the necessary background made things up that did not fit the situation depicted by the text, whereas the elaborations of the subjects with background information did fit. Everyone also recalled reasonably well—the difference was in what was recalled. Certain parts of the text—the description of the efforts of the Indian army to subdue the Tamil guerrilla forces—were easily understood by all groups: General knowledge about civil wars was sufficient for this portion of the text, which contains a great deal of concrete, salient, recallable detail. However, subjects with information about the goals of the warring partners and their allies were also able to reproduce a fair amount of information about the political situation, the treaty between the two governments involved, and the anomalous situation that an Indian army was fighting their own people. The subjects who were given the impoverished texts to read recalled much less from this section of the text, whereas the subjects with no background information mostly disregarded it. They apparently had only some very general ideas about the political situation and made little effort to understand it. Thus, one finds few specifics about this part of the text in their protocols. Finally, we observed a general trend to recall more general high-level units for the "political" part of the text and more low-level units for the war description. This interaction might represent a decision by all subjects to "fill in" general descriptions when they are perceiving a lacking ability to produce a large amount of idea units in detail. When a high number of lower level details can be remembered (from the war part of the text), they do not see the need to summarize this information in general terms.

The theory of text comprehension developed by Kintsch (1988, 1992; van Dijk & Kintsch, 1983) offers a framework within which these complex interactions can be understood. The theory distinguishes between different types of representations that are being generated in comprehension, specifically between the text base and the situation model. The text base is the representation of the meaning and structure (including rhetorical organization) of the text itself. If a text is well written and provides appropriate signals to the reader as to what is important and what is not, readers are generally able to form an adequate text base, even with minimal domain knowledge. Behaviors that are primarily based on the text base include recognition and reproductive recall, as well as summarization. The situation model, on the other hand, represents the content of the text, the situation described by it, and what is already known about it. The formation of a situation model is influenced by the amount and structure of the reader's domain knowledge. An appropriate situation model forms the basis for tasks that require one to apply the new knowledge in some way. However, although the distinction between text base and situation model is important for analytical purposes, the two representations are by no means independent, as the present results demonstrate.

In the present experiment, the target text was the same for all subjects. What differed was the amount of information subjects had received about the topic under discussion. Hence, differences were expected in the situation models that subjects constructed on the basis of reading the text. The full-information subjects ought to have been able to form an adequate, veridical situation model. As far as the text base is concerned, subjects did quite well with the part of the text that was in fact a war report. They missed out on the higher level generalizations about the war, but nevertheless were able to form a good retrieval structure on the basis of their general knowledge about wars that supported their recall. Thus, they reproduced as much concrete detail from this portion of the text as anyone else. These subjects are like readers of a complex story: Because they have no specific information about the topic, they miss some of the intricacies and implications, yet they have no trouble getting the main point and even a lot of the detail. For the politics-related portion of the text, however, the no-information subjects were at a loss. No general knowledge was available to compensate for the lack of specific information. All they understood were some broad generalizations (who was involved in the negotiations), but no well-formed structure that could support the retrieval of the lower level idea units. Hence the conspicuous lack of recall of details from this part of the text by the no-information subjects. Without specific background information, readers were unable to form an adequate text base for this part of the text because they could not fall back on their general knowledge. This observation extends the findings of Means and Voss (1985), who reported comprehension differences as a function of the quality of readers' knowledge schemata. Better recall was observed for readers with more specific, elaborate knowledge schemata than for readers who could rely only on very general schemata. In the present study, the readers' war schema was sufficient to understand one part of the text, at least superficially, whereas the politics schema was useless by itself and needed to be combined with specific prior information in order to support comprehension.

In some cases (e.g., Mannes & Kintsch, 1987) it has been observed that readers form good text bases without constructing an adequate situation model. That is, they are able to recall and summarize a text without really understanding it, as evidenced by their behavior on inferencing and problem solving tasks. In those cases, however, subjects did have the knowledge background required to form a text base; their understanding merely remained at a superficial level. In the present study, the lack of knowledge was more extreme, so that not even the text itself could be understood. The present study therefore illustrates the limits of purely text-based understanding (see also Moravcsik & Kintsch, 1993).

Although news stories have often been used in text research (for a general introduction see van Dijk, 1988), there has been relatively little psychological research in this area. Most of the existing research deals with questions of what is remembered and where comprehension problems exist (e.g., Larsen, 1983). The present results extend the existing research by showing how readers update their knowledge on the basis of news reports. News reports are written for all kinds of readers, not just knowledgeable ones. They are supposed to be understandable for everyone—though at different levels for the informed and uninformed. Our results indicate what kinds of information uninformed readers can and cannot assimilate.

One might object that the results of a controlled laboratory study cannot be readily extrapolated to reading newspapers in everyday life. This is not necessarily so, however, as Singer (1982) showed. In his experiment, similar outcomes were obtained whether subjects read in the laboratory or in real-life situations, as long as the conditions of reading remained comparable. Ecological validity is not simply a matter of laboratory versus nonlaboratory environment.

The generalizability of this study is limited in other ways, however. We used a topic about which our subject had no specific knowledge. They also lacked personal involvement and biases that could have influenced their understanding. As a result, they neglected the part of the text they were not prepared to understand. If the topic were of personal significance, eliciting emotional involvement, readers might have reacted quite differently.

ACKNOWLEDGMENTS

This research was supported by Grant MH 15972 from the National Institute of Mental Health. The paper was written while the first author enjoyed the hospitality of the Max Planck Institut für Psychologische Forschung in Munich. We thank Eileen Kintsch for her editorial comments.

REFERENCES

Beck, I. L., Omanson, R. C., & McKeown, M. G. (1982). An instructional redesign of reading lessons: Effects on comprehension. *Reading Research Quarterly, 17*, 462–481.

Eylon, B. S., & Reif, F. (1984). Effects of knowledge organization on task performance. *Cognition and Instruction, 1*, 5–44.

Kintsch, W. (1988). The use of knowledge in discourse processing: A construction-integration model. *Psychological Review, 95*, 163–182.

Kintsch, W. (1992). A cognitive architecture for comprehension. In H. L. Pick, Jr., P. van den Broek, & D. C. Knill (Eds.), *Cognition: Conceptual and methodological issues* (pp. 143–164). Washington, DC: American Psychological Association.

Kintsch, W. (1993). Information accretion and reduction in text procesing: Inferences. *Discourse Processes, 16*, 193–202.

Larsen, S. F. (1983). Text processing and knowledge updating in memory for radio news. *Discourse Processes, 6*, 21–38.

Mannes, S., & Kintsch, W. (1987). Knowledge organization and text organization. *Cognition and Instruction, 4*, 91–115.

Means, M., & Voss, J. (1985). Star Wars: A developmental study of expert and novice knowledge structures. *Memory and Language, 24*, 746–757.

Moravcsik, J. E. & Kintsch W. (1993). Writing quality, reading skills, and domain knowledge as factors in text comprehension. *Canadian Journal of Experimental Psychology, 47*, 360–374.

Pearson, P. D., Hanson, J., & Gordon, C. (1979). The effects of background knowledge on young children's comprehension of explicit and implicit information. *Journal of Reading Behavior, 11*, 201–209.

Perfetti, C. A., & McCutchen, D. (1987). Schooled language competence: Linguistic abilities in reading and writing. In S. Rosenberg (Ed.), *Advances in applied psycholinguistics* (pp. 105–141). New York: Cambridge University Press.

Schneider, W., Körkel, J., & Weinert, F. E. (1989). Domain-specific knowledge and memory performance: A comparison of high- and low-aptitude children. *Journal of Educational Psychology, 81*, 306–312.

Schneider, W., Körkel, J., & Weinert, F. E. (1990). Expert knowledge, general abilities, and text processing. In W. Schneider, & F. E. Weinert (Eds.), *Interactions among aptitudes, strategies, and knowledge in cognitive performance* (pp. 235–251). New York: Springer-Verlag.

Singer, M. (1982). Comparing memory for natural and laboratory reading. *Journal of Experimental Psychology: General, 111*, 331–347.

Spilich, G. J., Vesonder, G. T., Chiesi, H. L., & Voss, J. F. (1979). Text processing of domain related information for individuals with high and low domain knowledge. *Journal of Verbal Learning and Verbal Behavior, 18*, 275–290.

van Dijk, T. A. (1988). *News as discourse.* Hillsdale, NJ: Lawrence Erlbaum Associates.

van Dijk, T. A., & Kintsch, W. (1983). *Strategies of discourse comprehension.* New York: Academic Press.

18 Construction of a Mental Model

Caren M. Jones
University of Massachusetts—Amherst

Mental models have become ubiquitous in psychological research. Despite a vast literature on how mental models are used, relatively little work has been done on what mental models are, and even less research has investigated how mental models are generated. Mental models are messy, as everyone seems to have a different opinion of what they are. For example, mental models may be images (Denis & Denhiere, 1990; Ottosson, 1987; Rouse & Morris, 1986), propositional structures (Garnham, 1982), just like perceptions (Glenberg, Meyer, & Lindem, 1987), or none of these things (e.g., Craik, 1943; Johnson-Laird, 1983; McNamara, Miller, & Bransford, 1984; van Dijk & Kintsch, 1983). Perhaps the only generally agreed upon aspect of mental models is that they are representations in which the structure maps directly onto the structure of the real-world situation that is represented. That is, mental models represent things and their interrelations; they do not represent the description itself. This is a general claim that has been made many times (e.g., Johnson-Laird, 1983; McNamara et al., 1984; Morrow, Greenspan, & Bower, 1987; van Dijk & Kintsch, 1983). I return later to question the usefulness of this assumption. For now, though, I consider in more depth another basic question about mental models: How are they constructed? This topic has received even less attention than the question of format, both theoretically and empirically.

Currently, there is no well-specified theory of mental model construction and, as a result, the process of construction has been "left to the reader's imagination" (Johnson-Laird, 1983, p. 253). Although Johnson-Laird (1983) described an iterative process by which an existing model could be updated, he did not specify how the initial representation would be created. Garnham (1982) suggested that a mental model is created when some minimal amount of linguistic information is retrieved from memory and placed in the representation. However, Garnham assumed that mental models could be represented by an integrated set of propositions, whereas Johnson-Laird has argued repeatedly (e.g., Johnson-Laird, 1983; Mani & Johnson-Laird, 1982) that propositional information is lost as soon as a mental model is generated. The work of Garnham and Johnson-Laird highlight a major problem facing any theory of mental model construction; the basic units of the model (i.e., propositions or something else) remain uncertain.

Possibly, a theory of mental model construction has not been developed because mental models have been assumed to play a wide variety of roles in the comprehension process. For example, it has been argued that mental models are the basis of language comprehension (e.g., Bower & Morrow, 1990; Johnson-Laird, 1989), that they are fundamental to our understanding of the world (e.g., Johnson-Laird, 1983; Oden, 1987; Ottosson, 1987), that they are the mechanism by which we can reason about space (e.g., Ehrlich & Johnson-Laird, 1982; Mani & Johnson-Laird, 1982), and solve both physical (e.g., Hegarty, 1992) and syllogistic problems (e.g., Johnson-Laird, Byrne, & Tabossi, 1989). Given the multiple roles that mental models may serve, it may not be reasonable to assume a single type of representation. Thus, specifying the construction process to any serious degree may be difficult. I avoid many of these complex issues by considering the processes involved in the construction of only the simplest kind of mental model that can be derived from text descriptions: those that represent a small set of physical objects along with associated nonspatial attributes of those objects (e.g., colors and sizes).

Empirically, as theoretically, little effort has been devoted to the study of mental model construction. This may be due in part to the difficulty in establishing a sound methodology. The few studies that have investigated mental model construction have evaluated the process by measuring reading times on text descriptions. The logic behind these experiments is that the time to read a text reflects the ease with which the text is comprehended. It is assumed that a major portion of the comprehension process involves the construction of a mental representation and the integration of currently read text into that representation; longer reading times reflect greater difficulty in completing that integration (e.g., Johnson-Laird, 1983; Stenning 1986). Therefore, we may be able to learn about the construction of a mental representation by presenting subjects with various types of information that is organized in different ways. By evaluating reading times for carefully selected propositions, it should be possible to ask interesting questions about both the processes underlying the construction of a mental model as well as the nature of that representation. However, even this may prove difficult in light of the assumptions just given. For example, Bower and Morrow (1990) suggested that constructing a mental model may require more time than is reflected in the reading of a single (complex) sentence. Also, McKoon and Ratcliff (1992) argued that, in the absence of any specific comprehension goal, readers will engage in only minimal processing and will not establish a mental model of the text.

Typically, text descriptions used in mental model research have been written in naturalistic English. That is, the sentences have often contained more than one proposition about a described situation. For example, consider the following introductory sentence from a passage used in O'Brien and Albrecht (1992): "As Kim stood inside the health club she felt a rush of excitement" (p. 781). This sentence contains two important pieces of information about the protagonist: it positions Kim in space and tells the reader something about her mental state. This type of sentence can be used in research that is focused on the resulting representation, but it is too complex for evaluating the construction of the representation. Investigating the construction process requires presenting subjects with atomic propositions—single units of new information—such as, "The ball is blue," after the existence of the ball has been established. Each sentence must add only a single bit of new information to the mental representation. In that way, the difficulty of incorporating that proposition into the model can be assessed independent of the difficulty of adding any other proposition.

Of the previous studies on mental model construction, only two (Stenning 1986; Stenning, Shepard, & Levy 1988) used such atomic descriptions (but see also Schnotz, 1982, and Passerault, 1986, for studies with similar experimental designs but more naturalistic texts). For example, Stenning (1986; Stenning et al., 1988) presented subjects with descriptions of a small number of things (e.g., objects, people), each with a small number of associated features (e.g., color, size, temperament). The presented information was organized in one of two ways: either all of the features of one object were described before the second was mentioned (*object organized*), or the features of the two objects were presented in alternation (*feature organized*).

Presenting the information in these two organizations has the advantage of allowing one to evaluate the organization of the mental representation. If the representations are organized around the objects, then it should be easier to construct a mental model from an object-organized text than from a feature-organized text; reading times for object-organized descriptions should be faster than for feature-organized descriptions. Likewise, if the models are organized around features, then reading times should be faster for feature-organized texts than for object-organized texts.

The reading times for a single text can also provide information about the structure of the resulting model. If the representations are organized around objects, then it should be more difficult to integrate new features with an object in the representation than to add a new object to the representation. In that case, the first object and its features form a conceptual chunk and should have relatively little influence on the other parts of the model. Thus, the amount of time spent reading about each additional object should be roughly the same if each object has the same number of features. Similarly, if the representations are organized around features, then the amount of time spent reading about each feature should be relatively independent of the number of other features that have been learned.

On the assumption that mental models mirror the structure of the real-world situation that is described, one can predict that the representations will be organized around the objects when only objects and features are described. In real-world situations, features do not exist independently of objects; furthermore, there is considerable evidence suggesting that objects are more central than features (e.g., Baylis & Driver, 1993; Duncan, 1984; Kahneman, Treisman, & Gibbs, 1992). However, G. V. Jones (1976) found that an object's identity was no more central than its location or its color; a cued recall task revealed that an object's identity, color, and location were all equally good retrieval cues for the remaining details.

Schnotz (1982) presented subjects with long text passages about two types of psychotherapies and asked subjects to learn the material well enough to explain it to another student. Schnotz reported only overall reading times, which did not differ by text organization. However, subjects who read the object-organized texts tended to recall more of the information, suggesting that those descriptions were easier to learn. In a follow-up study, Passerault (1986) described two varieties of plants to his subjects, using the same object- or feature-organized text structures. Subjects were asked to learn the plants' similarities and dissimilarities. On average, subjects were slower to read about the first plant than the second when the text was object-organized. Passerault argued that because his subjects knew only two plants would be described, they established a skeletal representation for the second plant as they were learning about the first. Hence, reading times for the second plant were shorter because some of the construction had already been completed.

Stenning (1986; Stenning et al., 1988) used the same general experimental design as Schnotz (1982) and Passerault (1986). That is, he presented subjects with both object- and feature-organized descriptions of a small number of objects (Stenning, 1986) or people (Stenning et al., 1988), each with a small number of associated features. Subjects were asked to learn the information for a subsequent memory test. Unlike Schnotz (1982) and Passerault (1986), however, Stenning used atomic descriptions. His experiments also differed in that he presented subjects with a preview of the to-be-described objects and features immediately prior to each description. For example, subjects might read,

black/white, circle/square, large/small,

followed by this description:

There is a square.
The square is white.
The square is large.
There is a circle.

The circle is black.
The circle is small.

Subjects read the sentences one at a time, and reading times were recorded. Following each description, there were a few recognition questions and then a recall task. The results were identical for the two types of stimuli, so I discuss the data as if all the texts had been object/feature descriptions.

Stenning found that reading times for the objects did not depend on the text organization, nor did the reading time for any particular object depend on how many other objects had been described. Subjects were fastest to read about the first feature of each object and progressively slower to read about each additional feature. In other words, reading times for the first and third object were the same, but reading times for the first feature of any object were faster than for the third feature. The pattern of reading times is similar to a fan effect for a mental representation organized around objects, and Stenning (1986) described it in those terms. But unlike traditional fan effects, which occur during retrieval (e.g., Anderson, 1974; Radvansky & Zacks, 1991), Stenning found the fan-like pattern during encoding.

There are a couple of problems with Stenning's experiments. First, the same presentation order (the most linguistically natural order) was used for the features in each description. For objects, the order was always, shape, color, texture, size; for person descriptions it was, occupation, nationality, physical character, temperament. Although these orderings may have helped to make the descriptions more natural and less awkward, they made the pattern of reading times difficult to interpret. Do subjects take longer to learn each additional bit of information about an object, or are sizes simply more difficult to learn than colors?

A second problem in Stenning's experiments is the repetition of specific features in the description of different objects. For example, both a circle and a square might be black. Furthermore, immediately prior to reading a description, subjects were given a preview of the features and objects that would be described (see the example presented earlier). Thus, subjects knew how many objects would be described, and what the features would be; the only information the preview did not provide was the binding of particular features to particular objects. Although Stenning (1986) did not report how often the features matched across the objects, the descriptions used by Stenning et al. (1988) had objects with at least one identical feature in 75% of the descriptions. Thus, in the majority of descriptions presented to subjects, some sentences contained no new information. If subjects knew from the preview that only two objects would be described, a circle and a square, and that there were two black things, then reading that the circle is black or the square is black is redundant with their existing knowledge. Given that the reading times for those noninformative sentences were averaged with reading times for informative sentences, it is difficult to interpret the overall pattern of reading times. Although Stenning presented atomic descriptions, then, he did not take full advantage of their potential value.

My experiments were designed to replicate Stenning's, and to extend the results by tracking the representation over several exposures to the description. Previous research suggests that a mental model may not be completely formed after a single exposure to the information. Perrig and Kintsch (1985) found that when subjects were given a single exposure to a complex text, they were unable to make accurate spatial inferences based on the presented information. However, Taylor and Tversky (1992) found that when subjects were given as many as four self-paced exposures to a text, they were quite adept at making inferences from a variety of perspectives. The same appears to be true of simple descriptions: Subjects who were given as long as they liked to learn a simple spatial description were quite able to recognize a diagram that corresponded to the described layout (Mani & Johnson-Laird, 1982), but when the exposure time was limited and subjects were given a reproduction task, the apparent quality of their mental representations decreased dramatically (Ehrlich & Johnson-Laird, 1982). Therefore, in the present experiments, I presented descriptions several times and tested subjects after each repetition of the information to track any changes in the mental representation over time.

EXPERIMENT 1

In Experiment 1, subjects were presented with descriptions of two objects each with four features. The descriptions were atomic, and each object was described with a color, a size, a texture, and a motion. Unlike Stenning, I did not treat the object's identity as a feature. The order of the features was randomly determined for each repetition of each description. Thus, any difference in reading times to the first and later presented features is attributable to the process of adding the Nth feature, not to the particular feature type. The information in each description was shown four times in a different, randomly chosen presentation order each time. Example descriptions and repetitions are shown in Table 18.1. Subjects were tested on the descriptions after each repetition.

In addition, I presented features that were not predictable and that were never identical for both objects. For example, if one object was yellow, then the other object could not be yellow; moreover, its color could not be predicted with a probability greater than one third (there were four possible values for each of the features; associating one of them with an object left three alternatives for the remaining object). Thus, the features in my descriptions were much less predictable than in Stenning's descriptions. This is especially true because my subjects did not see a preview of the to-be-presented features and objects. As in Stenning's studies, subjects read one sentence at a time at their own pace, and reading

TABLE 18.1
Examples, Descriptions, and Questions for Experiment 1

Repetition	Object Organization	Questions	Feature Organization
1	There is a stick	jar lacy	There is a stick
	The stick is yellow	jumping tiny	There is a jar
	The stick is colossal	lacy yellow	The stick is yellow
	The stick is jumping	stick orange	The jar is purple
	The stick is smooth	purple rising	The stick is colossal
	There is a jar	wrinkled jumping	The jar is tiny
	The jar is purple	colossal smooth	The stick is jumping
	The jar is tiny		The jar is rising
	The jar is rising		The stick is smooth
	The jar is lacy		The jar is lacy
2	There is a jar	Rough rising	There is a jar
	The jar is rising	tiny yellow	There is a stick
	The jar is purple	lacy tiny	The jar is rising
	The jar is lacy	stick colossal	The stick is jumping
	The jar is tiny	jar falling	The jar is purple
	There is a stick	purple smooth	The stick is yellow
	The stick is jumping	jumping yellow	The jar is lacy
	The stick is yellow		The stick is smooth
	The stick is smooth		The jar is tiny
	The stick is colossal		The stick is colossal

times were collected. Eighteen subjects participated in exchange for course credit.

Following each repetition of a description, subjects were asked a series of yes–no questions about the most recently presented information. They were presented with pairs of feature names, such as *yellow tiny*, and were asked to press "1" if both features described the same object (half the subjects) or different objects (the remaining subjects) and to press "0" otherwise. For each description, there were also three questions that paired an object name with a feature (e.g., *stick yellow*); these were included so that subjects would learn the associations of the features to the objects and not just the interrelations of the features. The questions were randomly determined and randomly ordered for each repetition of each description, and were about half true and half false for both groups of subjects. Example questions are shown in Table 18.1.

Sentence reading times that were less than 300 ms or more than two standard deviations above the untrimmed mean for a given condition were excluded from the analyses. This cutoff procedure eliminated less than 6% of the data. The trimmed mean sentence reading times for the descriptions in Experiment 1 are shown in Fig. 18.1 as a function of repetition number (Panels a–d), text organization (object- or feature-organized), and sentence position within the description. The reading times for the sentences of the feature-organized texts were rearranged to allow direct comparison with the object-organized descriptions. Thus, the first five points along the x-axis correspond to reading times for

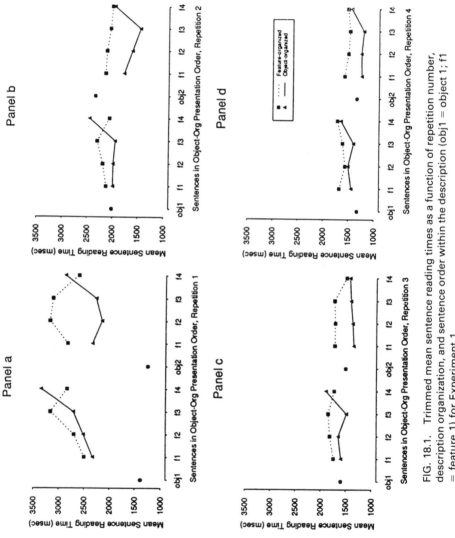

FIG. 18.1. Trimmed mean sentence reading times as a function of repetition number, description organization, and sentence order within the description (obj1 = object 1; f1 = feature 1) for Experiment 1.

sentences about the first object; the first point is the introduction of the object (e.g., "there is a jar"), and the remaining points are for sentences that added features to the object (e.g., "the jar is yellow").

As can be seen in Fig. 18.1, subjects were reliably faster to read the object-organized texts than the feature-organized texts on all repetitions of the descriptions [$F(1,17) = 9.17, p < .01, MS_e = 3221334$], suggesting that the representations were object based. A second indication that the representations have an object-based structure is that the reading times for the sentences that introduce an object are reliably faster than for those that add features to the object, even when the number of syllables in the two types of sentences is taken into account [$F(3,48) = 22.57, p < .001, MS_e = 32791$]. Finally, the reading times for the second object are relatively independent of those for the first object. That is, when the text is feature organized, the reading times for information about the two objects is read equally quickly, as if the two objects form independent conceptual chunks.

For the object-organized texts, the pattern is a bit more complicated. Subjects were faster to read about the features of the second object than to read about features of the first object. The interaction between description organization and reading times for each object is reliable, $F(1,17) = 7.18$, $p < .02$, $MS_e = 1182218$. However, that pattern only emerges after subjects have read enough descriptions to realize that each text would be about two and only two objects, and that the same types of features would be mentioned for each object. Once subjects drew that conclusion, a new strategy appeared in which they seemed to establish the representation for the second object as they were learning the details of the first object. Therefore, reading about the second object took less time because they could simply insert the actual values of the features into the previously created slots (see Passerault, 1986, for a similar argument). For the most part, then, these data replicate Stenning's (1986; Stenning et al., 1988) data, and suggest that objects are the conceptual units in a mental representation of this sort.

The memory data lend further support to the conclusion that the representations are object based. After each repetition of a description subjects were presented with a series of feature-pairs and asked to judge whether the features had been described of the same or different objects. For one-half of those questions, the features had in fact belonged to the same object. As can been seen in Table 18.2, subjects were reliably faster to correctly answer questions that were about one object than questions that were about two objects [$F(1,16) = 37.67, p < .001, MS_e = 196606$]. The response time advantage for single-object questions was the same for both groups of subjects ($p > .1$), and the number of errors was the same for one- and two-object questions ($p > .7$). Therefore, the effect probably should not be attributed to a general reaction time advantage to respond positively (e.g., Tversky, 1969).

Subjects who answered "same" did make fewer errors than those who an-

TABLE 18.2
Mean Reaction Time (ms) to Correctly Answered Questions in Experiment 1

	Repetition Number			
Number of Objects	1	2	3	4
One	3,252	3,028	2,796	2,536
Two	3,844	3,678	3,028	2,875
Difference	592	650	232	339

swered "different" [7.4% vs. 14.6%, respectively; $F(1,14) = 4.75, p < .05, MS_e = 9.08$], but no more errors were made on two- than one-object questions ($p > .7$). So the reaction time advantage should not be attributed to a speed–accuracy trade-off. There were a large number of errors made overall (19.4%, 12.0%, 9.1%, and 7.4% across the four repetitions) suggesting that subjects found this task quite difficult.

The reading times and question-answering times from Experiment 1 both suggest that subjects were creating central object nodes to organize the object and feature information. Experiment 2, however, demonstrated that objects are not always the central units of mental models of objects and features; a great deal depends on the relative topicality of the features.

EXPERIMENT 2

Experiment 2 was designed to evaluate the degree to which the structure of the mental representation depends on the structure of the text description. In other words, were the object-centered mental representations found in Experiment 1 a consequence of some descriptive bias toward the objects? Or, would such object-based representations have been generated from any description of objects and features? To answer these questions, the descriptive focus of the descriptions and the questions were reversed. Rather than reading descriptions of two objects each with four associated features, the 17 paid subjects read descriptions of two features, each with four associated objects.

The structure of the descriptions was as similar as possible across the two experiments. In Experiment 1, the features of the two objects were clearly related to each other (e.g., each object had an associated color). In order to mimic that relatedness for the objects in Experiment 2, pairs of objects were generated that were maximally related to each other and minimally related to other pairs of objects. One member of each object pair was assigned to one feature in a description. Thus, if *pen* was associated with the first feature, then *pencil* was associated with the second.

The questions in Experiment 2 also paralleled those in Experiment 1. Subjects were given pairs of objects (e.g., *pen scarf*) and asked to indicate whether or not the two objects shared a feature. The only other change in the stimuli for Experiment 2 was an attempt to make the sentences more natural without destroying their atomic nature. Rather than presenting things like "the yellow is a hat" (which would be exactly parallel to sentences in Experiment 1), subjects saw "one yellow thing is a hat." See Table 18.3 for example descriptions and questions.

The same cutoff procedure was used as in Experiment 1; less than 3% of the

TABLE 18.3
Example Descriptons and Test Questions for Experiment 2

Repetition	Object Organization	Questions
1	There are purple things	purple boat
	There are yellow things	scarf pencil
	One purple thing is a hat	rifle hat
	One yellow thing is a scarf	spoon pen
	One purple thing is a pen	scarf yellow
	One yellow thing is a pencil	fork gun
	One purple thing is a fork	orange pen
	One yellow thing is a spoon	
	One purple thing is a rifle	
	One yellow thing is a gun	
2	There are yellow things	pencil fork
	There are purple things	gun scarf
	One yellow thing is a spoon	basket purple
	One purple thing is a fork	hat spoon
	One yellow thing is a pencil	tan fork
	One purple thing is a pen	pen rifle
	One yellow thing is a gun	yellow pencil
	One purple thing is a rifle	
	One yellow thing is a scarf	
	One purple thing is a hat	

Repetition	Feature Organization	Questions
1	There are purple things	orange pen
	One purple thing is a hat	scarf purple
	One purple thing is a fork	purple boat
	One purple thing is a rifle	rifle hat
	There are yellow things	spoon pen
	One yellow thing is a scarf	scarf yellow
	One yellow thing is a pencil	fork gun
	One yellow thing is a spoon	
	One yellow thing is a gun	
2	There are yellow things	pencil fork
	One yellow thing is a spoon	yellow scarf
	One yellow thing is a pencil	purple sheet
	One yellow thing is a gun	gun scarf
	One yellow thing is a scarf	hat spoon
	There are purple things	pen rifle
	One purple thing is a fork	tan pen
	One purple thing is a pen	
	One purple thing is a rifle	
	One purple thing is a hat	

reading time data were excluded from the analyses. The trimmed mean sentence reading times for the descriptions in Experiment 2 are shown in Fig. 18.2 as a function of repetition number (Panels a–d), description organization, and sentence order within the description. Note that object- and feature-organized texts have different interpretations in this experiment; the first five points on the x-axis correspond to sentences about objects belonging to the first feature.

Figures 18.1 and 18.2 are quite similar. In Experiment 2, subjects were fastest to read sentences that introduced a feature, and slower to associate the objects with that feature [$F(1,15) = 8.79$, $p < .01$, $MS_e = 2269729$]. Subjects read about the second feature more quickly than the first [$F(1,15) = 4.97$, $p < .05$, $MS_e = 692503$], as if they were beginning to establish the representation for the second feature while they were reading about the first. Thus, when the topic of the descriptions switched from objects to features, the apparent structure of the resulting representation also shifted. Features might be somewhat less desirable as organizing units, though: There was no overall difference in the reading times for the two text organizations in Experiment 2. Because the reading times should be faster for texts that are structured more like the internal representation, a feature-based representation should result in faster reading times for feature-organized texts.

The reaction times to the correctly answered questions suggest that features were the central nodes in the representations. Subjects were presented with pairs of objects (e.g., *pen–scarf*), and were asked to judge whether they had shared a feature in the description. As can be seen in Table 18.4, response times to those single-feature questions were faster than to questions that involved two features [$F(1,15) = 7.18$, $p < .02$, $MS_e = 263958$], and both response groups showed the same reaction time advantage. This result is directly parallel to the single-object response time advantage found in Experiment 1. As with the reading-time data, there is some suggestion that features may be less desirable than objects as organizing units. However, this conclusion requires a comparison across experiments and should be viewed with caution.

The number of errors decreased across repetitions (17.0%, 13.1%, 12.2%, 10.2%, $F(3,39) = 3.46$, $p < .05$, $MS_e = 1.01$), but otherwise were not influenced by any experimental manipulation.

TABLE 18.4
Mean Reaction Time (ms) to Correctly Answered Questions in Experiment 2

Number of Features	Repetition Number			
	1	2	3	4
One	3,574	3,120	3,114	2,966
Two	3,904	3,362	3,311	3,137
Difference	330	242	197	171

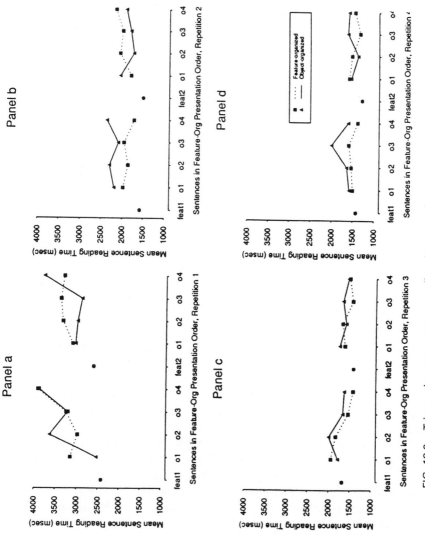

FIG. 18.2. Trimmed mean sentence reading times as a function of repetition number, description organization, and sentence order within the description (o1 = object 1; feat1 = feature 1) for Experiment 2.

347

DISCUSSION

One might want to argue from these data that subjects simply organize the information around the fewest possible conceptual units. In Experiment 1, subjects chose to organize the four features around the two objects, whereas in Experiment 2 they chose to organize the four objects around the two features. However, there are two reasons why this seems unlikely. First, Stenning (1986) presented subjects with descriptions of four objects each with one feature,[1] or three objects each with two features, in addition to descriptions of two objects with two or three features each. For all types of descriptions, the same pattern appeared: Reading times slowed as more information was learned about a given object, but not as more objects were added to the representation. Although those data suggest that subjects were organizing the representation around the objects even when using features would have resulted in fewer conceptual chunks, they are not conclusive. Stenning's 1986 study was modest ($N = 5$), and this aspect of the design was not replicated in his larger study (Stenning et al., 1988).

A second line of evidence that subjects were not simply organizing around the fewest chunks comes from more complex descriptions. In more complex representations, subjects show clear preferences for particular organizers (e.g., characters) both when each possible organizer would result in the same number of conceptual chunks and when an alternative organizer (e.g., time) would yield fewer chunks of information (Taylor & Tversky, 1994; see also Radvansky, Spieler, & Zacks, 1993). Thus, subjects showed organizational preferences for a given set of information, and that organization did not necessarily lead to the fewest number of conceptual chunks.

The willingness of subjects to mentally organize the described information in a variety of ways has implications for the nature of mental models. Probably the most commonly made claim about mental models is that their structure maps onto the real-world situation that is represented (e.g., Johnson-Laird, 1983). The problem with this idea, of course, is that the structure of the mental model can (and does) vary, but the world does not change. We can impose a particular organization on our perception of the world, but the world exists independently of such impositions. This realization reduces the force of the claim about mental models: Is it any surprise that our internal representation shows the same structure as the structure we impose on the world? This is an important issue. Without some objective measure of structure in the world (which may be impossible to obtain), suggesting that a mental model is like the world relies too heavily on intuition about exactly what structure is meant.

---

[1]Stenning (1986) referred to these descriptions as four-object, two-predicate descriptions. Unlike Stenning, I have not treated an object's identity as a feature (i.e., predicate) of an object.

WHAT ABOUT CONSTRUCTION?

I started this research with the aim of learning how mental models of objects and features are constructed. Several experiments later, there is still little that can be said with any certainty. The message in these data seems to be that the construction of a mental representation from simple texts involves establishing a central node (an object or a feature, depending on their relative importance) and associating attributes to that node. A central node plus its attributes and their links to the node forms a conceptual chunk that has little to no influence on the other chunks in the model.

Stenning (1986) suggested that the linkage of attributes to the central nodes is fan-like, but I am less certain. Data from a related experiment (C. M. Jones & Tversky, 1992) with a similar design suggest that later-mentioned attributes are linked to each other in a chain-like fashion, rather than being linked directly to the central node. In that experiment, reaction times to recognition questions (e.g., *bag purple* was presented and subjects were asked if the feature had been associated with the object) were an increasing function of the number of intervening features associated with the object. In other words, subjects were fastest to confirm the first-mentioned feature of an object and slowest to confirm the most recently described feature. For example, if subjects read,

> There is a circle
> The circle is yellow
> The circle is lacy
> The circle is jumping,

they were slower to respond to *circle jumping* than to *circle yellow*. This effect is the opposite of a recency effect, despite the fact that subjects could respond to *circle jumping* with only the information contained in that final sentence. The reaction time pattern suggests that the features form a chain leading back to the object node (which presumably contains identity information), and that no link can be skipped when making a judgment that involves the object's name.

The relationship among the central nodes is also uncertain. Although in these descriptions the object or feature information could be chunked into discrete and independent units, it is often the case that information about different objects must be integrated in some way. Perhaps the most straightforward example of this is the need to represent the spatial relations among objects. Of course, causal or spatio-temporal interrelations of objects can also be important to our understanding of a description.

What about the development of the representation over repetitions of the descriptions? This, too, is unclear. The structure of the representation does not change substantially across the repetitions, as is indicated by the faster reaction times to one-object and one-feature questions after each repetition (see Tables 18.2 and 18.4). However, the error rates to the questions do decrease across repetitions, suggesting that the representations became more complete or perhaps more elaborated as subjects had more exposure to the information. The present data do not allow further specification of the developing model.

THE FUTURE OF THE AREA

Perhaps the most important point in these data lies in what they do not and cannot tell us. Response times to questions cannot tell us about the construction of the representation, only about the structure of that representation. Sentence reading times do not tell us how the presented information is used, only that it was easier or more difficult to use than some other type of information. In fact, the construction of such simple mental representations may occur too quickly for simple reading times to detect. The high error rates, though, suggest that the mental representations of these descriptions are not particularly accurate or complete, regardless of their simplicity.

Even if these data could indicate clearly how mental models of objects and features were established, we might still know very little of how other sorts of mental models might be generated. Mental models themselves are both ill defined and highly varied, and there may be more than one way to create them.

Is this a fruitful area for future research? Until better techniques for online analysis of the representation are developed, and until mental models are more precisely defined, I will remain pessimistic.

ACKNOWLEDGMENTS

This chapter is based on part of a doctoral dissertation submitted to Stanford University. I would like to thank Barbara Tversky, Gordon Bower, and Herb Clark for their discussions of these data, and Evan Heit for helpful comments on the dissertation.

REFERENCES

Anderson, J. R. (1974). Retrieval of propositional information from long-term memory. *Cognitive Psychology, 6*, 451–474.

Baylis, G. C., & Driver, J. (1993). Visual attention and objects: Evidence for hierarchical coding of location. *Journal of Experimental Psychology: Human Perception and Performance, 19*, 451–470.

Bower, G. H., & Morrow, D. G. (1990). Mental models in narrative comprehension. *Science, 247*, 44–48.

Craik, K. J. W. (1943). *The nature of explanation*. Cambridge, England: Cambridge University Press.

Denis, M., & Denhiere, G. (1990). Comprehension and recall of spatial descriptions. *European Bulletin of Cognitive Psychology*, *10*, 115–143.

Duncan, J. (1984). Selective attention and the organization of visual attention. *Journal of Experimental Psychology: General*, *113*, 501–517.

Ehrlich, K., & Johnson-Laird, P. N. (1982). Spatial descriptions and referential continuity. *Journal of Verbal Learning and Verbal Behavior*, *21*, 296–306.

Garnham, A. (1982). *On-line construction of representations of the content of texts*. Bloomington, IN: Indiana University Linguistics Club.

Glenberg, A. M., Meyer, M., & Lindem, K. (1987). Mental models contribute to foregrounding during text comprehension. *Journal of Memory and Language*, *26*, 69–83.

Hegarty, M. (1992). Mental animation: Inferring motion from static displays of mechanical systems. *Journal of Experimental Psychology: Learning, Memory, and Cognition*, *18*, 1084–1102.

Johnson-Laird, P. N. (1983). *Mental models*. Cambridge, MA: Harvard University Press.

Johnson-Laird, P. N. (1989). Mental models. In M. I. Posner (Ed.), *Foundations of Cognitive Science* (pp. 469–499). Cambridge, MA: MIT Press.

Johnson-Laird, P. N., Byrne, R. M. J., & Tabossi, P. (1989). Reasoning by model: The case of multiple quantification. *Psychological Review*, *96*, 658–673.

Jones, C. M., & Tversky, B. (1992). [Chaining of features in mental model construction]. Unpublished raw data.

Jones, G. V. (1976). A fragmentation hypothesis of memory: Cued recall of pictures and of sequential position. *Journal of Experimental Psychology: General*, *105*, 277–293.

Kahneman, D., Treisman, A., & Gibbs, B. J. (1992). The reviewing of object files: Object-specific integration of information. *Cognitive Psychology*, *24*, 175–219.

Mani, K., & Johnson-Laird, P. N. (1982). The mental representation of spatial descriptions. *Memory and Cognition*, *10*, 181–187.

McKoon, G., & Ratcliff, R. (1992). Inference during reading. *Psychological Review*, *99*, 440–466.

McNamara, T. P., Miller, D. L., & Bransford, J. D. (1984). Mental models and reading comprehension. In P. D. Pearson, R. Barr, M. L. Kamil, & P. Mosenthal (Eds.), *Handbook of Reading Research* (pp. 490–511). New York: Longman.

Morrow, D. G., Greenspan, S. L., & Bower, G. H. (1987). Accessibility and situation models in narrative comprehension. *Journal of Memory and Language*, *26*, 165–187.

O' Brien, E. J., & Albrecht, J. E. (1992). Comprehension strategies in the development of a mental model. *Journal of Experimental Psychology: Learning, Memory, and Cognition*, *18*, 777–784.

Oden, G. C. (1987). Concept, knowledge, and thought. *Annual Review of Psychology*, *38*, 203–227.

Ottosson, T. (1987). *The world in mind: Mental models of spatial relations* (Tech. Rep. No. 1987:01). Gothenburg, Sweden: Gothenburg University, Department of Education and Educational Research.

Passerault, J. M. (1986). Organisation du texte et strategies d'integration [Text organization and integration strategies]. *Canadian Journal of Psychology*, *40*, 263–271.

Perrig, W., & Kintsch, W. (1985). Propositional and situational representations of text. *Journal of Memory and Language*, *24*, 503–518.

Radvansky, G. A., Spieler, D. H., & Zacks, R. T. (1993). Mental model organization. *Journal of Experimental Psychology: Learning, Memory, and Cognition*, *19*, 95–114.

Radvansky, G. A., & Zacks, R. T. (1991). Mental models and fact retrieval. *Journal of Experimental Psychology: Learning, Memory, and Cognition*, *17*, 940–953.

Rouse, W. B., & Morris, N. M. (1986). On looking into the black box: Prospects and limits in the search for mental models. *Psychological Bulletin*, *100*, 349–363.

Schnotz, W. (1982). How do different readers learn with different text organizations? In A. Flammer & W. Kintsch (Eds.), *Discourse Processing* (pp. 87–97). New York: North-Holland.

Stenning, K. (1986). On making models: A study of constructive memory. In T. Myers, K. Brown, & B. McGonigle (Eds.), *Reasoning and Discourse Processes* (pp. 165–185). London: Academic Press.

Stenning, K., Shepard, M., & Levy, J. (1988). On the construction of representations for individuals from descriptions in text. *Language and Cognitive Processes, 3*, 129–164.

Taylor, H. A., & Tversky, B. (1992). Spatial mental models derived from survey and route descriptions. *Journal of Memory and Language, 31*, 261–292.

Taylor, H. A., & Tversky, B. (1994). *Character and time as organizers of events in memory.* Manuscript submitted for publication.

Tversky, B. (1969). Pictorial and verbal encoding in a short-term memory task. *Perception and Psychophysics, 6*, 225–233.

van Dijk, T. A., & Kintsch, W. (1983). *Strategies of Discourse Comprehension.* New York: Academic Press.

19

The Role of Readers' Standards for Coherence in the Generation of Inferences During Reading

Paul van den Broek
Kirsten Risden
Elizabeth Husebye-Hartmann
University of Minnesota

One of the hallmarks of successful reading is the perception that various parts of the text belong together, that they form a connected whole. Despite the seeming ease with which readers perceive the connectedness, or *coherence*, of most texts, such perception is the outcome of an intricate interplay of cognitive processes that involve memory, background knowledge, textual constraints, processing limitations, and so on. The major reason for this is that relations in a discourse are underdetermined; that is, the coherence of a discourse often is not obvious from the immediate text alone. Crucial relations frequently are not explicitly described in the text and therefore need to be added by the reader, relations may connect ideas that are mentioned quite far apart in the text, and potential relations may even be contradictory and thus must be reconciled by the reader.

Because of the underdetermined nature of the relations in a text, it generally is assumed that coherence is heavily dependent on inferential processes on the part of the reader (Black & Bower, 1980; Graesser, 1981; Kintsch, 1988; Kintsch & van Dijk, 1978; Trabasso, Secco, & van den Broek, 1984).[1] One type of inferences that has received particular attention concerns those that identify causal relations between the various parts of a text. The general notion that causal coherence plays an important role in memory for texts has been supported in many empirical studies. For example, the more causal relations a statement has

---

[1]The term *inference* is used in various ways by researchers in the field of reading comprehension. Here, the term is used in a broad sense, referring to any information about events, relations, and so on that the reader adds to the information that is explicitly presented in the text. Conceived in this way, inferences refer not only to the addition of facts or events as nodes in the mental representation of the text, but also to the identification of relations between nodes that already exist. Thus, in terms of van Dijk and Kintsch (1983), they include both situation-model and text-base inferences.

the more often it is recalled (Goldman & Varnhagen, 1986; Graesser, 1981; Graesser & Clark, 1985; Trabasso et al., 1984; Trabasso & van den Broek, 1985; van den Broek, 1988; van den Broek, Rohleder, & Narváez, in press) and the more quickly it is accessed (O'Brien & Myers, 1987). As a second example, the extent to which one statement from a text primes memory for another is a function of the strength of their causal relation (Keenan, Baillet, & Brown, 1984; McKoon & Ratcliff, 1992; Myers, Shinjo, & Duffy, 1987).

As a result of these and other findings there is little doubt among researchers that causal structure is a strong determinant of memory for a text (e.g., Kintsch, 1992). They disagree considerably, however, about which of all possible causal relations actually are identified *during* reading.

One source of disagreement concerns the extent to which readers identify relations that connect what they are currently reading to prior text or events. From the perspective of a reader, at each point in a text such relations can take one of two forms:

1. *Local* relations connect information in the sentence or clause that is presently being read to information that is still activated from the previous reading cycle.

2. *Global* relations connect information in the present sentence or clause to information that currently is not activated. Global relations require (a) the reactivation of information that was activated at an earlier point in the text but subsequently was deactivated or (b) the activation of extratextual background knowledge.

These types of relations are best illustrated by a simple example. Consider the following story:

1. A young knight rode through the forest.
2. The knight was unfamiliar with the country.
3. Suddenly a dragon appeared.
4. The dragon was kidnapping a beautiful princess.
5. The knight wanted to free her.
6. The knight wanted to marry her.
7. The knight hurried after the dragon.
8. They fought for life and death.
9. Soon, the knight's armor was completely scorched.
10. At last, the knight killed the dragon.
11. He freed the princess.
12. The princess was very thankful to the knight.
13. She married the knight. (adapted from van den Broek & Trabasso, 1986)

In this story, the causal relation between the statements "He freed the princess" and "The princess was very thankful to the knight" is local because the two events are described consecutively and the knight's freeing the princess therefore is likely to still be activated when the reader encounters the princess' being thankful. In contrast, the causal relation between the statements "The knight wanted to marry her" and "She married the knight" is global because the knight's wanting to marry her has not been processed recently. Hence, it is not likely to still be activated and needs to be reinstated from memory. Similarly, comprehension of the statement "Soon the knight's armor was completely scorched" requires a global inference because the reader needs to draw on his or her background knowledge in order to provide sufficient explanation. The background knowledge that dragons tend to breath fire in combination with the prior sentence "They fought for life and death" provides such an explanation.

Local relations can be inferred rather quickly and effortlessly because they connect pieces of information that are already activated. Most, if not all, models of reading comprehension assume that local inferences are routinely made during reading. In contrast, the inference of global relations on the basis of information from the reader's background knowledge or from prior text will usually be more time consuming and effortful. The fact that the generation of global inferences is costly to the reader has led to substantial disagreement among researchers about whether global inferences actually are generated during regular reading and, if they are, under what circumstances (cf. O'Brien, Shank, Myers, & Rayner, 1988). In a recent article, Myers and his colleagues stated it concisely: "Although such [global] causal inferences seem intuitively to be a natural part of text comprehension, there is need to provide clear evidence that they occur and to systematically investigate the conditions under which they occur" (Dopkins, Klin, & Myers, 1993, p. 70).

A second source of disagreement concerns the extent to which readers make *forward* or predictive inferences.[2] These inferences occur when the reader anticipates aspects of events that are likely to be described in subsequent text. For instance, in the example story the statement "The dragon was kidnapping a beautiful princess" may lead the reader to anticipate that the knight will attempt to save the princess. There are several reasons that one might think that these inferences are not generated frequently during regular reading. Again, Myers and colleagues captured it nicely: "One [reason] is that it is not efficient for readers to use resources to draw forward inferences when the information they need will be provided in [subsequent] text. A second reason is that . . . readers run the risk of drawing the wrong inference" (cf. Murray, Klin, & Myers, 1993, p. 2). Yet, intuition suggests that forward inferences are not only drawn frequently but that they are part of what makes reading enjoyable. As a result, theoretical models of

---

[2]Forward inferences are sometimes classified together with global inferences. We differentiate between global and forward inferences because they are *functionally* distinct, as discussed later.

reading differ in the predictions they make concerning the generation of forward inferences. To make matters worse, empirical results likewise seem to be contradictory. With respect to forward inferences, as with global ones, it appears crucial to investigate systematically under what circumstances such inferences occur.

The central hypothesis in this chapter is that readers employ (often implicitly) *standards of causal coherence* and that these standards, together with the constraints provided by the information in the text, determine the inferential activities in which a reader engages during reading. This chapter consists of three sections. In the first section, we describe how the notion of readers' standards of causal coherence and textual constraints can be used to predict the circumstances under which local, global, and forward inferences are generated. The second section presents empirical evidence on the psychological validity of these predictions from a series of free-production experiments and from prior studies on on-line processing. In the third section, we discuss parallels between the findings on standards for causal coherence and those on referential coherence reported by other researchers, and suggest a general model of inference generation based on readers' standards of coherence.

MAINTAINING STANDARDS OF CAUSAL COHERENCE DURING READING

We propose that a reader entertains *standards for coherence* as he or she proceeds through a text (cf. van de Velde, 1989, for a detailed discussion of standards for coherence). These standards determine whether the reader feels that comprehension is complete or that additional inferential processes are required. At times the reader may be aware of his or her standards but more commonly the standards will be implicit, exerting their influence without the reader realizing it.

Several researchers have pointed out that requirements for comprehension play an important role in the generation of inferences but that it is crucial to find out exactly what these requirements are (e.g., Kintsch, 1988; McKoon & Ratcliff, 1992). The current model constitutes a first step toward the systematic study of reader's requirements or standards by placing these standards for coherence central in the description of the reading process. With respect to the causal structure of a text, we propose that the reader attempts to attain *causal sufficiency*: The reader has comprehended an event when, to his or her knowledge, the event receives sufficient causal explanation from the preceding events.[3] As the

---

[3]The term *sufficiency* is used here in a psychological rather than in a logical manner. In this sense it means that, against the combined background of the general text, the immediately preceding events, and any inferred information, the current event is adequately explained or could even have been expected (Mackie, 1980). This notion of sufficiency is neither as strict nor as objective as it is in formal logic. For example, it may vary as a function of inter- and intra-individual differences in motivation, reading purpose, and knowledge or familiarity with the topic(s) in the text.

reader proceeds step by step through the text, he or she engages in inferential processes in an attempt to establish a causal explanation for the events that are being read. This is accomplished most easily if the information that was processed during the immediately preceding reading cycle, and that hence still is activated, provides sufficient causal explanation for the current event. In this case the standard of causal coherence is met quickly and with little effort by means of the inference of a *local* relation, and reading can proceed to the next sentence or clause.

If the information in the prior reading cycle does not provide sufficient causal explanation for the current event, then further inferential processes take place. The aim of these processes is to identify additional events that, alone or in combination with already activated information, supply sufficient cause for the current event. These processes can involve a search of memory for the prior text and/or the activation of background knowledge. Memory searches result in the reactivation of events that were processed earlier during reading but since have become deactivated, whereas access of background knowledge results in the activation of new events or facts that are not described in the text. If the information that is activated through either of these processes increases the strength of the causal explanation for the current event, then one or more *global* relations are constructed. The inferential processes are complete and comprehension is successful when the local relations and any global relations that have been inferred together provide a causally sufficient explanation for the current event.

Thus, the standards that a reader adopts and the constraints that are provided by the text together determine whether local inferences will suffice for comprehension or whether global inferences are likely to be generated as well. In addition, they influence the content of the resulting inferences. Whenever global inferences *are* generated they will tend to supplement the causal explanation provided by the local inferences. The greater the sufficiency that is provided by local inferences, the smaller the need for strong sufficiency in global inferences and vice versa.

This account of the reading process emphasizes the *function* of inferential processes: It is the coherence-maintaining function of a potential inference rather than its local or global character that determines whether it will be generated or not. In this respect it is markedly different from models of reading that focus on categorical questions such as whether all possible inferences are drawn, whether global relations are or are not inferred, whether outcomes in a story are inevitably linked to their goals, and so on. In the current model, the emphasis shifts from questions such as these to a functional perspective on inference generation during reading. According to this model, the reader proceeds step by step through the text, at each point ascertaining whether the information that is being processed in that step has been adequately comprehended. Causal inferences are not made simply because they *can* be made; only a subset of all possible inferences is likely to be generated during regular reading. For example, outcomes tend to be related to their goals not because there is something magical about goals and outcomes, but because in narratives goals tend to serve a very strong explanatory function for the outcomes. The current model predicts that if an outcome is sufficiently explained by the immediately preceding text then no inference to an earlier mentioned goal is required for comprehension and hence such a relation is not likely to be inferred during regular reading. In contrast, if an event is not adequately explained by the information in the immediately preceding processing cycle then global inferences are likely to be made. Thus, inferences provide a major source of coherence to the reader, but the reverse also holds: The need for coherence drives the inferential process.

In addition to their influence on backward inferences, standards of coherence and textual constraints play an important role in the generation of forward inferences. First, a reader's standard of causal coherence may lead the reader to expect that the upcoming text will be a causally coherent continuation of the text that currently is being read. Second, the more strongly the constraints provided by the currently activated text point toward or are sufficient for a particular causal continuation, the more likely it is that the reader will infer that continuation (cf. van den Broek, 1990a). These two principles together determine both the likelihood and the content of a forward inference. They suggest, for example, that the statement "The angry husband threw the vase against the wall" (based on Potts, Keenan, & Golding, 1988) is more likely to evoke the inference that the vase broke than the statement "The angry husband threw the vase on the bed."

The model makes specific predictions about the circumstances under which the various types of inferences will be generated. With respect to backward coherence, the model predicts that if the current statement receives sufficient causal explanation from the statements that have just been processed then a local connection is inferred and no further inferences take place. If the already activated information does not yield sufficient explanation, however, then an attempt toward reinstatement of information from the prior text or elaboration on the basis of background knowledge will take place. This attempt will continue until the standard of coherence is reached or until it becomes obvious that reaching the standard requires more effort than the reader is willing to exert or is impossible no matter how much additional information will be (re)activated. With respect to the content of the inferences that are generated, the model predicts that the information in each inference will contribute to the sufficiency of the explanation for the current event.

With respect to forward inferences, the model predicts that readers anticipate that future events will be causally related to the current event. The constraints provided by the current event often are not strong enough, however, for the reader to generate a specific inference. The more sufficient a current event is for a particular consequence, the more likely it is that the consequence will be inferred.

Thus, the generation of backward inferences is constrained by the current event and by the extent to which the immediately preceding events provide sufficient explanation, whereas the likelihood and content of forward inferences are constrained by the extent to which the current event is sufficient for particular consequents. In this fashion, backward inferences directly contribute to the achievement of the standards of coherence, whereas forward inferences may facilitate achievement of those standards when the next sentence is encountered.

In the following section we explore these predictions. First, we present the results of a series of production studies in which we tested whether subjects indeed attempt to maintain causal sufficiency during reading. A production task was chosen because subjects are left free to generate whatever comes to their minds. This contrasts with tasks in which subjects are presented with response options that the experimenter has selected, thereby constraining the range of inferences for which evidence is gathered. An important disadvantage of production tasks, however, is that they may elicit responses that subjects would not have made spontaneously. For this reason, the description of the results in the production studies is followed by a review of studies on inference generation during reading that use less 'inviting' tasks. The results from these two types of tasks show remarkable convergence, thus providing a strong basis for drawing conclusions about inferential activities during reading (cf. Magliano & Graesser, 1991; van den Broek, Fletcher, & Risden, 1993).

THE ROLE OF CAUSAL STANDARDS IN THE GENERATION OF INFERENCES: EVIDENCE FROM PRODUCTION TASKS

A frequently used method for investigating inferences during reading is that of eliciting answers to questions. Question-answering protocols provide a useful source of data for determining the conceptual organization of narratives, particularly where inferences are concerned. Questioning techniques have been used extensively in order to identify this structure (Goldman & Varnhagen, 1986; Graesser & Clark, 1985; Graesser, Robertson, & Anderson, 1981; Magliano & Graesser, 1991). The purpose of the first study is to test the model's central assumption that many inferences during reading are causal in nature, as well as the specific predictions with respect to the role of necessity and sufficiency on forward and backward inferences. In the second and third studies, we examine in more detail the interplay between causal standards and textual constraints in the generation of forward and backward inferences, respectively.

Study 1: Are Inferences Causal in Nature?

In order to test the model's central assumptions about the causal nature of inferences, we reanalyzed a large corpus of question-answering protocols (Graesser & Clark, 1985). In the original study, Graesser and Clark (1985) obtained question-answering protocols from 10 college students. Immediately upon finishing reading a text, the subjects were asked a series of questions for each sentence (Why did X occur? How did X occur? What are the consequences of X? What is the significance of X? and What enabled X to occur?). In the present study, two raters used counterfactual tests to judge whether the answers given by the subjects indicated the presence of a causal relation (Hart & Honore, 1985; Mackie, 1980; van den Broek, 1990a, 1990b). If an answer reflected a causal relation, it was further analyzed to identify whether the antecedent was necessary and/or sufficient for the consequent. An antecedent is considered necessary for a consequent when, given the circumstances in the text, the consequent would not have occurred if the antecedent had not taken place. It is considered sufficient for a consequent if it is true that the antecedent, in the context of the prior text, is likely to be followed by the consequence. Interrater reliability on all judgments was high, $K = .82$, $p < .001$ (necessity $K = .85$, sufficiency $K = .81$).

The vast majority of responses (82%) were causal in nature. Within causal responses, most antecedents provided sufficiency for the consequent (81%), whereas a somewhat smaller proportion of antecedents was necessary for the consequent (72%). When the responses to backward and forward questions were analyzed separately, however, the patterns of sufficiency and necessity were found to be somewhat different. The results are displayed in Fig. 19.1. Backward inferences were more strongly determined by sufficiency (87%) than by necessity (67%). The reverse held for forward inferences: Responses were more strongly influenced by necessity (83%) than by sufficiency (67%).

These results show that when readers are asked to engage in inference generation the content of the resulting inferences is strongly determined by causality. As predicted, there was a strong tendency for backward inferences to provide sufficient causal explanation. Interestingly, in forward inferences the antecedents frequently were necessary for the inferred consequent but less often sufficient. The lesser importance of sufficiency for forward inferences may reflect the fact that the constraints provided by the current event may not be strong enough for the reader to infer exactly what event will follow. Instead, the reader recognizes that the subsequent event will somehow be dependent on the current event (i.e., the antecedent is necessary for the consequence) but does not have enough information to infer exactly which event will follow (i.e., the antecedent is not sufficient for a particular consequence). If this is true, then one would expect that increasing the sufficiency that the current event provides for a particular inference will affect the likelihood that this inference will be generated. This prediction was tested in the second study.

Although these results suggest that readers attempt to maintain causal coherence during reading, they do not allow one to draw firm conclusions about the spontaneous generation of causal inferences during reading. After all, questions such as "why . . . ?" and "what happened as a consequence of . . . ?" are likely

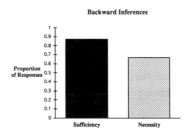

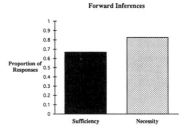

FIG. 19.1. Sufficiency and necessity of backward and forward inferences (Study 1, data
from Graesser & Clark, 1985).

to bias the reader toward providing causal answers. In addition, the question-
answer protocols were obtained after subjects had finished reading the entire
text, rather than as they were comprehending. Post-reading comprehension processes therefore may have influenced subjects' responses. In the second and third
studies these limitations are avoided by asking neutral questions immediately
upon reading of the relevant statement. The purpose of the second study is to
investigate the effect of causal constraints on forward inferences, whereas the
purpose of the third study is to examine the effects of causal coherence and
textual constraints on the generation of backward inferences.

Study 2: Causal Sufficiency and the Generation of Forward Inferences

A central assumption of the model is that the likelihood that a reader will make a
particular forward inference depends on the amount of sufficient causal support
that the current event provides for that inference. According to this assumption,
the more sufficient the current event is for a particular possible future event, the
more likely it is that this future event will be inferred. This assumption was tested
in the second study (van den Broek & Husebye, 1991, based on a subsample
from Husebye-Hartmann, 1992). In this study, 101 college students read 38 brief
story stems (based on McKoon & Ratcliff, 1989) and were asked to provide
continuations to each story stem. Subjects were instructed to indicate as quickly
as possible what event they thought would happen next. Thus, the instructions

did not bias toward causal relations. Three versions of these story stems were constructed by systematically varying the amount of sufficiency that was provided for a target inference. For example, consider the following example:

(1)   Story stem:
The angry wife could not hold her temper against her husband any longer; when he put his hand on her shoulder, she picked up a . . .

     High: letter opener
     Medium: fountain pen
     Low: crystal vase
     Target inference: *stab*

Interrater reliability on the three levels of sufficiency was high, $K = .81$, $p <$ .001 (Husebye-Hartmann, 1992). Each subject received only one version of each story stem with versions distributed randomly across subjects. The continuations provided by the subjects were scored with respect to whether they mentioned the target inference.

In general, causal coherence played an important role in the anticipation of upcoming events: 83% of the responses were causally related to their respective story stems. Of primary interest, however, is the frequency with which the target inference was given as a function of the amount sufficiency that the story stem provided, presented in Fig. 19.2. The probability that a particular target event was anticipated was strongly related to the strength of the sufficiency provided by the story stem. Conversely, the number of different nontarget causal inferences declined as the sufficiency for a particular inference increased: On average, the low sufficiency stems produced 6.1 nontarget inferences, the medium sufficiency stems 4.4, and the high sufficiency stems 3.2. Thus, both the probability of generating a particular target inference and the number of alternative inferences was found to be linearly related to the amount of causal support provided by the stem.

In order to rule out the possibility that these patterns were the result of differences in the associative strengths between the last part of each version and the target inference, a control study was conducted in which subjects generated associates to the final parts of the story stems (Husebye-Hartmann, 1992). The frequency with which the target inference was given was very low, $p = .04$, and did not differ across the levels of sufficiency. Thus the results just given are due to the variation in sufficiency, not to differences in word association.

These results support the notion that forward inferences during reading tend to preserve causal coherence. Furthermore, they indicate that the causal constraints provided by the text that has been read so far determine the likelihood that a particular forward inference will be generated. Thus, the expectation of causal

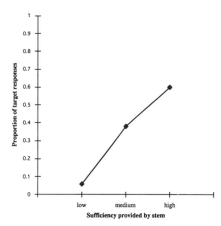

FIG. 19.2. Frequency of forward inferences as a function of high, medium, and low sufficiency provided by text (Study 2, data from Husebye-Hartmann, 1992).

coherence and the constraints provided by the text jointly determine the generation of forward inferences.

Study 3: Causal Sufficiency and Textual Constraints in the Generation of Backward Inferences

The purpose of the third experiment was to investigate the joint role that causal standards and textual constraints play in the generation of global backward inferences. According to the model, readers attempt to construct sufficient explanations for the events that they read. As a result, the model predicts that backward inferences should be causally related to the sentence that the reader is currently processing. In addition, the resulting global inferences should complement the local inferences so that the combination provides sufficient explanation for the sentence that is currently being read.

In order to investigate these two predictions, we reanalyzed the data on backward inferences by Myers and Duffy (1990). In this study, 40 college students read sentence pairs that varied systematically in the extent to which the first sentence (the antecedent) provided causal sufficiency for the second sentence (the consequent). Subjects read the sentence pairs at their own pace and were asked to write down a statement that could reasonably fit between the two sentences. Thus, subjects were prompted to generate backward inferences by accessing background knowledge. The responses were analyzed according to the same criteria for causality that were used in the previous studies.

With respect to the first prediction, the majority of backward inferences (82%) were causally related to the consequent. A large proportion (57%) provided strong sufficiency. The necessity and sufficiency provided by the first sentence influenced the extent to which the backward inferences were causally related to the consequent, however. Virtually all causal responses (93%) occurred when the first sentence provided partial, but not complete, sufficiency for the second sentence. Most responses that did not reflect a causal relation (90%) occurred when the story stem did not provide any causal support for the consequence or when it provided a completely sufficient explanation by itself, thereby obviating the need for additional inferences to provide sufficiency. When an inference *was* produced in the latter circumstances, it provided strong necessity and sufficiency for the current statement. In these cases, the backward inferences predominantly provided complete alternative explanations or were redundant with those provided in the prior text. Interestingly, Myers and Duffy (1990) found that it took subjects a significantly longer time to produce backward inferences in these two conditions. This suggests that backward inferences are likely to be causal when the statement that precedes the current statement provides partial causal explanation. When the preceding statement contains no seeds for causality, the elaboration is likely to not be causal either; conversely, when the preceding statement provides sufficient explanation for the current statement, no additional causal inferences are needed. These results concur with earlier suggestions that in such circumstances frequently no meaningful relation is established between preceding text and the current statement (cf. Myers et al., 1987; van den Broek, 1990b). This pattern of findings illustrates how textual support and standards of coherence together determine the generation of inferences.

If inferences are generated in order to attain standards for coherence, then the combination of local and global inferences should provide sufficient causal explanation for the consequent. Raters read subjects' responses and judged whether necessity or sufficiency were present. Fig. 19.3 displays the proportion of local/global inference combinations that provided complete necessity and sufficiency as a function of the necessity and sufficiency provided by local inferences (i.e., the first sentence) alone. Apparently, the combination of elaboration and story stem together tend to provide very strong necessity and sufficiency for the current statement, indicating that the global inferences indeed complemented the local inferences. The only exception concerned situations in which the story stem provided very little support for further causal explanation, although even here the increase in causal explanation provided by the elaboration was considerable.

These results suggest that global backward inferences tend to help the reader attain his or her standards of causal coherence. Backward inferences provide necessity and sufficiency for the statement that is currently being read but, as predicted by the model, the exact relation of the inferred global relations to the current statement is dependent on the amount of causal support that is provided by local inferences. Global inferences provide sufficiency and are generated quickly (Myers & Duffy, 1990) when the amount of causal support that is provided by the immediately preceding text is intermediate. When the preceding

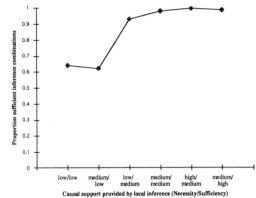

FIG. 19.3. The proportion of local/global inference combinations that provided complete necessity and sufficiency as a function of causal support provided by first sentence alone (Study 3, data from Myers & Duffy, 1990).

text has little or no causal relation to the current statement or provides a complete causal explanation, backward inferences are difficult to generate.

THE ROLE OF CAUSAL STANDARDS IN THE GENERATION OF INFERENCES: EVIDENCE FROM ON-LINE TASKS

The results obtained in the production tasks attest to the psychological validity of the reading model. When readers were asked to produce elaborations, they generated inferences that were causal in nature and, more specifically, that contributed to attaining the standard of causal sufficiency. In order to find out whether such inferences actually are generated spontaneously and effortlessly during reading, the model's predictions and the findings given earlier need to be tested by methods that do not explicitly prompt readers to generate elaborations. The results of several studies that use tasks requiring automatic responses provide evidence on the spontaneous generation of inferences. Space limitations prevent a complete discussion of these studies, so we now just summarize some of the findings that have an immediate bearing on the issue of standards of causal coherence (for reviews, see Singer, in press; van den Broek, in press).

The results of reading-speed studies indicate that reading slows down when the reader encounters a statement for which local causal coherence is either completely lacking (Bloom, Fletcher, van den Broek, Reitz, & Shapiro, 1990; Klin & Myers, 1993; Thurlow, 1991), or when an explanation is provided but is not sufficient, for example when the current event requires the reinstatement of a goal or of other prior text in order to be sufficiently explained (Bloom et al., 1990; Dopkins et al., 1993; Thurlow, 1991). The results of naming and lexical decision studies show that events that are predicted to be reinstated in order to provide sufficient explanation for a focal statement are more highly activated after the focal statement than before (Dopkins et al., 1993; Klin & Myers, 1993; Thurlow, 1991). Furthermore, such reinstatements occurred *only* when the immediately preceding statement did not provide full sufficiency (Thurlow, 1991). Similarly, verification times for facts from background knowledge are faster immediately following statements for which such background information provides sufficient explanation than following control statements (Singer, Halldorson, Lear, & Andrusiak, 1992). Findings such as these suggest that readers slow down when they encounter situations in which the current event is not sufficiently explained by the immediately preceding statement, and that they reinstate or draw on background knowledge to activate information that provides the missing sufficient explanation. In addition to being generated during reading, these inferences appear to be incorporated into the memory representation of the text. Events that are hypothesized to have been reinstated during initial reading speed up recognition of their consequences in subsequent memory tasks (van den Broek & Lorch, 1993).

With respect to forward inferences, the naming speed of target words for which the immediately preceding text provides highly sufficient explanation has been found to be shorter than that for the same items when the preceding text provides no sufficiency (Murray et al., 1993).

These findings converge nicely with those obtained in the production tasks. Backward inferences are generated when they are needed to provide sufficient causal explanation for the current event. The current event, in turn, elicits forward inferences for which it provides sufficient support. The convergence across experimental tasks provides strong evidence for the view that the reader attempts to achieve coherence and engages in inferential processes to do so.

STANDARDS OF REFERENTIAL COHERENCE

The findings on the inferential processes that take place in order to establish causal coherence have remarkable parallels to those on the processes that are involved in attaining *referential coherence*. Referential coherence is established when the reader is clear about to what or whom the referents in the current sentence refer. For example, in the statement pair "The doctor asked the patient to enter. She asked the child where he hurt", referential coherence would require the reader to identify that "she" refers to "the doctor" and "the child" to "the patient." *Anaphoric* relations connect referents to objects, persons, and so on in the prior text (analogous to backward causal inferences), whereas *cataphoric* relations refer to likely objects, persons, and so on in upcoming text (comparable to forward causal inferences).

The notion that readers actively pursue global inferences in order to attain anaphoric coherence has extensive empirical support. For example, there is ample evidence that readers engage in reinstatement searches in order to restore referential or anaphoric coherence to their understanding of a text. When anaphoric resolution is required to restore referential coherence, readers will slow their reading rates (Garrod & Sanford, 1990; Haviland & Clark, 1974) and differentially activate appropriate antecedents while simultaneously suppressing inappropriate antecedents (Gernsbacher, 1989; 1990; Gernsbacher & Faust, 1991; McKoon & Ratcliff, 1980; O'Brien, Duffy, & Myers, 1986). Such anaphoric resolution is carried out via a parallel backward search in which potential antecedents are activated (O'Brien, Plewes, & Albrecht, 1990). These findings demonstrate, first, that a breakdown of local anaphoric coherence evokes additional cognitive activity and, second, that this activity includes global inferences if these are required to restore referential coherence.

Similarly, cataphoric constructions prolong the activation of a referent, apparently because the reader expects that the referent will be a topic in subsequent sentences. For example, readers are more likely to sustain activation for *egg* in the cataphoric sentence "And then the man picked up *this* egg" than in the noncataphoric statement "And then the man picked up *the* egg" (Gernsbacher & Shroyer, 1989). Thus, the notion that readers' standards for referential coherence dictate the patterns of activations and inferences during reading has considerable psychological validity.

In sum, readers attempt to attain standards of referential coherence much in the same way as they attempt to construct causal coherence while they are reading. The similarity in findings for two different standards of coherence lends credence to the notion that the reader's assessment that he or she is comprehending the events in the text drives inferential processes.

DISCUSSION

In this chapter, we have argued that readers maintain standards of coherence that determine at each point in the text whether they have adequately understood what they are reading and whether they need to engage in further inference generation in order to achieve complete understanding. The results of the production task studies and those of studies that use less inference-provoking tasks indicate that readers attempt to maintain causal coherence as they proceed through a text. Remarkably similar results have been reported on referential coherence.

With respect to both causal and referential coherence, global backward inferences, in the form of reinstatements and elaborations, occur when a matching of the current statement and information that is still activated from the previous reading cycle does not meet the standard of sufficient explanation or anaphoric clarity. These global inferences, together with local inferences of relations between adjacent sentences in the text, attain the standards of causal and referential coherence.

Standards for causal and referential coherence also influence the generation of inferences about the upcoming text. With respect to causal coherence, readers expect upcoming text to be causally related to the text that they currently are reading. In particular, they expect that the current text is necessary, and thereby provides at least partial sufficiency, for the upcoming text. The stronger the sufficiency of the current text for a particular upcoming event, the more likely readers infer that event. With respect to referential coherence, cataphors create expectations that particular objects, persons, and so on will be mentioned in upcoming text and hence will result in continued activation.

Together, the findings on causal and referential relations demonstrate that inferential processes during reading are strongly determined by the extent to which they satisfy readers' need for coherence. Theoretical accounts of the reading comprehension process therefore need to include reference to the readers' needs for coherence. Inferences serve a *function*. Whether this function is fulfilled determines whether additional inferences will be generated.

The notion of readers' standards for coherence amplifies existing accounts of reading comprehension in several ways. First, the focus on function-driven inferential processes makes the reader central in the description of inferential processes. Although support from the text is vital, it is the reader who conducts the inferences and it is the reader who decides (implicitly or explicitly) when comprehension is adequate and when it is not.

Second, the model allows the reconciliation of two groups of process models that seem to give contradictory accounts of reading. Some theoretical models of reading comprehension (e.g., Kintsch, 1988; McKoon & Ratcliff, 1992) emphasize that inferential processes frequently are limited to those that identify local relations between the information that is currently being read and information that is still activated from the previous reading cycle. In these models, global relations to information that preceded the current event by several sentences or to background knowledge play a minor role. Thus, these models emphasize how comprehension in many circumstances involves a rather limited set of inferences. A second group of models (Graesser, 1981; Graesser & Clark, 1985; Singer, in press; Singer et al., 1992; Trabasso et al., 1984; Trabasso, van den Broek, & Suh, 1989) emphasizes the importance of global relations to successful comprehension. In contrast to the first group of models, these models are built on the assumption that readers frequently detect a wide variety of connections.

These two groups of models may not be as far apart as they seem. On the one hand, proponents of the models that emphasize local inferences state that time-consuming and effortful global inferences *can* occur, *provided that such inferences are required for comprehension* (Kintsch, 1988; McKoon & Ratcliff, 1992). On the other hand, proponents of models that emphasize the global inferences that readers may make generally describe the inferences that their models posit as constituting the *idealized* coherence that would be constructed by a motivated reader who has ample time and opportunity to identify all possible local and global relations between the various components of a text. Thus, models of reading comprehension that emphasize local relations leave open the possibility that other inferences are generated during reading, in particular when these "other" inferences are required for comprehension, whereas models that focus on global inferences acknowledge that, during regular reading, only a subset of all possible global inferences actually may be made. Thus, it would seem that the two types of models may bracket the inferential processes that take place during reading: "Local" models provide the lower boundary or bracket and "global" models provide the upper boundary or bracket on inferential processes during reading (cf. van den Broek et al., 1993). In this view, readers' inferential activities can range from those described by "local" models to those described by "global" models with most readers falling somewhere in between these extremes.

The question, then, is where these two types of models meet. What are the requirements for comprehension that make readers generate inferences beyond those described by "local" models? And what determines which subset of all possible inferences captured by "global" models are likely to be made? We propose that the standards for causal and referential coherence are prime candidates for the "requirements for comprehension". On the one hand, the standards dictate when a reader makes inferences beyond those that are local. On the other hand, they indicate that potential inferences differ in their importance for comprehension and thus in the likelihood that they are generated. In this view, "local" and "global" models of reading comprehension capture the lower and upper boundaries of a dimension of varying degrees of inferential activities. In describing the subset of possible inferences that are "required for comprehension," the current model describes the modal reader implied by both "local" and "global" models.

Third, the current model suggests that an important area of future research is the systematic investigation of factors that influence a reader's standards. Variations in standards may result from inter- and intra-individual differences as well as from differences in circumstances imposed by the task. Interindividually, readers may differ in the strictness of their criteria. For example, poor readers have been found to maintain lower standards for coherence and therefore may be satisfied more easily than good readers. But interindividual differences also occur within the group of good readers. For example, although most skilled readers are able to gain substantial understanding and appreciation of the coherence in novels such as Tolstoy's *Anna Karenin* and even Joyce's *Finnegan's Wake*, such understanding and perception of coherence is rather meager when compared to that of an expert in Russian or English literature. Intraindividually, readers may vary their criteria as a result of their current levels of motivation and their reading goals. Thus, standards of coherence may be set quite differently when one is reading an article while waiting in the airport for the arrival of a plane than when studying for an examination or reading a novel of high interest.

Fourth, regardless of intra- and inter-individual differences, the extent to which a reader will attain his or her desired levels of coherence is heavily influenced by the opportunities provided by the circumstances. For example, when the reader is encouraged to read as quickly as possible, the level of inference generation will be close to that posited by a "local" model of reading. In contrast, when ample time and opportunity are given or when additional inference generation is encouraged, then the "global" model of reading comprehension may provide a more accurate depiction of the inferential process. As a final example, because global inferences may require the reader to access his or her background knowledge, a reader's success in attaining standards for coherence will depend on his or her expertise in the domain described by the text.

The emphasis of this chapter has been on two standards of coherence, causally sufficient explanation and referential clarity, as determinants of inferential activity. Other standards may operate as well. Readers of fables, for example, may entertain the standard that the story contains some moral lesson, whereas readers of detective stories may set the additional standard that they identify the murderer. In addition, the standards not only influence what readers do to attain coherence, they also lead to some speculation as to what happens when the standards are explicitly contradicted. This occurs, for example, when the reader encounters *inconsistencies* in the text. The current model suggests that if the search for coherence takes the form of a spread of activation or construction-integration process (cf. Kintsch, 1988), as suggested by the findings on anaphoric resolution, then a reader will not only detect overlap or connections between activated concepts but also inconsistencies between these concepts. When an inconsistency is detected during the memory or background-knowledge search, additional inferential processes are likely to be conducted in order to resolve the inconsistency.

This account implies that inconsistencies are noticed when the two inconsistent pieces of information are active at the same moment. This is likely to happen when the inconsistent pieces of information are activated during consecutive comprehension cycles (i.e., when local coherence usually is established). It can also occur, however, when global inferences (re)activate information from the prior text or extratextual information, or when prior information is so strongly encoded that its activation easily reaches threshold (cf. Dopkins et al., 1993; Klin & Myers, 1993; O'Brien et al., 1990). In contrast, an inconsistency between the current event and information from prior text or background knowledge is unlikely to be detected if local relations provide adequate coherence for the current event. In this case, no search of memory for prior text or background knowledge is initiated and hence the inconsistent information will not be activated simultaneously with the current event. Thus, whether a global inconsistency is detected depends on the readers' standard of coherence and on the extent of the resulting inferential processes. This is nicely exemplified by an anecdote about Nobel-prize winning physicist Paul Dirac (Hovis & Kragh, 1993). One of Dirac's friends gave him Dostoevski's *Crime and Punishment* to read. After he had finished the book, the friend asked Dirac if he had enjoyed the book. Dirac's only comment was, " It is nice, but in one of the chapters the author makes a mistake. He describes the sun as rising twice in a day." For the highly mathematical mind of Dirac, the temporal information was strongly encoded and hence the inconsistency was glaring. Luckily, this inconsistency escapes most readers and therefore does not interfere with their enjoyment of the book.

In sum, readers do not make inferences simply because they are *there* to be made. Instead, they make backward and forward inferences in order to create a representation that is coherent vis à vis the standards of coherence that they employ. The inclusion of standards of coherence in models of reading not only extends the generality of existing models, but also facilitates the investigation of individual differences during reading. Only by including standards for coherence in our models can we identify the circumstances under which a reader is likely to generate global and local inferences.

ACKNOWLEDGMENTS

We would like to express our gratitude to Jerome L. Myers and Arthur C. Graesser for generously sharing their data with us, and to Robert F. Lorch, Jr. for his thoughtful comments on an earlier version of this paper. The research presented in this chapter was supported by the Center for Research in Learning, Perception, and Cognition at the University of Minnesota through a grant from the National Institute of Child Health and Human Development (HD-07151). Parts of this research was reported at the annual meeting of the American Educational Research Association, Chicago, 1991.

REFERENCES

Black, J. B., & Bower, G. H. (1980). Story understanding as problem solving. *Poetics, 9*, 223–250.

Bloom, C. P., Fletcher, C. R., van den Broek, P., Reitz, L., & Shapiro, B. P. (1990). An on-line assessment of causal reasoning during text comprehension. *Memory & Cognition, 18*, 65–71.

Dopkins, S., Klin, C., & Myers, J. L. (1993). The accessibility of information about goals during the processing of narrative texts. *Journal of Experimental Psychology: Learning, Memory and Cognition, 19*, 70–80.

Garrod, S., & Sanford, A. (1990). Referential processing in reading: Focusing on roles and individuals. In D. A. Balota, G. B. Flores d'Arcais, & K. Rayner (Eds.), *Comprehension processes in reading* (pp. 465–484). Hillsdale, NJ: Lawrence Erlbaum Associates.

Gernsbacher, M. A. (1989). Mechanisms that improve referential access. *Cognition, 32*, 99–156.

Gernsbacher, M. A. (1990). *Language comprehension as structure building*. Hillsdale, NJ: Lawrence Erlbaum Associates.

Gernsbacher, M. A., & Faust, M. (1991). The role of suppression in sentence comprehension. In G. B. Simpson (Ed.), *Understanding word and sentence* (pp. 97–128). North-Holland: Elsevier.

Gernsbacher, M. A., & Shroyer, S. (1989). The cataphoric use of the indefinite *this* in spoken narratives. *Memory & Cognition, 17*, 536–540.

Goldman, S. R., & Varnhagen, C. K. (1986). Memory for embedded and sequential story structures. *Journal of Memory and Language, 25*, 401–418.

Graesser, A. C. (1981). *Prose comprehension beyond the word.* New York/Heidelberg/Berlin: Springer-Verlag.

Graesser, A. C., & Clark, L. F. (1985). *The structures and procedures of implicit knowledge.* Norwood, NJ: Ablex.

Graesser, A. C., Robertson, S. P., & Anderson, P. A. (1981). Incorporating inferences in narrative representations: A study of how and why. *Cognitive Psychology, 13*, 1–26.

Husebye-Hartmann, E. A. (1992). *Causal elaborative inferences in text comprehension: Implications for psychology and education.* Unpublished doctoral dissertation, University of Minnesota.

Hart, M. L. A., & Honore, A. M. (1985). *Causation in the law.* Oxford: Clarendon.

Haviland, S. E., & Clark, H. H. (1974). What's new? Acquiring new information as a process in comprehension. *Journal of Verbal Learning and Verbal Behavior, 13*, 512–521.

Hovis, R. C., & Kragh, H. (1993). P. A. M. Dirac and the beauty of physics. *Scientific American, 268*, 104–109.

Keenan, J. M., Baillet, S. D., & Brown, P. (1984). The effects of causal cohesion on comprehension and memory. *Journal of Verbal Learning and Verbal Behavior, 23*, 115–126.

Kintsch, W. (1988). The role of knowledge in discourse comprehension: A construction-integration model. *Psychological Review, 95*, 163–182.

Kintsch, W. (1992). How readers construct situation models for stories: The role of syntactic cues and causal inferences. In A. F. Healy, S. M. Kosslyn, & R. M. Shiffrin (Eds.), *From learning processes to cognitive processes: Essays in honor of William K. Estes*, (Vol. 2, pp. 261–278). Hillsdale, NJ : Lawrence Erlbaum Associates.

Kintsch, W. A., & van Dijk, T. A. (1978). Toward a model of text comprehension and production. *Psychological Review, 85*, 363–394.

Klin, C. M. & Myers, J. L. (1993). Reinstatement of causal information during reading. *Journal of Experimental Psychology: Learning, Memory and Cognition, 19*, 554–560.

Mackie, J. L. (1980). *The cement of the universe.* Oxford: Clarendon.

Magliano, J. P., & Graesser, A. C. (1991). A three-pronged method for studying inference generation in literary text. *Poetics, 20*, 193–232.

McKoon, G., & Ratcliff, R. (1980). Priming in item recognition: The organization of propositions in memory for text. *Journal of Verbal Learning and Verbal Behavior, 19*, 369–386.

McKoon, G., & Ratcliff, R. (1989). Semantic associations and elaborative inference. *Journal of Experimental Psychology: Learning, Memory and Cognition, 15*, 326–338.

McKoon, G., & Ratcliff, R. (1992). Inferences during reading. *Psychological Review, 99*, 440–466.

Murray, J. D., Klin, C. M., & Myers, J. L. (1993). Forward inferences about specific events during reading. *Journal of Memory and Language, 32*, 464–473.

Myers, J. L., & Duffy, S. A. (1990). Causal inferences and text memory. In A. C. Graesser & G. H. Bower (Eds.), *Psychology of learning and motivation: Inferences and text comprehension* (Vol. 25, pp. 35–51). San Diego: Academic.

Myers, J. L., Shinjo, M., & Duffy, S. A. (1987). Degree of causal relatedness and memory. *Journal of Memory and Language, 26*, 453–465.

O'Brien, E. J., Duffy, S. A., & Myers, J. L. (1986). Anaphoric inference during reading. *Journal of Experimental Psychology: Learning, Memory, and Cognition, 12*, 346–352.

O'Brien, E. J., & Myers, J. L. (1987). The role of causal connections in the retrieval of text. *Memory & Cognition, 15*, 419–427.

O'Brien, E. J., Plewes, P. S., & Albrecht, J. E. (1990). Antecedent retrieval processes. *Journal of Experimental Psychology: Learning, Memory, and Cognition, 16*, 241–249.

O'Brien, E. J., Shank, D. M., Myers, J. L., Rayner, K. (1988). Elaborative inferences during reading: Do they occur occur on-line? *Journal of Experimental Psychology: Learning, Memory, and Cognition, 14*, 410–420.

Potts, G. R., Keenan, J. M., & Golding. J. M. (1988). Assessing the occurrence of elaborative inferences: Lexical decision versus naming. *Journal of Verbal Behavior and Verbal Learning, 27*, 399–415.

Singer, M. (in press). Inference generation during reading. In M. A. Gernsbacher (Ed.), *Handbook of psycholinguistics*. New York: Academic.

Singer, M., Halldorson, M., Lear, J. C., & Andrusiak, P. (1992). Validation of causal bridging inferences in discourse understanding. *Journal of Memory and Language, 31*, 507–524.

Thurlow, R. E. (1991). *The inference of causal antecedents during the reading of narratives.* Unpublished doctoral dissertation, University of Minnesota.

Trabasso, T., Secco, T., & van den Broek, P. W. (1984). Causal cohesion and story coherence. In H. Mandl, N. L. Stein, & T. Trabasso (Eds.), *Learning and comprehension of text* (pp. 83–111). Hillsdale, NJ: Lawrence Erlbaum Associates.

Trabasso, T., & van den Broek, P. W. (1985). Causal thinking and the representation of narrative events. *Journal of Memory and Language, 24*, 612–630.

Trabasso, T., van den Broek, P. W., & Suh, S. Y. (1989). Logical necessity and transitivity of causal relations in stories. *Discourse Processes, 12*, 1–25.

van den Broek, P. (1988). The effects of causal relations and hierarchical position on the importance of story statements. *Journal of Memory and Language, 27*, 1–22.

van den Broek, P. W. (1990a). The causal inference maker: Towards a process model of inference generation in text comprehension. In D. A. Balota, G. B. Flores d'Arcais, K. Rayner (Eds.), *Comprehension processes in reading* (pp. 423–445). Hillsdale, NJ: Lawrence Erlbaum Associates.

van den Broek, P. W. (1990b). Causal inferences in the comprehension of narrative texts. In A. C. Graesser & G. H. Bower (Eds.), *Psychology of learning and motivation: Inferences and text comprehension, 25*, 175–194. San Diego: Academic Press.

van den Broek, P. W. (in press). Comprehension and memory of narrative texts: Inferences and coherence. In M. A. Gernsbacher (Ed.), *Handbook of psycholinguistics*. New York: Academic Press.

van den Broek, P. W., Fletcher, C. R., Risden, K. (1993). Investigations of inferential processes in reading: A theoretical and methodological integration. *Discourse Processes, 16*, 169–180.

van den Broek, P. W., & Husebye, E. (1991), *Elaborative inferences in comprehension of narrative texts*. Paper presented at the Annual Meeting of the American Educational Research Association, Chicago, IL.

van den Broek, P. W., & Lorch, R. F., Jr. (1993). Causal relations in memory for narrative texts: Evidence from a priming task for network representations. *Discourse Processes, 16*, 75–98.

van den Broek, P. W., Rohleder, L., & Narváez, D. (in press). Causal inferences in the comprehension of literary texts. In R. J. Kreuz & M. S. McNealy (Eds.), *The empirical study of literature*. Hillsdale, NJ: Lawrence Erlbaum Associates.

van de Velde, R. G. (1989). Man, verbal text, inferencing, and coherence. In W. Heydrich, F. Neubauer, J. S. Petofi, & E. Sozer (Eds.), *Connexity and coherence: Analysis of text and discourse*. New York: Walter de Gruyter.

van Dijk, T. A., & Kintsch, W. (1983). *Strategies of discourse comprehension*. New York: Academic Press.

20 Distinctions Among Reading Situations

Robert F. Lorch, Jr.
Madeline A. Klusewitz
Elizabeth Pugzles Lorch
University of Kentucky

TWO MEANINGS OF STRATEGY IN READING RESEARCH

The concept of *strategy* plays an important role in theorizing about reading comprehension processes, but the term is employed in different senses by different theorists. One important use of the term is to refer to systematic ways in which readers process text in response to cognitive limitations. For example, Frazier and Rayner (1982) hypothesized that readers' sentence parsings are governed by preferences for structurally simple interpretations (e.g., late closure and minimal attachment strategies). In addition, several theorists have hypothesized that readers use strategies to cope with the capacity limits of working memory. These strategies involve simple rules for identifying information to be retained in memory that is likely to serve as an effective context for the integration of subsequent statements in the text (e.g., Albrecht & O'Brien, 1993; Fletcher, 1986; Fletcher & Bloom, 1988; Kintsch & van Dijk, 1978; O'Brien & Albrecht, 1992). In both of these examples, readers appear to follow simple processing principles for coping with memory limitations, probably without any awareness of doing so. It is this meaning of the term *strategy* that is most often intended by cognitive psychologists studying reading.

The term *strategy* is also frequently used by educational psychologists to refer to the adaptations that readers make to deal effectively with the demands of different reading situations. (We use the term *reading situation* to mean a specific type of text read for a specific purpose; e.g., "Read a short story to do a critique" or "Read a store catalog to window shop.") Although educational psychologists are very much interested in how readers cope with limitations on their processing abilities, they are equally concerned with the types of adjustments readers make to the specific requirements of different reading situations. Adults read many types of materials for many different purposes. Some reading situations entail the construction of a coherent text representation; some reading situations involve a search for specific information; other reading situations implicate study skills (e.g., memorization); and still other situations emphasize aesthetic purposes for reading. Taking a broad view of the variety of reading experiences familiar to mature readers, it is apparent that reading situations differ on a number of dimensions that are likely to affect the nature of reading behavior. Some texts genres have schematic structures, whereas other genres are less constrained. Some text content is abstract, whereas some is concrete. Some tasks demand close attention to the text, whereas other tasks permit less careful reading. Thus, over different reading situations, readers may adjust their reading speed, the way in which they distribute their attention over content, their use of study techniques, their standards of coherence (van den Broek, Risden, & Husebye-Hartmann, this volume), the nature and extent of the inferences they draw, and many other characteristics of reading behavior.

In this chapter, we are concerned with strategies in the sense of adjustments to different reading situations. Our goal is not to characterize the types of processing strategies readers use in different circumstances; that would be premature given our current state of knowledge. Rather, we will focus on the kinds of distinctions adult readers make across the range of reading situations with which they are familiar. Our goal is to present a typology of reading situations based on readers' introspections about the cognitive requirements of different reading materials and purposes for reading. Our belief is that a mature reader's selection of a processing strategy in a given reading situation depends on his or her individual typology of reading situations.

THE IMPORTANCE OF CONDITIONAL KNOWLEDGE TO STRATEGIC READING

Conditional knowledge (Paris, Lipson, & Wixson, 1983), or knowledge of when and why a given reading strategy should be employed, is essential to *strategic* reading. A reader with a wide repertoire of reading strategies cannot be an effective reader if he or she does not make relevant discriminations concerning when to apply particular strategies (Paris et al., 1983). Presumably, a reader's selection of a given strategy depends, at least in part, on an analysis of the cognitive requirements of the reading task at hand. Conversely, how people vary their reading behavior across different reading situations depends on distinctions they make among the situations. As Garner (1990) emphasized, strategies are goal driven and goals vary across different settings, or contexts. Therefore, attempts to understand strategic behavior must take the setting into account. Given this perspective, a reasonable first step toward a theory of strategy use in reading is to construct a typology of reading situations reflecting the distinctions readers make with respect to how they read.

RELATED RESEARCH

There is little research on the distinctions readers make among reading situations. One study by Greaney and Neuman (1990) examined various reading goals distinguished by children. Their data revealed three distinct reading goals: (a) reading for utility (e.g., "helps me at school"), (b) reading for enjoyment (e.g., "it is exciting"), and (c) reading to escape (e.g., "helps me relax"). Although experienced readers make similar distinctions among reading goals, they make many finer distinctions as well (Lorch, Lorch, & Klusewitz, 1993).

Lorch et al. (1993) examined distinctions college students make among reading situations. Readers sorted descriptions of reading situations (e.g., "Read a history book for a research paper"; "Read a bridal magazine to plan a wedding") according to how they believed they read in each situation. Hierarchical clustering analyses of the sorting data revealed 10 distinct categories of reading situations. Ratings of the cognitive demands of the situations supported the typology induced from the sorting data and suggested how readers may alter their reading behavior across the 10 reading situations.

There is reason to believe that the typology suggested by Lorch et al. (1993) underestimates the degree to which college readers discriminate among reading situations. The major distinction readers made was reading for school-related purposes versus reading by personal choice. These two superordinate clusters accounted for a large proportion of variance in the cluster analyses. Because of the salience of this dimension of variability, readers may not have made more subtle discriminations among reading situations. Also, in an attempt to present readers with a wide range of reading situations, some reading categories might not have been adequately represented in the stimulus set and thus never had an opportunity to be identified by the procedure.

The aim of the present study was to determine if readers make finer or different discriminations among reading situations than those identified by Lorch et al. (1993). One way to do this is to provide subjects with a relatively homogenous set of reading situations to categorize. In Experiment 1, subjects were asked to categorize reading situations pertaining to school-related reading only. In Experiment 2, subjects were asked to categorize reading situations pertaining to personal choice reading only. If the salience of the school versus personal choice distinction prevented subjects in the Lorch et al. study from making finer distinctions, then those finer distinctions should emerge in the present study.

EXPERIMENT 1

Of the 10 types of reading situations identified by Lorch et al. (1993), four types represented distinctions among school-related reading situations: (a) reading to prepare for an exam, (b) reading as research in preparation for writing a paper, (c) reading to prepare for class (e.g., preparing for a class discussion), and (d) reading to learn some specific subject matter (e.g., "Read a physics chapter to understand a topic"). Other potential distinctions that might have been anticipated a priori did not emerge. For example, subjects did not discriminate among the different types of exams for which a student might prepare (e.g., multiple choice versus essay). Also, there was no evidence of subjects categorizing reading situations by types of reading materials. For instance, no type emerged corresponding to reading for science courses or reading for English courses. The purpose of Experiment 1 was to determine whether college readers make finer distinctions among school-related reading tasks than were identified by Lorch et al. (1993).

The procedure in Experiment 1 was the same as that used by Lorch et al. (1993) except that subjects were only presented school-related reading situations to categorize. One group of college subjects sorted descriptions of 35 reading situations into categories based on their analysis of how they read in each situation; situations for which their reading behavior was the same were to be grouped together. A second group of subjects was presented the same set of reading situations (uncategorized) and asked to rate each situation on a set of six questions about how they read (e.g., "What is your reading speed?"). The sorting data were analyzed by a hierarchical clustering procedure to identify distinct types of reading situations; the rating data were used to characterize how subjects read for each distinct type.

Method

Phase 1: Sorting Reading Situations

Subjects. Subjects were 88 students from introductory psychology classes at the University of Kentucky. Participation in experiments was a course requirement.

Materials. The materials consisted of most of the reading situations identified as school-related reading situations in the Lorch et al. (1993) study. These situations were selected using the results of a multidimensional scaling analysis of the sorting data in the Lorch et al. study. The scaling results indicate that the major dimension on which reading situations were ordered was a discrimination between school reading tasks versus reading by personal choice. We selected the 35 reading situations that were the best examples of school reading tasks (i.e., most extreme scores on the school/non school dimension) according to the scaling analysis.[1]

Each reading situation specified a reading material (e.g., "Read a math text . . . ") and a purpose for reading the material (e.g., to prepare for an exam). The 35 reading situations were typed on 3" × 5" index cards, one situation per card (see Table 20.1 for a list of all the school-related reading situations). Ten sets of 35 cards were constructed. Finally, a response sheet was constructed containing spaces for subjects to record the results of their sorts. The sheet allowed up to 15 different reading categories to be listed, and also contained a space to list situations that were unfamiliar to the subject.

Procedure. Subjects were presented with a deck of cards and a response sheet. They were told that each index card contained a description of a type of reading material and a purpose for reading the material. Subjects were told to look through the cards and to think about how they read in each situation. The instructions emphasized that the subjects should think about what they do mentally when reading in each situation. Subjects were asked to then sort the cards into piles, putting situations in which they read similarly in the same pile and situations in which they read differently into different piles. Subjects were told not to group the cards together simply because they contained the same type of reading material or the same purpose, but to sort according to the strategies they used in each reading situation. Subjects were allowed to identify reading situations with which they were unfamiliar and omit those items from their sorts.

The only restrictions on sorting were that subjects were told that they had to sort the 35 cards into at least 2 piles and no more than 15 piles. Also, each card could only be included in one pile. The constraints on the number of categories allowed were intended to prevent subjects from being superficial in their judgments (i.e., failing to make any differentiations or judging every situation as unique). Although other investigators have often placed no restrictions on the number of sorting categories (e.g., Miller, 1969), it was decided that the con-

---

[1]The experiments of this study were designed and executed before publication of the Lorch et al. (1993) study. At the time of the design of the current study, the sorting data of the Lorch et al. study had been analyzed by multidimensional scaling analyses and overlapping cluster analyses. The multidimensional scaling analyses were thus used as the basis for identifying appropriate reading situations to include among the stimulus materials of the current study. Subsequently, in response to a reviewer's suggestions, we reanalyzed the sorting data in Lorch et al. using hierarchical cluster analyses. If those analyses had been available at the time we designed the current study, our procedure for selecting materials would have changed to include adequate representation of all the clusters identified in Lorch et al. (1993). Unfortunately, our sampling procedure systematically excluded reading situations from one school reading cluster and one personal choice reading cluster ultimately identified in Lorch et al. This happened because the two clusters were composed of reading situations that were not very extreme with respect to their scores on the major dimension of the multidimensional scaling analysis.

straints would be helpful to subjects given the relative novelty of both the stimulus materials and the judgments required in the task. In fact, there was little evidence that the restrictions on the number of sorting categories represented much of a constraint on subjects' performances. Only one subject used 2 categories and two subjects used all 15 categories. The modal number of categories used was 6; the mean was 7.86, with a standard deviation of 2.58 points.

Phase 2: Rating Reading Situations

Subjects.   Subjects were 23 students from introductory psychology classes at the University of Kentucky. The data of one subject were omitted from analyses because the subject failed to follow instructions. None of the subjects participating in the rating task had participated in the sorting task.

Materials.   A subset of 6 of the 21 questions from the Lorch et al. study was used for the present experiment. Only the 18 questions concerning processing demands of reading situations were considered for inclusion in Experiment 1. Given that the ratings for most of the questions were highly intercorrelated in the Lorch et al. (1993) study, six questions was deemed sufficient to characterize the reading types. The six questions chosen for inclusion were selected because they were useful in discriminating the 10 reading types in the Lorch et al. study and they represented reading behaviors that might easily be examined in a laboratory study. The six questions were:

1. What is your reading speed when you do this type of reading?
2. How much do you test your understanding as you do this type of reading?
3. How much do you use "supports" (e.g., outlining, highlighting, note-taking) when you do this type of reading?
4. How much do you reread when you do this type of reading?
5. How much do you attend to the major points when you do this type of reading?
6. What is your level of concentration when you do this type of reading?

Booklets were constructed for presenting the rating questions. The booklet began with instructions for the rating task, followed by a page containing the six rating questions and the 7-point scale associated with each question, followed by three pages containing the 35 reading situations to be rated.

Procedure.   Subjects were tested in three groups in sessions lasting approximately 1 hour. They were required to rate the 35 reading situations on each of six different questions. Each question was to be rated on a scale of 1 to 7, where 1 represented the minimum and 7 represented the maximum. For example, for the question, "What is your reading speed when you do this type of reading?" 1 would represent minimum speed, and 7 would represent maximum speed. Subjects were told to rate all of the reading situations with respect to the first question, then rate all of the situations with respect to the second question, and so on, until they had completed all six questions.

Results and Discussion

Phase 1: Cluster Analyses of the Sorting Task

The data from the sorting task were assembled into a 35×35 matrix of interitem distances. For each pair of reading situations, the percentage of subjects who sorted the two items into different categories was computed. These distance scores could range between a minimum of 0 (all subjects grouped the two items into the same category) and a maximum 100 (all subjects put the two items into different categories). In calculating these percentages, items that individual subjects indicated were unfamiliar were excluded from the computations (2.11% of the 3,080 items sorted).

A hierarchical cluster analysis (Ward's minimum variance method) was conducted on the sorting data. Clusters were fused if they either accounted for less than 2.5% of the variance in the squared interitem distances or if there were fewer than three items in the cluster. Using these criteria, a seven cluster solution resulted; this solution accounted for 70.6% of the variance in the squared interitem distances. The results of the cluster analysis are presented in Table 20.1. Given that the primary goal of Experiment 1 was to refine the typology of school reading situations identified in Lorch et al. (1993), we organize our descriptions of the seven clusters by reference to the typology in Lorch et al.

One of the four types of school reading situations identified by Lorch et al. (1993) is reading in preparation for an exam. All 14 of the reading situations comprising this type in the Lorch et al. study were included among the materials of Experiment 1. These items, along with one other, were grouped into a superordinate cluster replicating the exam preparation type of Lorch et al. However, the superordinate cluster divided into three subclusters representing distinctions readers make among exam situations. These clusters are labeled Types 1, 2, and 3 in Table 20.1. The first type listed is labeled *reading to memorize*. It consists of study situations that place a heavy emphasis on memory for details (e.g., vocabulary learning). The second type in Table 20.1 is labeled *reading for an essay exam* because each reading situation involves preparation for an essay exam. Finally, the third type is labeled *reading for objective exams*. This cluster consists primarily of reading in preparation for exams based on recognition (e.g., true/false) and cued recall (e.g., short answer). At first glance, this type appears very similar in its cognitive demands to reading to memorize. Perhaps the basis for the distinction is that the material to be tested is more clearly specified for the

TABLE 20.1
Types of School Reading Situations Identified by Cluster Analyses

Type 1: Reading to Memorize

Read a foreign language textbook to learn verb conjunctions
Read a chapter in a foreign language text to prepare for a vocabulary test
Read a geology text to prepare for a lab test on identifying minerals
Read a biology text to prepare for a lab exam on anatomy identification
Read a chemistry chapter to learn to identify particular compounds
Read a chemistry text to prepare for a lab exam on identifying compounds

Type 2: Reading for an Essay Esam

Read a history text to prepare for an essay exam
Read short stories to prepare for an essay exam in an English lit course
Read a biology text to prepare for an essay test

Type 3: Reading for Objective Exams

Read class notes to review for an exam
Read a chemistry text to prepare for a short-answer test
Read a psychology text to prepare for a true-false test
Read a physics text to prepare for a multiple-choice exam
Read a political science text to prepare for a short-answer exam
Read a math text to prepare for an exam

Type 4: Reading to Write Literature Papers

Read a Shakespeare play to write a paper on a character
Read a short story to do a critique
Read a novel to write a review paper for a literature class
Read a novel to write an essay
Read a selection of poems to write a critical essay

Type 5: Reading to Write Research Papers

Read an article in an encyclopedia to research a topic for a paper
Read a *Scientific American* article for research for a class
Read an article in a medical journal for a research paper
Read a psychology article for a research paper
Read a history book for a resarch paper

Type 6: Reading to Prepare for Class

Read a psychology chapter for a class discussion
Read a biology chapter to review basic concepts
Read class notes to prepare for class
Read a newspaper article on the Middle East for a political science class
Read a chapter in a sociology text to supplement lectures
Read a chapter of philosopy for a class discussion

Type 7: Reading Selectively

Read a psychology text in order to apply the information to a problem
Read a history chapter to do an outline
Read a math text to learn how to do a particular type of problem
Read a text on government to outline a chapter

reading to memorize type than for the reading for objective exams type. For example, students usually know quite precisely what vocabulary terms will be tested in a language class. In contrast, only the general domain relevant to the test is specified in the case of a multiple-choice exam in physics. In sum, the reading for exam preparation type of the Lorch et al. (1993) study was partitioned into three distinct types in the present experiment.

A second type identified by Lorch et al. (1993) was reading to research a topic, usually in preparation to write a paper. This type was clearly replicated in Experiment 1 by a superordinate cluster. The superordinate cluster contained 10 of the 11 reading situations from Lorch et al. that were included among the items sampled for Experiment 1. The superordinate cluster was divided into two distinct clusters in the present experiment, however, indicating that readers make finer discriminations among research reading situations than was evident in the Lorch et al. data. The first cluster is labeled *reading to write literature papers* and the second is labeled *reading to write research papers* in Table 20.1. Although both types involve reading in preparation for writing a paper, the type of reading differs for the two types. All of the reading situations listed under reading to write literature papers involve critical, subjective reading of English literature. In contrast, the situations listed under reading to write research papers involve critical, objective reading of scientific or factual materials.

A third type of reading identified by Lorch et al. was reading in preparation for a class. Of the seven reading situations sampled from this type for the current experiment, six were grouped together into the same cluster. This cluster is labeled *reading to prepare* in Table 20.1. Thus, this type was replicated in Experiment 1.

The fourth type identified in the Lorch et al. study was labeled *reading to learn*. Unfortunately, only three of the seven reading situations making up this type were included in the item sample of the current experiment (see Footnote 1). Two of these reading situations were grouped in the final type identified in Experiment 1, suggesting some connection between the two clusters. However, the overlap is insufficient to evaluate the relation between the clusters. The seventh cluster of Experiment 1 does appear to merit a different description than the fourth cluster of Lorch et al. We have labeled the type *reading selectively* because all four reading situations grouped in this category involve reading for specific information to be applied in a particular task. For example, reading to do an outline requires selecting out the most important ideas in a text and determining their relationships. Similarly, reading a math text to learn how to do a particular type of problem involves identifying the information relevant to the specific demands of the learning task. Finally, we should note that the selective reading type was grouped with the class preparation type into a superordinate cluster distinct from the other two superordinate clusters corresponding to research reading and exam preparation.

In sum, the typology of school reading situations that emerged from the sorting data of Experiment 1 replicates and extends the typology suggested in the Lorch et al. (1993) study. Lorch et al. distinguished four types of school reading situations. The results of Experiment 1 call for a partitioning of the exam preparation type of Lorch et al. into three distinct types of exam preparation. In addition, reading to research was partitioned into researching literature papers and researching objective factual papers. The class preparation type of Lorch et al. replicated in Experiment 1. Finally, the reading to learn type identified by Lorch et al. was not adequately represented in the item sample of Experiment 1, so it is difficult to assess its relation to the selective reading type identified in Experiment 1.

Phase 2: Rating Analyses

For each of the seven school reading types, the mean rating was computed across subjects and reading situations for each of the six questions. For each of the six questions, a multivariate analysis of variance was conducted to determine whether there were systematic differences among the seven types. All six of these preliminary tests demonstrated reliable differences among the seven types; smallest approximate F (6, 17) = 4.54, $p < .006$. Additional tests were conducted to determine the pattern of differences among the reading types. For each of the six questions, the mean rating for each type was compared with the mean rating across the remaining six types while controlling family-wise error rate at the .05 level for a set of seven contrasts (i.e., Bonferroni procedure). The results of these comparisons are summarized in Table 20.2.

The purpose of the rating data was to provide a characterization of reading for

TABLE 20.2
Mean Ratings by Question for the School Reading "Types"

	Questions					
Type	Speed	Test Understanding	Use Supports	Reread	Attend Major Points	Concentrate
Memory	2.862[b]	5.797[a]	5.442[a]	5.428[a]	5.877	5.696[a]
Essay exam	3.420	5.768[a]	4.971	4.536[a]	5.609	5.696[a]
Other exams	3.645	5.847[a]	4.949[a]	4.855[a]	5.891[a]	5.316
Literature	4.209	4.087[b]	3.183[b]	3.487	5.409	5.217
Research	4.374	4.052[b]	4.296	3.539	5.130	4.383
Prepare	4.957[a]	3.246[b]	3.326[b]	2.442[b]	4.768[b]	3.507[b]
Selective	4.000	4.163[b]	4.641	3.380[b]	5.446	4.011[b]
Mean	3.942	4.686	4.376	3.960	5.443	4.807

Note. Ratings typed in boldface and marked with letters are significantly different from the mean rating across the other six types; an "a" ("b") indicates the mean for the type was higher (lower) than the mean across the other six types. All t-tests were conducted on 22 df with family-wise error rate held at approximately the .05 level for a set of seven comparisons.

each of the seven types of reading situations. Although the rating profiles for the seven types differ in the questions on which they show significant deviations, two general patterns of ratings emerge across the seven types. One profile characterizes reading to prepare for exams, whereas the other profile characterizes reading for other purposes.

Reading to memorize and reading to prepare for essay exams and objective exams all have very similar rating profiles. Again, this is consistent with the fact that the three types comprise a superordinate cluster (i.e., reading to prepare for exams). The common characteristic uniting them is that they all require retention of text content. In general, readers rate all three types of reading as demanding. Compared to the average profile for school reading, reading for exams involves: slow reading, a great deal of testing for understanding and use of supports, much rereading, close attention to major points, and good concentration. This profile is completely consistent with the rating results from Lorch et al. (1993). Most of the comparisons of these three types with the average reading profile are significant, indicating that reading for exams is quite different from other types of school reading.

The four reading types that do not emphasize memory for content are generally similar in their rating profiles, but some finer distinctions may be made across these types. The ratings for the reading for literary writing and reading for research writing clusters are presented in the fourth and fifth rows of Table 20.2. The rating profiles for these two types are very similar, which is consistent with the findings from the cluster analyses that these two clusters comprise a superordinate cluster (i.e., reading to write papers). In general, both types of reading involve somewhat faster than average reading, relatively little testing of understanding, and relatively little use of supports, rereading, or attention to major points. This profile is completely consistent with the rating results for the reading to write type in the Lorch et al. (1993) study. Both types of reading are distinguished statistically from the average profile for school reading in that they involve little testing of understanding. In addition, reading to write humanities papers involves little use of supports (e.g., highlighting). If there is a distinction to be made between the two types of reading to write, reading for literary writing involves somewhat more concentration but less use of supports than reading for research writing. In sum, the rating profiles for these two types of reading imply that students treat the text as coherent material, but do not read the text particularly closely (i.e., little testing of understanding).

Reading to prepare for class is the least demanding type of school reading. Class preparation involves fast reading, little testing of understanding or use of supports, little rereading, and little attention to major points or concentration. This type is significantly different from the average rating profile on all six questions. Again, the rating profile is completely consistent with the findings for the class preparation type in the Lorch et al. (1993) study. When students read without a specific purpose and with the expectation that they will not be held immediately responsible for the material, they characterize themselves as reading superficially.

Finally, selective reading is distinct from the average rating profile in three respects. It involves little testing of understanding, little rereading, and little concentration. Reading speed, use of supports, and attention to major points are close to the means for other types of school reading. The profile is consistent with a mode of processing in which the reader is searching for specific information in the text and is processing irrelevant information superficially.

In sum, we have argued for four distinct modes of school reading based on the rating data. The rating profiles distinguish reading to prepare for various types of exams, reading to write various types of papers, reading to prepare for class, and selective reading. The rating profiles for the first three categories of reading were consistent with the rating profiles for the corresponding types of reading in Lorch et al. (1993). Although the cluster analyses indicate that readers distinguish two types of reading to write and three types of reading to prepare for exams, the rating data indicated more similarities than differences within the reading to write types and the exam reading types.

EXPERIMENT 2

The purpose of Experiment 2 was to carefully examine distinctions college readers make among different types of reading of their personal choosing. In the Lorch et al. (1993) study, six types of personal choice reading situations were identified:

1. Reading to apply acquired knowledge to a specific task (e.g., "Read a bridal magazine to plan a wedding").
2. Searching for information (e.g., "Read a *TV Guide* to see what is on TV").
3. Reading that is intellectually challenging (e.g., "Read a newspaper editorial for intellectual stimulation").
4. Light reading (e.g., "Read comics in the newspaper to relax").
5. Reading for affective stimulation (e.g., "Read a suspense story for excitement").
6. Reading to self-inform (e.g., "Read a pamphlet on health care for general information").

Experiment 2 investigated 34 reading situations sampled from five of these six categories of reading experience. The category of reading to self-inform was not represented (see Footnote 1). As in the first experiment, the rationale for using a relatively homogeneous set of reading situations was that it should encourage subjects to make fine discriminations among the situations. The results of Experiment 2 will be compared directly with the typology of personal choice reading situations found by Lorch et al. With the exception of the reading situations studied, the procedures for Experiment 2 were identical to those of Experiment 1.

Method

Phase 1: Sorting Reading Situations

Subjects. Subjects were 88 students from introductory psychology classes at the University of Kentucky. Participation in experiments was a course requirement.

Materials. The materials consisted of 34 reading situations in the Lorch et al. (1993) study that were identified as reading situations that were personally chosen by the readers, as opposed to being assigned as a class requirement. The procedure for the selection of items was analogous to the procedure of Experiment 1. As in Experiment 1, each reading situation specified a reading material (e.g., "Read a bridal magazine . . . ") and a purpose for reading the material (to plan a wedding). (See Table 20.3 for a list of all the personal choice reading situations).

Procedure. The procedure was identical to that of Experiment 1. As in the first experiment, there was little evidence that the restrictions on the number of sorting categories represented much of a constraint on subjects' performances. Only one subject used two categories and one subject used all 15 categories. The modal number of categories used was 7; the mean was 7.6, with a standard deviation of 2.35 points.

Phase 2: Rating Reading Situations

Subjects. Subjects were 23 students from introductory psychology classes at the University of Kentucky. The data of one subject were omitted from analyses because the subject failed to follow instructions. None of the subjects participating in the rating task had participated in the sorting task.

Materials and Procedure. With the exception that the set of reading situations differed, all aspects of the preparation of materials for the rating task were identical to those of Experiment 1. The rating procedure in Experiment 2 was also identical to Experiment 1.

Results and Discussion

Phase 1: Cluster Analysis of the Sorting Task

The data from the sorting task were reduced by the same procedures described for Experiment 1. Only a small percentage of the items were excluded from the

TABLE 20.3
Types of Personal Choice Reading Situations Identified by Cluster Analyses

---

Type 1: Reading to Apply

Read a bridal magazine to plan a wedding
Read a poster to learn about travel opportunities
Read a cookbook to find an interesting recipe
Read a "how to" book to find ideas
Read a hobby magazine to learn about a particular pasttime

Type 2: Search

Read a store catalog to window shop
Read a *TV Guide* to see what is on TV
Read over coupons in the newspaper to find ways to save money
Read advertisements to see if they are of interest to you
Read over sports articles in the paper to learn basketball scores
Read a fashion magazine to learn current styles

Type 3: Intellecutally Challenging Reading

Read a newspaper editorial for intellectual stimulation
Read over *Newsweek* magazine to find articles of interest
Read letters from friends to find out what they are doing
Read local news in the paper to stay up to date on the community
Read an article in a medical journal for personal interest

Type 4: Light Reading

Read comics in the newspaper to relax
Read a cookbook for enjoyment
Read an advice column in the newspaper for entertainment
Read *Time* magazine for pleasure
Read a travel brouchure for enjoyment
Read a sports magazine to relax

Type 5: Read to Kill Time

Read a campus newspaper to kill time
Read junk mail to kill time
Read *People* magazine to kill time

Type 6: Reading for Stimulation

Read a suspense story for excitement
Read a bestseller to escape
Read a romance for the emotional feeling it gives you
Read a Mark Twain novel for pleasure
Read science fiction to think about the future
Read fiction for enjoyment
Read humor to cheer up
Read an autobiography for inspiration
Read fantasy for fun

---

analyses because individual subjects indicated they were unfamiliar (2.17% of the 2,992 items sorted). The sorting data were analyzed using a hierarchical clustering procedure and followed the same criteria adopted in Experiment 1 for the identification of distinct clusters. The results of the analysis are presented in Table 20.3.

One of the six types of personal choice reading situations identified by Lorch et al. (1993) was reading for information to apply to a specific purpose (e.g.,

"Read a bridal magazine to plan a wedding"). This reading type was clearly replicated in the current experiment. Four exemplars of this reading type were sampled from the materials of Lorch et al. All four of these reading situations were grouped into a single cluster in Experiment 2, along with one additional reading situation (i.e., "Read a poster to learn about travel opportunities").

A second personal choice reading situation identified by Lorch et al. was reading to search for specific information (e.g., "Read a TV Guide to see what is on TV"). This type was also replicated in Experiment 2. Of the seven items sampled from Lorch et al. representing search reading, six formed a distinct cluster in the present experiment; the remaining item was categorized as a type of reading to apply. Search and reading to apply were clearly related types of reading in Experiment 2, both being grouped together under the same superordinate category. In both types of reading, the reader has an interest in a general category of information (e.g., TV listings, basketball scores, travel opportunities, recipes), and is searching the text for items of relevance. The apparent distinction between reading to apply and searching is in the extent to which the reader processes the text as coherent text. In reading to apply, the reader attends more closely to the text and the sought-for information constitutes coherent text (e.g., a recipe or a description of a hobby). In search reading, the reader is skimming the text for isolated, small bits of information (e.g., basketball scores or TV listings).

Intellectually challenging reading was identified as a third category of reading experience by Lorch et al. (1993). This type includes coherent text on topics of political or technical relevance. This reading type was inadequately represented in the item sample of Experiment 2 (see Footnote 1); nevertheless, the three representatives of this type formed the core of the third cluster listed in Table 20.3. One of the additional items grouped in this cluster could clearly be considered intellectually challenging (i.e., "Read an article in a medical journal for personal interest"). Thus, the cluster appears to replicate the intellectually challenging reading type identified in Lorch et al., although one of the items included in the cluster seems anomalous (i.e., "Read letters from friends to find out what they are doing").

A fourth type of reading was termed *light reading* by Lorch et al. It was represented by 12 items in Experiment 2, 6 of which were grouped into a single cluster corresponding to the light reading type identified by Lorch et al. All of the items grouped as light reading represent reading for diversion and positive affect. Of the remaining six items categorized as light reading in Lorch et al., three formed a distinct category of their own. These items involved reading to "kill time" and may have been grouped together simply on the basis of their superficial wording similarity (i.e., all three reading situations were described as "reading [some type of material] to kill time"). On the other hand, reading to kill time may deserve to be distinguished from light reading on substantive grounds. In the case of light reading, the reader is intrinsically interested in the reading activity and therefore is likely to have a reasonable degree of cognitive involvement. In the case of reading to kill time, the reader is not intrinsically motivated to read; rather, reading is a "filler" activity and therefore the reader's cognitive involvement is likely to be minimal.

The final type of reading from Lorch et al. (1993) that was represented in the item sample of Experiment 2 was reading for stimulation (e.g., "Read a suspense story for excitement"). This category of reading experience was represented in Experiment 2 by seven items from the Lorch et al. study. Six of the seven items were grouped together in the present experiment. In addition, two items that were classified as light reading in the Lorch et al. study were grouped with the six stimulating reading situations in Experiment 2 (i.e., "Read fantasy for fun; read humor to cheer up"). All of the reading situations grouped as stimulating reading in the current experiment share the characteristic that the texts are long and the motivation for reading is affective. This cluster was very clearly distinguished from the other five clusters in the cluster analysis for Experiment 2. The basis for the sharp distinction is apparently that subjects considered this final category of reading experience to be much more engrossing than other types of reading.

In sum, the clustering results of Experiment 2 essentially replicate the findings of the Lorch et al. study. Both studies are in agreement that readers distinguish several types of personal reading experiences: reading to find information to apply to a specific purpose, intellectually challenging reading, searching for specific information, light reading, and reading for affective stimulation. In addition, Experiment 2 produced a distinction between light reading and reading to kill time. This distinction probably had no opportunity to be identified by Lorch et al. because neither of the two replications of the sorting procedure in that study had a sufficient number of representatives of reading to kill time. Finally, a reading type identified by Lorch et al. (i.e., reading to self-inform) was not represented in the item sample of Experiment 2 (see Footnote 1).

Phase 2: Rating Analyses

For each of the six personal choice reading types, the mean rating was computed across subjects and reading situations for each of the six questions. For each of the six questions, a multivariate analysis of variance was conducted to determine whether there were systematic differences among the six types. All of these preliminary tests showed reliable differences among the reading types; smallest approximate F (5, 105) = 13.45, $p < .0001$. Additional tests were conducted to determine the pattern of differences among the reading types. For each of the six questions, the mean rating for each type was compared with the mean rating across the remaining five types while controlling family-wise error rate at the .05 level for a set of six contrasts. The results of these comparisons are summarized in Table 20.4.

The purpose of the rating data was to provide a characterization of reading for

TABLE 20.4
Mean Ratings by Question for the Personal Choice Reading "Types"

Type	Speed	Test Understanding	Use Supports	Reread	Attend Major Points	Concentrate
					Questions	
Apply	4.5	3.936[a]	3.609[a]	3.636[a]	4.691[a]	4.191[a]
Search	5.447[a]	2.758[b]	2.068	2.78	4.053	3.008[b]
Challenge	4.355	4.191[a]	2.454	3.4[a]	4.9[a]	4.554[a]
Light	4.545	3.22	1.78[b]	2.477[b]	3.485[b]	3.356[b]
Kill time	5.727[a]	2.182[b]	1.318[b]	1.803[b]	3.061[b]	2.152[b]
Stimulate	4.02[b]	3.318	1.667[b]	2.77	3.535	4.333[a]
Mean	4.635	3.321	2.128	2.855	3.946	3.746

Note. Ratings typed in boldface and marked with letters are significantly different from the mean rating across the other six types; an "a" ("b") indicates the mean for the type was higher (lower) than the mean across the other six types. All *t*-tests were conducted on 21 *df* with family-wise error rate held at approximately the .05 level for a set of six comparisons.

each of the six types of reading situations. Across the six types, two general rating profiles were observed. Reading to apply and challenging reading have similar profiles; both types of reading are perceived as relatively cognitively demanding. In contrast, search, light reading, reading to kill time, and stimulating reading are relatively undemanding. Although two general profiles serve to characterize the major distinctions across reading types, additional distinctions may be made among the six types.

The rating profiles for reading to apply and intellectually challenging reading are presented in the first and second rows of Table 20.4. Compared to other types of personal choice reading, subjects report that their reading speed is somewhat slower than average, they concentrate harder, and they are more likely to test their understanding, use supports, reread, and attend to major points. This profile exactly matches the rating profile found for reading to apply in the Lorch et al. (1993) study. However, the profile is not consistent with that found for intellectually challenging reading by Lorch et al. In the previous study, the profile for challenging reading was completely flat (i.e., did not differ from the mean across other types on any question). The likely reason for this discrepancy is that the Lorch et al. study included a type of reading situation (i.e., reading to self-inform) that was more cognitively demanding than either reading to apply or challenging reading. Averaging this additional type with the other types of reading by choice made the mean profile for choice reading more like the profile for challenging reading.

The one apparent distinction between reading to apply and challenging reading is that reading to apply involves more use of supports (e.g., underlining). This makes sense. Reading to apply involves a search for specific relevant information (e.g., a special recipe), which is then to be applied in a particular context. In challenging reading, no specific content has any special status with respect to the reader's goals; rather, the reader treats the entire text as coherent and relevant.

Searching for very specific information in a text represents a mode of reading that is probably quite distinct from other types of personal choice reading. The text involved is typically highly segmented and therefore is not read for understanding. Subjects read rapidly with little testing of understanding or concentration. On the other hand, they are average in their use of supports, rereading, and attention to major points. Because readers generally want to retain specific information from a search, they will sometimes use supports (e.g., circle an item in a store catalog); because they are reading quickly, they will occasionally reread to make certain they have not missed relevant information; and because content differs in its relevance, some content is attended more closely than other content.

Light reading involves reading coherent text for enjoyment, but the reader is not particularly cognitively or emotionally involved in the reading. This characterization is reflected in average ratings with respect to speed and testing of understanding, and below average ratings on use of supports, rereading, attention to major points, and concentration.

Reading to kill time has the most extreme rating profile of all six reading types, differing from the average of the other types on all six questions. This is clearly the most superficial of all the types. Reading is fast, with little concentration or testing of understanding, and minimal rereading, use of supports, or attention to major points. This is the only situation in which reading is not intrinsically motivated; reading is simply a convenient filler activity to occupy time rather than being motivated by a desire for information or affective stimulation.

Finally, the profile for stimulating reading indicates that it is more appropriately characterized in terms of its affective components than in terms of its cognitive demands. As in the Lorch et al. study, subjects rated this type of reading as being slow and involving close concentration, but as not involving use of supports. Subjects do not appear to perceive this type of reading as cognitively demanding; rather, they perceive it as engrossing.

GENERAL DISCUSSION

The purpose of this study was to generate a typology characterizing the range of reading experiences of college students. The results of Experiments 1 and 2 replicate and extend the typology of reading situations suggested by Lorch et al.

(1993). With only one exception, each type identified in the current study either replicated or was a subset of a type identified by Lorch et al. Combining the results of the current study with those of Lorch et al., we suggest that college readers distinguish at least 14 types of reading situations. These types and their organization are summarized in Table 20.5.

A Theory of Reading Settings

What is the relevance of the typology presented in Table 20.5? The subjects in our experiments claimed that they read differently across the distinct types of reading situations summarized in Table 20.5. Future research may, indeed, demonstrate that the distinctions among reading types identified in this typology correlate with different reading strategies. However, we do not present the typology as a theory of reading behavior. The typology is moot with respect to the nature of reading strategies that may be associated with specific types and we have not collected any behavioral data relevant to this issue. Both the sorting and rating procedures used in this study provide information regarding readers' *introspections* about how they read in different situations. Those introspections may or may not turn out to be valid predictors of readers' actual behavior (Nisbett & Wilson, 1977). However, introspections are a valid starting point for determining appropriate reading behavior. That is, a reader's perception of the cognitive demands of a given reading situation constitutes critical conditional knowledge

TABLE 20.5
Proposed Typology of 14 Reading Types and Their Hierarchical Organization

Superordinate	Category	Type
School	Exam	Memorization Essay exam Objective exam
	Writing	Literature papers Scientific papers
	Class	Preparation Selective
Personal	Selective	Application Search
	Serious	Challenging Self-informing*
	Diversion	Light reading Killing time
	Stimulation	Stimulation

*Reading to self-inform is the only type of reading in this typology that was not identified in the analyses of sorting data collected in the present study. The identification of this type is based on results reported in Lorch et al. (1993).

necessary for strategic reading. We present the typology in Table 20.5 as a theory of reading "settings" (Garner, 1990) that college students discriminate. As such, we expect that this typology will be useful in predicting when and why readers alter their reading behavior.

Relevance of the Typology to the Study of Strategies as Adjustments to Different Goals

The reading types summarized in Table 20.5 are associated with different reading goals and different types of texts. Both of these factors are likely to affect the strategic adjustments students make to read effectively in different reading situations. Although we lack the relevant behavioral data at this point, we speculate about some of the ways in which our typology might be found to relate to reading behavior.

There are at least four important dimensions along which the reading types in Table 20.5 appear to vary:

1. Reading materials vary across the types with respect to the degree of segmentation of the text. Some of the texts are relatively unsegmented (e.g., a novel) and some texts are composed of many brief and relatively unrelated segments (e.g., advertisements in a catalog or recipes in a cookbook).

2. The types vary in whether, and how closely, they are associated with an external evaluation of the products of reading.

3. The reading goals associated with different types vary with respect to how unambiguously they define the relevance of specific text content.

4. The reading goals associated with different types vary in the importance they assign to constructing a coherent representation of the information communicated by the author.

These dimensions of variation are likely to correlate with the types of strategic adjustments readers make to the demands of different reading situations.

The nature of the text to be read is likely to have a direct influence on a reader's processing strategy. To give some examples: readers have schemas for narrative structure that direct their attempts to comprehend stories (Trabasso, Secco, & van den Broek, 1984), scientific or technical text often requires particular attention to definitions of important concepts (Dee-Lucas & Larkin, 1988; Kieras, 1981), poetry requires processing strategies that are unique to the genre. Looking at the reading materials associated with the different types in Tables 20.1 and 20.3, one dimension along which texts vary is in their degree of segmentation. Although many of the texts are extended and cohesive (e.g., novels, chapters in textbooks), the content of many other texts is highly segmented (e.g., cookbooks, catalogs). Cohesive texts can be associated with a variety of reading goals and thus are likely to be processed in many different ways. However, texts consisting of brief, unrelated parts place greater constraints on what constitutes an appropriate reading goal and strategy. For instance, a listing of basketball scores cannot be processed as coherent text. Rather, highly segmented texts are likely to be associated with strategies such as skimming (e.g., finding out what TV shows are on) or searching for specific target information (e.g., the result of the Kentucky-Indiana basketball game in a newspaper listing of scores).

Reading in preparation for any kind of external evaluation calls for the use of study strategies that would not typically be used when doing reading that will not be evaluated. Both reading to prepare for an exam and reading in preparation for writing a paper involve subsequent evaluation by the course instructor. To take the example of exam preparation, this reading purpose emphasizes subsequent memory for text content and thus requires strategic adjustments in reading that will improve memory (e.g., slow reading, rereading, self-testing).

Some purposes for reading involve clear specification of goal-relevant text content, whereas other reading situations are much more ambiguous. Reading to memorize (e.g., reading a foreign language text to learn verb conjugations), selective reading (e.g., reading a history chapter to do an outline), and search reading (e.g., reading a *TV Guide* to see what is on TV) are all examples of types of reading where the relevant text content is well defined by the reading goal. These types of reading situations encourage various types of selective processing strategies. For example, situations associated with reading to memorize may involve the identification and selective rehearsal of test-relevant information. As another example, search reading presumably entails a strategy of text search that depends on the identification of well-specified target information related to the reader's goal. Both of these examples involve reading situations where the goal-relevant information is quite discrete and easily distinguished from irrelevant information. In many other situations, the relevance of any given content may vary more continuously because the reading goal does not specify relevance definitively. Still, a degree of selective processing is possible in such situations. For example, reading to do an outline or to give a summary emphasizes macrostructure-relevant information and encourages readers to construct a globally coherent representation at the expense of attention to detail (Lorch, Lorch, & Matthews, 1985).

Finally, given a type of reading where comprehension is a goal, readers may adopt different standards of coherence in different reading situations (van den Broek et al., this volume). In situations such as light reading or killing time, readers may construct a minimally connected representation based primarily on processing of local coherence relations (cf. McKoon & Ratcliff, 1992). In other situations, readers may construct a highly connected representation that includes global coherence relations and, perhaps, elaborative and predictive inferences (e.g., reading for stimulation).

In sum, the reading situations in our typology appear to vary along at least four major dimensions, including: the degree to which the materials to be read constrain the types of goals and processing strategies that are appropriate, the extent to which reading is done for evaluation, the precision of specification of goal-relevant information in the text, and the standards of coherence that readers are likely to adopt. We expect that these differences among reading situations will be found to relate to strategic adjustments that readers make in their reading behaviors.

Relevance of the Typology to the Study of Strategies for Coping with Capacity Limits

As we observed in the beginning of this chapter, cognitive scientists have generally not paid much attention to readers' macrostrategies (but see Kieras, 1982, Masson, 1982 for examples of exceptions to this generalization). Rather, they have typically preferred a more detailed level of analysis of reading behavior, including examination of the strategies used by readers to cope with basic cognitive capacity limitations. Towards this end, cognitive scientists have concentrated most of their efforts on the examination of basic reading processes (e.g., O'Brien, this volume) in the context of brief narrative (e.g., Fletcher & Bloom, 1988) or technical prose (e.g., Dee-Lucas & Larkin, 1988; Kieras, 1981) read for the purpose of an immediate test of memory or understanding. This rather narrow focus has led to excellent progress toward understanding the basic processes underlying the construction of a coherent representation of simple narrative and expository texts. However, the progress may be at the cost of generality of our theories of reading. For example, one influential theoretical position is that readers typically generate only those inferences necessary to maintain local coherence of their text representations (McKoon & Ratcliff, 1992). In addition, there is widespread agreement that readers typically do not generate predictive or elaborative inferences except under highly constrained circumstances (see Graesser, Bertus, & Magliano, this volume). The empirical foundation for these perspectives consists primarily of studies of how subjects read simple texts (e.g., 10-sentence stories) to perform simple tasks (e.g., word recognition). If our studies examined a wider range of materials and purposes for reading, our understanding of the nature and extent of inferencing during reading might be different. For example, readers may well engage in extensive forward inferencing when reading a mystery with the goal of anticipating its resolution.

If the typology we propose is demonstrated to relate to the reading strategies of college students, it is likely to be more closely related to the sense of strategies as adaptations to specific reading goals than to the sense of strategies as responses to cognitive limitations. However, the two senses of the term *strategy* are not unrelated because different reading tasks challenge different cognitive limits. For example, a search task places minimal demands on memory because it does not demand integration of information, whereas intellectually challenging reading requires a processing strategy that makes efficient use of working memory because it does demand integration. Thus, studying reading behavior across the range of types represented in Table 20.5 may most directly advance our understanding of the nature of readers' strategic adaptations to different reading goals. However, such an enterprise may also be productive with respect to advancing our understanding of the nature of readers' strategies for coping with the constraints of working memory.

ACKNOWLEDGMENTS

We would like to thank Edward J. O'Brien for his comments on an earlier version of this chapter. We also want to acknowledge Francis T. Durso for his contributions to the work reported in this chapter. His insightful comments as a reviewer of Lorch, Lorch, & Klusewitz (1993) led to a complete reanalysis and reorganization that substantially improved that article and indirectly influenced the current chapter for the better.

REFERENCES

Albrecht, J. E., & O'Brien, E. J. (1993). Updating a mental model: Maintaining both local and global coherence. *Journal of Experimental Psychology*, *19*, 1061–1070.

Dee-Lucas, D., & Larkin, J. H. (1988). Attentional strategies for studying scientific text. *Memory & Cognition*, *16*, 469–479.

Fletcher, C. R. (1986). Strategies for the allocation of short-term memory during comprehension. *Journal of Memory and Language*, *25*, 43–58.

Fletcher, C. R., & Bloom, C. P. (1988). Causal reasoning in the comprehension of simple narrative text. *Journal of Memory and Language*, *27*, 235–244.

Frazier, L., & Rayner, K. (1982). Making and correcting errors during sentence comprehension: Eye movements in the analysis of structurally ambiguous sentences. *Cognitive Psychology*, *14*, 178–210.

Garner, R. (1990). When children and adults do not use learning strategies: Toward a theory of settings. *Review of Educational Research*, *60*, 517–529.

Greaney, V., & Neuman, S. B. (1990). The functions of reading: A cross-cultural perspective. *Reading Research Quarterly*, *25*, 172–195.

Kieras, D. E. (1981). Topicalization effects in cued recall of technical prose. *Memory & Cognition*, *9*, 541–549.

Kieras, D. E. (1982). A model of reader strategy for abstracting main ideas from simple technical prose. *Text*, *2*, 47–81.

Kintsch, W., & van Dijk, T. A. (1978). Toward a model of text comprehension and production. *Psychological Review*, *85*, 363–394.

Lorch, R. F., Jr., Lorch, E. P., & Klusewitz, M. A. (1993). College students' conditional knowledge about reading. *Journal of Educational Psychology*, *85*, 239–252.

Lorch, R. F., Jr., Lorch, E. P., & Matthews, P. D. (1985). On-line processing of the topic structure of a text. *Journal of Memory and Language*, *24*, 350–362.

Masson, M. E. J. (1982). Cognitive processes in skimming stories. *Journal of Experimental Psychology: Learning, Memory, and Cognition, 8*, 400–417.

McKoon, G., & Ratcliff, R. (1992). Inference during reading. *Psychological Review, 99*, 440–466.

Miller, G. A. (1969). A psychological method to investigate verbal concepts. *Journal of Mathematical Psychology, 6*, 169–191.

Nisbett, R. E., & Wilson, T. D. (1977). Telling more than we can know: Verbal reports as data. *Psychological Review, 84*, 231–257.

O'Brien, E. J., & Albrecht, J. E. (1992). Comprehension strategies in the development of a mental model. *Journal of Experimental Psychology: Learning, Memory, and Cognition, 18*, 777–784.

Paris, S. G., Lipson, M. Y., & Wixson, K. K. (1983). Becoming a strategic reader. *Contemporary Educational Psychology, 8*, 293–316.

Trabasso, T., Secco, T., & van den Broek, P. (1984). Causal cohesion and story coherence. In H. Mandl, N. L. Stein, & T. Trabasso (Eds.), *Learning and comprehension of text* (pp. 83–111). Hillsdale, NJ: Lawrence Erlbaum Associates.

Author Index

Subject Index